JOURNAL FOR THE STUDY OF THE OLD TESTAMENT
SUPPLEMENT SERIES

395

A Royal Priesthood

Literary and Intertextual Perspectives on an Image of Israel in Exodus 19.6

John A. Davies

Published by T&T Clark International
The Tower Building, 11 York Road, London SE1 7NX
15 East 26th Street, Suite 1703, New York, NY 10010

www.tandtclark.com

British Library Cataloguing-in-Publication Data
A catalogue record for this book is available from the British Library

Typeset and edited for Continuum by Forthcoming Publications Ltd
www.forthcomingpublications.com

Printed on acid-free paper in Great Britain by The Bath Press, Bath

ISBN 0-8264-7157-9

CONTENTS

PREFACE

This book brings to fruition the ponderings and labours of many years on one small phrase in the Bible, and the imperfectly understood and neglected image it represents of the privileged relationship God grants to his people.

I take this opportunity to record a few expressions of thanks. The Presbyterian Theological Centre in Sydney (Australia) granted me a period of study leave which made it possible to devote some concentrated time to this research. I thank the Committee and staff for affording me this opportunity, for carrying the teaching and administrative load in my absence and for their encouragement to see the work through.

The work was originally submitted to the University of Sydney as a doctoral thesis. I am indebted to my supervisor Dr Ian Young and my associate supervisor, Emeritus Professor Alan Crown of the Department of Semitic Studies for their stimulation.

I thank those colleagues and friends who took the time to read through a draft form of this work and made useful suggestions, in particular Dr Ian Smith, Dr Greg Goswell and Mr Bernard Secombe.

I also record my indebtedness to Mr Andrew Lu, who well understands the needs of the visually challenged, for his generosity in making available an optical reader, without which much of the reading involved would have been impossible.

Finally I thank my wife Julie and children Kathryn, Timothy and Simon for their support and patience through this period of research and writing.

John A. Davies
April, 2003

ABBREVIATIONS

AAR	American Academy of Religion
AB	The Anchor Bible
ABD	David Noel Freedman (ed.), *The Anchor Bible Dictionary* (New York: Doubleday, 1992)
AnBib	Analecta biblica
ANET	James B. Pritchard (ed.), *Ancient Near Eastern Texts Relating to the Old Testament* (Princeton: Princeton University Press, 3rd edn, 1969)
AnOr	Analecta orientalia
AOAT	Alter Orient und Altes Testament
ASOR	American Schools of Oriental Research
ASV	American Standard Version
ATANT	Abhandlungen zur Theologie des Alten und Neuen Testaments
AusBR	*Australian Biblical Review*
BA	*Biblical Archaeologist*
BASOR	*Bulletin of the American Schools of Oriental Research*
BDB	Francis Brown, S.R. Driver and Charles A. Briggs, *A Hebrew and English Lexicon of the Old Testament* (Oxford: Clarendon Press, 1907)
BETL	Bibliotheca ephemeridum theologicarum lovaniensium
BEvT	Beiträge zur evangelischen Theologie
BHS	*Biblia hebraica stuttgartensia*
Bib	*Biblica*
BibOr	Biblica et orientalia
BibInt	*Biblical Interpretation: A Journal of Contemporary Approaches*
BJS	Brown Judaic Studies
BKAT	Biblischer Kommentar: Altes Testament
BSac	*Bibliotheca Sacra*
BSC	Bible Student's Commentary
BT	*The Bible Translator*
BTB	*Biblical Theology Bulletin*
BZ	*Biblische Zeitschrift*
BZAW	Beihefte zur *ZAW*
CAD	Ignace I. Gelb *et al.* (eds.), *The Assyrian Dictionary of the Oriental Institute of the University of Chicago* (Chicago: Oriental Institute, 1964–)

CAT	Commentaire de l'Ancien Testament
CBQ	*Catholic Biblical Quarterly*
CBSC	Cambridge Bible for Schools and Colleges
ConBOT	Coniectanea biblica, Old Testament
DCH	David J.A. Clines (ed.), *Dictionary of Classical Hebrew* (Sheffield: Sheffield Academic Press, 1993–)
DJD	Discoveries in the Judaean Desert
EBib	Etudes bibliques
EncJud	*Encyclopedia Judaica*
ETL	*Ephemerides theologicae lovanienses*
ETSMS	Evangelical Theological Society Monograph Series
FRLANT	Forschungen zur Religion und Literatur des Alten und Neuen Testaments
FzB	Forschung zur Bibel
GKC	*Gesenius' Hebrew Grammar* (ed. E. Kautzsch, revised and trans. A.E. Cowley; Oxford: Clarendon Press, 1910)
HAR	*Hebrew Annual Review*
HAT	Handbuch zum Alten Testament
HCOT	Historical Commentary on the Old Testament
HKAT	Handkommentar zum Alten Testament
HSM	Harvard Semitic Monographs
HSS	Harvard Semitic Studies
HTR	*Harvard Theological Review*
HUCA	*Hebrew Union College Annual*
ICC	International Critical Commentary
IDB	George Arthur Buttrick (ed.), *The Interpreter's Dictionary of the Bible*
IEJ	*Israel Exploration Journal*
Int	*Interpretation*
JAOS	*Journal of the American Oriental Society*
JBL	*Journal of Biblical Literature*
JCS	*Journal of Cuneiform Studies*
JETS	*Journal of the Evangelical Theological Society*
JJS	*Journal of Jewish Studies*
JNES	*Journal of Near Eastern Studies*
JNSL	*Journal of Northwest Semitic Languages*
JPS	Jewish Publication Society
JQR	*Jewish Quarterly Review*
JRH	*Journal of Religious History*
JRS	*Journal of Religious Studies*
JSNT	*Journal for the Study of the New Testament*
JSNTSup	*Journal for the Study of the New Testament*, Supplement Series
JSOT	*Journal for the Study of the Old Testament*
JSOTSup	*Journal for the Study of the Old Testament*, Supplement Series

JSP	*Journal for the Study of the Pseudepigrapha*
JSPSup	*Journal for the Study of the Pseudepigrapha*, Supplement Series
JSS	*Journal of Semitic Studies*
JTS	*Journal of Theological Studies*
KB	Ludwig Koehler and Walter Baumgartner (eds.), *Lexicon in Veteris Testamenti libros*
KHAT	Kurzer Hand-Kommentar zum Alten Testament
LCL	Loeb Classical Library
MT	Masoretic Text
NTAbh	Neutestamentliche Abhandlungen
NCB	New Century Bible
NEB	New English Bible
NovTSup	*Novum Testamentum*, Supplements
NICOT	New International Commentary on the Old Testament
NIDOTE	Willem A. VanGemeren (ed.), *New International Dictionary of Old Testament Theology and Exegesis*
NIV	New International Version
NRSV	New Revised Standard Version
OBO	Orbis biblicus et orientalis
OLZ	*Orientalistische Literaturzeitung*
Or	*Orientalia*
OTG	Old Testament Guides
OTL	Old Testament Library
OTP	James Charlesworth (ed.), *Old Testament Pseudepigrapha*
OTS	*Oudtestamentische Studien*
PEQ	*Palestine Exploration Quarterly*
PRU	Jean Nougayrol (ed.), *Le palais royal d'Ugarit. III. Textes Accadiens et Hourites des archives est, ouest et centrales* (Mission de Ras Shamra, 6; Paris: Imprimerie Nationale Librairie C. Klincksieck, 1955)
RB	*Revue biblique*
RevExp	*Review and Expositor*
RevQ	*Revue de Qumran*
RSV	Revised Standard Version
RTR	*Reformed Theological Review*
RV	Revised Version
SANT	Studien zum Alten und Neuen Testament
SBL	Society of Biblical Literature
SBLDS	SBL Dissertation Series
SBLMS	SBL Monograph Series
SBLSP	SBL Seminar Papers
SBLSS	SBL Semeia Studies
SBS	Stuttgarter Bibelstudien
SBT	Studies in Biblical Theology

SBTS	Sources for Biblical and Theological Study
ScEs	*Science et esprit*
SH	Scripta Hierosolymitana
SJLA	Studies in Judaism in Late Antiquity
SJOT	*Scandinavian Journal of the Old Testament*
SJT	*Scottish Journal of Theology*
SNTSMS	Society for New Testament Studies Monograph Series
SOTBT	Studies in Old Testament Biblical Theology
TynBul	*Tyndale Bulletin*
TDNT	Gerhard Kittel and Gerhard Friedrichs (eds.), *Theological Dictionary of the New Testament* (trans. Geoffrey W. Bromiley; 10 vols.; Grand Rapids: Eerdmans, 1964–76)
TDOT	G. Johannes Botterweck, Helmer Ringgren and Heinz-Joseph Fabry (eds.), *Theological Dictionary of the Old Testament*
TLOT	Ernst Jenni and Claus Westermann (eds.), *Theological Lexicon of the Old Testament*
TOTC	Tyndale Old Testament Commentaries
TRu	*Theologische Rundschau*
TTZ	*Trierer theologische Zeitschrift*
TZ	*Theologische Zeitschrift*
UF	*Ugarit-Forschungen*
VT	*Vetus Testamentum*
VTSup	*Vetus Testamentum*, Supplements
WBC	Word Biblical Commentary
WMANT	Wissenschaftliche Monographien zum Alten und Neuen Testament
WTJ	*Westminster Theological Journal*
ZAW	*Zeitschrift für die alttestamentliche Wissenschaft*
ZKT	*Zeitschrift für katholische Theologie*

Chapter 1

Introduction

1. *The Royal Priesthood in Exodus 19.6 and the Scope of this Study*

The designation of the people of Israel as a ממלכת כהנים in Exod. 19.6 has been and continues to be a *crux interpretum*. While the phrase is capable of a diversity of translations and paraphrases ('kingdom of priests', 'priestly kingdom', 'royalty [and] priests', 'administrative body of priests'), I offer at this stage (in anticipation of the discussion in Chapter 4) as a working translation, 'a royalty, or royal body of priests', or, more paraphrastically, 'a royal priesthood'.

These words form the climax of a brief divine declaration given to Moses, sometimes known as the 'eagle speech' (Exod. 19.4-6a), which he is to relay to the people of Israel upon his descent from Mt Sinai. Thus, according to the writer of Exodus, these words constitute a designation of Israel in the mind of God, his characterization of the elect people consequent upon the new or heightened relationship inaugurated at Sinai.

Both because of its position at the head of the extended Sinai pericope (Exod. 19.1–Num. 10.10) and because of its striking content, this declaration has come to be regarded by some within both the Jewish and the Christian traditions as a significant *locus* for the theology of the Hebrew Scriptures, enjoying paradigmatic status as the quintessential *Erwählungstradition*, the story behind Israel's awareness of being the elect people of God. Phillips considers that 'Ex 19.3-8 acts as a summary of the whole account of the covenant in Ex 19–24'.[1] Merrill writes, 'Without doubt Exodus 19.4-6 is the most theologically significant text in the book of Exodus'.[2] Muilenburg would extend even further the signficance of this unit of text, venturing that 'it is scarcely too much to say that [Exod. 19.3-6] is *in nuce* the *fons et origo* of the many covenantal pericopes which

1. Anthony Phillips, 'A Fresh Look at the Sinai Pericope', *VT* 34 (1984), pp. 39-52, 282-94 (51).

2. Eugene H. Merrill, 'A Theology of the Pentateuch', in Roy B. Zuck (ed.), *A Biblical Theology of the Old Testament* (Chicago: Moody Press, 1991), pp. 7-87 (32).

appear throughout the Old Testament'.[3] Similarly Elliott sees this passage as containing 'one of the most dominant and central expressions of Israel's theology and faith in the entire Old Testament'.[4]

Not all interpreters are as convinced of the prominence of this declaration, however. The monumental Old Testament theology of Gerhard von Rad contains not a single reference to Exod. 19.6 or the eagle speech.[5] There is as yet no consensus on the import and function of this declaration, and the situation is not helped by the fact that only once in the Hebrew Bible are the words ממלכת כהנים found in this combination. As one recent Old Testament theologian puts it, 'The phrasing is only a tease that is left unexplored'.[6] Whether it is as unexplored in the biblical tradition as Brueggemann imagines remains to be seen.

What meaning is to be attributed to the words translated 'royalty' (or 'kingdom') and 'priests'? How do they relate to each other? What light is shed on the meaning of the expression by the cotext,[7] both the immediate cotext in ch. 19, and the wider cotext of the Sinai narrative proper (Exod. 19–24), or the book of Exodus, or even the Pentateuch as a whole? Conversely, does the designation of Israel as a 'royal priesthood' contribute to a better understanding of the nature of the Sinai covenant? How might the covenant, understood in terms of such a declaration, relate to the significant corpus of laws embedded in the narrative matrix of the Pentateuch, particularly the so-called 'priestly' material? What place might the Sinai covenant, when seen in the light of this general royal-priestly declaration, occupy within the discussion on biblical covenants generally?

3. James Muilenburg, 'The Form and Structure of the Covenantal Formulations', *VT* 9 (1959), pp. 347-65 (352).

4. John Hall Elliott, *The Elect and the Holy: An Exegetical Examination of 1 Peter 2.4-10 and the Phrase βασίλειον ἱεράτευμα* (NTSup, 12; Leiden: E.J. Brill, 1966), p. 59.

5. Gerhard von Rad, *Old Testament Theology* (trans. D.M.G. Stalker; 2 vols.; New York: Harper & Row, 1962, 1965).

6. Walter Brueggemann, *Theology of the Old Testament: Testimony, Dispute, Advocacy* (Minneapolis, MN: Fortress Press, 1997), p. 431.

7. The term 'cotext' is used in some discussions of linguistic theory to mean the *literary* context of the discourse in which a particular item of text is set. In this sense it is distinguished from the more familiar term 'context', by which is meant the totality of the attendant circumstances to the discourse (including paralinguistic ones) which may be inferred either from the text itself, or drawn from other sources of knowledge; see, e.g., Peter Cotterell and Max Turner, *Linguistics and Biblical Interpretation* (London: SPCK, 1989), p. 16.

One motivation for this study is the observation that in the Christian tradition, the doctrine of the 'royal priesthood of the faithful' (in its Catholic form), or the 'priesthood of all believers' (as Protestants generally know it) has had a long pedigree and is a live issue in the Church. '[I]t has the unanimous consent of the Early Fathers, and is expounded by theologians up to the eighth century and after the twelfth century in both Eastern and Western Christendom. So prominent is it that it is rare for a church writer of importance to be silent about it.'[8] It is my observation that discussions of this issue have not always proceeded from the best exegetical foundations. It is beyond the scope of this book, however, to interact with these discussions as such,[9] or to consider any outcomes in terms of ecclesiastical structure or practice. So far as these discussions are exegetically based, they deal predominantly with the New Testament citations of or allusions to Exod. 19.6 found in 1 Pet. 2.5, 9; Rev. 1.6; 5.10; and 20.6, passages which will not be considered here in any depth.

The focus of this work will be to consider the meaning and use of the expression ממלכת כהנים as found in Exod. 19.6, within its literary cotext, both its immediate and its wider cotext, then to consider some thematic and ideological implications of this study for Israel's self-perception, and finally to explore some possible literary reflections upon Exod. 19.6 within the Hebrew Bible.

2. *A Survey of Relevant Literature*

On the questions posed above, much has been written from a wide diversity of perspectives. The literature survey below will concentrate on works from roughly the last one hundred years, with increasing attention to the

8. Cyril Eastwood, *The Royal Priesthood of the Faithful: An Investigation of the Doctrine from Biblical Times to the Reformation* (London: Epworth Press, 1963), p. 226; cf. also, for the post-Reformation period, Cyril Eastwood, *The Priesthood of All Believers: An Examination of the Doctrine from the Reformation to the Present Day* (London: Epworth Press, 1960). The most comprehensive catalogue of Christian reflections on the theme (mostly with reference to New Testament echoes of Exod. 19.6) is to be found in Paul Dabin, SJ, *Le sacerdoce royale des fidèles dans la tradition ancienne et moderne* (Museum Lessianum—Section Théologique; Brussels: Desclée, 1950).

9. For examples of the genre, see Donald C. Fleming, *The Priesthood of All Believers* (Brisbane: Christian Brethren Research Fellowship, 1983); Walter B. Shurden (ed.), *Proclaiming the Baptist Vision: The Priesthood of All Believers* (Macon, GA: Smyth & Helwys, 1993); Alwyn Marriage, *The People of God: A Royal Priesthood* (London: Darton, Longman & Todd, 1995).

more recent contributions. This is not meant to diminish the substantial and abiding contribution of earlier generations of interpreters. Quite the contrary, in fact, as the conclusions reached in this study will at times be seen to have affinities with earlier interpretations, such as those adopted by the versions, the targums and early Jewish and Christian commentators, but largely abandoned by modern interpreters, and to depart from aspects of the prevailing views of recent scholarship. From the moment the words of Exod. 19.6 were promulgated, the interpretative task began. This book aims to make a small contribution to the ongoing task, and to the extent that it has value, builds upon the foundation of those who have gone before.

a. *Commentaries*

Among the numerous commentaries on Exodus, we may note a few of the most significant ones from the past century or so as being those by Keil,[10] Holzinger,[11] Chadwick,[12] McNeile,[13] Driver,[14] Beer,[15] Noth,[16] Cassuto,[17] Hyatt,[18] Childs,[19] Schmidt,[20] Gispen,[21] Durham,[22] Fretheim,[23] Sarna,[24]

10. C.F. Keil and F. Delitzsch, *Commentary on the Old Testament* (trans. James Martin; 10 vols.; repr.; Grand Rapids: Eerdmans, 1983).

11. H. Holzinger, *Exodus* (KHAT, 2; Tübingen: J.C.B. Mohr, 1900).

12. G.A. Chadwick, *The Book of Exodus* (The Expositors Bible; London: Hodder & Stoughton, 1903).

13. A.H. McNeile, *The Book of Exodus with Introduction and Notes* (Westminster Commentaries; London: Methuen, 1908).

14. S.R. Driver, *The Book of Exodus in the Revised Version with Introduction and Notes* (CBSC; Cambridge: Cambridge University Press, 1911).

15. Georg Beer, *Exodus, mit einem Beitrag von K. Galling* (HAT, 3; Tübingen: J.C.B. Mohr, 1939).

16. Martin Noth, *Exodus: A Commentary* (trans. J.S. Bowden; OTL; London: SCM Press, 1962).

17. U. Cassuto, *A Commentary on the Book of Exodus* (trans. I. Abrahams; Jerusalem: Magnes Press, 1967).

18. J. Philip Hyatt, *Commentary on Exodus* (NCB; London: Oliphants, 1971).

19. Brevard S. Childs, *Exodus: A Commentary* (OTL; Philadelphia: Westminster Press, 1974).

20. Werner H. Schmidt, *Exodus* (BKAT, 2; 2 vols.; Neukirchen–Vluyn: Neukirchener Verlag, 1974).

21. W.H. Gispen, *Exodus* (BSC; Grand Rapids: Zondervan, 1982).

22. John I. Durham, *Exodus* (WBC, 3; Waco, TX: Word Books, 1987).

23. Terence E. Fretheim, *Exodus* (Int; Louisville, KY: John Knox Press, 1991).

24. Nahum M. Sarna, *Exodus: The Traditional Hebrew Text with the New JPS Translation* (The JPS Torah Commentary; Philadelphia: Jewish Publication Society of America, 1991).

Jacob,[25] Houtman,[26] Gowan[27] and Propp.[28] The nature of commentaries is such that rarely will there be more than a brief discussion under a verse such as Exod. 19.6. The chief value of the commentaries lies in the fact that in general they deal with the whole book, and the structure of the commentary is usually (though not always) dictated by the received form of the textual tradition.

Most of the commentaries named fall broadly within the tradition of critical scholarship, which for much of the past century has meant working within the canons of the historicist framework and its principal artefact of Hebrew Bible studies, the documentary hypothesis made popular by Wellhausen in his *Prolegomena to the History of Israel*.[29] This work represented both a culmination of nineteenth-century scholarship on the Pentateuch and a new point of departure for much of its subsequent study, indeed much of the study of the Hebrew Bible generally. A consequence is that few commentators have felt their job has been done unless each unit of text has been assigned to one or other of the continuous sources or one of the many redactions through which the Pentateuch passed on its journey to the form in which we know it. A notable gap in the list above is an Exodus commentary in the International Critical Commentary series, as the projected volume by A.R.S. Kennedy never appeared. This series has generally represented for the English-speaking world the classical outworking of the Wellhausen approach to Pentateuchal studies. One major exception to the observation above regarding the dominance of the documentary hypothesis is the work of Cassuto, who sought to give a unified reading of the book of Exodus. Perhaps the most groundbreaking of the commentaries is the one by Childs,[30] who is more candid than has been customary among serious commentators about the pre-commitments of

25. Benno Jacob, *The Second Book of the Bible: Exodus, Interpreted by Benno Jacob* (trans. with an introduction by Walter Jacob in association with Yaakov Elman; Hoboken, NJ: Ktav, 1992).

26. Cornelis Houtman, *Exodus* (trans. Johan Rebel and Sierd Woudstra; HCOT; 3 vols.; vols. 1 and 2: Kampen: Kok, 1993; vol. 3: Leuven: Peeters, 2000).

27. Donald E. Gowan, *Theology in Exodus: Biblical Theology in the Form of a Commentary* (Louisville, KY: Westminster/John Knox Press, 1994).

28. William H. Propp, *Exodus 1–18: A New Translation with Introduction and Commentary* (AB, 2A; New York: Doubleday, 1998).

29. Julius Wellhausen, *Prolegomena to the History of Israel* (trans. J. Sutherland Black and Allan Menzies; Edinburgh: A. & C. Black, 1885).

30. Childs, *Exodus*, p. xiii.

the exegete and the way these do and must affect the interpretative task. Childs gives ample space to historical-critical issues, but, unlike some commentators, does not feel that the exegete's task ends when he has fragmented the text into myriad constituent parts. His approach will be considered further below.

b. *Monographs on the Sinai Pericope*

More scope for treatment of literary and thematic issues is afforded by the monographs on the section of Exodus which deals with the encounter between Israel and the God Yhwh on Mt Sinai, or with various portions of the narrative of this encounter, particularly chs. 19–24. With their interweaving of narrative and law, these chapters present the interpreter with a formidable task to analyze their literary structure in any satisfying way. Principal among these monographs are the works of Beyerlin,[31] Eissfeldt,[32] Zenger,[33] Nicholson,[34] Schmidt,[35] Renaud[36] and Niehaus.[37] These approach the Sinai material from some different perspectives. The Sinai pericope has been the most notoriously difficult portion of the Pentateuch with which to grapple from a source-critical perspective. Eissfeldt's *Die Komposition der Sinai-Erzählung* and Zenger's *Die Sinaitheophanie* in particular represent a developed stage of this approach as applied to the

31. Walter Beyerlin, *Origins and History of the Oldest Sinaitic Traditions* (trans. S. Rudman; Oxford: Basil Blackwell, 1965).

32. Otto Eissfeldt, *Die Komposition der Sinai-Erzählung: Exodus 19–34* (Sitzungsberichte der sachsichen Akademie der Wissenschaften zu Leipzig, philologisch–historische Klasse, 113.1; Berlin: Akademie Verlag, 1966).

33. Erich Zenger, *Die Sinaitheophanie: Untersuchung zum jahwistischen und elohistischen Geschichtswerk* (FzB, 3; Würzburg: Echter Verlag, 1971); *idem*, *Israel am Sinai: Analysen und Interpretationen zu Exodus 17–34* (Altenberge: CIS-Verlag, 1982); cf. also *idem*, 'Wie und wozu die Tora zum Sinai kam: Literarisch und theologische Beobachtung zu Exodus 19–34', in Marc Vervenne (ed.), *Studies in the Book of Exodus: Redaction, Reception, Interpretation* (BETL, 126; Leuven: Leuven University Press, 1996), pp. 265-88.

34. Ernest W. Nicholson, *Exodus and Sinai in History and Tradition* (Richmond, VA: John Knox Press, 1973).

35. Werner H. Schmidt, *Exodus, Sinai und Mose: Erwägungen zu Ex 1–19 und 24* (Erträge der Forschung, 191; Darmstadt: Wissenschaftliche Buchgesellschaft, 1983).

36. Bernard Renaud, *La théophanie du Sinai, Ex 19–24: Exégèse et théologie* (Cahiers de la Revue biblique, 30; Paris: J. Gabalda, 1991).

37. Jeffrey J. Niehaus, *God at Sinai: Covenant and Theophany in the Bible and Ancient Near East* (SOTBT; Grand Rapids: Zondervan, 1995).

Sinai pericope. Zenger's work is particularly useful in giving a digest of the major contributions to the discussion to the 1960s. Beyerlin is more concerned to consider the form-critical background to the component units of the Sinai material, considered against the background of the ancient Near Eastern treaties and their possible origin in festival contexts. Schmidt's contribution is to evaluate the traditions linking Moses with both the Exodus and the Sinai traditions. The work by Niehaus, while containing substantial material on the Sinai encounter, uses the genre of the theophany account to investigate other biblical passages and ancient Near Eastern parallels.

c. *Essays on the Sinai Pericope*

There have been countless essays and articles on the Sinai pericope or aspects of it. Mention can only be made here of a few. Among the most influential has been von Rad's essay, 'The Form Critical Problem of the Hexateuch',[38] the German original of which appeared in 1938. Other contributions include those by Van Seters,[39] Blum,[40] Sonnet,[41] Rendtorff,[42] Otto[43] and Alexander.[44] In addition, one finds substantial sections on the Sinai pericope in monographs on the Pentateuch (or Hexateuch) as a

38. Gerhard von Rad, 'The Form Critical Problem of the Hexateuch', in *idem*, *The Problem of the Hexateuch and Other Essays* (trans. E.W. Trueman Dicken; London: SCM Press, 1966), pp. 1-78.

39. John Van Seters, '"Comparing Scripture with Scripture": Some Observations on the Sinai Pericope of Exodus 19–24', in Gene M. Tucker, David L. Petersen and Robert R. Wilson (eds.), *Canon, Theology and Old Testament Interpretation: Essays in Honor of Brevard S. Childs* (Philadelphia: Fortress Press, 1988), pp. 111-30.

40. Erhard Blum, 'Israël à la montagne de Dieu: Remarques sur Ex 19–24, 32–34 et sur le contexte littéraire et historique de sa composition', in Albert de Pury (ed.), *Le Pentateuque en question: Les origines et la composition des cinq premiers livres de la Bible à la lumière des recherches récentes* (Geneva: Labor et Fides, 1989), pp. 271-95.

41. Jean-Pierre Sonnet, SJ, 'Le Sinaï dans l'événement de sa lecture: La dimension pragmatique d'Ex 19–24', *Nouvelle revue théologique* 111 (1989), pp. 321-44.

42. Rolf Rendtorff, 'Der Text in seiner Endgestalt: Überlegungen zu Exodus 19', in Dwight R. Daniels, Uwe Glessner and Martin Rösel (eds.), *Ernten, was man sät: Festschrift für Klaus Koch zu seinem 65. Geburtstag* (Neukirchen–Vluyn: Neukirchener Verlag, 1991), pp. 459-70.

43. Eckart Otto, 'Kritik der Pentateuchkomposition', *TR* 60 (1995), pp. 163-91.

44. T.D. Alexander, 'The Composition of the Sinai Narrative in Exodus xix 1–xxiv 11', *VT* 49 (1999), pp. 2-20.

whole, such as those by Carpenter and Harford,[45] Noth,[46] Whybray,[47] Blum[48] and Rendtorff.[49] Again, some of this material shows a preoccupation with the pre-history of the text, in terms of source-analysis, form-criticism or tradition-criticism rather than with interpreting the text as a literary unity, though the contributions of Whybray, Blum, Rendtorff and Alexander represent different stages of a move away from the earlier consensus.

d. *Literature on Exodus 19.4-6*

On the specific passage which concerns us, Exod. 19.6 and its immediate cotext in Exodus 19, there has been a steady stream of articles in the years since the turn of the twentieth century, the main contributions of which will be considered under Chapter 4. Principal among these are those by Klopfer,[50] Caspari,[51] Scott,[52] Bauer,[53] Moran,[54] Fohrer,[55] Mosis,[56] Rivard,[57]

45. J. Estlin Carpenter and George Harford, *The Composition of the Hexateuch: An Introduction with Select Lists of Words and Phrases* (London: Longmans, Green & Co., 1902).

46. Martin Noth, *A History of Pentateuchal Traditions* (trans. Bernhard W. Anderson; Scholars Press Reprints and Translations Series; repr.; Atlanta: Scholars Press, 1981).

47. R.N. Whybray, *The Making of the Pentateuch: A Methodological Study* (JSOTSup, 53; Sheffield: JSOT Press, 1987).

48. Erhard Blum, *Studien zur Komposition des Pentateuch* (BZAW, 189; Berlin: W. de Gruyter, 1990).

49. Rolf Rendtorff, *The Problem of the Process of Transmission in the Pentateuch* (trans. John J. Scullion; Sheffield: JSOT Press, 1990).

50. Richard Klopfer, 'Zur Quellenscheidung in Exod. 19', *ZAW* 18 (1898), pp. 197-235.

51. Wilhelm Caspari, 'Das priesterliche Königreich', *Theologische Blätter* 8 (1929), cols. 105-10.

52. R.B.Y. Scott, 'A Kingdom of Priests (Exodus 19.6)', *OTS* 8 (1950), pp. 213-19.

53. J.B. Bauer, 'Könige und Priester, ein heiliges Volk (Ex 19,6)', *BZ* 2 (1958), pp. 283-86.

54. W.L. Moran, SJ, 'A Kingdom of Priests', in John L. McKenzie, SJ (ed.), *The Bible in Current Catholic Thought* (New York: Herder & Herder, 1962), pp. 7-20.

55. Georg Fohrer, '"Priestliches Königtum" (Ex 19.6)', in Georg Fohrer, *Studien zur alttestamentlichen Theologie und Geschichte (1949–1966)* (BZAW, 115; Berlin: W. de Gruyter, 1969), pp. 149-53.

56. Rudolf Mosis, 'Ex 19,5b.6a: Syntaktischer Aufbau und lexikalische Semantik', *BZ* 22 (1978), pp. 1-25.

57. Richard Rivard, 'Pour une relecture d'Ex 19 et 20: Analyse sémiotique d'Ex 19,1-8', *ScEs* 33 (1981), pp. 335-56.

Le Roux,[58] Cazelles,[59] Kleinig,[60] Barbiero,[61] Ska,[62] Dozemann[63] and Schenker.[64]

Since questions of source are generally dealt with more substantially in studies of larger units of text (see above), these more specific studies, while usually containing some material relating to source-analysis, deal with syntactic and lexical issues (Caspari, Scott, Bauer, Moran, Fohrer, Mosis, Cazelles and Barbiero), with issues of social or theological provenance (Ska, Barbiero), with literary form, function and redaction (Rivard, Kleinig, Dozemann, Le Roux), and with aspects of the history of translation and interpretation (Cerfaux, Schenker). The chief issue addressed in not a few of these studies is the identity of the referent of the expression ממלכת כהנים. As we shall see in Chapter 4, the two substantive issues to be determined are whether the words ממלכת כהנים refer to Israel collectively, or only to a priestly elite, and the more commonly overlooked question of to whom an attribution of royalty is being made.

Finally, attention must be drawn to the monograph of Jo Bailey Wells which is based on Exod. 19.5-6.[65] Wells is primarily interested in the

58. J.H. Le Roux, 'A Holy Nation Was Elected (The Election Theology of Exodus 19.5-6)', in W.C. van Wyk (ed.), *The Exilic Period: Aspects of Apocalypticism* (Old Testament Essays; Pretoria: Die Ou-Testamentisse Werkgemeenskap in Suid-Afrika, 1984), pp. 59-78.

59. Henri Cazelles, PSS, '"Royaume de prêtres et nation consacrée" (Exode XIX,6)', in Henri Cazelles, PSS, *Autour de l'Exode (Etudes)* (Sources bibliques; Paris: J. Gabalda, 1987), pp. 289-94.

60. John W. Kleinig, 'On Eagles' Wing: An Exegetical Study of Exodus 19.2-8', *LTJ* 21 (1987), pp. 18-27.

61. Gianni Barbiero, '*Mamleket kohanîm*: (Es 19,6a): I sacerdoti al potere?', *Rivista Biblica* 37 (1989), pp. 427-46.

62. Jean Louis Ska, SJ, 'Ex 19,3-8 et les parénèses deutéronomiques', in Georg Braulik, OSB, Walter Gross and Sean McEvenue (eds.), *Biblische Theologie und gesellschaftlicher Wandel* (Festschrift Norbert Lohfink, SJ; Freiburg: Herder, 1993), pp. 307-14; *idem*, 'Exode 19,3b-6 et l'identité de l'Israël postexilique', in Vervenne (ed.), *Studies in the Book of Exodus*, pp. 289-317.

63. Thomas B. Dozeman, 'Spatial Form in Exod. 19.1-8a and in the Larger Sinai Narrative', *Semeia* 46 (1989), pp. 87-101.

64. Adrian Schenker, OP, 'Besonderes und allgemeines Priestertum im Alten Bund: Ex 19,6 und Jes 61,6 im Vergleich', in Alois Schifferle (ed.), *Pfarrei in der Postmoderne? Gemeindebildung in nachchristlicher Zeit* (Festschrift Leo Karrer; Freiburg: Herder, 1997), pp. 111-16; *idem*, 'Drei Mosaiksteinchen: "Königreich von Priestern", "Und ihre Kinder gehen weg", "Wir tun und wir hören" (Exodus 19,6; 21,22; 24,7)', in Vervenne (ed.), *Studies in the Book of Exodus*, pp. 367-80.

65. Jo Bailey Wells, *God's Holy People: A Theme in Biblical Theology* (JSOTSup,

theme of holiness as an attribute and aspiration of the people of God for which she sees this passage as foundational. After a literary analysis of Exod. 19.5-6 and its setting in the book of Exodus, Wells considers the relationship of priesthood and holiness, and addresses the development of these interrelated themes in the Hebrew canon and the New Testament, particularly 1 Peter. There is thus some overlap of interest with the present work. The focus differs, however, in that Wells does not treat in any depth the privileged status of Israel described in terms of royalty which is a major theme of the present work, and the intertextual studies are consequently different.

e. *Old Testament Theologies*

A further genre of literature relevant to this study for the treatment generally given to the themes of covenant, election, people of God, worship and related *loci* which are raised by the Sinai encounter is that of Old Testament theology, or history of Hebrew religion.[66] Among these, the comprehensive work of Eichrodt and the more focussed studies of Dumbrell and McComiskey in particular devote considerable attention to the notion of covenant, seeing it as a significant structuring device for their consideration of thematic development within the Hebrew Bible. No study of Old Testament theology, with the exception, to a degree, of the work of

305; Sheffield: Sheffield Academic Press, 2000). The present work in its phase as a doctoral thesis was completed without the benefit of Wells's helpful study.

66. Among the more relevant theologies may be listed those of Edmond Jacob, *Theology of the Old Testament* (New York: Harper & Row, 1958); Th.C. Vriezen, *An Outline of Old Testament Theology* (trans. S. Neuijen; Oxford: Basil Blackwell, 1958); George A.F. Knight, *A Christian Theology of the Old Testament* (London: SCM Press, 1959); Walther Eichrodt, *Theology of the Old Testament* (trans. D.A. Baker; OTL; 2 vols.; London: SCM Press, 1961, 1967); Gerhard von Rad, *Old Testament Theology* (trans. D.M.G. Stalker; 2 vols.; New York: Harper & Row, 1962, 1965); Walther Zimmerli, *Old Testament Theology in Outline* (trans. David E. Green; Edinburgh: T. & T. Clark, 1978); William J. Dumbrell, *Covenant and Creation: An Old Testament Covenantal Theology* (Exeter: Paternoster Press, 1984); Ronald E. Clements, *Old Testament Theology: A Fresh Approach* (Marshall's Theological Library; London: Marshall, Morgan & Scott, 1978); Thomas Edward McComiskey, *The Covenants of Promise: A Theology of the Old Testament Covenants* (Grand Rapids: Baker Book House, 1985); Horst Dietrich Preuss, *Old Testament Theology* (trans. Leo G. Perdue; OTL; 2 vols.; Louisville, KY: Westminster/John Knox Press, 1995, 1996); John H. Sailhamer, *Introduction to Old Testament Theology: A Canonical Approach* (Grand Rapids: Zondervan, 1995); Brueggemann, *Theology of the Old Testament*.

Dumbrell who devotes more than passing attention to Exod. 19.3b-6,[67] has made use of the *locus* of Israel's royal priesthood as a central element in its treatment of Israel's religious thought.[68]

f. *Literature on Israel's Priesthood and Cult, Election and Covenant*

As will be argued in Chapter 6, any understanding of the 'royal priesthood' declaration must take account of the ideology behind Israel's cult. Among the more specific studies which deal with the theme of priesthood and the cult generally, we may note at this stage the works of de Vaux,[69] Kraus,[70] Rowley,[71] Cody,[72] Haran,[73] Jenson,[74] Nelson[75] and Longman,[76] and from a more comparative stance, those of James,[77] Clifford[78] and Henshaw.[79] These works set Israel's cult in the context of the cultic ideology and practice of the ancient world, outline the details of Israelite practice as

67. Dumbrell, *Covenant and Creation*, esp. pp. 84-90.

68. Despite its title, the Old Testament theology by Eugene H. Merrill, *Kingdom of Priests: A History of Old Testament Israel* (Grand Rapids: Baker Book House, 1987), is no exception to this observation.

69. Roland de Vaux, OP, *Ancient Israel* (2 vols.; New York: McGraw–Hill, 1965).

70. Hans-Joachim Kraus, *Worship in Israel: A Cultic History of the Old Testament* (trans. Geoffrey Buswell; Oxford: Basil Blackwell, 1966).

71. H.H. Rowley, *Worship in Ancient Israel: Its Forms and Meaning* (London: SPCK, 1967).

72. Aelred Cody, OSB, *A History of Old Testament Priesthood* (AnBib, 35; Rome: Pontifical Biblical Institute Press, 1969).

73. Menahem Haran, *Temples and Temple Service in Ancient Israel: An Inquiry into Biblical Cult Phenomena and the Historical Setting of the Priestly School* (Winona Lake, IN: Eisenbrauns, 1985).

74. Phillip P. Jenson, *Graded Holiness: A Key to the Priestly Conception of the World* (JSOTSup, 106; Sheffield: JSOT Press, 1992).

75. Richard D. Nelson, *Raising Up a Faithful Priest: Community and Priesthood in Biblical Theology* (Louisville, KY: Westminster/John Knox Press, 1993).

76. Tremper Longman, III, *Immanuel in our Place: Seeing Christ in Israel's Worship* (The Gospel According to the Old Testament; Phillipsburg, NJ: P. & R. Publishing, 2001).

77. E.O. James, *The Nature and Function of Priesthood: A Comparative and Anthropological Study* (Studies in the History of Religions; Numen Supplements, 25; London: Thames & Hudson, 1955).

78. Richard J. Clifford, *The Cosmic Mountain in Canaan and the Old Testament* (HSM, 4; Cambridge, MA: Harvard University Press, 1972).

79. Richard A. Henshaw, *Female and Male, the Cultic Personnel: The Bible and the Rest of the Ancient Near East* (Princeton Theological Monograph Series, 31; Pittsburgh, PA: Pickwick Press, 1994).

recorded in the literary texts or as reconstructed from archaeological studies and to some extent endeavour to develop a rationale for Israel's cult and priesthood.

Israel's understanding of its relationship with Yhwh, particularly as expressed in the concepts of election and covenant, has generated a vast literature, some of which will be considered in Chapter 7. While from the perspective adopted in this work, election and covenant are closely interrelated themes,[80] they have for the most part been treated separately. By some, the 'kingdom of priests' passage is treated as a key passage in expounding Israel's belief in its special status or calling as Yhwh's chosen people, notably by Wildberger and Fuhs.[81] It is surprisingly omitted by Sohn from his otherwise comprehensive catalogue of images of election, perhaps because the rich extended metaphor lying behind the notion of Israel as a royal priesthood has not been fully appreciated. There have been a number of significant monographs as well as some influential essays on the nature of Israel's covenant(s) with Yhwh over the past half century commencing with Mendenhall's *Law and Covenant in Israel and the Ancient Near East*.[82] The steady stream of monographs[83] and articles[84] has

80. Cf. Rolf Rendtorff, *The Covenant Formula: An Exegetical and Theological Investigation* (trans. Margaret Kohl; Edinburgh: T. & T. Clark, 1998), p. 3.

81. Hans Wildberger, *Jahwes Eigentumsvolk: Eine Studie zur Traditionsgeschichte und Theologie des Erwählungsgedankens* (Zurich: Zwingli-Verlag, 1960), esp. pp. 9-16 and 80-95; Hans F. Fuhs, 'Heiliges Volk Gottes', in J. Schreiner (ed.), *Unterwegs zur Kirche: Alttestamentliche Konzeptionen* (Freiburg: Herder, 1987), pp. 143-67 (154-59). Among the more significant contributions on the election theme are those of Kurt Galling, *Die Erwählungstraditionen Israels* (BZAW, 48; Giessen: Alfred Töpelmann, 1928); H.H. Rowley, *The Biblical Doctrine of Election* (Louisa Curtis Lectures, 1948; London: Lutterworth, 1950); Robert Martin-Achard, 'La signification théologique de l'élection d'Israël', *TZ* 16 (1960), pp. 333-41; *idem*, 'Israël, peuple sacerdotal', *Verbum Caro* 18 (1964), pp. 11-28; Georges Auzou, *De la servitude au service: Etude du livre de l'Exode* (Connaissance de la Bible, 3; Paris: Editions de l'Orante, 1961); Peter Altmann, *Erwählungstheologie und Universalismus im Alten Testament* (BZAW, 92; Berlin: Alfred Töpelmann, 1964); Seock-Tae Sohn, *The Divine Election of Israel* (Grand Rapids: Eerdmans, 1991).

82. George E. Mendenhall, *Law and Covenant in Israel and the Ancient Near East* (Pittsburgh: The Presbyterian Board of Colportage of Western Pennsylvania, 1955); cf. *idem*, *The Tenth Generation: The Origins of the Biblical Tradition* (Baltimore: The Johns Hopkins University Press, 1973).

83. Dennis J. McCarthy, SJ, *Treaty and Covenant: A Study in Form in the Ancient Oriental Documents and in the Old Testament* (AnBib, 21; Rome: Pontifical Biblical Institute Press, 2nd edn, 1981); Lothar Perlitt, *Bundestheologie im Alten Testament*

canvassed such issues as the degree to which Israel's understanding of its relationship with Yhwh is parallelled within ancient Near Eastern religious or royal conventions, the degree of continuity/discontinuity within the Israelite covenants and the tension between conditionality and unconditionality in the covenants, with the result that no clear consensus has emerged.

g. *Literature on New Testament Citations of Exodus 19.6*

One final category of literature must be mentioned at this point. Because the New Testament books of 1 Peter (2.5, 9) and Revelation (1.6; 5.10; 20.6) quote or make clear allusion to Exod. 19.6, treating the theme of the corporate royal priesthood of Christians as a significant aspect of Christian reflection on this unit of text and tradition, a major monograph has been written on each of these. Both the work of Elliott on the 1 Peter *locus*, and

(WMANT, 36; Neukirchen–Vluyn: Neukirchener Verlag, 1969); Delbert R. Hillers, *Covenant: The History of a Biblical Idea* (Baltimore: The Johns Hopkins University Press, 1969); Klaus Baltzer, *The Covenant Formulary in Old Testament, Jewish and Early Christian Writings* (trans. David E. Green; Oxford: Basil Blackwell, 1971); E. Kutsch, *Verheissung und Gesetz: Untersuchungen zum sogenannten 'Bund' im Alten Testament* (BZAW, 131; Berlin: W. de Gruyter, 1973); Paul Kalluveettil, CMI, *Declaration and Covenant: A Comprehensive Review of Covenant Formulae from the Old Testament and the Ancient Near East* (AnBib, 88; Rome: Pontifical Biblical Institute Press, 1982); Jon D. Levenson, *Sinai and Zion: An Entry into the Jewish Bible* (New Voices in Biblical Studies; Minneapolis: Winston Press, 1985); Ernest W. Nicholson, *God and His People: Covenant and Theology in the Old Testament* (Oxford: Clarendon Press, 1986); Rendtorff, *The Covenant Formula*.

84. Among the more influential articles, we may include George E. Mendenhall, 'Ancient Oriental and Biblical Law', in Edward F. Campbell and David Noel Freedman (eds.), *The Biblical Archaeologist Reader 3* (Garden City, NY: Doubleday, 1970), pp. 3-24; Muilenburg, 'Form and Structure'; David Noel Freedman, 'Divine Commitment and Human Obligation: The Covenant Theme', *Int* 18 (1964), pp. 419-31; Moshe Weinfeld, 'The Covenant of Grant in the Old Testament and in the Ancient Near East', *JAOS* 90 (1970), pp. 184-203; H.H. Schmid, 'Ich will euer Gott sein und ihr sollt mein Volk sein: Die sogenannte Bundesformel und die Frage nach der Mitte des Alten Testaments', in Dieter Luhrmann and Georg Strecker (eds.), *Kirche* (Festschrift Günther Bornkamm; Tübingen: J.C.B. Mohr, 1980), pp. 1-25; Erich Zenger, 'Die Bundestheologie', in *idem* (ed.), *Der Neuer Bund im Alten: Studien zur Bundestheologie der beiden Testamente* (Quaestiones disputatae, 146; Freiburg: Herder, 1993), pp. 13-49; Menahem Haran, 'The *berît* "Covenant": Its Nature and Ceremonial Background', in Mordechai Cogan, Barry L. Eichler and Jeffrey H. Tigay (eds.), *Tehillah le-Mosheh: Biblical and Judaic Studies in Honor of Moshe Greenberg* (Winona Lake, IN: Eisenbrauns, 1997), pp. 203-19.

that of Schüssler Fiorenza on the Revelation passages discuss in some depth the Hebrew text of Exod. 19.6, the versional evidence, and some of the ancient quotations and allusions.[85]

3. *Method and Format of this Study*

Our task, then, will be to focus on the interpretation of Exod. 19.6. The next chapter will consider the main contours of the source-critical approach to the Sinai pericope which has been dominant for over a century. Noting the failure of this approach to produce satisfying results, we will consider the newer literary criticism with its emphasis on the integrity of the discourse and outline the approach to be taken in this book. In keeping with the (nuanced) 'final form' approach to be adopted (as outlined in Chapter 2), we will not deal with form-critical or tradition-historical matters except to the extent that these are related to the discussion on the meaning of 'covenant' (Chapter 7). Chapter 3 will present an exegesis of the passage Exod. 19.1-8 with particular attention to vv. 4-6a in an endeavour to understand the functioning of the phrase ממלכת כהנים in relation to that cotext. The interpretation of the phrase itself will occupy our attention in Chapter 4. The discussion will then be extended to take in some considerations from the structure of the book of Exodus as a whole and the bearing these may have on the interpretation of Exod. 19.6. These matters will be dealt with Chapter 5 which will focus in particular on the unit Exod. 24.1-11. This passage, it is argued, presents the 'ordination' rite for the priesthood of the community of Israel, and the culmination of the preparations of ch. 19 in the consummation of the divine vision and the meal as honoured guests in God's heavenly palace.

Chapter 6 will outline something of the rationale of the priestly legislation, principally as this is found in Exodus 25–31, though drawing on other relevant passages of the Hebrew Bible and beyond. What was the nature and function of the tabernacle and the Levitical or Aaronic priesthood which functioned within it?[86] How do such priests relate to the

85. Elliott, *The Elect and the Holy*, pp. 50-128; Elisabeth Schüssler Fiorenza, *Priester für Gott: Studien zum Herrschafts- und Priestermotiv in der Apokalypse* (NTAbh, 7; Münster: Aschendorff, 1972), pp. 78-166.

86. The epithets 'Levitical' and 'Aaronic' are used here interchangeably to denote the specially designated class of cultic officials within Israel and to distinguish them from the general priesthood to which Israel as a whole is called. The discussion as to whether other Levite families legitimately filled the priestly office, or whether the

'priests' of Exod. 19.6? It will be suggested that the Aaronic priests are intended by the writer of Exodus to present a concretization of the image of Israel's royal priesthood, a visual lesson on the ideal prospect set before the nation as a whole. This chapter will include more comparative material on priesthood and cult in the ancient Near East. There is no intention to assume a 'history of religions' approach and imply that Israel's understanding must conform to a general cultural pattern. Such parallels as we observe are intended to act as catalysts and prompts for our closer investigation of the sources which are specific to Israel's cultic theory and practice.

Although it is beyond the scope of this work to present a comprehensive interpretation of the Sinai covenant, Chapter 7 will suggest ways in which an understanding of the 'royal priesthood' declaration may elucidate the Sinai covenant as one in which the notion of a grant to Israel of a privileged position predominates. This grant is understood to entail, in some metaphorical sense, something of the status and prerogatives of royalty as well as priesthood. These metaphors are seen as drawing their content from the cosmic cultic ideology as this is presented within Israel's religious tradition, and as pointing to the restoration of access to God's presence as he is conceived of as enthroned in his heavenly temple.

The phrase ממלכת כהנים or echoes of it occurs in a number of later Jewish and Christian writings. Besides the New Testament references cited above, we may note some of the principal references to be found in 2 Macc. 2.17; *Jub*. 16.18; 33.20; Philo, *Abr*. 56; *Sobr*. 66; 4Q504 7.4 and some possible allusions in texts relating to the *Testament of Levi* (both a Greek fragment and the *Aramaic Levi* texts from Qumran). However, as these have mostly been treated (albeit sometimes briefly) in discussions on the background to the New Testament passages,[87] and as any substantial treatment of these would significantly alter the focus of the present work, there will not be a detailed study of these here, though reference will be made to them, particularly in Chapter 4, primarily for the light they cast on the state of the text of Exod. 19.6 in Second Temple times.

restriction of priesthood to the Aaronides was a late development will be taken up again briefly below, but will not be a major issue for this study. For the writer of Exodus, only the sons of Aaron, of the tribe of Levi, were eligible to serve as priests.

87. Elliott, *The Elect and the Holy*, pp. 78-101; Schüssler Fiorenza, *Priester für Gott*, pp. 90-94; Martin McNamara, MSC, *Targum and Testament: Aramaic Paraphrases of the Hebrew Bible—A Light on the New Testament* (Shannon: Irish University Press, 1972), pp. 151-53.

There are, however, a number of possible echoes of the 'royal priesthood' image of Exod. 19.6 within the Hebrew Bible, and with the exception of Isa. 61.6, which is frequently considered in relation to Exod. 19.6,[88] most of these have received scant attention from the perspective of their intertextual or thematic relationship with the Exodus passage. As used in this book, 'intertextuality' refers to the way texts draw on one another's language, images and conceptual worlds.[89] It is not laden with a particular philosophical content,[90] but is used in much the same way as the phrase 'inner-biblical exegesis' is used by Fishbane.[91] Among the passages to be considered for their links with Exod. 19.6 are Numbers 16; Hos. 4.4-9; Isa. 61.6; Mic. 4.6-14; Ps. 114.2 and Zechariah 3. These generally short studies are not intended to be exhaustive, but indicative of possible fruitful lines of inquiry. Other possible connections will be mentioned more in passing. In looking at these passages, it is the aim of this study to demonstrate that the notion of Israel as a corporate royal-priestly entity is not a passing metaphor, but represents a richer and more sustained ideology which has left its mark at a number of places within the Hebrew Bible and beyond. We will also be interested to note the light that one text may shed upon the interpretation of another.

88. Even the Isaiah passage is not universally considered to have any relationship with Exod. 19.6. See Elliott, *The Elect and the Holy*, pp. 61-62; Henri Cazelles, PSS, 'Alliance du Sinai, alliance de l'Horeb et renouvellement de l'alliance', in H. Donner, Robert Hanhart and Rudolf Smend (eds.), *Beiträge zur alttestamentlichen Theologie* (Festschrift Walther Zimmerli; Göttingen: Vandenhoeck & Ruprecht, 1977), pp. 69-79 (77).

89. For this broad definition, cf. Gail R. O'Day, 'Jeremiah 9.22-23 and 1 Corinthians 1.26-31: A Study in Intertextuality', *JBL* 109 (1990), pp. 259-67 (259).

90. For a general introduction to the theory of intertextuality, see Michael Worton and Judith Still (eds.), *Intertextuality: Theories and Practices* (Manchester: Manchester University Press, 1990).

91. Michael Fishbane, *Biblical Interpretation in Ancient Israel* (Oxford: Oxford University Press, 1985), pp. 1-19.

Chapter 2

OLD AND NEW IN LITERARY CRITICISM: METHODOLOGIES IN THE INTERPRETATION OF EXODUS 19.6

1. *Literary Criticism in its Older Guise: Source and Redaction Criticism*

As has been noted in Chapter 1, much of what has been written on the Sinai pericope has addressed source-critical, form-critical and tradition-historical concerns, though with no sign of any significant consensus. The following section will briefly survey the main contours of the discussion on the source criticism of Exod. 19.4-6a (or, including the quotative frame and response, vv. 3b-8).

Exodus 19–24 presents the reader with an array of puzzling difficulties. These include the apparent misplacement of the Decalogue in 20.1-17, the confusing number of ascents and descents of the mountain on the part of Moses, the tensions regarding the nature and degree of proximity of the encounter between God and Israel, the character of the theophany event (Is it storm?, volcanic activity?) and the role and identity of the various representative or mediatorial figures in the encounter. Most typically, scholars have had recourse to source-critical solutions to these tensions, identifying the apparent disjunctures in the flow of the text as the seams marking the transitions to a different underlying source. The results of such studies have been less than satisfying, as evidenced by the lack of consensus as to an overall analysis after well over a century of such scrutiny of the text. McCarthy's comment would meet with substantial acceptance: 'The Sinai narrative is a *locus classicus* for the difficulties of traditional source criticism'.[1]

There is widespread agreement that 19.4-6a, at least, is from a single source, with possibly a degree of redactional reworking, or alternatively that it is in its entirety the contribution of a single redactor. Muilenburg,

1. McCarthy, *Treaty and Covenant*, p. 256; cf. Dale Patrick, 'The Covenant Code Source', *VT* 27 (1977), pp. 145-57 (145).

for example, believed that 'the composition of Exod. xix 3-6 is so closely woven and the structure so apparent that the excision of any line of verse actually mars its unity and destroys its literary character'.[2] While some forty years later it may seem strange to observe a scholar almost apologizing for maintaining the literary integrity of such a small unit of text, such of course was the climate in which Muilenburg wrote. Yet, for this particular unit, his comment is not unrepresentative of the views of scholars working in the area of Pentateuchal criticism.[3]

All semblance of agreement ends at that point, however, for the attribution of 19.4-6a to one or other of the commonly identified Pentateuchal sources (continuous parallel narrative strands) or redactional (editorial) additions to the Pentateuch in the form in which we have it has proved one of the most elusive of all source-critical quests. Even scholars normally confident in their attribution of passages to sources are sometimes hesitant, and sometimes confusing when it comes to this portion of the Pentateuch.

Those who have seen in the expression ממלכת כהנים at least an echo of an ancient liturgical formula have tended to attribute it either to the Yahwist (J) or, more commonly, to the Elohist (E) source. The J source has traditionally been regarded as the earliest of the Pentateuchal sources (as early as the tenth century). Its distinguishing feature for the Sinai complex is considered to be its depiction of Yhwh as one who descends to Mt Sinai in theophany, as distinct from having his permanent abode there. The J source is associated with the warnings about crossing over to see God.[4] Among those who support the attribution of Exod. 19.4-6 to J, we may include Carpenter and Harford,[5] S.R. Driver,[6] Gressmann,[7] Oesterley

2. Muilenburg, 'Form and Structure', p. 351.

3. For similar views see Beer, *Exodus*, p. 96; Cuthbert Aikman Simpson, *The Early Traditions of Israel: A Critical Analysis of the Pre-Deuteronomic Narrative of the Hexateuch* (Oxford: Basil Blackwell, 1948), p. 199; Noth, *Exodus*, p. 154; Otto Eissfeldt, *Hexateuch-Synopse: Die Erzählung der fünf Bücher Mose und des Buches Josua mit dem Anfange des Richterbuches* (Darmstadt: Wissenschaftliche Buchgesellschaft, 1962), p. 146*; Beyerlin, *Origins*, pp. 67-77; Zenger, *Sinaitheophanie*, p. 58; Childs, *Exodus*, p. 360; McCarthy, *Treaty and Covenant*, p. 155; Barbiero, '*Mamleket kohanîm*', p. 430.

4. Noth, *Exodus*, p. 154.

5. Carpenter and Harford, *Composition*, pp. 515-17.

6. S.R. Driver, *Introduction to the Literature of the Old Testament* (Edinburgh: T. & T. Clark, 9th edn, 1913), p. 31.

7. Gressmann regards Exod. 19.3-6 as originally an introduction to the Book of the Covenant: Hugo Gressmann, *Die Anfänge Israels, von 2 Mose bis Richter und*

and Robinson[8] and von Rad.[9] While the J authorship of the unit 19.4-6a has not been popular, it has recently been revived by Van Seters, although in a rather different cast.[10] Van Seters's Yahwist is a post-exilic writer, hence one who *ex hypothesi* is amenable to Deuteronomic influences.

The majority of interpreters over the past century have favoured an Elohist (E) source for 19.4-6a (or 3b-8), conventionally dated about a century after J. The Elohist is identified with the view that Mt Sinai is God's permanent abode, and gives prominence to the figure of Moses as a mediator. Those who adopt this position include Galling,[11] Muilenburg,[12] Weiser,[13] Eichrodt,[14] Newman,[15] Eissfeldt,[16] Beyerlin,[17] Kuntz,[18] Childs[19] and Hanson.[20]

With the growing loss of confidence regarding the existence of an E source in recent decades, there has been a heightened interest in one or other of the alternative traditional sources or redactions, and new sources proposed.

Some see these verses as old (pre-Deuteronomic) yet as not belonging to either the J or E epic sources. For Wildberger, the discourse constitutes an

Ruth: Übersetzt, erklärt und mit Einleitung versehen (Die Schriften des Alten Testaments, 1.2; Göttingen: Vandenhoeck & Ruprecht, 1914), p. 61.

8. W.O.E. Oesterley and Theodore H. Robinson, *An Introduction to the Books of the Old Testament* (Living Age Books; New York: Meridian Books, 1953), p. 37.

9. Von Rad, 'The Form Critical Problem', p. 40.

10. John Van Seters, *The Life of Moses: The Yahwist as Historian in Exodus–Numbers* (Louisville, KY: Westminster/John Knox Press, 1994), p. 251.

11. Galling, *Erwählungstraditionen*, p. 27.

12. Muilenburg, 'Form and Structure', p. 351.

13 Artur Weiser, *Introduction to the Old Testament* (trans. D.M. Barton; London: Darton, Longman & Todd, 1961), p. 115.

14. Eichrodt, *Theology*, I, p.40.

15. Murray Lee Newman, Jr, *The People of the Covenant: A Study of Israel from Moses to the Monarchy* (Nashville: Abingdon Press, 1962), p. 40.

16. Eissfeldt, *Hexateuch-Synopse*, p. 146*, and *The Old Testament—An Introduction: The History of the Formation of the Old Testament* (New York: Harper & Row, 1965), p. 201.

17. Beyerlin, *Origins*, p. 11.

18. J. Kenneth Kuntz, *The Self-Revelation of God* (Philadelphia: Westminster Press, 1967), pp. 75-80.

19. Childs, *Exodus*, p. 61. Childs guardedly posits a Deuteronomic redaction to an underlying E source for these verses.

20. Paul D. Hanson, *The People Called: The Growth of Community in the Bible* (San Francisco: Harper & Row, 1986), p. 39.

independent election source.[21] McCarthy links 24.1-2, 9-11; 24.3-8; and 19.3b-8, and sees them as stemming from a source independent of J or E.[22] Likewise Patrick sees 19.3b-8, taken together with 20.22–23.19 and 24.3-8, as constituting a connected account of the Sinai event, distinct from J and E, and probably of northern provenance, composed prior to 721 in order to provide a narrative setting for the Covenant Code.[23]

There is no Deuteronomic (D) source as such postulated for this section of the Pentateuch, though the Deuteronomic school is widely regarded as having a significant redactional role in relation to the shaping of the J and E traditions.

In the complex process of weaving together the separate strands, one or more interim redactional stages are posited before the final redaction. Typically, there was a JE redaction, followed by one or more Deuteronomic redactions, with the resulting material undergoing a final redaction at the hands of the Priestly school. Exodus 19.4-6a has been regarded as a product of redactional activity on the part of each of the major editorial hands. Thus Bennett has it as the work of a pre-Deuteronomic redactor of the JE material.[24] More commonly, there has been a sustained acceptance of the view, first propounded by Wellhausen, that vv. 4-6a are in some way Deuteronomic.[25] The use of 'Deuteronomic' in this context has conventionally referred to a redaction of the (already combined) JE material which has theological and stylistic affinities with the bulk of the book of Deuteronomy. Such activity is usually associated with the Josianic reforms which date from 621, though some proto-Deuteronomic activity has been attributed to the period of Hezekiah a century earlier, and later dates are also proposed.

Principal among the reasons advanced for detecting a Deuteronomic redaction at Exod. 19.4-6a are its affinities in vocabulary and style with passages in Deuteronomy, such as the reference to Israel 'seeing' a past event (cf. Deut. 4.3, 9; 10.21; 11.7), the carrying of Israel on eagles' wings (cf. 32.11), the use of סגלה (cf. 7.6; 14.2; 26.18), the conditional covenantal

21. Wildberger, *Jahwes Eigentumsvolk*, pp. 9-16.

22. McCarthy, *Treaty and Covenant*, pp. 264-73.

23. Patrick, 'The Covenant Code Source'.

24. W.H. Bennett (ed.), *Exodus, Introduction: Revised Version with Notes, Giving an Analysis Showing from which of the Original Documents Each Portion of the Text is Taken* (Century Bible; Edinburgh: T.C. & E.C. Jack, 1910), p. 30.

25. Wellhausen's views underwent some modification between the editions of his *Die Composition des Hexateuchs und der historischen Bücher des Alten Testaments*; see Childs, *Exodus*, p. 345.

idea of v. 5, considered by many a Deuteronomic innovation (cf. 11.13; 15.5; 28.1), and the characterization of Israel as a 'holy' nation, though the use of גוי rather than עם is sometimes seen as a difficulty (cf. 7.6; 14.2, 21; 26.19; 28.9).

Wellhausen has been followed in his perception of Deuteronomic influence by such interpreters as Klopfer,[26] McNeile,[27] Steuernagel,[28] Beer,[29] Simpson,[30] Noth,[31] Haelvoet,[32] Jacob,[33] Auzou,[34] Perlitt,[35] Zenger,[36] Hyatt[37] and Nicholson.[38] For Blum, who has made a significant contribution to the study of Pentateuchal composition, Exod. 19.3b-8 marks a stage in the compositional history between the D and P redactions.[39]

Least prominent among candidates for the source of 19.4-6a has been the Priestly source (P). Such a source has (following Wellhausen) generally been regarded as containing little of the Sinai narrative material (often no more of chs. 19–24 than 19.1-2a, and 24.15b-18a), though much of the legal and cultic material of the Pentateuch is attributed to P. It has generally been considered to be post-exilic, and theologically sterile. The post-exilic dating of P has, however, been challenged by a number of scholars on linguistic and other grounds.[40]

26. Klopfer, 'Quellenscheidung', pp. 201-202.

27. McNeile, *Exodus*, p. xxvii.

28. D. Carl Steuernagel, *Lehrbuch der Einleitung in das Alte Testament: Mit einem Anhang uber die Apokryphen und Pseudepigraphen* (Tübingen: J.C.B. Mohr, 1912), p. 150.

29. Beer, *Exodus*, p. 97.

30. Simpson, *Early Traditions*, p. 199.

31. Noth, *Pentateuchal Traditions*, p. 31.

32. Marcel Haelvoet, 'La théophanie du Sinaï: Analyse littéraire des récits d'Exode 19–24', *ETL* 29 (1953), pp. 374-97 (374-78).

33. E. Jacob, *Theology*, p. 204.

34. Auzou, *De la servitude*, p. 245.

35. Perlitt, *Bundestheologie*, pp. 171-74. Perlitt's work significantly raised the profile of the D redactor.

36. Zenger, *Sinaitheophanie*, pp. 57-58.

37. Hyatt, *Exodus*, p. 197.

38. Nicholson, *Exodus and Sinai*, p. 31.

39. Blum, *Komposition des Pentateuch*, p. 99.

40. Yehezkel Kaufmann, *The Religion of Israel from its Beginnings to the Babylonian Exile* (trans. and abridged M. Greenberg; London: George Allen & Unwin, 1961), pp. 175-200; Avi Hurvitz, 'The Evidence of Language in Dating the Priestly Code: A Linguistic Study in Technical Idioms and Terminology', *RB* 81 (1974), pp. 24-56; Menahem Haran, 'Behind the Scenes of History: Determining the Date of the Priestly Source', *JBL* 100 (1981), pp. 321-33; Gary Rendsburg, 'Late Biblical Hebrew and the

The traditional view of P as originally constituting an independent narrative strand has also over recent decades to some extent given way to the view that the Priestly contribution to the process of Pentateuchal formation was one of redactional activity, particularly the final shaping of the Pentateuch in much the form in which we have it,[41] though an independent P source has still had its recent defenders.[42]

Any understanding of ממלכת כהנים which involves the notion of the collective priesthood of the whole community is not felt to sit well with the more exclusive priestly agenda. However, for those who understand כהנים in Exod. 19.6 in a more restricted sense, the P source, or a post-exilic priestly reshaping of earlier material is an attractive possibility, and such viewpoints have been espoused by such scholars as Winnett,[43] Fohrer,[44] Cazelles,[45] Dozemann[46] and Ska.[47]

In recent decades there has been a growing level of dissatisfaction with the method and results of traditional source criticism as applied to the Pentateuch and alternative approaches have been considered. In particular the contributions of Schmitt,[48] Knierim,[49] Whybray,[50] Rendtorff[51] and

Date of "P"', *JAOS* 102 (1982), pp. 65-80; Ziony Zevit, 'Converging Lines of Evidence Bearing on the Date of "P"', *ZAW* NS 94 (1982), pp. 481-511; cf. Robert Polzin, *Late Biblical Hebrew: Toward an Historical Typology of Biblical Hebrew Prose* (HSM, 12; Missoula, MT: Scholars Press, 1976).

41. E.g. Frank Moore Cross, Jr, 'The Priestly Work', in his *Canaanite Myth and Hebrew Epic: Essays in the History of the Religion of Israel* (Cambridge, MA: Harvard University Press, 1973), pp. 293-325 (293-94).

42. Klaus Koch, 'P—kein Redaktor!', *VT* 37 (1987), pp. 446-67; G.I. Davies, 'The Composition of the Book of Exodus: Reflections on the Theses of Erhard Blum', in Michael V. Fox *et al.* (eds.), *Texts, Temples and Traditions: A Tribute to Menahem Haran* (Winona Lake, IN: Eisenbrauns, 1996), pp. 71-85; Baruch J. Schwartz, 'The Priestly Account of the Theophany and Lawgiving at Sinai', in Fox *et al.* (eds.), *Texts, Temples and Traditions*, pp. 103-34.

43. Frederick Victor Winnett, *The Mosaic Tradition* (Near and Middle East Series, 1; Toronto: University of Toronto Press, 1949), pp. 163-64.

44. Georg Fohrer, *History of Israelite Religion* (London: SPCK, 1973), p. 299.

45. Cazelles, 'Alliance du Sinai', p. 78, and '"Royaume de prêtres"', p. 290.

46. Dozemann attributes only vv. 5bβ-6a to P (embedded in a D matrix): Thomas B. Dozeman, *God on the Mountain: A Study of Redaction, Theology and Canon in Exodus 19–24* (SBLMS, 37; Atlanta: Scholars Press, 1989), pp. 93-98.

47. Ska, 'Exode 19.3b-6'.

48. Hans-Christoph Schmitt, 'Redaktion des Pentateuch im Geiste der Prophetie: Beobachtungen zur Bedeutung der "Glaubens"—Thematik innerhalb der Theologie des Pentateuch', *VT* 32 (1982), pp. 170-89.

49. Rolf P. Knierim, 'The Composition of the Pentateuch', in Kent Harold

Blum[52] represent various degrees of movement in the direction of a focus on the redactional or final form of the text. The hypothesis involving the redaction of several documents along the lines popularized by Graf and Wellhausen has undergone some significant modifications—some adjustment of dates, some new sources, the virtual disappearance of the E source, and a greater emphasis on the role of the redactor(s). Yet it remains in its essentials as the dominant position in Pentateuchal studies. For how long remains to be seen.

Whatever advantages historical criticism as traditionally practised may have for other portions of the Pentateuch, it has been singularly disappointing as a means of elucidating the origins (and hence perhaps the significance) of the Sinai complex in general and Exod. 19.4-6a in particular. The comment of Gunn expresses a growing realization on the part of Old Testament scholarship: 'It is no exaggeration to say that the truly assured results of historical critical scholarship concerning authorship, date and provenance would fill but a pamphlet'.[53] Certainly there is little by way of positive result to report after more than a century of source-critical endeavour so far as the Sinai complex is concerned. The lack of methodological controls evident in much of the literature would suggest that little progress is to be expected from further efforts along the lines of traditional source criticism. Thus Rendtorff concludes that 'the criteria for source criticism have proved unsuitable to explain the literary problems of the Sinai pericope'.[54]

The approach in its earlier stage of development depended on an assumption of the minimally creative role of the redactors, who (apparently without noticing) left glaring inconsistencies of plot, character and theology in their redaction, to be discovered by scholars from a time and culture far removed from theirs. Yet when a greater role is given to the redactors, the very criteria which were used to distinguish their sources begin to evaporate. The comment of Gowan is worth repeating: 'Redaction certainly took

Richards (ed.), *Society of Biblical Literature 1985 Seminar Papers* (SBLSP, 24; Atlanta, GA: Scholars Press, 1985), pp. 393-415.

50. Whybray, *The Making of the Pentateuch.*

51. Rendtorff, *Process of Transmission.*

52. Blum, *Komposition des Pentateuch.*

53. David M. Gunn, 'New Directions in the Study of Biblical Hebrew Narrative', in Paul R. House (ed.), *Beyond Form Criticism: Essays in Old Testament Literary Criticism* (Sources for Biblical and Theological Study, 2; Winona Lake, IN: Eisenbrauns, 1992), pp. 412-22 (413).

54. Rendtorff, *Process of Transmission*, p. 112.

place in the creation of the Old Testament books, but there are too few objective criteria for determining what is redactional, and the failure to find agreement on the composition of Exodus 19–24 is proof that most of the decisions being made are subjective'.[55] Moreover, even if we could get behind the text to its sources, it would do little for our understanding of the text as a literary document. It would simply push the questions back to an earlier stage, and would still call for something much more than an identification of a unit of text as 'E' or 'redactional' or 'priestly', or as 'misplaced'. Knierim is only marginally overstating the case when he writes: 'Traditional historical exegesis has for good reasons been preoccupied with the layers and developments before the latest composition. At the same time, however, it has behaved as if the final composition was not worth discussing.'[56] The text as we have it is reduced to the status of a witness to something else, and at times a very indirect witness at that, rather than being treated as literature with its own integrity and worthy of study in its own right.

2. *A Paradigm Shift: The Newer Literary Criticism and the 'Final Form'*

This leads us to a consideration of the approach to the text to be adopted in this study. Recent decades have begun to witness something of a sea-change in approaches to the literature of the Hebrew Bible. There has been an increasing emphasis on more holistic literary approaches to the text as we have it, where the integrity of the discourse is axiomatic to a serious reading. Even as early as 1938, von Rad observed:

> A process of analysis, doubtless almost always interesting, but nevertheless highly stylised, has run its course, and a more or less clear perception of its inevitability handicaps many scholars today… On almost all sides the final form [*Letztgestalt*] of the Hexateuch has come to be regarded as a starting-point barely worthy of discussion, from which the debate should move away as rapidly as possible in order to reach the real problems underlying it.[57]

Developments in biblical interpretation over recent decades, particularly with regard to biblical narrative, have their roots in general literary theory,

55. Gowan, *Theology in Exodus*, p. 282 n. 13.

56. Knierim, 'Composition', p. 393.

57. Von Rad, 'The Form Critical Problem', p. 1. In practice, von Rad himself continued to treat the final form more as a window through which one looked for evidence of how it came to be there.

drawing on the work of literary critics such as Frye, who states one of the central tenets of his approach:

> The primary understanding of any work of literature has to be based on an assumption of its unity. However mistaken such an assumption may eventually prove to be, nothing can be done unless we start with it as a heuristic principle. Further, every effort should be directed toward understanding the whole of what we read, as though it were all on the same level of achievement.[58]

The Presidential address of James Muilenburg delivered to the Society of Biblical Literature in 1968 signalled something of a turning point in Old Testament scholarship in this regard.[59] While wishing to remain very much in continuity with form criticism, Muilenburg issued 'an appeal to venture beyond the confines of form criticism into an inquiry into other literary features which are all too frequently ignored today'.[60] Adopting the phrase 'rhetorical criticism' for the approach he advocated, Muilenburg wished to place greater emphasis on the distinctive contribution of each particular text, rather than generalize about its literary affinities, and to observe its structural and aesthetic features. It was this address which introduced such literary terms as *chiasmus* and *inclusio* into the general vocabulary of scholars of the Hebrew Bible.

Another proposal for a more integrated reading of the texts of the Hebrew Bible, one less reliant on a speculative reconstruction of sources, was put forward in 1978 by McCarthy: 'The object of exegesis, then, is primarily the text as it stands, not possible origins or historical referent'.[61] This approach has been expounded and applied (in different ways) within the context of Hebrew Bible studies generally by such writers as Polzin,[62] Licht,[63] Clines,[64] Childs,[65] Alter,[66] Berlin,[67] Sternberg[68] and Rendtorff,[69] to

58. Northrop Frye, 'Literary Criticism', in James Thorpe (ed.), *The Aims and Methods of Scholarship in Modern Languages and Literatures* (New York: Modern Language Association of America, 1963), pp. 57-69 (63).

59. James Muilenburg, 'Form Criticism and Beyond', *JBL* 88 (1969), pp. 1-18.

60. Muilenburg, 'Form Criticism and Beyond', p. 4.

61. Dennis J. McCarthy, SJ, 'Exodus 3.14: History, Philology and Theology', *CBQ* 40 (1978), pp. 311-22 (320).

62. Robert Polzin, *Biblical Structuralism: Method and Subjectivity in the Study of Ancient Texts* (Semeia Supplement Series, 5; Philadelphia: Fortress Press, 1977).

63. Jacob Licht, *Storytelling in the Bible* (Jerusalem: Magnes Press, 1978).

64. David J.A. Clines, *The Theme of the Pentateuch* (JSOTSup, 10; Sheffield: JSOT Press, 1978).

name but a few. It provides the editorial rationale for some relatively recent literary introductions to the books of the Bible.[70] Such study is concerned not so much with the pre-history of the text, or with uncovering the *Sitz im Leben* of its component forms, or with the pre-literary traditions which may underlie the text, all of which are ultimately of limited value in explaining the function of a unit of discourse within the matrix of its surrounding cotext. Rather, it accepts the text as a given, and endeavours to discern its inner coherence and meaning, to appreciate the artistry which has shaped it, and to consider it in relation to texts which appear to have some interrelationship with it (intertextuality).

Rendtorff traces the course of traditional historical-critical inquiry, noting the continuum between redaction criticism (with its emphasis on process) and what has become known as a 'final form' approach, with its emphasis on product, and makes the following observation:

> What will continue, I hope, is the attitude of taking the text seriously in its given form, in its final shape... [T]aking a synchronic approach to the text in its given shape is a task Old Testament scholarship has neglected too long and too intentionally. Scholars still seem to be proud of knowing things better than the final redactors or compilers. This is a kind of nineteenth-century hubris we should have left behind us. The last writers, whatever we want to call them, were, in any case, much closer to the original meaning of the text than we can ever be.[71]

65. Brevard S. Childs, *Introduction to the Old Testament as Scripture* (Philadelphia: Fortress Press, 1979).

66. Robert Alter, *The Art of Biblical Narrative* (New York: Basic Books, 1981).

67. Adele Berlin, *Poetics and Interpretation of Biblical Narrative* (Bible and Literature Series, 9; Sheffield: Almond Press, 1983); *idem*, 'A Search for a New Biblical Hermeneutics: Preliminary Observations', in Jerrold S. Cooper and Glenn M. Schwartz (eds.), *The Study of the Ancient Near East in the Twenty-First Century: The William Foxwell Albright Centennial Conference* (Winona Lake, IN: Eisenbrauns, 1996), pp. 195-207.

68. Meir Sternberg, *The Poetics of Biblical Narrative: Ideological Literature and the Drama of Reading* (Indiana Literary Biblical Series; Bloomington: Indiana University Press, 1985).

69. Rolf Rendtorff, 'The Paradigm is Changing: Hopes—and Fears', *BibInt* 1 (1993), pp. 34-53.

70. Robert Alter and Frank Kermode (eds.), *The Literary Guide to the Bible* (Glasgow: Fontana, 1989); Leland Ryken and Tremper Longman, III (eds.), *A Complete Literary Guide to the Bible* (Grand Rapids: Zondervan, 1993).

71. Rendtorff, 'Paradigm', p. 52.

Berlin articulates some principles relevant to her proposal for 'a new biblical hermeneutics' which are worth itemizing in their summary form:

1. Respect the integrity of the text...
2. Assume the text makes sense in its present form...
3. Take the wording of the text seriously...
4. Take the literary context seriously...
5. Take the historical and social context seriously...
6. Is the text to be read literally or metaphorically?...
7. Decide which features of the text are hermeneutically significant and how they are to be used in the interpretive process.[72]

The present study proceeds from a position which is in general accord with these principles with one reservation. The reservation relates to what is meant by the integrity of the text as this affects textual criticism (taken up below). On a 'final form' approach, the notion of what we are calling cotext becomes much more important than it has traditionally been. Words, expressions, whole speeches derive their meaning not merely from the lexicon, or the sum of their constituent parts. They take on meaning in relation to the text around them. Thus, for example, when we come to consider the meaning of the oracle in Zech. 3.8-10, we will not be looking for its meaning in isolation, or in relation to a hypothetical 'oracles source',[73] but in relation to the preceding vision account (Zech. 3.1-7) and ultimately the book of Zechariah as a whole.

Utzschneider[74] and Vervenne[75] both note the paradigm shift as this applies to the study of Exodus. The Exodus commentaries by Childs,[76] Durham,[77] Fretheim,[78] Houtman[79] and Propp[80] represent, to varying degrees, more integrated literary approaches to the text. The Sinai complex

72. Berlin, 'Search', pp. 201-206.

73. Albert Petitjean, *Les oracles du Proto-Zacharie: Un programme de restauration pour la communauté juive après l'exil* (EBib; Paris: J. Gabalda, 1969), p. 179.

74. Helmut Utzschneider, 'Die Renaissance der alttestamentlichen Literaturwissenschaft und das Buch Exodus: Überlegungen zu Hermeneutik und Geschichte der Forschung', *ZAW* NS 106 (1994), pp. 197-223.

75. Marc Vervenne, 'Current Tendencies and Developments in the Study of the Book of Exodus', in *idem* (ed.), *Studies in the Book of Exodus*, pp. 21-59.

76. Childs, *Exodus*.

77. Durham, *Exodus*.

78. Fretheim, *Exodus*.

79. Houtman, *Exodus*.

80. Propp, *Exodus 1–18*.

has not received the same attention from the perspective of a holistic literary approach as other portions of the Hebrew Bible, perhaps because of the special problems associated with the interweaving of story with law.[81] The following treatments of the Sinai material exemplify some, at least, of the characteristics outlined above: Licht,[82] Rivard,[83] Greenberg,[84] Moberly,[85] Chrichigno,[86] Blum,[87] Dozemann,[88] Rendtorff,[89] Sailhamer[90] and Wells.[91] We will be considering some of these contributions at relevant points.

a. *Textual Criticism and the 'Final Form'*

Though the approach adopted here has sometimes been called a 'final form' or *Endgestalt* approach,[92] this may not prove to be a particularly helpful description. Given the diversity of textual traditions of a document such as the book of Exodus, 'final form' becomes a matter of choice—the choice of the individual interpreter or the tradition of one's faith community—as to which particular text-form or even version will be adopted as the basis for one's literary analysis. Pushed to its ultimate limit, this may even mean settling on one manuscript or printed edition as being normative. Insofar as the expressions 'final form' or 'the text as we have it' may be used in this book, they are used somewhat more loosely, more in the manner of their use by Childs and Rendtorff to refer to the broad contours

81. Cf. Gabriel Josipovici, *The Book of God: A Response to the Bible* (New Haven: Yale University Press, 1988), p. 90.

82. Jacob Licht, 'גילוי שכינה במעמד הר סיני (The Sinai Theophany)', in Yitschak Avishur and Joshua Blau (eds.), *Studies in the Bible and the Ancient Near East Presented to Samuel E. Loewenstamm* (Jerusalem: Rubinstein, 1978), pp. 251-68.

83. Rivard, 'Relecture', *ScEs* 33 (1981), pp. 335-56.

84. Moshe Greenberg, 'Exodus, Book of', in *EncJud*, VI, pp. 1050-67.

85. R.W.L. Moberly, *At the Mountain of God: Story and Theology in Exodus 32–34* (JSOTSup, 22; Sheffield: JSOT Press, 1983).

86. G.C. Chirichigno, 'The Narrative Structure of Exod. 19–24', *Bib* 68 (1987), pp. 457-79.

87. Blum, 'Israël à la montagne', and *Komposition des Pentateuch.*

88. Dozeman, 'Spatial form', and *God on the Mountain.*

89. Rendtorff, 'Der Text in seiner Endgestalt', pp. 459-70.

90. John H. Sailhamer, *The Pentateuch as Narrative: A Biblical-Theological Commentary* (Library of Biblical Interpretation; Grand Rapids: Zondervan, 1992), pp. 281-98.

91. Wells, *God's Holy People.*

92. Childs, *Introduction to the Old Testament*, p. 75; Rendtorff, 'Der Text in seiner Endgestalt'.

of the text accepted as 'canonical' within the Jewish and Christian traditions, without restricting that to one precise text-form. The approach adopted here will be open to textual criticism, as traditionally practised in connection with the Hebrew Bible. That is (*pace* Berlin), there will be at least a readiness to consider the evidence not only of the Masoretic Text (MT) but also the witness of other manuscript traditions, the versions, and the targums for such evidence as they may suggest for readings, possibly earlier, besides those of MT. In particular, the Masoretic vocalization will be regarded as a helpful interpretative overlay on the consonantal text (the proto-Masoretic text), but will not be treated as definitive. Thus to some extent, this study seeks to work from a reconstructed text, though only insofar as there is reasonable evidence to support a particular reading.

The attempt to reconstruct hypothetical earlier forms of the text (the continuous narrative sources, or earlier redactions) involves a greater degree of subjectivity. It is not to be denied that the enterprise of combining sources and editing earlier works was a feature of Hebrew historiography,[93] nor that there is to some extent a continuum between text-critical and source-critical analyses. Both seek to establish earlier forms of the text as part of the quest for historical authenticity. The question might be posed, however, whether 'earlier' inevitably means 'better', that is, whether particular forms of a text are amenable to this sort of value judgment. In part, the distinction between source- and text-criticism involves a distinction between the activity of an editor and that of a scribe. To the extent that textual variations are deliberate (editorial), they have signficance. Insofar as they are thoughtless scribal accidents, they are of limited value for the reading of texts, though they may shed light on scribal techniques, or the development of the Hebrew language.

It is an axiom of the method adopted here that the final form (barring scribal lapses) is a literary work worthy of our attention. There will be a predisposition to accept the coherence of any text; that is, whatever its background in terms of sources, its author or editor consciously shaped the work to suit authorial or editorial purposes. If the observance of features of coherence and aesthetic qualities in the text may be queried as springing from a desire to find unity, so equally may the discovery by others of discrepancies and doublets (the stock-in-trade of the older source-critical

93. See, e.g., William Johnstone, 'Reactivating the Chronicles Analogy in Pentateuchal Studies, with Special Reference to the Sinai Pericope in Exodus', *ZAW* NS 99 (1987), pp. 16-37.

approaches) be seen as arising from an overly historicist need to get beyond the text. Within the Sinai pericope, one may take the example of the paradox of seeing God or being face-to-face with God, and not seeing God, particularly his face (Exod. 19.21; 24.11; 33.11, 20, 23). These references will either be regarded as constituting a discrepancy and hence suggestive of different sources brought together in such a manner that the editor was unaware of, or unable to control the result, or alternatively, they may be seen as a conscious reflection of the inherent tension in a divine–human encounter, and the inadequacy of language to convey both the transcendence and the immanence of such an experience.

b. *Historicity and the 'Final Form'*

Is the method adopted here then to be excluded from an engagement with history? This is a serious issue on which not a great deal has yet been written.[94] The more one simply opts for a synchronic as opposed to a diachronic reading of a given text, with minimal attention to the process of formation and transmission of the text and its underlying traditions, the less safe might appear to be one's conclusions as to the way that text connects with real events or with other texts. Applied to the Bible, this means, for example, that an approach which assumes the integrity of the text may of necessity be more tentative about issues of dating and the priority of one text over another than has often been the case. But it is not thereby ahistorical in character. Childs, who prefers to call his approach a 'canonical' approach, identifies the failures of the historical critical method, while at the same time endeavouring to take Israel's history seriously.[95]

In some ways, the contribution to historiography of the newer literary approaches will be less assertive and confident than has been true of much of the literary criticism of the previous century, but the widely divergent conclusions reached about so many issues over this period suggest that it is time for a more modest and realistic assessment of our abilities to reconstruct both texts and events.[96] At least an approach which deals with the texts we possess has some claim to historicity and is inherently less prone to fragile hypothetical reconstructions. The evidence of the texts themselves is more tangible than the reconstructions which attempt to reach back beyond them. In the end there will hopefully be a better balance

94. See David Damrosch, *The Narrative Covenant: Transformations of Genre in the Growth of Biblical Literature* (San Francisco: Harper & Row, 1987).

95. Childs, *Introduction to the Old Testament*, p. 71.

96. Cf. Berlin, 'Search', pp. 195-97.

resulting from the newer literary emphases, without an abandonment of historical enquiry in the process.

This work is primarily literary and thematic in its concerns. However, it proceeds from an assumption that literature and history cannot be divorced. If historical comments are at times confined to footnotes, this is not an indication of their intrinsic insignificance, but is because their injection into the body of the text would interrupt the flow of the discussion.

Chapter 3

THE ROYAL PRIESTHOOD IN ITS IMMEDIATE COTEXT: EXODUS 19.1-8

1. *The Literary Structure of Exodus 19.1-8*

Our primary concern is to explore the significance of the expression ממלכת כהנים in Exod. 19.6a. We must therefore make some judgment as to the limits of the unit of discourse which can be considered the more immediately relevant cotext of this expression. Source-critical criteria have frequently been invoked in determining these boundaries. Despite the many uncertainties of source criticism, there is, as noted in the previous chapter, a significant consensus in identifying a unit which is regarded as enjoying 'compositional integrity' which extends from v. 3b to v. 8 or at the very least which includes vv. 3-6.[1] Where a wider cotext than these verses is sought, Exod. 19.3b-8 is sometimes held to belong most closely with 24.3-8, perhaps as part of a common source, which has been inserted in its present setting in ch. 19 as part of the redactional process, or alternatively, composed as an anticipatory summary with the conclusion of 24.3-8 in mind.[2]

Whatever may prove to be the case regarding the source of the unit (if anything approaching proof should ever eventuate), and with whatever other portion of text these verses may once have been closely associated, a hypothesis regarding an earlier stage of the text is not an adequate criterion for determining the limits or function of a passage in its present literary setting. Accordingly, we will need to seek a more objective criterion, one based on a literary analysis of the present form of Exodus 19.

1. Childs, *Exodus*, p. 360; cf. Muilenburg, 'Form and Structure', p. 351.

2. Beyerlin, *Origins*, p. 69; Nicholson, *Exodus and Sinai*, pp. 30-31; *idem*, *God and His People*, p. 164; Patrick, 'The Covenant Code Source'; McCarthy, *Treaty and Covenant*, pp. 264-73; Levenson, *Sinai and Zion*, p. 24; Fuhs, 'Heiliges Volk Gottes', pp. 154-59; Blum, *Komposition des Pentateuch*, pp. 51-52; Ska, 'Ex 19,3-8 et les parénèses'.

The words ממלכת כהנים occur in the final stich of the report of a divine speech (vv. 4-6a) imparted to Moses on Mt Sinai and which he in turn is charged with relaying to the people of Israel gathered at the base of the mountain:

> (4a) You yourselves saw what I did to Egypt, (4b) and how I lifted you up on eagles' wings and brought you to myself. (5a) Now, if you will pay heed to my voice, and keep my covenant, (5b) you will be mine as a special treasure in distinction from all the peoples. That is, the whole earth is mine, (6a) but you will be mine as a royal priesthood and a holy nation.

The divine speech constitutes a coherent unit, as is evident from the *inclusio* formed by the repetition of the (emphatic) personal pronoun (ו)אתם ('you [yourselves]') as subject, followed by a finite verb in the second person plural, in both the opening and closing lines. The rubrics giving directions to Moses concerning the delivery of the message form an envelope structure around this unit:

> (3b) This is what you are to say to the house of Jacob and declare to the Israelites. (6b) These are the words which you are to speak to the Israelites.

The use of both initial and final quotative frames for a speech of only five lines is noteworthy, though it appears to have escaped the attention of interpreters.[3] Certainly in all other cases where the expression כה תאמר or כה תאמרו(ן) ('Thus you shall say') occurs, followed by direct speech, there is no closing frame, while the only other occurrences of the expression אלה הדברים ('These are the words') with direct speech are as initial frames (Deut. 1.1; Jer. 30.4), not, as here, a final frame after the embedded speech. The twofold frame is probably to be understood as an indicator of the *gravitas* of the enclosed speech, or as Cassuto expresses it, the final frame 'is a solemn, concluding formula'.[4] Note the repetition of בני ישׂראל ('the Israelites') and the second person singular verbs of saying, תאמר (v. 3b) and תדבר (v. 6b), which stand in contrast with the plurals of the verses they enclose. The former of these two rubrics (v. 3b) is in the form

3. For quotative frames in Hebrew narrative see Samuel A. Meier, *Speaking of Speaking: Marking Direct Discourse in the Hebrew Bible* (VTSup, 46; Leiden: E.J. Brill, 1992); Cynthia L. Miller, 'Introducing Direct Discourse in Biblical Hebrew Narrative', in Robert D. Bergen (ed.), *Biblical Hebrew and Discourse Linguistics* (Winona Lake, IN: Eisenbrauns, 1994), pp. 199-241; *idem*, *The Representation of Speech in Biblical Hebrew Narrative: A Linguistic Analysis* (HSM, 55; Atlanta: Scholars Press, 1996). Miller does not list any examples of a twofold frame.

4. Cassuto, *Exodus*, p. 227.

of parallel couplets which prepare the reader for the somewhat poetic language of vv. 4-6a (for which see below).

Verses 3b-6 are then further bracketed by narrative sections which relate Moses' ascent (עלה) to God on Mt Sinai, and God's summons (ויקרא) to him (v. 3a), followed by Moses' descent (ויבא), his summons (ויקרא) to the elders of the people (v. 7) and his recounting of the words (דברים) of Yhwh according to instructions (v. 7, cf. v. 6). The expression אל־האלהים ('to God') in conjunction with a verb of motion is generally avoided in the Hebrew Bible, as it may imply a heavenly journey. Such passages as Deut. 30.12 and Prov. 30.4 indicate that such a journey can be contemplated, if only to be dismissed as out of the realistic reach of mortals. The LXX avoids the implication by its rendering εἰς τὸ ὄρος τοῦ θεοῦ ('to the mountain of God'). Commentators usually draw attention to the apparent confusion over the location of God throughout the Sinai pericope. Is he resident on the mountain (as v. 3aβ), or in heaven (as implied by v. 11)? The question may not be as meaningful as it first appears. The limitations of language to describe a divine–human encounter will be evident not least in the terminology relating to the geography of the encounter. In much of ancient religious thought, heaven may fuse with the sacred mountain, or with the sanctuary of the god on earth. In Isaiah's oracle concerning the king of Babylon, he is likened to a 'morning star' who attempted to gain by his own efforts precisely what appears to be on offer to Israel in Exod. 19.3b-6: 'You said in your heart, "I will ascend to heaven; I will raise my throne above the stars of God; I will sit enthroned on the mount of assembly, on the extremities of Zaphon"' (Isa. 14.13).[5] Kleinig remarks on Exod. 19.3a: 'It is as if Moses had thereby entered the heavenly realm, but only because heaven had come down to earth on the mountain'.[6]

Moving one further layer out from the core, vv. 1-2 provide an indication of the setting in both place and time of the events to follow. They serve to link the preceding account of the events of the Israelites' departure from Egypt and encampment at Sinai, the initial goal of the exodus (chs. 1–18) with the following discourse—whether this is understood more

5. On the theme of heavenly invasion, see David J. Halperin, 'Ascension or Invasion: Implications of the Heavenly Journey in Ancient Judaism', *Religion* 18 (1988), pp. 47-67.

6. Kleinig, 'On Eagles' Wing', p. 20. For the notion of the cosmic mountain, the divine abode, see Isa. 14.13; cf. S. Talmon, 'הר', in *TDOT*, III, pp. 441-42; Clifford, *Cosmic Mountain*.

narrowly as being vv. 3-8, or a more extended unit such as Exodus 19–24, or even the remainder of the book of Exodus in its entirety.

Spatially, the setting is ההר ('the mountain', v. 2), an expression which draws the reader back to previous references to the mountain (3.1, 12; 4.27; 18.5) and so sets up an expectation that what follows is the significant divine encounter anticipated by these earlier references. The phrase used to indicate the temporal setting ביום הזה ('on this day') also appears laden. The only other uses of this expression in the Pentateuch are found at Gen. 7.11 (the first day of the flood), Lev. 8.34 (the day of the ordination of the priests) and Lev. 16.30 (the Day of Atonement), all days of significant divine activity.[7]

In these introductory verses to ch. 19, Israel as a whole is active as the subject of third person verbs (באו, ויסעו, ויבאו and ויחנו). By v. 8a, the whole people, who in the intervening verses have been passive onlookers, resume their active participation in the events in the words ויענו, ויאמרו and נעשה in which they respond to the terms of the divine initiative. There are thus clear indications of a deliberate envelope pattern to the section from 1-8a:

A People of Israel camp at the mountain (third person plural verbs) (vv. 1-2).
  B Moses' ascent and Yhwh's summons (third person singular verbs) (v. 3a).
    C Divine instruction regarding delivery of message to Israel (second person singular verbs) (v. 3b).
      D Divine declaration concerning Israel (second person plural verbs) (vv. 4-6a).
    C′ Divine instruction regarding delivery of message to Israel (second person singular verbs) (v. 6b).
  B′ Moses' descent and summons to the elders (third person singular verbs) (v. 7).
A′ People of Israel respond (third person plural verbs) (v. 8a).

If the references to Moses' movements up and down the mountain serve as rhetorical devices, marking the larger structural divisions of the Sinai pericope,[8] then his 'returning' (וישב, hiphil, transitive) of the people's response to Yhwh in v. 8b (necessitating another trip up the mountain) is probably best seen as marking a new unit, or at least a transitional unit, commencing at v. 8b. Note the *inclusio* formed by the repetition of the

7. See Dozeman, *God on the Mountain*, p. 92. Dozemann considers this to be evidence for an original cultic setting for these words.

8. Dozeman, *God on the Mountain*, p. 14; Daniel C. Arichea, Jr, 'The Ups and Downs of Moses: Locating Moses in Exodus 19-33', *BT* 40 (1989), pp. 244-46.

phrase את־דברי־העם אל־יהוה ('the words of the people to Yhwh', vv. 8b, 9b) with Moses as the subject of a verb of reporting in each instance. These formulas bracket the announcement of the theophany (v. 9a).

We may thus be confident that we have identified a unit extending from the beginning of the chapter to the end of v. 8a, and this coincides with the first of Dozeman's six units covering the whole Sinai pericope.[9] What is not clear is whether this unit describes the first of a number of separate divine encounters which ensue in sequence through chs. 19–24, or whether (as appears more likely) it constitutes a synopsis or summary of these episodes.[10] In Chapter 5 we will consider the wider cotext of 19.1-8a, particularly its setting in chs. 19–24. For the moment, we have a sufficient feel for the immediate cotext to proceed to a closer reading of the divine speech encompassed in vv. 3b-6.

2. *The Literary Texture of Exodus 19.3b-6*

Verses 3b-6 (or 3b-8a) are frequently regarded as having some poetic characteristics. Childs, for example speaks of their 'poetic symmetry and artistic beauty'[11] or of 'the elevated style of the prose, which approaches poetry in its use of parallelism and selected vocabulary'.[12] Cross detects an ancient epic poem behind the existing more prosaic form of these verses. It is an instance of those prose passages which 'when stripped of a few prose particles become exquisite poetry in epic style'.[13] Muilenburg expresses a similar view when, speaking of the studied balance and assonance of 19.3-6, he writes: 'Whoever has undertaken a study of Hebrew literary composition and rhetoric will be quick to see that such phenomena are by no means fortuitous and that they may be illustrated by scores of examples, not least of all in the context of the covenant message'.[14]

9. Dozeman, *God on the Mountain*, p. 14.

10. See Noth, *Exodus*, p. 154; Childs, *Exodus*, p. 360; Phillips, 'A Fresh Look', p. 51; Chirichigno, 'Narrative Structure'; Dozeman, 'Spatial Form'; Arichea, 'Ups and Downs'.

11. Childs, *Exodus*, p. 360.

12. Childs, *Exodus*, p. 366.

13. Frank Moore Cross, Jr, 'The Epic Traditions of Early Israel: Epic Narrative and the Reconstruction of Early Israelite Institutions', in Richard Elliott Friedman (ed.), *The Poet and the Historian: Essays in Literary and Historical Biblical Criticism* (HSS, 26; Chico, CA: Scholars Press, 1983), pp. 13-39 (21).

14. Muilenburg, 'Form and Structure', p. 353. The identification of the unit as poetic is frequently associated with a cultic origin; cf. Noth, *Exodus*, p. 157; Beyerlin, *Origins*, p. 70; Cassuto, *Exodus*, p. 223; McCarthy, *Treaty and Covenant*, p. 272.

Several characteristics are suggestive of a verse idiom:

(1) *Parallelismus membrorum* is discernible at some points. We note, for example, the grammatical as well as semantic parallelism of the expressions תאמר לבית יעקב ('you are to say to the house of Jacob') and ותגיד לבני ישראל ('and declare to the Israelites', v. 3b). The close pairing of בני ישׂראל ('Israelites') with בית יעקב ('house of Jacob') occurs elsewhere only in poetry at Amos 9.7-8. The כה ('thus', v. 3b) does double duty whereas in prose we might have expected it to be repeated (e.g. 1 Sam. 3.17). In v. 4b, we find two hemistichs with closely parallel syntactic patterns—both are introduced by a *wayyiqtol* verb form followed by the pronominal object אתכם ('you') and a prepositional phrase. Note also the parallelism in v. 5 where אם־שׁמוע תשׁמעו בקלי ('if you will pay heed to my voice') is paralleled by ושׁמרתם את־בריתי ('and keep my covenant'), again with אם doing double duty. We might also detect a loose parallelism between והייתם לי סגלה מכל־העמים ('you will be mine as a special treasure in distinction from all the peoples') and כי־לי כל־הארץ ('that is, the whole earth is mine') with the repetition of לי, and כל־העמים paralleling כל־הארץ (v. 5).

(2) The object marker את (a 'prose particle') is absent before אשׁר in v. 4.[15]

(3) The syntax of v. 4b is paratactic in character, where the *wayyiqtol* forms ואשׂא ('I lifted') and ואבא ('I brought') can be construed as logically subordinate (though formally parallel) to the verb of perception ראיתם of v. 4a. Thus we might read: 'You yourselves have seen what I did, and (have seen) how (or: that) I carried you…and how (or: that) I brought you…' An alternative way of expressing this is to say that the relative אשׁר does triple duty for the clauses containing the verbs ראיתם, אשׂא and אבא.

(4) The bold image of God carrying his people on eagles' wings as a metaphor for the whole exodus experience suggests the language of poetry (as Deut. 32.11-12, where a similar image is used, is poetry). The striking nature of the expression was not lost on the translators of the LXX who added ὡσεί ('as if') to soften what might seem an unacceptable 'ornithomorphism'.

15. Francis I. Andersen and A. Dean Forbes, '"Prose Particle" Counts in the Hebrew Bible', in Carol M. Meyers and M. O'Connor (eds.), *The Word of the Lord Shall Go Forth: Essays in Honor of David Noel Freedman in Celebration of his Sixtieth Birthday* (Winona Lake, IN: Eisenbrauns, 1983), pp. 165-83.

The unit also has some prosaic features such as the object marker את before בריתי ('my covenant') in v. 5a. and the two instances of its suffixed form אתכם in v. 4b. We note also the 'prose particle' אשׁר in vv. 4a and 6b. In v. 4a, where it lacks an antecedent, it is less easily avoided. At v. 6b the LXX and Peshitta may attest to a Hebrew *Vorlage* which lacked the אשׁר.

The most we may safely conclude regarding the literary texture of Exod. 19.3b-6 is that it is a relatively tightly constructed rhetorical unit with a number of poetic features which place it more towards the poetic end of the poetry–prose continuum. When we come to consider v. 6a more closely, therefore, we may be disposed to look for poetic features.

3. *Interpretation of Exodus 19.4-6a*

a. *Exodus 19.4*

We come now to a consideration in greater detail of the content of the divine words which Moses is instructed to relay to the people of Israel (19.4-6a). Verse 4 provides a summary of the exodus and wilderness experience from the point of view of God's initiative and action on behalf of his people.

> (4a) You yourselves saw what I did to Egypt, (4b) and how I lifted you up on eagles' wings and brought you to myself.

The plural אתם ('you', referring to Israel, the ultimate addressee) is emphatic and draws attention to the Israelite's undeniable experience of God's activity on their behalf (cf. Deut. 4.3; 10.21; 11.7; 29.2). This activity is summed up in the three cola marked by the verbs עשׂיתי ('I did'), ואשׂא ('I lifted up') and ואבא ('I brought'). It is a highly compressed account of Israel's threefold experience to date. First, there is God's activity with regard to Egypt.[16] By such words the reader of Exodus would recall the plagues, the victory over Pharaoh's army at the Reed Sea, and the evident distinction made between God's dealings with Egypt and with Israel in these events.

Secondly, there is God's activity with regard to Israel in the period of the wanderings. It is in this connection that the image of the eagle is introduced. Strictly speaking, the bird in question may be a form of vulture, though this may have some unintended negative connotations for the

16. Or perhaps the Egyptians (*Targum Pseudo-Jonathan* reads למצראי and LXX reads τοῖς Αἰγυπτίοις from the same consonantal Hebrew text).

English reader and is unlikely to become accepted into the translations.[17] A more extended example of vulture–eagle imagery in connection with Israel is seen in Deut. 32.10-12:

> He found him in a desert land, in a barren and howling waste. He shielded him and cared for him; he guarded him as the apple of his eye, as an eagle (נֶשֶׁר) stirs up its nest and hovers over its young, and spreads its wings (כְּנָפָיו) to catch them and carries them on its pinions. Yhwh alone led him; there was no foreign god with him.

It would be easy to make some simplistic assumptions concerning the function of the metaphor in Exod. 19.4. While divine tutelage and protection in a general sense are undoubtedly factors, they may not be central, and a moment's reflection should be enough to show that it is not the case that Israel is learning to be less and less dependent on God just as the fledglings eventually learn to 'fly for themselves'![18] Such a metaphor needs to be read in the light of the vulture iconography of the ancient world. Representations of such birds are found in close association with royalty in both Egypt and Mesopotamia. A series of temple scenes in Egypt depicts such a bird on the central axis of the temple ceiling in successive stages of escorting the Pharaoh as he makes his way through to the god in the *adytum*.[19] The Assyrian king is depicted in battle with the god Aššur taking the form of a vulture or eagle over his head, or wearing the wings of such a bird himself.[20] The eagle or vulture is a symbol of transcendence over the earthly sphere of events, and applied to royalty, an indication that the king is invited to participate in a dominion normally beyond the level of human capacity. There is a close association with warfare and with the divine guarantee of success.

Some other biblical passages may help to fill out our understanding of the eagle (נֶשֶׁר) in association with Israel. Proverbs 23.5 employs the

17. For the meaning and iconic use of נֶשֶׁר see BDB, pp. 676-77; KB, pp. 640-41; S.R. Driver, *Exodus*, p. 170; G.R. Driver, 'Birds in the Old Testament. II. Birds in Life', *PEQ* 20 (1955), pp. 129-40 (140); Kleinig, 'On Eagles' Wing', pp. 21, 26; N. Kiuchi, 'נשׁר', in *NIDOTE*, III, pp. 200-201.

18. Fretheim, *Exodus*, p. 210.

19. Harold H. Nelson, 'The Egyptian Temple', in David Noel Freedman and G. Ernest Wright (eds.), *The Biblical Archeologist Reader* (Garden City, NY: Doubleday, 1961), pp. 147-57 (151).

20. Othmar Keel, *Jahwe-Visionen und Siegelkunst: Eine neue Deutung der Majestätsschilderungen in Jes 6, Ez 1 und Sach 4* (SBS, 84-85; Stuttgart: Katholisches Bibelwerk, 1977), pp. 207-16; Kleinig, 'On Eagles' Wing', p. 21; Niehaus, *God at Sinai*, p. 153.

image of riches spouting wings like an eagle and soaring to the sky, as the ultimate vanishing point. Proverbs 30.19 includes the way of an eagle in the sky in a list of things beyond human comprehension. The eagle is proverbial for building its nest in high and inaccessible places (Job 39.27-30; Obad. 1.4; Jer. 49.16). The only other reference to Israel in connection with eagles' wings is Isa. 40.31, where those in exile who place their hope in Yhwh 'will soar on wings like eagles' in the jubilant return to Jerusalem and the land. The point, then, of the 'eagle' image in Exod. 19.4 would seem to be the divinely granted ability to 'fly' or be transported in flight to the heights where God dwells—a region normally inaccessible to human endeavour and beyond human comprehension. Thus while the expressions ואשׂא אתכם על־כנפי נשׁרים ('I lifted you up on eagles' wings') and ואבא־אתכם אלי ('and brought you to myself') may refer to two phases of the divine activity, on this view they are considered to belong closely together in climactic parallelism.

The third expression of v. 4 ואבא־אתכם אלי ('and I brought you to myself') is without parallel in the Hebrew Bible. The hiphil form of בוא ('come, enter') could cover a range of nuances of causation from permission to effectuation. Even in its weaker nuances (permission, encouragement) it would convey the idea of great favour. In close association with ואשׂא ('I lifted up') it must include the idea of a more direct divine agency in the entry of the people into God's presence. Elsewhere, where God is the subject of a hiphil form of בוא, the destination is generally the land, or God's holy hill (e.g. Deut. 31.20, 21; Josh. 24.8; Judg. 2.1; Jer. 2.7; Ezek. 20.28; 34.13; Zech. 10.10; Ps. 43.3). The boldness of the language of the Hebrew text, where God himself is the destination, was not lost on *Targum Onqelos*, which paraphrased it by וקריבית יתכון לפולחני ('and brought you near to my service') in order to soften the anthropomorphic element.[21]

Leibowitz draws attention to the comment of Rashbam who cites the 'covenant formula' להיות אני לכם לאלהים ('that I might be your God') by way of explanation of the expression.[22] That is, the 'bringing to myself' expresses the underlying motivation of the preceding divine actions and focuses on relationship rather than location. For a moment the mountain and all terrestrial indicators fade from view, such that we are not sure where God is to be located. Is it in the heights of the mountain, where

21. For the use of בוא (in both qal and hiphil) as a *terminus technicus* for entry to the sacral sphere see Horst Dietrich Preuss, 'בוא', in *TDOT*, II, pp. 22-25.

22. Nehama Leibowitz, *Studies in Shemot (The Book of Exodus)* (2 vols.; Jerusalem: World Zionist Organization, 1976), I, pp. 296-97.

eagles have their nests (Job 39.27-30; Obad. 1.4; Jer. 49.16)? Or is it in heaven, or among the stars, where eagles venture (Prov. 23.5; 30.19; Lam. 4.19)? If an answer is felt to be needed, possible support for the latter alternative is to be found at Exod. 20.22 where again we have a recitation of divine acts which employs a closely parallel introductory formula: 'Yhwh said to Moses, "This is what you are to say to the house of Israel, 'You yourselves saw that it was from heaven that I spoke with you'"'. Thus, while the evidence is slender at this stage, it would at least be a consistent reading of the text of Exod. 19.4 to picture Israel as in some way caught up to the heavenly realm as the invited guest of God. What is more important than the location of the encounter of 19.4, however, is the transcendent relationship so depicted. The reader has been prepared to some extent for this language by v. 3 which speaks of Moses' ascent אל־האלהים ('to God'). So the divine encounter which Moses is said (in the narrative framework, v. 3) to have experienced, has its counterpart (in the divine discourse, v. 4) in the experience of the people. It is this privilege of nearness, or access (בוא) to the presence of God (perhaps as a king might invite his favoured courtiers to draw near to him) which serves as the setting for the declarations of vv. 5-6. There are of course inherent tensions. For one, God has accompanied Israel on the journey as well as being the goal of the journey. For another, the notion of Israel's unqualified access to God does not sit comfortably with the subsequent narrative which will introduce obstacles to Israel's full enjoyment of God's presence, calling for mediation or representation. But these must not be allowed to obscure the fact that in this central summary declaration giving, as it purports, a divine perspective on the exodus experience with its climax at Sinai, it is the resulting heightened *proximity* of Israel to God which is paramount, a proximity which is the result of divine initiative and accomplishment.

b. *The Syntax of Exodus 19.5-6a*

Verses 5 and 6 follow the brief divine rehearsal of the events of the exodus and encounter at Sinai and give the content of the divine declaration regarding Israel:

> (5a) Now, if you will pay heed to my voice, and keep my covenant, (5b) you will be mine as a special treasure in distinction from all the peoples. That is, the whole earth is mine, (6a) but you will be mine as a royal priesthood and a holy nation.

The macrosyntactic introductory particle ועתה[23] ('now') has the rhetorical effect of drawing attention to the change of subject from the first person clauses of v. 4 (recounting divine activity) to the second person clauses (referring to Israel), as well as marking a temporal shift from the narration of past events to the setting forth of present and future consequences, particularly, as Kalluveettil notes, in covenantal settings (Deut. 4.1; 10.12; Josh. 24.14; 1 Sam. 12.13; 1 Chron. 22.11).[24]

Verses 5-6a have the structure of a conditional sentence, with v. 5a constituting the protasis, and the apodosis commencing with והייתם ('you will be') at v. 5b. Syntactically there are theoretically other possible readings, such as commencing the apodosis with ושׁמרתם ('then you will keep', v. 5aβ) or including the whole of v. 5b in the protasis and commencing the apodosis with ואתם ('then you', v. 6a). None of the alternative readings is semantically a real option. The clause of v. 5aβ is so closely parallel in meaning to v. 5aα that it must continue the protasis. On the other hand, to attempt to extend the protasis into v. 5b results in linking the heeding of God's voice and the keeping of his covenant with the notion of Israel being or becoming a סגלה ('special treasure'), as though the latter state (being or becoming God's special treasure) were similarly Israel's responsibility to achieve. Then, either embedded within the apodosis or appended to it is a clause commencing with כי (v. 5bβ). This כי clause is either contained within v. 5bβ, thus forming a parenthesis within the apodosis which then would resume with ואתם (v. 6a), or it extends to the end of v. 6a. The extent and nature of the כי clause is discussed below. Thus on any reasonable reading, the declaration of v. 5b is in some way formally contingent upon the parallel hemistichs: 'Now, if you will pay heed to my voice//and keep my covenant'.

Opinions differ on the real nature and logic of the conditional sentence. Muilenburg speaks of the 'covenant contingency' here,[25] seeing it as closely analogous to the many other biblical passages which set out a reward conditional on obedience.[26] Mosis takes issue with the lack of careful

23. For the macro-syntactic function of ועתה, see Wolfgang Schneider, *Grammatik des biblischen Hebräisch* (Munich: Claudius-Verlag, 1974), pp. 261-64.

24. Kalluveettil, *Declaration and Covenant*, p. 115; cf. Bruce K. Waltke and M. O'Connor, *An Introduction to Biblical Hebrew Syntax* (Winona Lake, IN: Eisenbrauns, 1990), §38, p. 634; §39.3.4.f., p. 667.

25. Muilenburg, 'Form and Structure', p. 352.

26. Muilenburg ('Form and Structure', p. 355), cites as representative examples Gen. 26.26-30; 31.44-50; Exod. 15.22-26; 23.22; Lev. 26.2-45; Num. 32.20-27; Deut. 8.11-20; 9.13-15, 22-25, 26-28; 28.1-6, 15-19, 58-60; 30.15-20; Josh. 24; Judg. 9.15,

syntactic and semantic study of vv. 4-6. He regards v. 5a as the key to the meaning of vv. 4-6a: 'Yhwh's declaration in vv. 4-6a is in essence neither proclamation, nor promise for the future, but *paraenesis*'.[27] In this, Mosis is following von Rad, for whom vv. 4-6 are 'part of the paraenetic pronouncement' which precedes the proclamation of the law in a liturgical setting'.[28] For von Rad, it is this passage, which approximates to the 'original liturgical form' of the exhortation—promising blessing as a reward for obedience—which 'was particularly well suited to an increasingly wide variety of adaptations'.[29] Among these adaptations, von Rad cites Pss. 81.7, 8; 95; and Mic. 6.3-5, along with the paraenetic sections of Deuteronomy with which he is primarily dealing at this point (particularly Deut. 7.1-11).

Patrick has pointed to a weakness in this understanding of the conditional in Exod. 19.5-6. The protasis does not so much lay down a precondition for certain benefits which will follow as a consequence if the precondition is met, but rather defines the nature and content of the appellations in the apodosis, or, at least in the first instance, of סגלה מכל־העמים ('special treasure in distinction from all the peoples'). Patrick paraphrases it thus: 'Being Yhwh's own possession, his holy nation and kingdom of priests, entails submitting to his will'.[30] The clauses of Exod. 19.5a-5b (or 5a-6a) are, on this view, more in the nature of a proclamation of favour—an offer which the people are expected to embrace.[31] The emphasis on this reading falls on the divine initiative, not on a *quid-pro-quo* arrangement. The relationship already exists and is the basis for the appeal for (continued) loyalty. Perhaps, to use a mundane analogy (imperfect, as all such analogies are), the difference in understanding the conditional can be illustrated by comparing the two sentences: 'If you accept my offer to teach you, and you devote yourself to learning Hebrew and other cognate languages, you will get a well-paid university position and a

16-20; 1 Sam. 7.3-4; 12; 1 Kgs 6.12-13; 9.1-9; 11.38-39; 1 Chron. 28.2-10; 2 Chron. 7.11-22; Neh. 1.8-10; Pss. 81; 89.30-37; 132.11-19; Jer. 4.1-2; 7.1-15; 12.16-17; 17.24-27; 18.7-11; 22.4-5; 26.4-6; 31.36-37; 33.19-26; and Mal. 2.1-5. For similar views see Beyerlin, *Origins*, p. 69; Baltzer, *The Covenant Formulary*, pp. 28-29; McComiskey, *The Covenants of Promise*, p. 171.

27. Mosis, 'Ex 19,5b.6a', p. 8 (original emphasis).

28. Von Rad, 'The Form Critical Problem', p. 33.

29. Von Rad, 'The Form Critical Problem', p. 33.

30. Patrick, 'The Covenant Code Source', p. 149; cf. Moberly, *At the Mountain of God*, pp. 226-27.

31. Cf. Nicholson, *Exodus and Sinai*, p. 31.

rewarding superannuation package', and 'If you accept my offer to teach you and you devote yourself to learning Hebrew and other cognate languages, you will have the satisfaction of being a Semitics scholar'. The latter is a definitional condition, where the apodosis spells out what is inherent in the protasis.

Fretheim follows Patrick, noting the close parallel in overall structure between the Sinaitic and the Abrahamic covenants.[32] As with Israel in Exod. 19.4-6, that Abraham will obey the covenant God initiated with him is linked with his relationship with the nations (Gen. 22.18; 26.4-5). Wildberger characterizes this passage as Yhwh's 'election proclamation'.[33]

This understanding of the protasis as a declaration requiring a response is confirmed by the report of the people's acceptance in v. 8a. The covenant thus comes into effect no later than the moment when the people pledge their commitment to it. The honorific designation of Israel in the apodosis is in force from that point on, not after sufficient time has elapsed for testing Israel's level of obedience.

Support for the understanding of these verses as proclamation may be found in the somewhat parallel passages in Deut. 7.6-11, 14.2 and 26.18-19. Deuteronomy 7.6-11 links the notions of Israel as God's holy people (עם קדוש), his treasure in distinction from all the nations (סגלה מכל־העמים), with an explicit reference to election (בחר), with God's action in redeeming them from slavery in Egypt, with his commitment to his covenant (שׁמר הברית והחסד) and with the consequent need on Israel's part to keep (שׁמר) God's requirements. Deuteronomy 14.2 is likewise set in the context of the call to heed God's commands (13.19 [ET 13.18]). This verse again links the notion of Israel as עם קדקשׁ ('a holy people') and סגלה מכל־העמים ('a special treasure in distinction from all the peoples') with the idea of election (בחר). The closest parallel to Exod. 19.5 is found at Deut. 26.18-19:

> (18) Yhwh has declared today that you are his people (עם), his treasure (סגלה), as he said to you, and that you are to keep (שׁמר) all his commands, (19) and that you will be exalted above all the nations (הגוים) he has made, in praise, reputation and honour, and that you will be a holy people (עם־קדשׁ) to Yhwh your God as he said.

Note the similar concepts and terminology to those found in Exod. 19.5 (קדשׁ, סגלה מכל־העמים, בריתי, שׁמרתם, תשׁמעו בקולי).

32. Fretheim, *Exodus*, p. 213.

33. *Erwählungsproklamation*, Wildberger, *Jahwes Eigentumsvolk*, p. 16; cf. Zenger, *Sinaitheophanie*, p. 102.

There are thus clear indications of an intertextuality between Exodus and Deuteronomy at this point, which may aid the interpretative task. To be sure, there is some difference in style, such as the Deuteronomic preference for עם for Israel, compared with the use of גוי in Exod. 19.6. Beyerlin draws attention to what he regards as a more significant contrast in content between the unconditional affirmations of the Deuteronomy passages and the 'cultic–hortatory' language of Exod. 19.5 with its emphatic '*If*'.[34] In none of the Deuteronomy passages is the סגלה status of Israel made conditional on the requirement to obey. Rather the כי which introduces both Deut. 7.6 and 14.2 suggests the converse. Israel is to obey *because* they are the chosen treasure. They will demonstrate and live out the unique relationship with Yhwh as they listen and obey. Fretheim also draws attention to Deut. 4.40, 6.20-24 and 11.7-8, passages where the motivation for keeping God's commandments is given in terms of a relationship already established by virtue of God's saving activity.[35] For many interpreters who recognize some form of affinity between Exod. 19.5-6 and the paraenetic passages of Deuteronomy, it is the Exodus passage which is treated as a result of Deuteronomic redaction.[36] Whether this is the case, or whether, with those who posit an E or J or independent source with no Deuteronomic redaction, we take the Exodus passage to be primary, the employment of the same body of material in Deuteronomy, with no hint of a notion that the status of Israel before Yhwh is a reward for faithfulness to the covenant, should be sufficient to make us wary of reading such a notion into the conditional protasis of Exod. 19.5.

Weinfeld argues that the direction of dependence is from Exod. 19.5-6 to the Deuteronomy passages.[37] The twice repeated phrase of Deut. 26.18, 19, 'as he promised', points to some familiar reference to a divine declaration regarding the 'treasure' status of the people of Israel, their unique position as a holy people, with perhaps further honorific designnations, coupled with a call to keep God's requirements. The reference may simply be to the earlier Deuteronomy passages (7.6; 14.2), both of which contain some of these elements. But we cannot rule out the possibility that the Deuteronomy passages are a conscious reflection both of the wording and of the theological thrust of the Exodus passage.

34. Beyerlin, *Origins*, pp. 67-68.

35. Fretheim, *Exodus*, p. 210.

36. See the section on the source analysis of Exod. 19.4-6 in the preceding chapter.

37. Moshe Weinfeld, *Deuteronomy 1–11: A New Translation with Introduction and Commentary* (AB, 5; New York: Doubleday, 1991), p. 367.

The suggestion, advanced by Beyerlin, among others,[38] that both the Exodus and Deuteronomy uses of the expression derive from an expression of the cult liturgy cannot be elevated beyond a conjecture in the absence of any clearer corroborations of the content of any such liturgy. One might surmise that such a central formula as סגלה מכל־העמים appears to have been in the view of Beyerlin, would not easily have been understood in two radically different ways—as a contingent declaration by the writer of Exodus and as an unconditional promise by the writer of Deuteronomy.

Whatever view one takes of the relationship between the Exodus and the Deuteronomic uses of the סגלה expression, the absolute form of the promise in Deuteronomy lends at least *prima facie* support to Patrick's understanding of the relationship between protasis and apodosis in Exod. 19.5-6a. The position of סגלה is not something Israel might attain by future acts of obedience, but something which is theirs by divine favour and which is manifested in the relationship which involves an unwavering loyalty.

Perhaps in the end not too much weight should be placed on the distinction between a reward based on the condition of faithful service (as Muilenburg), and a favour which entails elevation to a position calling for honoured and faithful service (as Patrick). Within Israel, there existed a form of piety which regarded the keeping of God's commands not as a burden, or as a means to the end of obtaining some other blessing, but as something which was its own reward (Ps. 19.12 [ET 19.11]). The possession of the commandments was not to be seen as a burden, but a privilege in itself: 'What other nation is so great as to have such righteous decrees and statutes as this law I am setting before you today?' (Deut. 4.8; cf. 30.11); 'Direct me in the path of your commands, for there I find delight' (Ps. 119.35).

There would be no significant weakening of the case being presented below for the meaning and function of the honorific designations of Israel in vv. 5-6a if one were to read some form of conditional reward at v. 5, provided this is understood to be within the framework of an already established relationship. An instructive parallel is found in the angel's charge to the high priest Joshua at Zech. 3.7: 'This is what Yhwh of hosts

38. Beyerlin, *Origins*, pp. 67-77. Von Rad ('The Form Critical Problem', pp. 33-40) associates the festival with Shechem. Wildberger (*Jahwes Eigentumsvolk*, pp. 40-62) associates the celebration of the proclamation of Israel's election with the festival of Unleavened Bread at Gilgal, seeing it as originally independent of the Sinai traditions.

says: "If you walk in my ways and keep (שׁמר) my charge, then you shall exercise authority over my house and take charge of my courts, and I will grant you people who gain access among these standing here"'.[39] Here we find the same structure of protasis, setting forth in general terms the requirement of loyalty to Yhwh (note the verb שׁמר), and an apodosis, which outlines in honorific language the nature of the reward. The reward consists of yet further opportunity for service. To 'stand' before the divine throne is to occupy the position of a faithful servant (as Elijah in 1 Kgs 17.1; 18.15). The fact that in both Zech. 3.7 and Exod. 19.5 it is *priestly* service which is in view, and that Joshua is envisaged as taking his place among the heavenly attendants only adds, on the interpretation being developed here, to the closeness of the parallel.

c. *The Conditional Protasis: Exodus 19.5a*

The expression שׁמוע תשׁמעו (Exod. 19.5a) is an instance of the *figura etymologica* with the infinitive absolute in prepositive position, which generally has the effect of intensifying or imparting a modal character to the expression. It may in some instances intensify the meaning of the verbal stem.[40] Such a use here would result in a meaning like 'obey me fully' (NIV). However, this would be a rare use of the infinitive, and is denied altogether by Jenni.[41] More commonly it is the effect of the clause as a whole which is affirmed or intensified, particularly any modal force which may be inferred.[42] While it commonly adds an asseverative force to indicate the certainty of the proposition stated, such a notion is of course inappropriate in a conditional protasis.[43] Could the infinitive perhaps strengthen the element of uncertainty inherent in a conditional sentence? This notion would seem to lie behind the NEB rendering, 'If only you will now listen to me...' Similarly KJV, RV, ASV and NASB all add an adverbial 'actually' or 'indeed' indicating a perceived significant level of doubt that the condition of the protasis will be met. GKC speaks of the use of the infinitive absolute after אם as emphasizing 'the importance of the

39. For discussion of this translation, see Chapter 12.

40. So Paul Joüon, SJ, *Grammaire de l'hébreu biblique* (Rome: Pontifical Biblical Institute Press, 1923), §123j, p. 351; Waltke and O'Connor, *Biblical Hebrew Syntax*, §35.3.1c, p. 585.

41. Ernst Jenni, *Lehrbuch der hebraischen Sprache des Alten Testaments* (Basel: Helbing & Lichtenhahn, 1981), p. 117.

42. T. Muraoka, *Emphatic Words and Structures in Biblical Hebrew* (Jerusalem: Magnes Press, 1985), pp. 83-92.

43. Waltke and O'Connor, *Biblical Hebrew Syntax*, §35.3.1g, p. 587.

condition on which some consequence depends'.[44] However, while in most if not all cases it is quite possible to translate the passages with such a force, a perusal of the contexts of the 64 instances in the Hebrew Bible where conditional אם is followed by the *figura etymologica* fails to offer convincing evidence that any such emphasis is necessarily or consistently present.

Nor does the context of Exod. 19.5 suggest any such focus on Israel's waywardness which is the assumption behind the translations of KJV, RV, ASV, NASB and NEB. To be sure, Israel's grumblings *en route* to Sinai have been noted—in the Desert of Sin (ch. 16) and at Massah and Meribah (ch. 17). But the only explicit reference to Israel's negative response to the *commands* of God prior to this point is found at 16.28 where the incident involved a breach of the prohibition on gathering manna on the Sabbath: 'How long will you refuse to keep (שׁמר) my commands and my instruction?' However, it is not likely that this incident is in view at 19.5. Apart from the use of שׁמר, there is no close verbal parallel, and any stress on a propensity to rebellion on the part of Israel would seem out of place after the heightened language regarding the encounter between God and Israel in v. 4. There is a dual tradition regarding Israel's potential for adherence to the Sinai covenant (cf. Deut. 30.11-14 with Judg. 24.19), and there is no *a priori* reason to prefer the pessimistic outlook to the more positive one at Exod. 19.5.[45] Whatever may have been the case in the subsequent outworking of the covenant, there is no focus in ch. 19 on Israel's failure to heed the voice of God. Indeed, the account of the dire apostasy into which Israel fell at Aaron's instigation in ch. 32 has the greater impact on the reader for the fact that it is *not* the anticipated response after the theophany encounter and the provisions made for perpetuating its effect in chs. 19–31.

Some recognize a use of the infinitive absolute to express duration of action, though this does not appear to have been proposed as a meaning for Exod. 19.5. While this usage has sometimes been claimed only for the postpositive position of the infinitive absolute,[46] Joüon,[47] Riekert[48] and

44. GKC, §113 o [2], pp. 342-43.

45. See George W. Coats, *Rebellion in the Wilderness: The Murmuring Motif in the Wilderness Traditions of the Old Testament* (Nashville: Abingdon Press, 1968); Michael DeRoche, 'Jeremiah 2.2-3 and Israel's Love for God during the Wilderness Wanderings', *CBQ* 45 (1983), pp. 364-76.

46. GKC, §113 r, p. 343.

47. Joüon, *Grammaire*, p. 349.

48. S.J.P.K. Riekert, 'The Struct Patterns of the Paronomastic and Co-ordinated Infinitives Absolute in Genesis', *JNSL* 7 (1979), pp. 69-83 (76-77).

Muraoka[49] fail to find any such distinction based on word order. Waltke and O'Connor do not recognize the existence of a category of duration for the idiom.[50]

No comprehensive categorization is possible for the nuances of the infinitive when used as an absolute complement, and its precise force must be determined by context in each case.[51] Of the eleven other occurrences of the qal infinitive absolute of שׁמע in the *figura etymologica*, seven are in a conditional protasis (Exod. 15.26; 23.22; Deut. 11.13; 15.5; 28.1; Jer. 17.24; Zech. 6.1). The remaining four occurrences are in postpositive position following the imperative (Isa. 55.2; Job 13.17; 21.2; 37.2) and thus presumably serve to strengthen the element of obligation. If word order carries no semantic significance, perhaps the conditional uses of this form of this verb have as their deep structure an imperatival force and hint at an obligation ('If, *as you ought*, you pay heed...'). That is, what is offered to Israel in Exod. 19.5 is not on a take-it-or-leave-it basis as though God is indifferent to the outcome, but comes as an authoritative word.[52] However, there can be no certainty on this point, and it may be preferable in the absence of any clearly discernible pattern in the force of the *figura etymologica* with other verbal roots after conditional אם to leave it without specific representation in the translation (as RSV, JB, NRSV).

The rather abrupt introduction of בריתי ('my covenant') in v. 5a has frequently been remarked upon by commentators. The implication of the pronominal suffix is that the covenant is identifiable and familiar to the recipient of the message (if not to the reader). It is generally taken to refer to the Sinai covenant. Thus Cassuto, following Rashi and Ibn Ezra, glosses it 'the covenant that I intend to make with you'.[53] No specific content (in terms of stipulations) has been given to this covenant in the text to this point. They will form the substance of much of the subsequent material in Exodus. So, can Israel be giving informed consent (v. 8) to the call to 'keep' such a covenant? Childs asserts that the introduction of בריתי here assumes the ratification of the covenant, which does not take place until

49. Muraoka, *Emphatic Words*, p. 89.

50. Waltke and O'Connor, *Biblical Hebrew Syntax*, §35.3.1d, p. 585.

51. Solá-Solé identifies thirteen: J.M. Solá-Solé, *L'infinitif sémitique: Contribution à l'étude des formes et des fonctions des noms d'action et des infinitifs sémitiques* (Bibliotheque de l'école pratique des hautes études. Section des sciences historiques et philologiques, 315; Paris: H. Champion, 1961), pp. 98-100.

52. Cf. Jon D. Levenson, *Creation and the Persistence of Evil: The Jewish Drama of Divine Omnipotence* (San Francisco: Harper & Row, 1988), pp. 141-42.

53. Cassuto, *Exodus*, p. 227; cf. Childs, *Exodus*, p. 367.

24.3-8.[54] Most solutions proposed are along source-critical lines, but in terms of the methodology outlined in the previous chapter, such solutions fail to satisfy the reader of the book of Exodus who assumes that the author or redactor was a competent literary craftsman.

Dumbrell, following Nachmanides, understands בריתי as a reference to the Abrahamic covenant.[55] The few previous references to ברית in Exodus are references to the covenant with the patriarchs (2.24; 6.4-5). Moreover, wherever the phrase שׁמר ברית ('to keep a covenant') occurs elsewhere with reference to the human response appropriate to a divinely initiated arrangement, it is an already established covenant which is in view (Gen. 17.9, 10; 1 Kgs 11.11; Ezek. 17.14; Pss. 78.10; 103.18; 132.12). The Exodus event was in fulfilment of the covenant with Abraham (Exod. 6.4), and it is this event which lies behind the poetic language of 19.4. Israel is not to become for the first time a people in covenant relationship with Yhwh at Sinai. They are already a believing and worshipping people (Exod. 4.31; 12.27; 14.31; 15.1-21).[56]

While Dumbrell has correctly queried the sharp distinction which is often made between the Abrahamic and the Sinai covenants, it may be an oversimplification to understand בריתי in 19.5 to refer exclusively to the patriarchal covenant. The Abrahamic covenant undoubtedly provides a backdrop to the exodus experience (Exod. 2.7, 20; 3.6-17). Moreover Israel's projected worship of God at the mountain in 3.12 is certainly set in the context of fulfilment of the Abrahamic promises. However, with this continuity in mind, it may nevertheless be preferable to read 19.4-6a as an anticipatory summary of the terms of the new development of the Sinai covenant, and therefore read בריתי in a somewhat proleptic sense.[57] Perhaps the most felicitous expression of the meaning of בריתי is captured by Fretheim when he observes that 'the covenant at Sinai is a specific covenant within an already existing covenant with an elected, redeemed, believing, worshiping community'.[58]

54. Childs, *Exodus*, p. 360; cf. Noth, *Exodus*, p. 154; Zenger, *Sinaitheophanie*, p. 58.

55. Dumbrell, *Covenant and Creation*, pp. 80-81, and *The Search for Order: Biblical Eschatology in Focus* (Grand Rapids: Baker Book House, 1994), p. 44.

56. For the relationship of the Sinai and Abrahamic covenants (particularly in relation to source criticism of the Sinai pericope, see Walther Zimmerli, 'Sinaibund und Abrahambund: Ein Beitrag zum Verständnis der Priesterschrift', *TZ* 16 (1960), pp. 268-80.

57. Phillips, 'A Fresh Look', p. 51.

58. Fretheim, *Exodus*, p. 209.

The call to listen to God's voice involves a more fundamental and comprehensive commitment than adherence to the specific provisions of the Sinai covenant which follow. Thus the response of the people to this summons in v. 8 ought not simply to be equated with the more specific response to the covenant stipulations at 24.3-7. The former is an acknowledgment in principle of Yhwh's sovereignty over them, an agreement to pay heed to whatever Yhwh may utter, which constitutes the basis for the particularities which follow. The requirement for unquestioning obedience might be compared with the command in the garden in Gen. 2.16-17. In view of the other creation motifs to be observed in the compositional design of the book of Exodus (to be considered in Chapter 6), this parallel may be significant.

A more extended discussion of the notion of covenant in relation to the Sinai pericope will be deferred to a later point (Chapter 7). What is clear from the suffix and from the parallel with בקלי ('to my voice') is that it is a divinely enunciated arrangement. It is equally clear (ושׁמרתם) that Israel has responsibilities with regard to this covenant.

d. *The Apodosis: Exodus 19.5b-6a*

We now turn our attention to the apodosis commencing at v. 5b. As translated above, these verses describe the covenant people by means of a single image ('special treasure') with expansionary or explanatory glosses in vv. 5bβ and 6a. Israel is, or is to be, or become a סגלה. The LXX has λαὸς περιούσιος which might imply the reading עם סגלה (as in Deut. 7.6; 14.2; 26.18). While there is little difference in the end result, there is no warrant, with McNeile,[59] for seeking to bring the Exodus text into line with those of Deuteronomy. It is more likely that the more familiar phrase from Deuteronomy has influenced the LXX rendering.

The word סגלה refers at the core of its semantic domain to some form of personal property. While not a common word in Biblical Hebrew (eight instances), it is common in Mishnaic Hebrew as a commercial–legal term where it refers to the personal property of a social inferior (such as a wife, or a slave).[60] The only two instances of סגלה in the Bible in a more literal sense, to denote property in the form of goods or accumulated wealth, are found in 1 Chron. 29.3 and Eccl. 2.8, both of which refer to the personal

59. McNeile, *Exodus*, p. 110.

60. See Samuel E. Loewenstamm, 'עם סגלה', in M. Bar Asher *et al.* (eds.), *Hebrew Language Studies Presented to Professor Zeev Ben-Hayyim* (Jerusalem: Magnes Press, 1983), pp. 321-28.

treasure of kings, seemingly as distinct from the wealth of the realm. Its principal use in the Hebrew Bible is as a metaphorical designation of the people of Israel in relation to God (Deut. 7.6; 14.2; 26.18; Mal. 3.17; Ps. 135.4). Thus the word is used in covenantal or election contexts within the Bible. Psalm 135.4, for example, would seem to echo the סגלה reference in Exod. 19.5.[61] 'Yah chose Jacob for himself // Israel as his treasure (סגלה)'. The use of a commercial term to refer to God's estimate of his people is hardly likely to be an original and independent metaphor in each of the biblical books where it is used. We must assume either that there is an intertextual relationship of some kind, or that the metaphor was part of the conventional language of divine or royal favour (or both).

Greenberg posits a connection between Hebrew סגלה and Akkadian *sikiltu*,[62] a word found in Old, Middle and Standard Babylonian, at Nuzi and in Middle Assyrian texts.[63] This is an acceptable cognate in phonological terms. While some scholars prefer the reading *siqiltu* (cognate with *saqālum*) rather than *sikiltu* (*sakālum*) in the Akkadian texts,[64] the identification of this word in one form or another with סגלה has been widely accepted, and has generated a significant amount of comment in relation to its biblical use.[65] *CAD* gives the meaning for *sikiltu* as 'possession, acquisition', first in the sense of illegally acquired goods, then in the sense of private possessions in distinction from those possessions which form

61. Cf. Leslie C. Allen, *Psalms 101–150* (WBC, 21; Waco, TX: Word Books, 1987), p. 225.

62. Moshe Greenberg, 'Hebrew *segulla*: Akkadian *sikiltu*', *JAOS* 71 (1951), pp. 172-74.

63. *CAD*, XV, p. 244; Moshe Held, 'A Faithful Lover in an Old Babylonian Dialogue', *JCS* 15 (1961), pp. 1-26 (11).

64. Benno Landsberger, 'Assyrische Königsliste und "Dunkeles Zeitalter"', *JCS* 8 (1954), pp. 47-73 (58); M.-J. Seux, *Epithètes royales Akkadiennes et Sumériennes* (Paris: Letouzer & Ané, 1967), pp. 261-62.

65. Held, 'A Faithful Lover', pp. 11-12; J.A. Thompson, *The Ancient Near Eastern Treaties and the Old Testament* (Tyndale Lecture in Biblical Archaeology, 1963; London: Tyndale Press, 1964), p. 13; Herbert B. Huffmon and Simon B. Parker, 'A Further Note on the Treaty Background of Hebrew *yāda'* ', *BASOR* 184 (1966), pp. 36-38; Seux, *Epithètes royales*, pp. 261-62; Weinfeld, 'The Covenant of Grant', p. 195; M. Dietrich, O. Loretz and J. Sanmartín, *Die keilalphabetischen Texte aus Ugarit: Einschließlich der keilalphabetischen Texte außerhalb Ugarits*. I. *Transkription* (AOAT, 24; Neukirchen–Vluyn: Neukirchener Verlag, 1976), col. 544; Loewenstamm, 'עם סגלה'; Sarna, *Exploring Exodus*, p. 131; Hans Wildberger, 'סגלה', in *TLOT*, II, pp. 791-93. For an alternative etymology, see Pietro Magnanini, 'Sull'origine letteraria dell'Ecclesiaste', *Annali* 18 (1968), pp. 363-84 (374).

part of an estate.[66] As with סגלה in Mishnaic Hebrew, *sikiltu* can be set aside for a good or bad purpose, and may be legitimately or illegitimately acquired or hoarded.[67]

While such literal uses broaden our understanding of the probable commercial background of the word, more important for our purposes is the use of *sikiltu* with a transferred meaning to express personal relationships in a royal or divine context. We find it so used in the Old Babylonian period (no later than the fifteenth century) by a god to refer to an honoured king. The Alalakh tablets contain a number of seal impressions of kings, or in one case of a vizier. One such contains the following designation of King Abban: 'Abban, the mighty king, son of Šarran, the servant of the god...the beloved of the god...the treasure of the god...'[68]

Less extensively treated in the secondary literature, but no less illuminating, is the parallel with Ugaritic *sglt*. Text 60 (18.38) of *PRU* 5 dates from the early twelfth century BCE and is a copy of a letter (no doubt a translation of the original Akkadian) from the Hittite suzerain to Ammurapi, the last king of Ugarit. It describes the vassal king in relation to the suzerain as both his 'servant ([ʻ]*bdh*) and *sglth*'.[69] This spelling out of the relationship between the two kings is a preface to a reproach by the suzerain for the failure of the Ugaritic vassal king to pay the customary visits of homage. Dahood draws attention to two biblical passages where he observes the same pairing of סגלה with עבד ('servant') in Eccl. 2.7-8 and Mal. 3.17.[70] Ecclesiastes 2.7-8 can hardly qualify as a valid parallel word pair in the strict sense, since עבדים ('servants') and סגלת מלכים ('treasure of kings') occur in an extensive list of possible acquisitions

66. *CAD*, XV, p. 244.

67. Held, 'A Faithful Lover', p. 11.

68. D.J. Wiseman, *The Alalakh Tablets* (Occasional Publications of the British Institute of Archaeology at Ankara; London: British Institute of Archaeology at Ankara, 1953), pl. III 1.76, pp. 28-30; cf. p. 113 for other instances; cf. Seux, *Epithètes royales*, p. 261. It is difficult to be certain of the identity of the god or gods.

69. Charles Virolleaud, *Le palais royal d'Ugarit*. V. *Textes en cunéiformes alphabétiques des archives sud, sud-ouest et du petit palais* (Mission de Ras Shamra, 6; Paris: Imprimerie Nationale Librairie C. Klincksieck, 1965), p. 84 line 6 (cf. line 12); for description see Cyrus H. Gordon, *Ugaritic Textbook* (AnOr, 38; Rome: Pontifical Biblical Institute Press, 1965), §17.1, no. 2060, p. 283; Huffmon and Parker, 'A Further Note', p. 37.

70. Mitchell Dahood, SJ, 'Ugaritic Hebrew Parallel Pairs', in Loren R. Fisher (ed.), *Ras Shamra Parallels: The Texts from Ugarit and the Hebrew Bible* (AnOr, 49-51; 3 vols.; Rome: Pontifical Biblical Institute Press, 1975), II, pp. 1-33 (24-25).

which might serve as a gauge of wealth. The סגלת מלכים here is presumably to be understood in its more literal sense, following as it does כסף וזהב ('silver and gold'). The other of Dahood's parallels, Mal. 3.17, reads as follows: 'They will be mine says Yhwh of hosts on the day when I make up my treasure (סגלה); I will spare them just as a man spares his son (בן) who serves (עבד) him'. Here, while it is with בן ('son') that סגלה is more formally parallel, the verb עבד ('to serve') is a significant qualifier of the type of filial relationship, just as בן is a qualifier of the type of service involved. Here is no menial servitude, but the honorific service of a devoted son. This parallel may then elucidate the nature of a סגלה relationship in Exod. 19.5 as being one where filial loyalty would be an appropriate response.

Israel is סגלה מכל־העמים ('a special treasure in distinction from all the nations'). Inherent in the word סגלה is the concept of distinction or separation from other property or relationships. Israel is a סגלה for God in some manner in distinction from, or rather than (מן) all the other nations. This concept of Israel's distinctiveness or separation for this status or role thus carries forward the special relationship which has already been brought to our attention in the brief resumé of v. 4, where Egypt is the only other nation in view.

The מן here might perhaps be interpreted in a somewhat more inclusive sense as 'from among', that is, as a reference to Israel's membership in the commonality of humanity, and hence, perhaps, as a pointer to Israel's function or mission in relation to all of humanity which some find in v. 6a (as RSV, NRSV).[71] While this is certainly possible grammatically, it seems to weaken the inherently distinctive status of a סגלה. Nor can the מן be understood as a מן *comparationis* ('a סגלה to a greater extent than the other nations'), as may be inferred in the paraphrase of *Targum Pseudo-Jonathan*, for the same reason. We will need to suspend judgment on Israel's role in relation to the other nations until we deal with v. 6a. Some close parallels for the use of מן *separationis* in relation to Israel's election may be found at Deut. 7.6 and 14.2, both also in relation to סגלה, and Amos 3.2. The latter passage reflects the same note of exclusivity in the relationship: 'You only have I known, in distinction from (מן) all the families of the earth'.

There is in fact one biblical passage which may be consciously epexegetic of the phrase סגלה מכל־העמים. Solomon's dedicatory prayer for the temple speaks of Israel in these words: 'For you distinguished (בדל)

71. Cf. Dumbrell, *Covenant and Creation*, pp. 86, 89.

them for yourself as an inheritance (נחלה) in distinction from (מן) all the nations of the earth, just as you declared by your servant Moses when you brought our fathers out of Egypt, Lord Yhwh' (1 Kgs 8.53). The hiphil of בדל brings out the notion of exclusivity, while another commercial–legal term נחלה ('inheritance') appears to substitute for the less familiar סגלה. Similarly, the Qumran text 4Q504 is a prayer which in part is an expansionary reflection on Exod. 19.4-6. Fragment 6.9 follows a paraphrastic expansion of the eagle image of Exod. 19.4 with a clear allusion to Num. 23.9:

[...ש]כנו בדד ובגוים לא תתחשב וא[...],

We remain aloof and one does not count us among the nations.[72]

The same sentiment is expressed at *Jub.* 16.17-18, a passage similarly dependent on Exod. 19.4-6.

We may summarize our discussion of the סגלה clause by emphasizing both its distinctive character and its royal associations—both in its biblical and extrabiblical instances alike. We will thus be disposed to seek a compatible royal context for its use in Exod. 19.5. Israel, the recipient of the title סגלה is the 'cherished possession' of the divine king, enjoying the status at least of a favoured royal retainer, if not royal status themselves, and doing so uniquely among the nations.

e. *Interpretation of the* כי *Clause: Exodus 19.5b*

The clause כי־לי כל־הארץ (v. 5b) has been understood in a number of ways. Ibn Ezra offers two interpretations. It might on the one hand be construed as a causal clause, or alternatively, it might be regarded as a concessive clause. We will consider each of these possibilities, and two others, that it is an asseverative clause, or an explanatory clause.

(1) *Causal interpretation*. Among those who take the כי clause as causal are *Targums Onqelos* and *Neofiti*, the *Fragment Targum*, the Peshitta,[73] KJV, RV, RSV, ASV, NASB, NEB, JB, Keil,[74] Beyerlin,[75] Perlitt,[76] Zenger[77] and

72. Florentino García Martínez and Elbert J.C. Tigchelaar (eds.), *Dead Sea Scrolls Study Edition* (2 vols.; Leiden: E.J. Brill, 1997, 1998), II, pp. 1008-1009.

73. See Israel Drazin, *Targum Onkelos to Exodus: An English Translation of the Text with Analysis and Commentary* (New York: Ktav, 1990), p. 191.

74. Keil and Delitzsch, *Commentary on the Old Testament*, I (Exodus), p. 96.

75. Beyerlin, *Origins*, p. 71.

76. Perlitt, *Bundestheologie*, p. 172.

77. Zenger, *Sinaitheophanie*, p. 167.

Patrick.[78] If it is a causal clause, for what does it offer the reason or motive? As the position or status of a סגלה is not something which the people of Israel set out to achieve, it logically cannot refer to any motivation on their part, though they form the subject of the verb הייתם. The כי clause is sometimes taken to provide the motive for the assertion of divine sovereignty involved in the first clause of v. 5b: 'You will be for me a treasure in distinction from all the peoples of the earth, (as is my sovereign right) since the whole world is mine (to deal with as I choose)'.[79] In other words, Yhwh, on this view, would be reinforcing his prerogative to make the offer of the covenant to Israel and to no other nation.[80] Wildberger understands ארץ here to refer to the land, rather than the earth—a reference to Israel's territory west of the Jordan.[81] This would still constitute a motive clause, establishing Yhwh's prior ownership of the land and hence his right to grant it to whomever he wished. For a contrary view, however, on the universal scope of the territory envisaged, see Perlitt, who connects the sentiment with that of Isa. 42.5.[82]

Dumbrell offers a somewhat modified version of the motive clause. While rejecting any suggestion that the clause provides a defence of God's choice of Israel, Dumbrell sees the כי clause as testifying 'to the purpose for which the exodus redemption was instituted by God: Israel is called because the whole world is the object of Yhwh's care'.[83] This relates closely to the somewhat functional interpretation which Dumbrell adopts at v. 6a, that of Israel's implied mission to the nations, an interpretation which will be considered below.

We have already canvassed the possibility that the כי clause extends to the end of v. 6a. On a causal reading of the כי, in this case, the assertion of the סגלה status of Israel would be based not only on Yhwh's ownership of the world (or the land), but also on the already established fact (on this view) of Israel's identity as 'a royal priesthood and a holy nation'. This

78. Patrick, 'The Covenant Code Source', p. 148.

79. E.g. John William Wevers, *Notes on the Greek Text of Exodus* (Septuagint and Cognate Studies, 30; Atlanta: Scholars Press, 1990), p. 295.

80. Holzinger interprets the phrase as 'die Begründung des Rechts Jahwes, Israel aus der Zahl der Völker heraus zu seinem besondern Eigentum zu machen, spricht, vom Standpunkt des absoluten Monotheismus aus, die Souveränität Gottes gegenüber der Völkerwelt aus' (Holzinger, *Exodus*, p. 67).

81. Wildberger, *Jahwes Eigentumsvolk*, p. 76.

82. Perlitt, *Bundestheologie*, p. 172.

83. Dumbrell, *The Search for Order*, pp. 44-45.

reading will hardly stand up, however. The designations of v. 6a are just as unprecedented as is the סגלה declaration of v. 5b, and hence cannot constitute a motive or reason for such a declaration. Thus on either view of the extent of the כי clause, a causal interpretation seems unlikely.

Mosis correctly rules out any interpretation of the כי clause involving an explanation of God's motivation, on the basis that nowhere else do we find such a motive given when divine prerogatives are in view.[84] Yhwh apparently needs no self-justification for his choices, and is only ever represented as grounding them in his own character (Deut. 7.7-8; Ezek. 20.9, 14, 22; 36.22-23).

(2) *Concessive interpretation*. The כי clause has also been understood in a concessive sense. As such, it could be taken either with the first clause of v. 5b (as in MT) and hence rather parenthetically to the flow of vv. 5b-6a: 'You will be for me a treasure in distinction from all the nations—even though the whole earth is mine'. Or the כי clause may be taken as concessive before the clause of v. 6a, as NIV: 'Although the whole earth is mine, you will be for me a kingdom of priests and a holy nation'. Neither of the two concessive interpretations is logically satisfying. For Yhwh to have Israel as a 'special treasure' or as a 'royal priesthood and holy nation' in no way sits uncomfortably with the notion of his universal ownership of the world such that a concessive clause would be felt to be needed. Rather, for Yhwh to have a special relationship with Israel (which appears to be inherent in all of these phrases) *implies* the existence of other categories of relationship, and the notion of a סגלה in particular implies other forms of possession and relationship. Muilenburg observes that the line '"for all the earth is mine"...serves to set [the declaration concerning Israel] apart and yet to relate it to the whole'.[85] Similarly Auzou understands the expression, whether it is taken more closely with the preceding or the following clause, as indicating that the privileged choice of Israel is made 'in view of all the nations'.[86]

(3) *Asseverative interpretation*. Dozeman draws attention to the problem of logic in treating a statement of universal sovereignty in v. 5bβ as a basis

84. Mosis, 'Ex 19,5b.6a', p. 13. For a study of the contexts in which motivation clauses are found, see James Muilenburg, 'The Linguistic and Rhetorical Usages of the Particle כי in the Old Testament', *HUCA* 32 (1961), pp. 135-60.

85. Muilenburg, 'Form and Structure', p. 353.

86. 'Dans la perspective de tous les peuples', Auzou, *De la servitude*, p. 250.

for the particularism of v. 5bα.[87] He treats the phrase כי־לי כל־הארץ as an asseverative clause (as NRSV),[88] though offers no satisfactory reason why an asseverative clause which introduces such a seemingly disparate element after the preceding clause would have been added, except to say that the two are 'distinct units of tradition which are presently juxtaposed to each other', that is, simply drawing attention to the lack of explanation.[89] So also Childs, who translates it 'surely all the world is mine', labels it a 'parenthetic remark' which upsets the poetic balance of the sentence.[90]

(4) *Explanatory interpretation.* A fourth possibility is that the clause is explanatory. Mosis draws attention to the strongly adversative ואתם ('but you') of v. 6a in his syntactic analysis of vv. 5-6 (cf. LXX ὑμεῖς δέ).[91] He rightly rejects the view that the ואתם serves a similar function to the emphatic אתם of v. 4a where (analogous with other instances of אתם ראיתם, 'you yourselves have seen', Deut. 29.1 [ET 29.2]; Josh. 23.3; Jer. 44.2) the emphasis is on the fact that it was not a different generation which witnessed the redemptive events of the exodus. With Dozeman,[92] we note that the adversative function of ואתם is underscored by the word order of ואתם תהיו ('but it is you who will be'). Thus there is a disjunction between the status of כל־הארץ ('all the earth') and that of Israel represented by the אתם. Though both stand in some relation to Yhwh (לי), they must stand in relation to Yhwh in contrasting ways.

Mosis then proposes to read the כי clause as an explanation clause, similar to those found after parables, to express the reality behind the similitude.[93] Such an example is found in Isa. 5.7, where after the description of Yhwh's vineyard we find these words, 'Now (כי) the vineyard of Yhwh of hosts is the house of Israel, and the people of Judah his pleasant garden'.[94] Mosis also takes the כי clause as extending to include v. 6a, seeing the expressions of vv. 5b and 6a as in antithetic parallelism, with

87. Dozeman, *God on the Mountain*, p. 95.

88. For the use of כי in asseverative clauses, see Carl Brockelmann, *Hebräische Syntax* (Neukirchen: Verlag der Buchhandlung des Erziehungsvereins, 1956), §31b, pp. 28-29.

89. Dozeman, *God on the Mountain*, p. 95.

90. Childs, *Exodus*, p. 367.

91. Mosis, 'Ex 19,5b.6a', pp. 13-14.

92. Dozeman, *God on the Mountain*, p. 95.

93. Mosis, 'Ex 19,5b.6a', p. 16; cf Muilenburg, 'The Particle כי', p. 146.

94. Cf. KB, p. 432, where this verse is given as an example under the category of 'introducing an interpretation'.

both clauses dependent on כי. These explanatory clauses serve to fill out the negative and positive meanings inherent in the image of a סגלה. We would then be dealing with two contrasting levels of ownership or relationship, which in any case is inherent in our understanding of the concept of a סגלה. There is the public ownership of the realm which the king administers (in this case כל־הארץ), and there is his intimate and exclusive claim on his personal property (Israel, the second person subject of הייתם). This explanation is appealing. The כי clause would thus set forth the twofold notion of Yhwh's ownership of or sovereignty over both all creation in general and Israel in particular. That is, Yhwh is understood as king, and this understanding is fundamental to the interpretation of this passage (see further below, Chapter 4).

One possible objection to the reading of Mosis is that the two clauses are not syntactically parallel. The first (v. 5bβ) is verbless, while the second (v. 6a) includes a form of the verb היה. This is not a serious obstacle, however. The כי clause in offering the more general background is more in the nature of a circumstantial clause, while the more substantive equivalent to the notion of Israel as a סגלה resumes the verbal clause form, picking up on the use of the verb היה in v. 5bα.

We may note then the *chiasmus* or inverted parallelism formed by the four hemistichs of the apodosis of vv. 5b-6a:

A	והייתם לי סגלה
B	מכל העמים
B′	כי־לי כל־הארץ
A′	ואתם תהיו־לי ממלכת כהנים וגוי קדוש

where כל־הארץ ('all the earth') in the explanation corresponds to כל־העמים ('all the peoples'), while תהיו־לי ('you will be mine') in the explanation picks up on the והייתם לי. The word סגלה is then glossed by the phrase ממלכת כהנים וגוי קדוש. This interpretation suggests that the notion of a סגלה, while enjoying some currency as a diplomatic term, was not such a cliché as not to warrant some form of explanatory note by the author of Exodus. The fact that it receives no such gloss in Deuteronomy might then suggest that its Deuteronomic usage is secondary, and may assume some familiarity with its prior use and the explanation clause in Exodus. The interpretation of ממלכת כהנים offered below will be influenced by this reading of the syntax of vv. 5b-6a. It will be read not as constituting a separate reward, or honour, or duty incumbent on Israel, but, in part at least, as spelling out, and giving substance to what it means to be Yhwh's סגלה.

One final observation in terms of structure may be in order. It does not follow that because vv. 5bβ-6a (the כי clause) is probably to be understood as structurally dependent on v. 5bα that it is somehow anticlimactic, or that the focus must be on the main clause containing the סגלה declaration. Muilenburg's observation that the stress of the passage falls 'more emphatically still on the ממלכת כהנים and גוי קדוש' is still valid,[95] since it is these words which climactically elucidate the otherwise somewhat allusive epithet סגלה.

4. *Conclusion*

Exodus 19.6 is set in a matrix of a divine declaration to Israel, cast in a semi-poetic idiom, of its favoured status as a nation. The people of Israel have enjoyed the intervention of Yhwh on their behalf in relation to the Egyptians. These attentions have also involved a privilege normally accorded only to royalty in ancient Near Eastern iconography of being carried aloft on eagles' wings. God himself is the destination of Israel's wilderness pilgrimage. Furthermore, Israel is favoured with a 'covenant', which, unlike a typical vassal treaty, seems designed not for the advantage of the suzerain, but for the benefit of the grantee. It is a covenant which, if accepted, involves Israel being considered in a most favourable light, in distinction from the other nations. Such a covenant involves submission to Yhwh, but, since Israel has already experienced the good hand of God in fulfilment of earlier covenant commitments, God and his requirements are not unknown quantities. The covenant and the honorific declarations have force as Israel heeds the voice of Yhwh. A key term employed to express the honorific status of Israel in relation to Yhwh is the commercial–legal term סגלה which is applied to royalty to express their relation to a higher royal power. Because this term appears not to have been a cliché, it may be felt to call for some further explanation. This explanation is forthcoming in the form of the כי clause of vv. 5b-6a. The meaning of what it is to be God's treasured possession is spelled out in the further designation of Israel as a 'royal priesthood and holy nation'. It is the content of these expressions which will occupy our attention in the following chapter.

95. Muilenburg, 'Form and Structure', p. 353.

Chapter 4

THE GRANT OF ROYAL PRIESTHOOD TO ISRAEL: EXODUS 19.6

1. *The Syntax of Exodus 19.6a*

The central concern of this work is with the expression ממלכת כהנים contained in Exod. 19.6. As noted earlier, it is part of a divine declaration which spells out what it means for Israel, as distinct from the other nations, to be God's special treasure. The MT of v. 6a reads וְאַתֶּם תִּהְיוּ־לִי מַמְלֶכֶת כֹּהֲנִים וְגוֹי קָדוֹשׁ, for which we have adopted as a working translation: 'But you will be mine as a royal priesthood and a holy nation'.

The ואתם is adversative and (followed by a finite *yiqtol* form) somewhat emphatic, drawing attention to the change of subject from that of the preceding clause 'the whole earth is mine' (v. 5bβ). We might almost translate: 'But as for you…' The verbal force of this clause is sometimes overlooked. It is not, as the preceding clause, a nominal sentence, but resumes the verbal clause with היה in v. 5bα. The words ואתם תהיו־לי could constitute a complete clause, and do not require the following words in order to make a syntactically coherent unit: 'But as for you, you will be mine'. These words are thus reminiscent of one half of what has become known as the 'covenant formula' of which the complete form is והייתי לכם לאלהים ואתם תהיו־לי לעם ('I will be your God and you shall be my people', Lev. 26.12; Jer. 7.23; cf., with variations, Jer. 11.4; 30.22).[1] When this formula is turned on its head in Hos. 1.9: אתם לא עמי ואנכי לא־אהיה לכם ('You will not be my people and I will not be yours [or: I will not be (there) for you]'), the lack of the expected לאלהים in the

1. Cf. Levenson, *Sinai and Zion*, p. 31. Opinions differ on whether the 'covenant formula' and the covenant (ברית) have any intrinsic connection. Good denies a connection: Robert McClive Good, *The Sheep of his Pasture: A Study of the Hebrew Noun* 'am(m) *and its Semitic Cognates* (HSM, 29; Chico, CA: Scholars Press, 1983), p. 75, though Deut. 29.11-12 (ET 29.12-13) seems to provide an undeniable association. See also Rudolf Smend, *Die Bundesformel* (Theologische Studien, 68; Zurich: EVZ-Verlag, 1963); Schmid, 'Ich will euer Gott sein'.

second colon suggests that the היה is more than a copula in the formula, but carries a force such as 'be present, be in relationship with'. This, in turn, is perhaps also the nuance to be understood in the explanation given of the divine name יהוה in the expression אהיה אשׁר אהיה ('I will be present [in relationship] with whomever I will be present [in relationship] with', Exod. 3.14). While there is no scope for developing the argument here, there are good grounds for the view that the writer of Exodus connects the divine name with the qal of the archaic form of the verb 'to be', understood not as detached existence, but as presence.[2] The point of the assurance given to Moses in Exod. 3.12-15 is that the God who was in relationship with (construct state) Abraham, Isaac and Jacob is the one who will now be present with Moses (כי־אהיה עמך, v. 12). Something of the same verbal force 'to be present', then, may be intended at Exod. 19.6. Similarly, the inclusion of לי ('to me' [when an alternative is available])[3] and its positioning before the noun phrases should be seen as slightly emphatic. Thus תהיו־לי would have the force of 'you (will) belong to me (as...)' rather than simply 'you will be my...' This is supported by the cotextual consideration that the expression is in close association with 'I brought you to myself' (v. 4). It is also supported by a comparison with a closely analogous expression in Num. 8.14, והיו לי הלוים ('and the Levites will be mine').[4] The phrases ממלכת כהנים and גוי קדוש in Exod. 19.6 thus appear to have some adverbial force in relation to their clause,[5]

2. The word 'connects' is used carefully, as it is not intended to comment on the etymology of the name. The connection may well be paronomastic, as with many 'explanations' of names in the Hebrew Bible. The significance of the divine tetragrammaton has been much discussed. See, e.g., Childs, *Exodus*, pp. 60-70, and the literature cited there, together with J.A. Motyer, *The Revelation of the Divine Name* (London: Tyndale Press, 1959); Barry J. Beitzel, 'Exodus 3.14 and the Divine Name: A Case of Paronomasia', *Trinity Journal* NS 1 (1980), pp. 5-20; Dumbrell, *Covenant and Creation*, pp. 83-84; Tryggve N.D. Mettinger, *In Search of God: The Meaning and Message of the Everlasting Names* (trans. Frederick. H. Cryer; Philadelphia: Fortress Press, 1988), pp. 14-49; William Johnstone, *Exodus* (Old Testament Guides, 2; Sheffield: JSOT Press, 1990), pp. 101-105; David Noel Freedman, 'The Name of the God of Moses', in John R. Huddleston (ed.), *Divine Commitment and Human Obligation: Selected Writings of David Noel Freedman*. I. *Israelite History and Religion* (Grand Rapids: Eerdmans, 1997), pp. 82-87.

3. A construction with possessive suffixes would have been possible: ממלכת כהני וגוי קדשי; cf., e.g., Ps. 2.6 for the construction.

4. Barbiero ('*Mamleket kohanîm*', p. 433) draws attention to the close syntactic parallels between Num. 8.14-18 and Exod. 19.5b-6a.

5. Mosis, 'Ex 19,5b.6a', pp. 24-25.

which may be paraphrased: 'you will belong to me *in this way or in this sense*—as a royal priesthood and a holy nation', or even, (taking the clause as resumptive of v. 5b and epexegetic of סגלה) 'you will belong to me as a special treasure...in the sense of a royal priesthood and a holy nation'.

2. *The Phrase* ממלכת כהנים

We take up, then, our consideration of the phrase ממלכת כהנים. We will first survey the textual evidence, then consider in some detail the semantic–syntactic values of this phrase and finally consider its relationship with the following phrase, וגוי קדוש.

a. *The Textual Evidence for* ממלכת כהנים *and its Understanding in Antiquity*

(1) *Hebrew Bible texts and citations*. Exodus 19.6 and the immediately surrounding verses are not extant among the Qumran Exodus texts, so our earliest Hebrew biblical texts attesting this passage are the manuscripts of the Masoretic tradition. These show no variation from the text exhibited for example by codex Leningrad מַמְלֶכֶת כֹּהֲנִים. The Samaritan Pentateuch preserves an identical consonantal reading to that of MT for this phrase.

There is a direct Hebrew citation of the phrase in the Qumran Cave 4 text known as the *Words of the Luminaries* (4Q504 4.10). The line reads כוהנים וגוי קדוש [...]. As Exod. 19.6 is the only occurrence of וגוי קדוש in conjunction with כהנים in the Hebrew Bible, ממלכת may safely (with Martínez and Tigchelaar) be supplied in the lacuna,[6] and thus, apart from the *plene* spelling of כוהנים, the text is identical to the proto-Masoretic text of Exod. 19.6. The context of the citation is a prayer which rejoices in the various privileges of the chosen race expressed particularly in terms of the exodus and Sinai experience. Most pointedly, there is a clear expansionary comment on Exod. 19.4-5 at fragment 6.6-9, which, if Martínez and Tigchelaar are correct in their reconstruction, comes before fragment 4. Besides its textual information, corroborating the form of MT, this Qumran text, which characterizes the whole elect community by this expression, will have a bearing on our subsequent interpretation of Exod. 19.6.

(2) *Versions, versional citations and allusions*. The ancient versions and versional citations in ancient texts show considerable variation.[7] The

6. Martínez and Tigchelaar, *Dead Sea Scrolls*, II, p. 1010.

7. For discussion on the witnesses to the text of Exod. 19.6 see Scott, 'A Kingdom of Priests', pp. 213-14; Fridericus Field (ed.), *Origenis Hexaplorum quae supersunt*

following survey is restricted to those references which are direct citations or translations or paraphrases or may reasonably be regarded as direct allusions to Exod. 19.6. Principal among these are the following:

LXX (followed by 1 Pet. 2.9)	βασίλειον ἱεράτευμα[8]
Aquila	βασιλείαν ἱερέων
Symmachus and Theodotion	βασιλεία ἱερεῖς[9]
Vulgate	*regnum sacerdotale*[10]
Peshitta	*mlkwt' wkhn'*
Syro-hexapla	*mlkwt' khn'* and *mlkwt' dkhn'*[11]
Jewish targums[12]	מלכין [ו]כהנין
Samaritan *Targum*	ממלכת כהנים.[13]
2 Macc. 2.17	τὸ βασίλειον καὶ τὸ ἱεράτευμα[14]

sive veterum interpretum Graecorum in totum Vetus Testamentum fragmenta (Hildesheim: Georg Olms, 1964), p. 114; Drazin, *Targum Onkelos to Exodus*, p. 191. There is a thorough study of the Greek sources in particular in Lucien Cerfaux, 'Regale sacerdotium', in *Recueil Lucien Cerfaux: Etudes d'exegèse et d'histoire religieuse* (BETL, 6-7, 18; 3 vols.; Gembloux: Duculot, 1954–62), II, pp. 283-315.

8. Cf. also Exod. 23.22 (LXX) which is a Septuagintal expansion based on Exod. 19.5-6. On the LXX text see Elliott, *The Elect and the Holy*, pp. 63-76; Schüssler Fiorenza, *Priester für Gott*, pp. 82-88. On the expansion of Exod. 23.22 see Schenker, 'Besonderes und allgemeines Priestertum', pp. 113, 116; McNamara, *Targum and Testament*, pp. 153-54.

9. Field, *Origenis Hexaplorum fragmenta*, p. 114. An alternative reading of Symmachus and Theodotion is given, however, on the basis of Vatican manuscript Gr 330 as βασιλεί[α] ἱερέων by Alan England Brooke and Norman McLean (eds.), *The Old Testament in Greek* (London: Cambridge University Press, 1909), I.2, p. 216. For discussion on the text-form, see especially Schüssler Fiorenza, *Priester für Gott*, p. 89.

10. Schüssler Fiorenza, *Priester für Gott*, p. 90.

11. Field, *Origenis Hexaplorum fragmenta*, p. 114; Holzinger, *Exodus*, pp. 63, 67.

12. The Jewish Targums all have מלכין [ו]כהנין or a further expansion on these words. McNamara, *Palestinian Targum*, p. 228; Elliott, *The Elect and the Holy*, pp. 76-78; Schüssler Fiorenza, *Priester für Gott*, pp. 79-81.

13. At least this is the reading of *Samaritan Targum* J. The *Samaritan Targum* A text has a lacuna at the final letter of the second word. It would have been interesting to know whether this was the Hebrew plural ending ם– or the Aramaic plural ן–. The incorporation of the (Hebrew) text of the Samaritan Pentateuch unchanged for the whole phrase ממלכת כהנים וגוי קדש in J may suggest that the expression had to some extent become a fixed part of the liturgical language of the Samaritans and hence there was no need to translate the phrase into Aramaic; see Abraham Tal, *The Samaritan Targum of the Pentateuch: A Critical Edition*. I. *Genesis, Exodus* (Tel-Aviv: Tel-Aviv University Press, 1980 [Hebrew]), pp. 298-99.

14. The text of 2 Maccabees can be dated to c. 124 BCE and the letter cited in 1.10–2.18 purports to have been written in 164. While the conjunction of 'kingship' and

Philo, *Abr.* 56	βασίλειον καὶ ἱεράτευμα
Philo, *Sobr.* 66	βασίλειον καὶ ἱεράτευμα θεοῦ[15]
Rev. 1.6	βασιλείαν, ἱερεῖς[16]
Rev. 5.10	βασιλείαν καὶ ἱερεῖς[17]

More indirect allusions are perhaps to be seen in

Aramaic *Levi* 1Q21.2	מלכות כהנותא[18]
and a Greek fragment relating to *T. Levi* 11.4-6, line 67	αὐτὸς καὶ τὸ σπέρμα αὐτοῦ ἔσονται ἀρχὴ βασιλέων ἱεράτευμα τῷ Ἰσραήλ.[19]

'priesthood' here is doubtless influenced by contemporary political events, it seems clear that there is an allusion to the LXX text of Exod. 19.6. Among the cotextual considerations we might include the fact that the words καὶ τὸ βασίλειον καὶ τὸ ἱεράτευμα καὶ τὸν ἁγιασμόν appear to be epexegetic of the preceding κληρονομίαν πᾶσιν ('an inheritance *for all*'). This would echo the structure I am suggesting for Exod. 19.5-6 where ממלכת כהנים וגוי קדוש is epexegetic of סגלה. We have noted in the previous chapter how סגלה and נחלה are closely associated or interchangeable terms. The word ἁγιασμόν ('sanctity') would then correspond to גוי קדוש. Finally, it is difficult to envisage any other passage in the law (v. 18) where such blessing is promised to faithful Israel. For discussion, see McNamara, *Targum and Testament*, p. 152; Jonathan A. Goldstein, *2 Maccabees* (AB, 41A; New York: Doubleday, 1984), p. 188.

15. Cerfaux, 'Regale sacerdotium', pp. 293-95; Martin McNamara, MSC, *The New Testament and the Palestinian Targum to the Pentateuch* (AnBib, 27; Rome: Pontifical Biblical Institute Press, 1966), p. 229; *idem*, *Targum and Testament*, p. 153; Philo explains βασίλειον thus: βασίλειον γὰρ δήπουθεν οἶκος.

16. The Byzantine textual tradition has βασιλεῖς καὶ ἱερεῖς here and at Rev. 5.10, which may be the result of smoothing of the asymmetry of the word classes in βασιλείαν [καὶ] ἱερεῖς.

17. Von Soden supports the Byzantine text-form for this verse: Hermann Freiherr von Soden, *Die Schriften des Neuen Testament in ihrer ältesten erreichbaren Textgestalt* (2 sections in 4 vols.; Berlin: Alexander Duncker, 1902–13), Section II, p. 854); cf. also Keil and Delitzsch, *Commentary on the Old Testament*, I (Exodus), p. 98. For the text-forms in Revelation, see also Wilhelm Bousset, *Die Offenbarung Johannis* (Göttingen: Vandenhoeck & Ruprecht, rev. edn, 1906), pp. 148-59.

18. D. Barthélemy, OP, and J.T. Milik, *Qumran Cave 1* (DJD, 1; Oxford: Clarendon Press, 1955), p. 88. I have not included here 4Q213 frag. 5 column 2 line 15, which reads אף כהנין ומלכין (Martínez and Tigchelaar, *Dead Sea Scrolls*, I, p. 448). The reversal of order and the fact that the phrase occurs as part of a list of officials which includes chiefs, judges and servants make it highly improbable that there is any association with Exod. 19.6.

19. R.H. Charles, *The Greek Versions of the Testaments of the Twelve Patriarchs* (Oxford: Clarendon Press, 1908), p. 253; Elliott, *The Elect and the Holy*, pp. 85-90.

Jub. 16.18	a kingdom, priests[20]
Jub. 33.20	a priestly and royal nation
and Rev. 20.6	ἀλλ' ἔσονται ἱερεῖς τοῦ θεοῦ καὶ τοῦ Χριστοῦ καὶ βασιλεύσουσιν μετ' αὐτοῦ.

The versions and citations are of course both indirect witnesses to the Hebrew text and interpretations of it. Hence it is not an easy matter to determine a Hebrew *Vorlage* in each case, though it will be of considerable help if we are mindful of a particular version's general translational philosophy. Nor in all cases is it clear what the versions mean. This is particularly so in the case of the LXX (quoted in 1 Pet. 2.9), where βασίλειον ἱεράτευμα may be understood either as a single constituent (adjective plus noun): 'a royal priesthood', or as two nouns in apposition: 'a royal residence, a priesthood'.[21]

The evidence of the Aramaic and Greek *Levi* texts also needs special mention, as it is not clear that there is an intended reference to Exod. 19.6. In the case of the 1Q21 fragment and the Greek fragment, the reference would appear to be to a promise to Levi's son Kohath. Thus, though it is possible that there has been some influence on the form of words used, great caution would be needed in drawing any inference as to the way Exod. 19.6 may have been understood by the authors of these documents.[22]

20. The Ethiopic version of *Jubilees* preserves the reading with two absolutes, as the Peshitta, the targums and Revelation; see Cerfaux, 'Regale sacerdotium', p. 285; McNamara, *Targum and Testament*, pp. 151-52. The Latin version has *regnum sacerdotale* and appears to have been assimilated to the form of the Vulgate (McNamara, *Targum and Testament*, p. 152).

21. For discussion on the LXX text-form see Cerfaux, 'Regale sacerdotium', pp. 287-92; Elliott, *The Elect and the Holy*, pp. 63-76; McNamara, *Palestinian Targum*, p. 229; Schüssler Fiorenza, *Priester für Gott*, pp. 82-88; Wevers, *Greek Text of Exodus*, p. 295. See especially Dan. 5.30 for the meaning 'royalty' for βασίλειον.

22. The full text of fragment 1 of 1Q21 (following Barthélemy and Milik, *Qumran Cave 1*, p. 88) reads: [מן די להוין תליתין] // [ביך מלכות כהנותא רבא מן מלכות] // [ל[ ]ל[ ]ל]. The operative words in line 2 are 'The sovereignty of the priesthood will be greater than the sovereignty of…' Barthélemy and Milik are probably correct in linking this with *T. Levi* 8.11 in the *Testaments of the Twelve Patriarchs*, where the context is a comparison of the respective future roles of Levi's three sons (note תליתין). The 'sovereignty of the priesthood', therefore, would be a reference to the prerogatives of the priestly office granted to Kohath as distinct from a military sovereignty. Grelot also discusses this text in relation to the *Aramaic Levi* text from the Cairo Geniza and reaches a similar conclusion: Pierre Grelot, 'Notes sur le Testament araméen de Levi', *RB* 63 (1956), pp. 391-406 (395-97). See also Elliott, *The Elect and the Holy*, p. 89.

This much is clear from the versions and other ancient citations. The text of Exod. 19.6 contains a noun phrase consisting of two nouns—one from the root מלך and the other from the root כהן. Beyond this basic commonality, a rather surprising number of variations is evident. Were the nouns ever joined by ו in a Hebrew text, as might be suggested by the Peshitta, *Palestinian Targums*, 2 Macc. 2.17, Rev. 5.10 and the citations in Philo? Are the nouns singular or plural in form? Are they concrete or abstract in meaning? Are they in apposition or in a bound construction? If they are in a bound construction, which noun serves to qualify the other?

We may broadly classify the versional data into two streams. One, which includes Symmachus, Theodotion, Peshitta, Syro-hexapla, the Jewish targums and possibly LXX, together with Rev. 1.6 and 5.10, provides evidence of an understanding of the Hebrew text which gives each term in the expression an independent and parallel force—'a kingdom (or: kings), and (or: namely) priests' or the like.[23] On the other hand Aquila, the Vulgate and perhaps the LXX indicate an understanding of the Hebrew words which treats the nouns as belonging in a bound construction such that one term has an adjectival force. The close formal-equivalence translation style of Aquila in particular means that this translation, at least, is almost certainly operating from a proto-MT.

It is possible that the group represented by the Jewish targums and the Syriac version indicates an underlying absolute form ממלכה, rather than ממלכת, which is most naturally taken as a noun in construct with כהנים. However, it is also possible to read ממלכת as a feminine absolute form with a northern or Phoenician type ending. The two-constituent reading is seen in its strongest form in the Peshitta, *Palestinian Targums*, 2 Macc. 2.17, Rev. 5.10 and the citations in Philo, with the addition of the copula between the two nouns. However, as will be seen below, the versional variations reflect the degree of ambiguity inherent in the MT, and thus do not necessarily constitute evidence that the Hebrew text ever read anything other than the tradition preserved by the Masoretes. The addition of the copula in the Peshitta at least is probably best regarded as an interpretative attempt to deal with the perceived awkwardness of the collocation of what appears to be a singular abstract or collective noun from מלך and a concrete plural noun from כהן. The first constituent of the Jewish Targumic readings (and the Byzantine text of Rev. 5.10) might be felt to reflect an

23. Cf. also Philo, *Sobr.* 66; *Abr.* 56; H.S. Horovitz and I.A. Rabin, *Mechilta d'Rabbi Ismael cum variis lectionibus et adnotationibus* (Jerusalem: Wahrmann, 1970), pp. 208-209; Saadya, *ad loc.*; see Drazin, *Targum Onkelos to Exodus*, p. 191.

original Hebrew form מלכים, a concrete plural noun in apposition with כהנים. However, it is suggested by some that ממלכת may sometimes have the concrete meaning 'king', as discussed below. Regardless of whether the targumists were aware of this, their rendering may easily be accounted for as asimplification, giving two concrete nouns in place of the more obscure abstract plus concrete expression. Add to this the fact that ממלכת כהנים is a somewhat difficult reading, a unique and syntactically awkward expression, and the case for the MT reading is strong.

b. *The Interpretation of* ממלכת כהנים *in Recent Literature*

As indicated above in connection with the versional evidence, the meaning of the phrase ממלכת כהנים is by no means clear. Scott speaks for all exegetes when he comments 'the Hebrew is in fact highly ambiguous'.[24] A glance through the major translations and commentaries will reveal something of the range of understandings this phrase has generated, though translations sometimes mask interpretative differences by multivalent English words such as 'kingdom'.

The questions raised by this one phrase seem interminable. Are the phrases ממלכת כהנים and גוי קדוש to be understood as coreferential? That is, do they each refer separately to Israel as a whole? Or do the noun phrases identify two subgroupings of Israel, which only when taken together refer to the totality of Israel? Is the meaning of ממלכת derivative from an active sense of the underlying root מלך or a passive one? Is ממלכת absolute or construct in form? If construct, what is the nature of its relationship with כהנים? Which noun is *regens* and which is *rectum*? If כהנים is a genitive after ממלכת, is it a subjective genitive, an objective genitive, a genitive of apposition, or perhaps some other type of genitive? Is ממלכת to be understood as *abstractum pro concreto*, or is כהנים to be understood as *concretum pro abstracto* (cf. Vulgate)? Fortunately, not all of the theoretically possible permutations are internally coherent, hence we are reduced to several main options. These have been variously enumerated as being four,[25] five[26] or eight.[27] Of the categorizations of the

24. Scott, 'A Kingdom of Priests', p. 215. Cf. Fuhs, 'Heiliges Volk Gottes', p. 156. It is a *crux interpretum* for Moran ('A Kingdom of Priests', p. 7) and a 'minefield' for Dumbrell, (William J. Dumbrell, 'The Prospect of Unconditionality in the Sinaitic Covenant', in Avraham Gileadi [ed.], *Israel's Apostasy and Restoration: Essays in Honor of Roland K. Harrison* [Grand Rapids: Baker Book House, 1988], pp. 141-55 [146]).

25. Gowan, *Theology in Exodus*, p. 177.

realistic options for the meaning of ממלכת כהנים, the list put forward by Scott may be taken as representative. According to Scott, ממלכת כהנים may mean:

1. 'a kingdom composed of priests' (by which Scott understands those who individually have access to God as may be implied by the New Testament references); or
2. 'a kingdom possessing a legitimate priesthood'; or
3. 'a kingdom with a collective priestly responsibility on behalf of all peoples'; or
4. 'a kingdom ruled by priests'; or
5. 'a kingdom set apart and possessing collectively, alone among all peoples, the right to approach the altar of Yahweh'.[28]

If each feasible subcategory of interpretation were to be itemized, the number would be somewhat in excess of these five. However, in order to differentiate more sharply the options which are advocated, it is proposed here to treat them under two broad categories. These two categories also have an advantage over Scott's summary in that they make clearer that the differences do not simply hinge on an understanding of the word כהנים, but in fact primarily divide over their understanding of whether there is a passive or an active force to the verbal notion which underlies ממלכת. Does ממלכת refer to the position of the ruled or the ruler? Scott, it is to be noted, blurs these distinctions by translating all options by means of the word 'kingdom' though understood in somewhat different senses. Only when we have canvassed the options for ממלכת will we return to a more detailed consideration of the meaning of כהנים. Some caution is needed in adopting this method, as we cannot in the end interpret either ממלכת or כהנים independently of the other term, as Perlitt reminds us.[29] Consequently, we will at times be considering the effect of a particular reading of one term on the other term in the expression. On the other hand, while it is true that the meaning of the phrase may be greater than the sum of its parts, composite expressions may legitimately be approached via their constituent terms, and analogies sought for each usage as a first step in understanding the total expression.

26. Scott, 'A Kingdom of Priests', p. 216.
27. Fohrer, '"Priestliches Königtum"', pp. 149-50.
28. Scott, 'A Kingdom of Priests', p. 216. Scott's own position is his fifth option.
29. Perlitt, *Bundestheologie*, pp. 172-73.

c. *The Meaning of* ממלכת

(1) *Outline of the passive interpretation of* ממלכת. The noun ממלכת is one of a number of noun forms from the root מלך which has to do with the exercise of kingship or royal office. Besides the common nouns מלך ('king'), מלכה and מלכת ('queen'), there are several related abstract and collective nouns with overlapping semantic domains: מלוכה ('kingship, royalty'), מלכת/מלכות ('royalty, royal power, reign, kingdom'), ממלכה ('kingdom, sovereignty, royalty dominion, reign') and a conflated form ממלכות with a similar range of meaning.[30] ממלכת in Exod. 19.6 is most naturally taken as a construct form of ממלכה, though, as noted above, it is possible to take it as a by-form or dialectal form of the absolute, equivalent to ממלכה. It is to be noted that ממלכה, though capable of an abstract meaning (as, e.g., ממלכתך, 'your kingship', 1 Sam. 13.14) is more commonly employed as a collective noun. The most common English translation of ממלכה at Exod. 19.6 is 'kingdom', which may predispose the reader to understand it as having a passive force, that is, the object of a monarch's rule—either the territory, or the people who are its citizens—passive, that is, with respect to the 'you' being addressed. Those who adopt a passive interpretation of the notion of מלך in ממלכת כהנים would understand the phrase to mean 'a kingdom or realm whose citizens are (in some sense) priests'. There would thus be a rough synonymous parallelism between the words ממלכת and גוי.[31] On this view, the word ממלכת would probably be the more neutral and colourless of the two nouns in the phrase ממלכת כהנים, being employed as a convenient collective term to denote corporate Israel. Greater weight would then fall on the term כהנים. It is the word כהנים which would define and give character to the corporate entity.

For many, even the notion that this entity is one ruled by a monarch (human or divine) is not in view ממלכת is simply an equivalent term to

30. BDB, pp. 572-75; KB, pp. 529-34.

31. So Cassuto, *Exodus*, p. 227. The terms synonym and synonymous will be used somewhat loosely to refer to words which belong to a common or to overlapping semantic domains. Alter denies the existence of genuine synonymous parallelism: Robert Alter, *The Art of Biblical Poetry* (New York: Basic Books, 1985), pp. 3-26; cf. James Kugel, *The Idea of Biblical Poetry: Parallelism and its History* (New Haven: Yale University Press, 1981), pp. 1-58. The term, if not pressed too far, still seems to me to be a useful category for the description of Hebrew poetry; see, e.g., Wilfred G.E. Watson, *Classical Hebrew Poetry: A Guide to its Techniques* (JSOTSup, 26; Sheffield: JSOT Press, 1984), p. 131.

'nation' or 'state'.[32] For others, it is more specifically the sphere or populace ruled by a king (מלך). Junker, who wrote in defence of the passive reading after Holzinger proposed an alternative interpretation,[33] expresses it this way: 'ממלכת "kingdom" is understood as a country, or here rather as a people under the rule of a king'.[34] Elliot glosses ממלכת as 'the community of the sovereign's (JHWH's) subjects'.[35] This reading would perhaps permit a slightly stronger emphasis to fall on this word. That is to say, part of the blessing promised to Israel would be the fact that they would be the subjects of a monarchy, whether that monarchy be human or divine. Who then is the implied king on this view? Since of course Israel lacked a human monarch at the point of the setting of this pericope (Sinai), such a reference to Israel being the domain of a king would either be proleptic, or must be taken as a reference to the kingship of God. Any notion of human kingship, even projected into the future, seems far removed from the context and (on this passive reading) seems to lack supporters.

One who has laid considerable stress on the divine kingship in this context is Martin Buber. For Buber, what is being offered to Israel is 'the *melekh*-ship of JHWH, in the form of the *mamlakha*, of the domain of the kingly rule'.[36] Buber compares this usage with 2 Sam. 3.28 where David says אני וממלכתי ('I and my realm'), that is, the body over which David exercises sovereignty.[37] Likewise, Patrick speaks of the 'royal imagery' of 19.3b-8, which suggests that 'Israelites will become Yahweh's subjects and he their sovereign'.[38] Among those who read ממלכת this way, it would generally be taken as being in a construct relationship with כהנים,

32. Noth (*Exodus*, p. 157) speaks for not a few exegetes when he takes ממלכת as equivalent simply to the 'state' as a term to denote the organized political entity which is Israel, with no particular emphasis on the notion of kingship; cf. Scott, 'A Kingdom of Priests'; Hans-Joachim Kraus, 'Das heilige Volk: Zur alttestamentlichen Bezeichnung *'am qādōš*', in Johann J. Stamm and Ernst Wolff (eds.), *Freude am Evangelium* (Festschrift Alfred de Quervain; BEvT, 44; Munich: Chr. Kaiser Verlag, 1966), pp. 50-61 (59); Vogels, *God's Universal Covenant*, p. 48; Barbiero, '*Mamleket kohanîm*', p. 440.

33. Holzinger, *Exodus*, p. 67; see below.

34. Hubert Junker, 'Das allgemeine Priestertum. I. Das allgemeine Priestertum des Volkes Israel nach Ex. 19,6', *TTZ* 56 (1947), pp. 10-15 (11).

35. Elliott, *The Elect and the Holy*, p. 52.

36. Martin Buber, *Kingship of God* (trans. Richard Scheimann; London: George Allen & Unwin, 3rd edn, 1967), p. 129.

37. Martin Buber, 'Holy Event (Exodus 19–27)', in Harold Bloom (ed.), *Exodus* (New York: Chelsea House, 1987), pp. 45-58 (49).

38. Patrick, 'The Covenant Code Source', p. 151.

which has traditionally been understood then to be a genitive of apposition.[39] That is, this domain or body of subjects consists of or is characterized by 'priests'.

Is there a difficulty, however, in envisaging a notion of God's kingship before Israel had a king? Von Rad, for example, presumes that the kingship of God in Israel must be a post-monarchy religious idea.[40] Such need not be the case. On a unified reading of Exodus, Israel has had experience of being under one king (Exod. 1.8, 15, 17, 18; 2.23; 3.18, 19; 5.4; 6.11, 27, 29; 14.5, 8). Thereafter, it has been made clear that יהוה ימלך לעלם ועד ('Yhwh is king for ever and ever', Exod. 15.18). By his victory over the primaeval forces of chaos represented by Pharaoh's hosts at the Reed Sea, Yhwh is demonstrably Israel's king.[41]

The notion of God as king is ancient, and מלך or its equivalent is found among Israel's neighbours as a designation or epithet of deity, as in the gods Milkom, Melkart and Chemosh-Melek.[42] At Ugarit, Baal is acclaimed as *mlk*.[43] Marduk of Babylon is, according to the *Enuma Elish*, king of the entire universe.[44] There is no reason to suppose that the characterization and worship of God as king would necessarily be dependent on the possession of kingship as a political institution. It may rather be seen as a part of the common cultural heritage of Israel's environment.[45] Lipiński, for

39. This is frequently to be inferred from the various translations and comments, though Moran makes this observation explicit ('A Kingdom of Priests', p. 10).

40. Gerhard von Rad, 'βασίλευς: B. מלך and מלכות in the Old Testament', in *TDOT*, I, pp. 565-71; cf. Albrecht Alt, 'Gedanken über das Königtum Jahwes', in *idem*, *Kleine Schriften zur Geschichte des Volkes Israel* (2 vols.; Munich: Beck, 1953), I, pp. 345-57 (348); Herbert Schmid, 'Jahwe und die Kultustraditionen von Jerusalem', *ZAW* NS 68 (1955), pp. 168-97; Kraus, *Worship in Israel,* p. 203; Werner H. Schmidt, *Königtum Gottes in Ugarit und Israel zur Herkunft der Königsprädikation Jahwes* (BZAW, 80; Berlin: W. de Gruyter, rev. edn, 1966), p. 69; Preuss, *Old Testament Theology*, I, pp. 153-54.

41. Junker, 'Das allgemeine Priestertum', p. 11.

42. Gudea, for example, calls Ningirsu his 'king': F. Thureau-Dangin (ed.), *Die sumerischen und akkadischen Königsinschriften* (Vorderasiatische Bibliothek, 1.1; Leipzig: J.C. Hinrichs, 1907), pp. 88-89; cf. Buber, *Kingship of God*, pp. 85-98.

43. E.g. *The Palace of Baal* (3) E, 40. All references to Ugaritic literature, unless otherwise specified, are to the titles as given by J.C.L. Gibson, *Canaanite Myths and Legends* (Edinburgh: T. & T. Clark, 2nd edn, 1978), with the Herdner numbers in brackets.

44. *Enuma Elish* 4.1.14 (*ANET*, I, p. 66).

45. For the kingship of God in relation to notions of the kingship of the gods in the ancient Near East, see Mendenhall, *The Tenth Generation*, pp. 1-31; J. de Fraine, SI,

whom Exod. 19.6 is the decisive text for the notion of the kingship of God at Sinai, sees a close connection with Psalm 47 which connects the notion of God's kingship (v. 3 [ET v. 2]) with the exodus–Sinai tradition.[46] Whether this sovereignty of Yhwh is inextricably linked with the notion of the vassaldom of Israel through the instrument of the covenant, as is also commonly held, is another matter, however, and will be discussed in Chapter 7.

(2) *Outline of the active-elite interpretation of* ממלכת. The major alternative view on the interpretation of ממלכת is one which takes it in an active sense. Rather than 'kingdom' in the sense of a territory or body of subjects, it is '(the office or exercise of) kingship, royalty, sovereignty', which either by denotation or by an extension of meaning from abstract to concrete might then be understood in the sense of 'king' or collectively 'kings, royal house, dynasty'.

An active reading of the verbal idea in ממלכת allows for two different syntactic understandings of its relationship to כהנים. If ממלכת is taken as an absolute form, then the words ממלכת and כהנים stand in apposition as two independent ways of characterizing the recipients of the covenant—an active kingship (or company of royal persons) and (i.e. who are also) priests, as apparently understood by the Jewish targums, Peshitta, Symmachus, Theodotion, *Jubilees* and Revelation. This reading, as noted above,

L'aspect religieux de la royauté Israélite: L'institution monarchique dans l'Ancien Testament et dans les textes Mésopotamiens (AnBib, 3; Rome: Pontifical Biblical Institute Press, 1954), pp. 119-22; Schmid, 'Jahwe und die Kultustraditionen'; Wildberger, *Jahwes Eigentumsvolk*, p. 83; Auzou, *De la servitude*, pp. 250-51; Otto Eissfeldt, 'Jahwe als König', in *idem*, *Kleine Schriften* (eds. Rudolf Sellheim and Fritz Maass; 2 vols.; Tübingen: J.C.B. Mohr, 1962–79), I, pp. 172-93; Buber, *Kingship of God*, pp. 85-93; E.F. Campbell, 'Sovereign God', *McCormick Quarterly* 20 (1967), pp. 173-86; E. Lipiński, *La royauté de Yahwé dans la poésie et le culte de l'Ancien Israël* (Verhandelingen van de Koninklijke Vlaamse Academie voor Wetenschappen, Letteren en Schone Kunsten van Belgie. Klasse der Letteren, 27.55; Brussels: Paleis der Academiën, 2nd edn, 1968); E. Theodore Mullen, Jr, *The Divine Council in Canaanite and Early Hebrew Literature* (HSM, 24; Chico, CA: Scholars Press, 1980); Gary V. Smith, 'The Concept of God/The Gods as King in the Ancient Near East and the Bible', *Trinity Journal* NS 3 (1982), pp. 18-38; Johannes C. de Moor, *The Rise of Yahwism: The Roots of Israelite Monotheism* (BETL, 91; Leuven: Leuven University Press, 1990); Niehaus, *God at Sinai*, pp. 84-94; Helmer Ringgren, K. Seybold and H.-J. Fabry, 'מלך', in *TDOT*, VIII, pp. 346-75.

46. Lipiński, *La royauté de Yahwé*, p. 425; cf. also Deut. 33.2-5; Judg. 8.22-23; 1 Sam. 12.12; Isa. 6.5; Pss. 24.7-10; 68.25; 93; 97; 99.

is syntactically awkward, a point perhaps felt by the targums, Rev. 5.10 (Byzantine text) and 4Q213, which render the Hebrew expression by two concrete nouns, and by 1Q21, which (if in fact alluding to this verse) renders it by two abstracts.

If on the other hand the phrase is taken as a construct expression, כהנים could be understood either as an appositional genitive, which would be indistinguishable in meaning from the appositional phrase (above); or as a subjective genitive: 'a reigning group of priests', with perhaps slightly more emphasis on the verbal idea in the root מלך. This appears to be the reading which underlies the use of the verbal forms of βασιλεύω in Rev. 5.10, 'And you appointed them for God a kingdom (βασιλείαν) and priests, and they will reign (βασιλεύσουσιν) on the earth', and Rev. 20.6, 'but they will be priests of God and of Christ and will reign (βασιλεύσουσιν) with him'.

Who then is the referent of the phrase ממלכת כהנים taken in this active sense? Most of those who support an active reading of ממלכת take it as a political reference to the ruling class within Israel, namely, its priesthood. This view that the phrase ממלכת כהנים refers to a priestly elite was put forward by Holzinger in 1900,[47] though it was Caspari who spelled out a semantic basis for the view,[48] followed by Moran who strengthened the case with better biblical examples.[49] On this understanding, the two expressions ממלכת כהנים and גוי קדוש are not synonymously parallel, but are complementary halves of the whole, analogous with other common Hebrew expressions for totality by means of polar opposites such as עשׁיר ואביון ('rich and poor', e.g. Ps. 49.3 [ET 49.2]) or מנער ועד זקן ('young and old', e.g. Gen. 19.4). They would refer to the ruler and the ruled who thus would comprise the hierocratic state. That is, Israel is promised that it will be a priestly monarchy. It is to be a nation ruled by priest-kings, or an aristocratic priestly caste, who will impart something of the characteristic quality of priesthood, perhaps its 'holiness', to the people they govern. While Caspari's position has been modified and supplemented by others, in essence it remains an influential view.[50]

47. Holzinger, *Exodus*, p. 67.

48. Caspari, 'Das priesterliche Königreich'; Caspari was followed by Winnett (*The Mosaic Tradition*, pp. 163-64) who argues that Exod. 19.3b-8 is the work of the Priestly writer and reflects the struggle for priestly power in the Second Temple period.

49. Moran, 'A Kingdom of Priests'.

50. Beyerlin, *Origins*, pp. 71-73; R. Van de Walle, 'An Administrative Body of Priests and a Consecrated People', *Indian Journal of Theology* 14 (1965), pp. 57-72;

(3) *Outline of the active-corporate interpretation of* ממלכת. Thus far we have seen in broad perspective the two dominant positions on the meaning of ממלכת כהנים. Our discussion, while no doubt not doing full justice to some nuanced variations, brings into relief the major differences between them. One sees the phrase as referring to the whole of Israel as the citizens of a domain characterized by the qualities of priesthood, with or without an inherent notion of divine suzerainty. This I have called the passive understanding of ממלכת. The other prominent position, active with respect to ממלכת, sees as the referent of that word a subgroup within Israel being identified as a ruling priestly elite.

Before we proceed to evaluate these, there is another perspective which has not received much attention in recent decades, but which combines some features of both major views. This interpretation sees in ממלכת כהנים a metaphorical designation of all Israel as those who in some way have attributes of royalty or sovereignty in an active sense and who are also identified as 'priests'. There would thus be in a sense a 'democratization' of the notion of royalty, just as it will be maintained below that the use of כהנים is in some sense a democratization of the notion of priesthood. By the use of the term 'democratization', there is no intention to imply a critique of the Israelite monarchy or institutional priesthood and no comment is made as to whether such a notion fits best in a pre-monarchic or post-monarchic setting. The words ממלכת and כהנים as applied to Israel will be understood as having a metaphorical or honorific value rather than a political or cultic one.

On this reading, ממלכת would either be in apposition with כהנים (as understood by Theodotion; Rev. 1.6; *Jub*. 16.18): 'a kingship (or: kings), (i.e.) priests', the view supported by Bauer,[51] or as having כהנים as its appositional or subjective genitive: 'You (all Israel) are mine as a kingship/royal company consisting of priests', as supported, for example, by Durham and Dumbrell. Durham formally adopts an active reading of ממלכת, without developing the argument, though significantly softens the

von Rad, 'The Form Critical Problem', p. 40; Fohrer, '"Priestliches Königtum"'; Cazelles, 'Alliance du Sinai'; *idem*, '"Royaume de prêtres"'. Fohrer's comment would be typical: 'Und da ist es evident, 1. daß *mămlækæt kohanîm* zwar nicht eine sachlich-inhaltliche, wohl aber eine sprachliche Parallele zu *gôj qadôš* bildet und 2. daß *kohanîm* in der gleichen Weise eine nähere Bestimmung oder ein Attribut zu *mămlakā* enthält wie *qaôš* zu *gôj*: Wie die Nation heilig sein wird, so seine *mămlakā* d.h. sein Königtum bzw. sein König, priesterlich' ('"Priestliches Königtum"', p. 151).

51. Bauer, 'Könige und Priester'.

active force of 'ruling'. The reference is not to 'a royal elite, whether among kings *or* priests', but to 'the whole of the people'. Yet Israel is 'a kingdom run not by politicians depending upon strength and connivance but by priests depending on faith in Yhwh, a servant nation instead of a ruling nation'.[52] Dumbrell has devoted considerable attention to Exod. 19.4-6 in several publications.[53] Though at one point he appears to endorse Scott's interpretation of the phrase (see above),[54] Dumbrell's reading of ממלכת is not only a corporate understanding (as Scott's), but is also a more active understanding of the verbal notion. It is 'the institution of kingship' as well as 'the royal domain'.[55] He gives as a gloss for ממלכת כהנים—'kings and priests'[56] or 'a worshipping company of priests, who are also kings'[57]—which might lead us to expect that, like Bauer, he takes the nouns as absolutes in apposition. This is not the case, however, as is made clear by his explanation of כהנים as a 'genitive' with adjectival force, which makes for a close parallelism with גוי קדוש, thus a 'priestly royalty', as the best understanding.[58]

On this view, a greater emphasis may fall on the word ממלכת than would normally be the case on a passive reading, and it might be given equal weight with כהנים. The resultant meaning would be that Israel is a royalty or royal house of priests or a priesthood with royal characteristics (as perhaps LXX βασίλειον ἱεράτευμα). This understanding demonstrably underlies those citations and allusions which render ממלכת either by a concrete noun ('kings') or introduce a verbal notion of the exercise of kingship (the Jewish targums; Rev. 20.6). We may call this the active-corporate interpretation. This reading will be supported in the discussion which follows. We need then to consider the strength and weakness of each of the major possibilities. In particular, how do these interpretations relate to the cotext of Exod. 19.6?

(4) *Evaluation of the passive interpretation of* ממלכת. A passive reading of ממלכת has the advantage that it takes the address to all Israel seriously,

52. Durham, *Exodus*, p. 263.

53. Dumbrell, *Covenant and Creation*, pp. 84-89, 'The Prospect of Unconditionality', pp. 143-47, and *The Search for Order*, pp. 43-46.

54. Dumbrell, 'The Prospect of Unconditionality', p. 146.

55. Dumbrell, *The Search for Order*, p. 45.

56. Dumbrell, *The Search for Order*, pp. 104, 122.

57. Dumbrell, 'The Prospect of Unconditionality', p. 147.

58. Dumbrell, *Covenant and Creation*, p. 86; cf. Schüssler Fiorenza, *Priester für Gott*, pp. 141-42.

and better suits the immediate cotext than does the 'active-elite' view. It may indirectly affirm the kingship of Yhwh, which is at least implicit in the notion that the covenant is something Yhwh is capable of granting to a people at his initiative and on his terms.

Yet if ממלכת, on this view, is taken as absolute (rather than in construct with כהנים), by itself it seems inadequate to convey clearly any notion of Yhwh's rule. The most natural reading of the phrase is as a construct expression. A study of such construct expressions with ממלכת, however, has shown that the dominant construction is with a subjective genitive, whereas the passive view requires an objective or at least an appostional genitive. Thus, for example, ממלכת עוג is 'the kingdom of (i.e. ruled by) Og' (Num. 32.33), and ממלכת צדקיה is 'the reign of (the kingship exercised by) Zedekiah' (Jer. 28.1). Similarly, the suffixed forms are all best understood as active, for example, ממלכתך 'your kingship/dynasty' (1 Sam. 13.13-14). The one contrary example in the singular cited in the discussions is ממלכת ישׂראל ('the kingdom of Israel', 1 Sam. 24.20), that is, the kingdom of which Saul is king and the Israelites are subjects.[59] However, it may be better to understand both 'kingdom' and 'Israel' here as geographical terms, 'the kingdom which is co-extensive with the region Israel'. This usage would be similar to some instances of the plural construct, such as the common expression ממלכות הארץ ('kingdoms of the earth', e.g. Deut. 28.25) or ממלכות צפונה ('kingdoms of the north', Jer. 1.15).[60] The preponderance of its usage in the construct singular inclines the reader of Exod. 19.6 to expect a subjective genitive following ממלכת. Certainly a 'geographical' meaning is precluded by the class of nouns to which כהנים belongs. An objective genitive, that is, 'a body of priests subject to kingly rule', as Keil notes, hardly suits the cotext. It would not convey the notion of fellowship with Yhwh (rather than simply subjection to him) which seems to be required by the cotext.[61] We will thus be inclined to look for an alternative to the passive reading of ממלכת.

(5) *Evaluation of the active-elite interpretation of* ממלכת. There is substance to the arguments for an active-elite interpretation of ממלכת. In

59. Moran, 'A Kingdom of Priests', p. 10. Cazelles (cited by Moran, p. 10, but poorly referenced) studied the use of ממלכת in the singular in construct with a following noun, or with a possessive suffix and found that of 24 cases, all but one (1 Sam. 24.21) are active in force. That is, the noun following the construct, or the suffixed pronoun, is the one reigning.

60. Cazelles, '"Royaume de prêtres"', pp. 293-94.

61. Keil and Delitzsch, *Commentary on the Old Testament*, I (Exodus), p. 97.

particular, it would enable the reader to understand כהנים in its normal sense of a designated priesthood, an elite subset of Israelite society. Caspari finds support for this understanding in the occurrence of ממלכת in Phoenician in the sense of 'king'. The Karatepe inscription, for example, includes the expression כל ממלכת וכל אדם (also found in some other Phoneician inscriptions). Caspari understands the normally abstract ממלכת in the concrete sense of *Regent*, the one who exercises the office of kingship.[62] Finding a similar meaning in 1 Sam. 10.18 (where הממלכות is modified by a masculine participle), he consequently adopts the closely allied meaning *Regierung* ('government, administration') in Exod. 19.6.[63]

Moran also finds the meaning 'king' for ממלכה in 1 Sam. 10.18; 1 Kgs 5.1; 10.20; Isa. 13.4; Jer. 1.15; 25.26; Amos 7.13; Pss. 68.33; 135.11; Lam. 2.2; 2 Chron. 12.8; and 17.10.[64] Not all of these are equally convincing as instances of the concrete meaning 'king'.[65] The clearest examples of ממלכה in the sense of 'king' are in 1 Kgs 5.1, for which 2 Chron. 9.26 substitutes מלכים, and Jer. 1.15, where ממלכות is resumed by the distributive איש כסאו ('each [king]...his throne', noting the masculine forms). More commonly, ממלכה, when active in its underlying verbal idea, is better rendered by a more institutional term like 'dynasty' or 'royal house' (e.g. 1 Sam. 13.13-14; 2 Sam. 3.10, 28; 5.12; 7.12, 13, 16; 1 Kgs 2.46; 11.11; 2 Kgs 11.1). If ממלכת כהנים is taken as a construct phrase, which is the most natural reading, the concrete reading 'king' will not suit, as 'king(s) of priests' yields little sense. Childs is prepared to accept the possibility of the meaning 'king' for ממלכה, though remains unconvinced by its appropriateness here,[66] and it is in a collective and more abstract, yet active sense that ממלכה is most naturally capable of sustaining the construct relationship with 'priests'.

62. Caspari, 'Das priesterliche Königreich', col. 105; cf. Beyerlin, *Origins*, pp. 1-73; Fohrer, '"Priestliches Königtum"', p. 151; Cazelles, '"Royaume de prêtres"', p. 293. A similar usage is found in other Phoenician and Punic texts: H. Donner and W. Röllig, *Kanaanäische und aramäische Inschriften, mit einem Beitrag von O. Rössler*. I. *Texte* (Wiesbaden: Otto Harrassowitz, 4th edn, 1979), 10.2, 11; 14.4; 101.1-4; 111.5; 112.6; 141.3; 161.2.

63. Caspari, 'Das priesterliche Königreich', col. 107.

64. Moran, 'A Kingdom of Priests', p. 11; Cazelles, '"Royaume de prêtres"', pp. 292-93; Dumbrell, 'The Prospect of Unconditionality', pp. 146-47.

65. The standard lexicons BDB (p. 585) and KB (pp. 533-34) do not recognize a meaning 'king' for ממלכה, though Zorell does: Franciscus Zorell (ed.), *Lexicon hebraicum et aramaicum Veteris Testamenti* (Rome: Pontifical Biblical Institute Press, 1984), p. 445.

66. Childs, *Exodus*, p. 374.

The other argument adduced by Caspari in support of his active reading of ממלכת is that words for 'king' and 'people' or a particular king and a particular people are frequently found in close relationship as complementary terms (e.g. 2 Sam. 17.16; 1 Kgs 8.65; 2 Kgs 11.17; 2 Chron. 5.6; Jer. 25.14; Neh. 9.24; Eccl. 2.8; Est. 4.11).[67] Moran discusses more fully the passages where ממלכה or מלך is used in association with, or as a parallel term to גוי, and supports Caspari's conclusion that the two words are to be seen as complementary rather than synonymous. They refer, on this view, to the king or royal house on the one hand, and the subject people on the other.[68]

In Gen. 17.6, 16 and 35.11, גוים is linked with מלכים ('kings') as an aspect of the divine grant to Abraham. While Moran finds significance in the fact that a similar pairing of מלכים is not found with the word עם ('people') when this is used in parallel passages (Gen. 28.3; 48.4), it should be noted that עם is no less capable of being linked with the root מלך (as in Gen. 17.16; 2 Sam. 17.16).[69] As these Genesis passages are capable of sustaining another interpretation from that of 'kings' as a component of the totality of Israel, one consistent with the understanding of Exod. 19.6 being expounded here (i.e. they may in fact refer to the corporate sovereignty of Israel), further discussion on them will be left until Chapter 7.

1 Kings 18.10 links גוי and ממלכה as places where Ahab has searched for Elijah and made enquiry after his whereabouts. The terms are thus at one level geographical (cf. שׁם, 'there') and yet also refer to persons who are capable of being adjured. While it is possible, as Moran claims,[70] that we have here two components of a whole (the subject population and the king), this again is not the only possible reading. Each term could simply be used as an approximate synonym meaning 'country' (both in the sense of a region and its population, without a specific focus on the king), both words being employed together for emphasis in Obadiah's protestation.[71]

67. Caspari, 'Das priesterliche Königreich', cols. 106-107.

68. Moran, 'A Kingdom of Priests', pp. 13-17.

69. Thus the view of Cody cannot be sustained, who sees the fact that ממלכת and גוי are a familiar word pair as the motivation for the choice of גוי over עם in Exod. 19.6: Aelred Cody, OSB, 'When Is the Chosen People Called a *gôy*?', *VT* 14 (1964), pp. 1-6.

70. Moran, 'A Kingdom of Priests', p. 14.

71. See James A. Montgomery and Henry Snyder Gehman, *A Critical and Exegetical Commentary on the Books of Kings* (ICC; Edinburgh: T. & T. Clark, 1951), p. 309.

Isaiah 61.11 refers to חיל גוים ('the wealth of the nations') and מלכיהם ('their kings') led in triumphal procession into restored Zion. It is highly improbable that in this case we are to see מלך and גוי as polar opposites. The wealth would hardly be that of the subject populations in contrast to royal wealth, but would at least encompass the bounty of the kings.

When in Jer. 18.7-8 and 27.7-8 the words גוי and ממלכה are linked, in each case a subsequent occurrence of the word גוי is sufficient to refer back to the national entity. It is unlikely that in these cases the word גוי would have both a restricted sense (part of the totality) and an inclusive sense (the totality) in such close proximity.

Moran admits that the remaining passages where ממלכה and גוי occur together are inconclusive, or in at least one case (Ps. 105.13 = 1 Chron. 16.20), the words are used synonymously. Synonymous parallelism would even appear to be the simplest explanation of such passages as Jer. 29.18, 51.20 and Ps. 46.7 (ET 46.6), where the remaining terms in each hemistich are synonymously parallel.

If Moran's examples discussed above are his strongest evidence, then that evidence will not support his conclusion that ממלכה in Exod. 19.6 must refer to the king rather than the people as a whole. Even if it could be shown that in every other example ממלכה and גוי were separate constituent entities of the body politic, we would need to note the dangers of a mechanical application of the notion of word pairs and what they may and may not signify.[72] By the nature of the case, where ממלכה has an active force, it will not ordinarily be co-referential with the people, for democracy as a political institution was in scarce supply in the ancient world.[73] If, however, one wished to assert something without precedent—that (in some sense) the 'royalty' or 'sovereignty' resided in the people, how else would one express this, other than by bringing into close relationship the words ממלכה and גוי (or their synonyms)?

72. James Barr issues a typically cautionary comment on the application of the notion of parallelism in semantic discussions in his *Comparative Philology and the Text of the Old Testament* (London: SCM Press, 1983), pp. 277-82.

73. See, however, Thorkild Jacobsen, 'Primitive Democracy in Ancient Mesopotamia', in William L. Moran (ed.), *Toward the Image of Tammuz and Other Essays on Mesopotamian History and Culture* (HSS, 21; Cambridge, MA: Harvard University Press, 1970), pp. 157-70; Robert Gordis, 'Democratic Origins in Ancient Israel: The Biblical *'edah*', in Saul Liebermann (ed.), *Alexander Marx Jubilee Volume on the Occasion of his Seventieth Birthday* (New York: Jewish Theological Seminary of America, 1950), English section pp. 369-88.

It is difficult to see how the notion of rule by a priest-king, or a priestly elite suits the cotext (rather than an assumed historical setting).[74] It fails to pay sufficient attention to the syntax of the clause. As noted above, the words ואתם תהיו־לי ('and you will be mine') are to be given some weight. The emphasis is on the mode of Israel's belonging to Yhwh, not on its mode of government. As Houtman observes, it would be a 'strained interpretation' to identify the corporate 'you' of the subject with the complement ממלכת...וגוי understood not as a homogeneous unit, but as a polarity.[75] This is particularly the case, we might add, since the speaker Moses is excluded from the second person address, whereas it is Moses himself who might be thought to represent any priestly elite at this stage of the narrative. It would appear rather anticlimactic, if, after the narrative build-up to this point, what Israel is promised is a particular form of administration—a priestly aristocracy—which in any event is hardly unique in the ancient world. Barbiero aptly asks the question, 'In which part of our text does the writer address the distinction between governors and subjects?'[76] A purported distinction between ruler and ruled does not sit well as an explanation of the סגלה notion, where Israel is *contrasted* with the nations. Nor does it do justice to the syntax of the verbal clause ואתם תהיו־לי..., discussed above, where the phrase ממלכת כהנים וגוי קדוש functions as a modifier of the manner in which the second person subject belongs to or relates to Yhwh (לי) not to one another. Above all, a polarized interpretation of this expression bears little relationship to the awesome theophanic presence of God with his people which is the focus of the chapter. It is commonly held that vv. 3b-8 must in some way be an introduction to the theophany, yet, on the active-elite interpretation, these verses are seen as rather intrusive.[77]

74. The setting for such a notion has been variously placed as the pre-monarchy period, as a product of the Israelite amphictyony (e.g. Moran, 'A Kingdom of Priests', pp. 17-20; Beyerlin, *Origins*, pp. 67-77) as coming from the late monarchy or exile (Fohrer, '"Priestliches Königtum"', p. 152) or most commonly as fitting the hierocracy of the post-exilic community (Ska, 'Exode 19,3b-6'; Le Roux, 'A Holy Nation Was Elected'; Fuhs, 'Heiliges Volk Gottes'; Barbiero, '*Mamleket kohanîm*').

75. Houtman, *Exodus*, II, p. 445.

76. Barbiero, '*Mamleket kohanîm*', p. 439.

77. McCarthy senses some incongruity and is somewhat apologetic as to the contribution that vv. 3b-8 make to this focus: 'Indeed, even as it stands with 3b-8 included, c. 19 is preoccupied with the tremendous presence of Yahwe' (*Treaty and Covenant*, p. 247).

(6) *Evaluation of the active-corporate interpretation of* ממלכת. We take up consideration of our third major possibility for the force of the word ממלכת—the active-corporate interpretation. Though this view has been largely unsupported in recent decades, the active interpretation traditionally regarded the whole people of Israel as the referent of ממלכת כהנים. That is, the phrases ממלכת כהנים and גוי קדוש were, for most of the period for which we have access to interpretations, understood to be synonymously parallel. Either phrase alone would have sufficed for the divine characterization of Israel, though both together reinforce and nuance that designation. This understanding characterizes most ancient readings (regardless of their other differences),[78] and was the common view within the Jewish and Christian traditions until comparatively recent times.[79]

78. Possibly a different interpretation lies behind the Aramaic and Greek *Levi* fragments cited above, where the priesthood in question appears to be that of Kohath, not the collective people of Israel. However, it is not clear that there is in these texts an intended reference to Exod. 19.6. Christian applications of the passage, beginning with the New Testament citations, of course broaden the referent to include peoples of all nations. See, e.g., G.K. Beale, *John's Use of the Old Testament in Revelation* (JSNTSup, 166; Sheffield: Sheffield Academic Press, 1998), pp. 100-110.

79. See, e.g., Hermann L. Strack and Paul Billerbeck, *Kommentar zum Neuen Testament aus Talmud und Midrasch* (5 vols.; Munich: C.H. Beck, 1922–28), III, pp. 788-89; Horovitz and Rabin, *Mechilta*, pp. 208-209; Rashi, *ad* Exod. 19.6; Ramban (Nachmanides), *Exodus* (trans. Charles B. Chavel; Commentary on the Torah; New York: Shilo Publishing House, 1973), p. 274; Maimonides, *The Guide to the Perplexed* 2.35 (Moses Maimonides, *The Guide to the Perplexed* [trans. Shlomo Pines; 2 vols.; Chicago: University of Chicago Press, 1963], II, p. 368). For early Christian and Reformation interpretations of Exod. 19.6 or derivative New Testament passages, see Justin Martyr, *Dialogue with Trypho* 116 (Alexander Roberts and James Donaldson [eds.], *The Ante-Nicene Fathers* [10 vols.; Grand Rapids: Eerdmans, 1980–83], I, p. 257); Irenaeus, *Adv. Haereses* 8.3 (*Ante-Nicene Fathers*, I, p. 471); Tertullian, *De oratione* 28 (*Ante-Nicene Fathers*, III, p. 690; *idem*, *De monogamia* 12 (*Ante-Nicene Fathers*, IV, p. 69); Cerfaux, 'Regale sacerdotium', pp. 308-13; Eastwood, *The Priesthood of All Believers*; John Calvin, *Commentaries on the Last Four Books of Moses Arranged in the Form of a Harmony* (trans. Charles William Bingham; 4 vols.; repr. Grand Rapids: Eerdmans, 1979), I, pp. 319-20; Keil and Delitzsch, *Commentary on the Old Testament*, I (Exodus), p. 97; Scott, 'A Kingdom of Priests', pp. 214-15. For typically nineteenth-century Protestant understandings, see George Bush, *Notes on Exodus* (2 vols.; New York: Newman & Ivison, 1852), I, p. 239; Charles A. Briggs, *Messianic Prophecy: The Prediction of the Fulfillment of Redemption through the Messiah* (New York: Charles Scribner's Sons, 1886), pp. 102-103; Keil and Delitzsch, *Commentary on the Old Testament*, I (Exodus), pp. 95-101. BDB (under כהן, p. 463) glosses ממלכת כהנים ('priests and kings at once in their relation to the nations').

Bauer is one of the few relatively recent interpreters who defend such an understanding.[80] He finds support for an active and concrete understanding of the normally abstract ממלכת as meaning 'kings' in the analogy with משמעת (e.g. 2 Sam. 23.23) which may carry the concrete sense of 'body of subjects' or 'bodyguard'.[81] This analogy is rather weak, however, as משמעת is *only* used (in our existing texts) in this concrete sense, so is not a good example of *abstractum pro concreto*.[82]

Bauer's analysis of the structure ממלכת כהנים // גוי קדוש as absolute noun + absolute noun // absolute noun + adjective in Exod. 19.6, with two absolute nouns in apposition balancing a phrase with noun followed by adjective, is awkward. Bauer seeks support for his analysis of this structure by reference to three analogous syntactic expressions which he finds in Prov. 5.19, Ps. 48.17 and Zech. 1.13.[83] However, the alleged parallels are not convincing. In the first (Prov. 5.19), אילת אהבים ויעלת חן ('a loving doe, a graceful deer'), each pair is most naturally construed as a construct relationship. The latter two examples are more difficult to explain and appear to be absolute plural nouns in apposition: הרים גבננים (Ps. 68.17 [ET 68.16]) and דברים נחנים (Zech. 1.13). Joüon finds both of these examples 'strange'.[84] A possible alternative explanation is that each pair is introduced by a plural construct followed by an enclitic mem.[85] In any event, the structure of the balancing hemistichs in each case does not provide a close parallel to Exod. 19.6 and they are a slender basis for Bauer's understanding of the structure of that verse.

Given the semi-poetic character of the unit Exod. 19.3b-6 as discussed above (Chapter 3), the reader will be predisposed to see balancing

80. Bauer, 'Könige und Priester'; cf. also Levenson, *Sinai and Zion*, p. 31.

81. Bauer, 'Könige und Priester', p. 283. See also the Mesha inscription, where משמעת (line 28) is probably to be read as 'a body of subjects', (J.C.L. Gibson, *Textbook of Syrian Semitic Inscriptions*. I. *Hebrew and Moabite Inscriptions* [Oxford: Clarendon Press, 1971], pp. 77, 82); Kent P. Jackson and J. Andrew Dearman, 'The Language of the Mesha Inscription', in J. Andrew Dearman (ed.), *Studies in the Mesha Inscription and Moab* (ASOR/SBL Archaeology and Biblical Studies, 2; Atlanta: Scholars Press, 1989), pp. 96-130 (120).

82. BDB, p. 1036; KB, p. 578.

83. Bauer, 'Könige und Priester', p. 284.

84. Joüon, *Grammaire*, p. 397.

85. On enclitic mem, see Horace D. Hummel, 'Enclitic *mem* in Early Northwest Semitic, Especially Hebrew', *JBL* 76 (1957), pp. 87-107; Moran, 'A Kingdom of Priests', p. 8; J.A. Emerton, 'Are there Examples of Enclitic Mem in the Hebrew Bible?', in Fox *et al.* (eds.), *Texts, Temples and Traditions*, pp. 321-38.

hemistichs here and to look for further elements of cohesion such as semantic or grammatical parallelism. The terms ממלכת and גוי are a natural word pair (as discussed above), while the terms כהנים and קדוש belong to closely related semantic domains. These facts serve to confirm our impression that the noun phrases in which they occur are best understood as balancing each other structurally, and that we should therefore read ממלכת כהנים as a single constituent to match the single constituent גוי קדוש. On this reading, each phrase is an epithet of the addressee, Israel, further defining the manner in which the nation will relate to God. We can thus also expect the phrases to be mutually explicative.

While our conclusions can only be tentative at this stage, the active-corporate reading of ממלכת cannot easily be dismissed and is a more natural reading of the syntax of the semi-poetic lines.

A further possibly fruitful line of inquiry for understanding the referent of ממלכת in Exod. 19.6 would be to look for intertextual links which might indicate how the passage was understood by other writers of the biblical period. Besides the versions and passages in intertestamental literature and the New Testament cited above, intertextual links may be found in such passages as Ps. 114.2 and Mic. 4.8. In order that our discussion of Exod. 19.6 might not become too convoluted, however, it is proposed to take up consideration of these passages in more detail at a later point (Chapter 10). For the moment, I simply note in anticipation of my conclusions to be drawn from such passages, that biblical writers, quite probably reflecting on Exod. 19.6, were comfortable with the application of sovereignty language in an active sense to Israel as a whole.

(7) *Ambivalent readings—ממלכת as active and passive and the relation of Israel's royalty to divine kingship*. A final possibility arises. Two commentators expressly raise the possibility that ממלכת is ambivalent as to an active or a passive force (which may also be implicit in Dumbrell's comments).[86] Thus Kleinig writes with reference to Exod. 19.6:

> The Hebrew word for 'kingdom' normally denotes the institution of the monarchy. This includes the royal court with all its personnel and administrative apparatus, controlled by the king and used by him for ruling his people. But the word can also denote the area and people ruled by a king. Israel was God's kingdom in these two senses of the word.[87]

86. See particularly *Covenant and Creation*, p. 90.
87. Kleinig, 'On Eagles' Wing', p. 22.

Gispen also takes ממלכת in this verse both as passive: ‘the service that was required of them as subjects of God’s kingdom was thus priestly in nature’, and at the same time as active: ‘Then Israel would be a kingdom also in the sense that they would rule with him…’[88] These observations could have merit. Perhaps no single perspective is adequate to do justice to such a complex passage. The choice of a unique expression with inherently ambivalent meaning may well be a literary device to entice the reader to see more than one angle to its meaning. Thus, while the emphasis in the discussion that follows will be on the active-corporate aspect of ממלכת, as a neglected or denied reading, there is no quarrel with those who would wish to see a passive force as well, though, as noted above, it represents a statistically improbable reading of the syntax of the composite expression. Israel, on this ambivalent reading, is both royal and a royal subject.

Whether we accept an ambivalent reading, or simply an active-corporate reading, we must still ask what could be meant by an active sense of kingship or royalty applied to Israel collectively and how might such regal status enjoyed by Israel relate to the (at least implied) kingship of God? Is there room for God to be sovereign and for Israel in some sense also to be sovereign?

Though it has been largely and inexplicably overlooked, an answer lies ready to hand in the accounts of royal or divine grant of kingly authority such as are found in numerous ancient Near Eastern texts, including the Bible. In such texts either the great king or the god grants the office of kingship to a specific mortal king or lesser deity who then exercises his rule under the aegis and protection of the deity or monarch. Israel, on this analogy, would be a corporate monarch, enjoying the grant of this status and the patronage of Yhwh. Because this grant is not to be seen in isolation from the corresponding grant of priesthood, and because this understanding of the nature of the Sinai covenant represents a departure from the prevailing understanding, it is proposed to defer further discussion of the covenant as a grant until Chapter 7.

What would the exercise of royalty on the part of Israel entail? For Bauer, the sovereignty of Israel is exercised over the nations.[89] They are

88. Gispen, *Exodus*, p. 180.

89. Addressing the analogy by which Israel stands in relation to the nations as the priests stand in relation to Israel, Bauer (‘Könige und Priester’, p. 286) remarks: ‘Analog dazu wird auch das Verständnis des Königtums der Israeliten zu suchen sein: Gott teilt seinem Volk seine Regierungsgewalt, seine Herrschermacht mit, wenn er vor diesem schwachen Volk die mächtigsten Feinde niederzwingt; er macht Israel zum

kings, according to Bauer, because they have the rule of the divine king mediated through them, as is evidenced by their victories over the nations, such as the Amalekites (Exod. 17) and in line with those passages where military superiority is predicated of Israel (Num. 24.8, 17-19; Deut. 33.29; Dan. 7.27).

It is to be doubted, however, that the other nations are really in view as the objects of such kingly rule in Exodus 19.[90] That is not to say that there is no seed for development of the potential inherent in the idea at a later point. Briggs may well be correct in seeing here the origin of the notion of the kingdom of God as the people who are not only 'subjects of their holy King' but who actively exercise 'sovereignty' by participating in God's reign.[91] Dumbrell regards Israel's kingship as being related to the tradition which sees Adam as king in the garden,[92] and (like Briggs) as that upon which are built eschatological expressions of the notion of the kingdom of God.[93] However, we should be careful not to read too much into the notion of kingship, and it does need to be taken closely with the notion of priesthood. The primary thrust of the cotext of Exod. 19.6 suggests that the 'royalty' or 'sovereignty' enjoyed by Israel is an honorific status—an endowment which enhances their perception of the privileged and treasured relationship being granted them, and which, in association with the grant of 'priesthood' equips Israel to participate in the royal court of the divine king. We may tentatively conclude that there are good reasons to take ממלכת כהנים to mean a collective royal company consisting of 'priests'. Israel is designated as royal by one who supremely holds the position of Israel's king. It is the people of God as a whole who bear this royal dignity and honour. Individuals enjoy these privileges only insofar as they belong to the group.

d. *The Meaning of* כהנים

Interpreters are divided over whether כהנים in Exod. 19.6 has a literal or an extended meaning. Does it refer to a particular class of individuals within Israel who were recognized by the community as its 'priests' or

König unter den Völkern, und die einzelnen Volksgenossen nehmen an dieser Königsmacht teil'.

90. Wildberger stresses the honorific nature of the declaration (*Jahwes Eigentumsvolk*, pp. 80-95).

91. Briggs, *Messianic Prophecy*, p. 102.

92. Dumbrell, *The Search for Order*, p. 104.

93. Dumbrell, *The Search for Order*, p. 46.

does it refer in a more metaphorical way to all Israel as having some characteristic or prerogative or function *analogous* to that of its cultic personnel? While to some extent this division falls along the same lines as the division between an active and a passive understanding of ממלכת, to some extent it cuts across these lines. Those who, like Caspari, Moran and Fohrer, adopt an active-elite interpretation of ממלכת understand כהנים in its regular literal sense as the Levitical priests who exercised not only cultic but, at times, a measure of civil authority in Israelite society. Because such a notion does not sit comfortably with the political institution of the monarchy, it is felt to pertain either to a period before the rise of monarchy, or more commonly, after the demise of monarchy in Israel.[94]

Those who adopt a passive or active-corporate interpretation will see כהנים as a more extended or metaphorical designation for Israel, and that is the position taken here.[95] As the arguments for these positions have been well canvassed above, our focus here is on a different question. If כהנים has an extended or metaphorical sense, what is the background and meaning of that extended use and its application here to all of Israel? What image is conveyed by 'priests' and how does their presence qualify or relate to the kingdom or royalty envisaged? At a later point, I will consider briefly some comparative material on priesthood in the ancient Near East, and the wider context of the cult in which priests operated (Chapter 6). At this point, my method will be

1. to survey the uses of כהן and its cognates in the Hebrew Bible, with a view to delineating the dominant characteristic(s) of 'priesthood'; and
2. to determine from cotextual criteria which aspect(s) of the resultant semantic field are likely to be most relevant to an understanding of Exod. 19.6.

The word כהן occurs some 741 times in the Hebrew Bible, where it most commonly identifies a holder of the religious office which had the responsibility for the maintenance of the cult of Yhwh, particularly at the central shrine which housed the ark.[96] It is in fact the only single term specifically

94. Caspari, 'Das priesterliche Königreich'; Moran, 'A Kingdom of Priests'; Cody, 'When Is the Chosen People Called a *gôy*?'; *idem*, *History*, p. 178; Fohrer, '"Priestliches Königtum"'; Cazelles, 'Alliance du Sinai'.

95. Schüssler Fiorenza has a useful discussion of the interpretative options (*Priester für Gott*, pp. 115-17).

96. See BDB, pp. 463-64; KB, pp. 424-25; *DCH*, IV, pp. 364-70.

used for Israelite priests.[97] It may also be used to refer to non-Israelite priests (e.g. Gen. 41.45; 1 Sam. 5.5).[98] There is also a denominative verb form כהן (piel, 'to act as priest', used 23 times),[99] and a cognate abstract noun כהנה ('priesthood, priestly office', used 14 times).[100] The etymology of the word is unknown,[101] and would be unlikely to be of great value in determining meaning, given the high number of cotexts in which to study its semantic range.

The expectation of the reader will be to understand a given reference to 'priests' in the light of its preponderant usage unless the cotext of that reference suggests otherwise. When the writer and readers wrote or read כהנים what was the resultant conceptual image? We are particularly concerned to elicit relevant information from the semantic range of כהן and its cognates for determining its meaning in Exod. 19.6.

Elliott objects at the outset to such a procedure.[102] For him, the כהנים of this passage are of such a different order that it will be misleading to bring into the purview the more regular use of the term which denotes the Levitical priestly office within Israel. With this assertion I must take issue. To be sure, we should be alert to any possible secondary meaning or nuance of the word. In particular, it may be used in an extended or metaphorical sense, as is commonly held by those who adopt either a passive or an active-corporate understanding of ממלכת. If it is used in a more inclusive sense, then כהנים cannot have an identical denotational and connotational range as when used more restrictively of the Aaronic priesthood or

97. Some (following Wellhausen) might wish to include the term לוי ('Levite') as effectively another Hebrew word for priest. The word לוי is ambiguous, referring both to a member of the tribe of Levi and to the occupant of a lesser cultic office restricted, according to the Pentateuchal legislation, to members of the Levi tribe. The relationship between priests and Levites has been the subject of much discussion over the past century. Levites are not said to serve as priests (the verb כהן) except in 2 Chron. 11.14, where the reference may be to the tribal identity of the Aaronic priesthood rather than indicating the identity of Levitical and priestly ministry. Deuteronomy several times joins the terms הכהנים הלוים (17.9, 18; 18.1; 24.8; 27.9). The variant הכהנים בני לוי suggests that this too is to be taken as a tribal identification, rather than a *terminus technicus* (21.5; 31.9). See Cody, *History*, pp. 29-33.

98. See Chapter 6 for a brief discussion of the Israelite conception of non-Israelite priests.

99. BDB, p. 464; KB, p. 424; *DCH*, IV, p. 364.

100. BDB, p. 464; KB, p. 425; *DCH*, IV, p. 370.

101. De Vaux, *Ancient Israel*, II, p. 346; KB, p. 424.

102. Elliott, *The Elect and the Holy*, pp. 57-58.

other priestly elites. However, the accepted canons of lexicography dictate that unless we are to posit a root כהן II, bearing no relationship to כהן I (and this is nowhere suggested), then the usage of Exod. 19.6 must be brought into some correlation with other uses of כהן. On any view of Pentateuchal origins, Israel had a recognized priesthood by the time of the composition of the Sinai pericope. The reader of Exodus 19 is assumed to have knowledge of some form of institutional priesthood (vv. 22, 24). It is difficult to believe, then, that Israelite readers were not to make a conceptual connection between כהן in Exod. 19.6 and the priesthood of their experience, or with the other occurrences of the word in the same document. That which is less familiar (the notion of a priesthood co-extensive with the nation, a position Elliott accepts) will inevitably be read in the light of an understanding of that which is more familiar (the incumbents of the special priestly office).

Some interpreters do see in a few instances of the word כהנים a meaning which is only distantly related to its more common meaning of a cultic official. This secondary meaning is that of a court official, or royal retainer. Rashi glosses כהנים in Exod. 19.6 with שׂרים ('princes') on the basis of the passage in 2 Sam. 8.18 where David's sons are designated as כהנים. The parallel account in 1 Chron. 18.17 substitutes for כהנים the phrase הראשׁנים ליד המלך ('the foremost ones at the king's hand'). Baudissin supported a secular understanding of כהן by reference to 1 Kgs 4.5, כהן רעה המלך ('the priest, the friend of the king'), seeing in this phrase not a reference to personal friendship but to a civic office.[103] On this view, כהנים may be ministers of state rather than ministers of religion, an elite circle of royal advisors and functionaries. Clearly by the time of the Chronicler, there was felt to be some awkwardness about the application of the term כהן to a non-Aaronide. However, was this (as on Wellhausen's view) because the circle of those who could exercise cultic office had become more circumscribed,[104] or simply because of semantic shift—that is, that a word which once may have had a wider application was no longer used for a secular court official? Our sources do not seem adequate fully to resolve the question of whether there is a completely 'secular' meaning of כהן. Perhaps we ought not to draw too sharp a contrast between secular and cultic functions in an ancient context, and between the respon-

103. Wolf Wilhelm Grafen Baudissin, *Die Geschichte des alttestamentlichen Priesterthums* (Osnabrück: Otto Zeller, 1967), pp. 191-92; cf. H. Donner, 'Der "Freund des Königs"', *ZAW* NS 73 (1961), pp. 269-77.

104. Moran, 'A Kingdom of Priests', p. 9.

sibilities of the royal court and the priesthood.[105] It is true of course that in the 'constitution' of Israel there was a differentiation of function, such that the king (and his court officials) did not generally perform certain cultic activities, or ran foul of the hereditary priesthood, with their perception of a divine mandate, should he attempt to do so (e.g. 1 Sam. 13.9-14; 2 Chron. 26.16-20). However, kings did engage in aspects of cultic activity without priestly condemnation (e.g. 2 Sam. 6.14) and were of course patrons of the official cult.[106] It is conceivable that the references to David's sons or 'friends' as priests is to be seen as in part a delegation of some royal cultic prerogative in the same manner in which Micah, at an earlier period, felt it within his power to appoint one of his sons as his priest (Judg. 17.5).

In several writings on the Sinai pericope Martin Buber has championed the position that the background to the image (which he takes to be applied to all Israel) is found in its secular usage.[107] Taking this closely with his advocacy of the prominence of the kingship of Yhwh in ממלכת, he sees Israel as the retainers in the court of the divine king. Thus, on Buber's view, the notion is one of privileged service, an honorific designation which will involve Israel in access to the court of the divine king.

Unless we are to insist on a literal and restricted reference to a particular class of individuals in Exod. 19.6, there may not be much to be gained by pursuing too rigorously a difference between a 'secular' and a 'cultic' background to the word כהנים. A very similar picture emerges on both a cultic and non-cultic understanding of the image. However, given that Yhwh is a God as well as a king, and his abode is therefore a temple as well as a palace, and that the worship of Yhwh by his people has been the objective of the Sinai journey, and given that כהנים is here parallel with קדוש, it is hardly feasible to rule out any cultic background to the word 'priests' as Buber would seek to do. This is not to suggest that we should attempt to read every aspect of the account of the Levitical priesthood, its status and functions, into Exod. 19.6, but we cannot rule out *a priori* any

105. See Carl Edward Armerding, 'Were David's Sons Really Priests?', in Gerald F. Hawthorne (ed.), *Current Issues in Biblical and Patristic Interpretation: Studies in Honor of Merrill C. Tenney Presented by his Former Students* (Grand Rapids: Eerdmans, 1975), pp. 75-86.

106. Cody, *History*, pp. 100-107.

107. Martin Buber, *The Prophetic Faith* (New York: Harper & Brothers, 1949), p. 160; *idem*, *Kingship of God*, pp. 130, 209; *idem*, 'Holy Event', p. 49; *idem*, *Moses: The Revelation and the Covenant* (Atlantic Highlands, NJ: Humanities Press International, 1989), p. 106. A similar view is espoused by Wildberger, *Jahwes Eigentumsvolk*, pp. 80-95.

characteristic or combination of characteristics of such priesthood as having no relevance to our passage.[108]

As the priesthood meant a variety of things and exercised a range of functions, it will be necessary to ask which particular aspect or aspects of priesthood may be intended by the use of the word in Exod. 19.6. The predominant impression gained from a reading of the passages which relate to the priesthood in the Hebrew Bible is a positive one. There is a strand of prophetic denunciations of priests (along with other officials, including other prophets!) for failing to live up to their high image and responsibility (e.g. Jer. 5.31; 6.13; 8.10; Ezek. 22.26; Hos. 6.9; 10.5; Zeph. 1.4; Mal. 1.6), but indirectly such passages simply serve to reinforce the perception of the honoured position the priest held in society. It is not for being priests that they are condemned, but precisely for *failing* to be priests.

The glowing portrayal Ben Sira (c. 200 BCE) provides of Simon the high priest officiating in the temple is noteworthy for its adulation of the priesthood (Sir. 50.5-21).[109] How closely does this sentiment match the perceptions of priesthood within the texts of the Hebrew Bible itself? Haran notes the essentially aristocratic or noble status enjoyed by the priests, and their priority in rank over prophets.[110] It will be instructive to note those passages where the image or functions of the priesthood are mentioned more or less in passing, as being the features of priesthood which most readily spring to mind, regardless of the immediate context. Thus the oracle of Yhwh delivered to Eli in 1 Sam. 2.28 contains a brief summary of the nature of priesthood: 'I chose him [your ancestor] from all the tribes of Israel to be my priest, to go up to my altar, to burn incense (להקטיר קטרת),[111] and to wear an ephod in my presence. I also gave your father's house all the fire-offerings of the Israelites.' It is the last-named perquisite

108. On the danger of 'illegitimate identity transfer', see James Barr, *The Semantics of Biblical Language* (London: Oxford University Press, 1961), p. 218; cf. Moisés Silva, *Biblical Words and their Meaning: An Introduction to Lexical Semantics* (Grand Rapids: Zondervan, rev. edn, 1994), pp. 25-27.

109. Cf. also 7.29-31; 45.8-26. For Ben Sira's perspective on the priesthood, see Saul M. Olyan, 'Ben Sira's Relationship to the Priesthood', *HTR* 80 (1987), pp. 261-86.

110. Menahem Haran, 'Temple and Community in Ancient Israel', in Michael V. Fox (ed.), *Temple in Society* (Winona Lake, IN: Eisenbrauns, 1988), pp. 17-25 (19); on rank and privilege generally within Israelite society, see Saul M. Olyan, *Rites and Rank: Hierarchy in Biblical Representations of Cult* (Princeton: Princeton University Press, 2000).

111. The root קטר may refer to any sacrifice consumed in smoke (1 Sam. 2.16; Ps. 66.15), though in this expression it seems always to refer to the burning of incense.

which is immediately in view as the one being honoured in the breach by Eli's sons. The other aspects of priesthood mentioned are thus a summary of the essence of priesthood. First, the priest was a priest because he (or his ancestor) was chosen (בחר) by Yhwh. Then the priest belonged to Yhwh (לי, cf. the idiom in Exod. 19.5-6) and had the privilege of approaching the incense altar, where the symbolism is the offering of that which will be acceptable to God. That this honour was highly esteemed is seen from accounts of the Korah incident (Num. 16, see below, Chapter 8) and the Uzziah incident (2 Chron. 26.16-21). The priest is said to come into the presence of (לפני) Yhwh, wearing an ephod, the most distinctive item of the priestly regalia, and the means of gaining access to the divine will.

Another passage which encapsulates the essence of priesthood is Ezek. 45.4: 'it shall be for the priests, who serve in the sanctuary, who draw near (הקרבים) to serve Yhwh'. Notions of access to the sanctuary or drawing near, in order to serve or attend on Yhwh, are central to Israel's perception of the priestly office.

Priests had the quality of קדשׁ ('holiness') which means that, after due process of 'consecration' (קדשׁ, piel) they shared an inherent characteristic of God (Lev. 21.6; 1 Sam. 7.1; cf. Isa. 5.16; 6.3; Ezek. 39.7; Ps. 99.5).[112]

Within the Mosaic blessing on the tribe of Levi (Deut. 33.8-11) there may be found a brief description of priestly responsibilities. These include possession of the sacred dice, the Urim and Thummim, to assist in the priest's juridical role, teaching the law to Israel, and offering incense 'in the nose' of God and burnt offerings on his altar. Such privileges are linked with Levi's zeal in his self-sacrificial guardianship of the covenant: 'they kept (שׁמרו) your word and guarded your covenant (בריתך)' (v. 9). This association of שׁמר...ברית ('keeping the covenant', cf. Exod. 19.5, though here the expression is distributed over two hemistichs), with the grant of the priestly privileges is to be noted.

On a view of the compositional unity of Exodus, the notion that Israel is being addressed as 'priests' should be brought into relation with other references to 'priest' in the book, and perhaps the Pentateuch as a whole. On this view, it is improbable that the reference in Exod. 19.6 is to be seen as in any way a polemic against, or to be in conflict with the instructions for the setting apart of Aaron and his sons recounted in ch. 28. Even within the chapter itself (19.22, 24) reference is made to a recognized group within

112. For the correlation of priesthood and holiness see, e.g., Wells, *God's Holy People*, pp. 98-129; Olyan, *Rites and Rank*, pp. 15-37.

Israel, the 'priests'. Whatever their identity in relation to the family of Aaron, they are evidently to be viewed as a subset of Israelite society, with distinctive cultic responsibilities.[113] Just as we have observed a wider and more extended application of the notion of royalty to Israel (which was later to have a monarchy), so it appears Israel is to be, as well as to have, a priesthood. Whether this duality will become a cause of tension remains to be seen.

(1) *The relationship of* כהנים *to* ממלכת. Consistent with the view adopted above that 'royalty' is an attribute of Israel collectively, it is proposed here that the word כהנים is to be taken as a further qualification of the nature of that royalty, and that taken together the phrase ממלכת כהנים is a powerful image of the grant of position or standing in relation to God which is being offered to Israel. 'Royalty' and 'priesthood' might be felt to be an awkward collocation, a combination of offices which were largely differentiated in Israelite society. However, the combination of royal and priestly images simply reflects a general ancient Near Eastern cultural background where royalty and priestly functions were felt to belong closely together, a collocation personified in Israelite thought by such a figure as the priest-king of Salem, Melchizedek (Gen. 14.18; Ps. 110.4).[114] While in the theocracy of Israel priests and kings were to be differentiated, in the reference to Israel's collective status, they apparently may be brought together, particularly in a text whose literary setting is prior to the account of the establishment of both the kingship and the Levitical system. The only references to כהן in Exodus prior to this point are those referring to Jethro, the 'priest' of Midian, who is clearly the civic leader of the community as well as having religious functions (Exod. 2.16; 3.1; 18.1), not dissimilar to the role of Israel's patriarchs in the familiar stories of Abraham, Isaac and Jacob, though these individuals are never called כהן within the biblical text.

The word כהנים is often taken as having a somewhat adjectival force qualifying ממלכת as קדוש qualifies גוי. It is a 'plural of abstraction',

113. See below for discussion of this verse.

114. For the background to the notion of the king as a priest, see Sidney Smith, 'The Practice of Kingship in Early Semitic Kingdoms', in Samuel H. Hooke (ed.), *Myth, Ritual and Kingship: Essays on the Theory and Practice of Kingship in the Ancient Near East and in Israel* (Oxford: Clarendon Press, 1958), pp. 22-73 (31-32); Cody, *History*, pp. 98-107.

according to Mosis.[115] This would result in a meaning 'priestly kingship', or 'priestly royalty'.[116] Scott writes: 'The attributive idea 'of priests' is to be understood in the light of the many references to the ritual sanctification of the priesthood'.[117] He offers as grammatical analogies for such an attributive or extended use of a noun of this type (designating a class of people) in this position, the word נגידים (regularly 'leaders'), perhaps in the extended sense of 'noble things' in Prov. 8.6,[118] and גיא שמנים ('fertile valley') in Isa. 28.1, 4. Scott's understanding of the first of these is difficult to sustain, as נגידים is a noun standing alone as object of אדבר ('I will speak'), not an attributive of another noun in apposition. In the Isaiah references, the word שמנים appears to be a plural of שָׁמָן for which KB gives the meaning 'fat (field)', and lists Gen. 27.28 and 39 as the only other occurrences.[119] With such a meaning, it is difficult to see a close analogy with Exod. 19.6, where כהנים is used to refer to a corporate body of people.[120] The resultant meaning 'priestly kingship' or the like may be virtually indistinguishable from 'kingship of priests', and is preferable to any endeavour to limit from the outset the reader's options to one characteristic of the notion of priesthood by translating כהנים as 'sanctified'.[121] Yet a more natural reading is simply to take the noun כהנים as a genitive of apposition after the collective ממלכת ('royalty, royal body, royal house') and to see in כהנים a collective reference to all Israel as being in some sense 'priests'.

(2) *Priesthood in relation to the nations*. The reader is then faced with an interpretative decision. In what sense could all Israel be said to be priests? It is a widespread practice of commentaries at this point to speak in terms of Israel's priestly role in relation to the world. Israel is to serve the

115. *Abstraktplural*: Mosis, 'Ex 19,5b.6a', p. 21; cf. Schüssler Fiorenza, *Priester für Gott*, p. 142; Kleinig, 'On Eagles' Wing', p. 27; Dumbrell, 'The Prospect of Unconditionality', p. 147.

116. Junker, 'Das allgemeine Priestertum'; Bauer, 'Könige und Priester'; Wildberger, *Jahwes Eigentumsvolk*, p. 81; Mosis, 'Ex 19,5b.6a', p. 22; Schüssler Fiorenza, *Priester für Gott*, pp. 141-42; Kleinig, 'On Eagles' Wing', p. 27.

117. Scott, 'A Kingdom of Priests', p. 218.

118. KB (p. 592) suggests that this instance of נגידים is to be regarded as a form of נֶגֶד with the sense 'by letter'.

119. KB, p. 990.

120. For further comment on the notion of כהנים as adjectival, see Moran, 'A Kingdom of Priests', p. 9.

121. Scott, 'A Kingdom of Priests', p. 218.

nations as priests as the Levitical priesthood was to serve Israel.[122] That is to say, there is commonly a functional understanding of כהנים. Thus Kleinig asks: 'How could a person be a priest without functioning as a priest?'[123] This priestly ministry is variously specified as service to the nations,[124] mediation of blessing or redemption to the nations,[125] intercession for the nations,[126] teaching the will of God to the nations,[127] or a liturgical mission to the nations.[128] Auzou is perhaps the most explicit in seeing a full range of priestly activity which Israel is to exercise on behalf of the nations: 'What the Israelite priests are for their brothers in the holy community, Israel as a whole was to become for the other peoples in the world'.[129] Auzou supports this with a number of references to the mission of Israel from Isaiah: 41.8-9; 42.19; 43.10; 44.1-2, 21; 45.4; 48.20; 49.3; 54.17; cf. also 56.6; 63.17; 65.8-9, 13-15; 66.14. However, a perusal of the cotext of each of these will show that the primary reference is to the privilege and delight of serving Yhwh directly, and the nations are hardly in view. Rather the focus is on Israel as the object of Yhwh's choice and attention, the one he created and redeems, the one on whom he bestows

122. BDB, p. 463; Noth, *Exodus*, p. 157; Cassuto, *Exodus*, p. 227; W. Gunther Plaut, Bernard J. Bamberger and William W. Hallo, *The Torah: A Modern Commentary* (New York: Union of American Hebrew Congregations, 1981), pp. 363-730 (522); Deryck Sheriffs, 'Moving On with God: Key Motifs in Exodus 13–20', *Themelios* 15 (1990), pp. 49-60 (56); Fretheim, *Exodus*, p. 212.

123. Kleinig, 'On Eagles' Wing', p. 27.

124. Childs, *Exodus*, p. 367; Barbiero, '*Mamleket kohanîm*', p. 444.

125. Junker, 'Das allgemeine Priestertum', p. 14; Vogels, *God's Universal Covenant*, p. 48; Walter C. Kaiser, Jr, 'Israel's Missionary Call', in Ralph D. Winter and Stephen C. Hawthorne (eds.), *Perspectives on the World Christian Movement: A Reader* (Pasadena, CA: William Carey Library, 1981), pp. A25-33 (A29); McComiskey, *The Covenants of Promise*, pp. 68-69; Albert Vanhoye, SJ, *Old Testament Priests and the New Priest According to the New Testament* (trans. J. Bernard Orchard, OSB; Studies in Scripture; Petersham, MA: St Bede's Publications, 1986), pp. 31-34; Barbiero, '*Mamleket kohanîm*', p. 443; Graeme Goldsworthy, 'The Great Indicative: An Aspect of a Biblical Theology of Mission', *RTR* 55 (1996), pp. 2-13.

126. Merrill, *Kingdom of Priests*, p. 80; Auzou, *De la servitude*, p. 251; Vogels, *God's Universal Covenant*, pp. 48-49.

127. McNeile, *Exodus*, p. 111; Walter Harrelson, *Interpreting the Old Testament* (New York: Holt, Rinehart & Winston, 1964), p. 62; Thomas D. Lea, 'The Priesthood of All Christians According to the New Testament', *Southwestern Journal of Theology* 30 (1988), pp. 15-21 (16).

128. Kleinig, 'On Eagles' Wing', p. 18.

129. Auzou, *De la servitude*, p. 251.

honour and in whom his glory is reflected. Thus, for example, 'You, Israel, my servant, Jacob whom I chose, the seed of Abraham my friend' (Isa. 41.1), and, 'You are my servant, Israel, in whom I will display my splendour' (Isa. 49.5).

If Christian interpreters have tended to see priesthood in terms of missionary service, a typically Jewish reading is to see it in terms of suffering. Rabbi J.H. Hertz comments: 'Israel's call has not been to privilege and rulership, but to martyrdom and service'.[130] Such a comment, if somewhat out of place in connection with Exod. 19.4-6, is eminently understandable in the light of centuries of suffering on the part of the Jewish people. Somewhat closer to the mark is the observation of Durham: 'Israel as a "kingdom of priests" is Israel committed to the extension throughout the world of the ministry of Yahweh's Presence'.[131] This at least brings service into closer relation to the 'proximity of Yhwh' theme of the chapter.

As many interpreters have observed, the meaning of כהנים in Exod. 19.6 should be brought into some relationship with the meaning of קדוש. קדוש is a frequent epithet of all things related to priestly activity. Given the fact, as we have noted, of the correlation of the words ממלכת and גוי as paired terms, there is a presumption of some form of synonymous parallelism between כהנים and קדוש as well. Kraus seeks to bring the notion of Israel's holiness into relationship with the nation's perceived mission to the nations.[132] He cites Isa. 43.10 and 44.8, which introduce the notion of Israel as witness (עד), but do not in fact bring this into close relation with the idea of holiness. Nor do such references as Ezek. 39.7 turn Israel's holiness into a charter for a mission to the nations. In this passage, Yhwh is said to reveal his holy name among his people Israel, that the nations may recognize that he is the Holy One in Israel. Israel does not participate in any active mission other than, in the eschatological vision, to plunder the abandoned spoils of war (vv. 9-10). Kraus's best example is Ezek. 36.22-23: 'when I reveal my holiness in you before their eyes'. There is here a sense in which Israel's character as special to Yhwh (holiness or priesthood) has a role in revealing to the nations his unique character. We might then say there is an eschatology implicit in the declaration of Exod. 19.6. The full realization of this declaration will ultimately involve the recognition of the holiness of God by the nations who are in

130. J.H. Hertz, CH (ed.), *The Pentateuch and Haftorahs: Hebrew Text, English Translation and Commentary* (London: Soncino, 1952), p. 291.

131. Durham, *Exodus*, p. 263.

132. Kraus, 'Das heilige Volk', pp. 58-61.

the background in Exod. 19.5-6, and they will recognize the holiness of God because they see Israel's holiness. This falls somewhat short, however, of giving Israel an active mission to the nations at the point of the inauguration of the covenant, and such 'missionary' notions tend to obscure the primary thrust of the declaration as one of grant rather than obligation.

Dumbrell is on surer ground, then, with a moderate 'service to the nations' position, seeing the service as somewhat passive in character. That is, it is by being who they are in relation to God that Israel serves the nations. Dumbrell ties this notion to the role of Abraham as the one through whom the nations would find blessing (Gen. 12.2-3; 18.18; 22.18; 26.4).[133] Dumbrell, however, regards any notion of status in v. 6 as being anticlimactic because status has already been dealt with in the word סגלה. Yet if my understanding of the syntax is correct, the expressions ממלכת כהנים and גוי קדוש are epexegetic of סגלה, and spell out further dimensions for the reader's understanding of the extent of the privilege it is to be Yhwh's 'special treasure'.

The problem with those perspectives which see Israel's relation to the nations as portrayed through the image of priesthood is that they assume, in most cases without feeling the need for any exegetical justification, that one must define priesthood in terms of what it is that priests *do*, particularly what it is they do in relation to other people. It may also owe something to a modern religious sensitivity that there is something inherently distasteful about the concept of election to privilege without quickly quailfying that notion with the addition of an obligation of service to others.[134]

Yet the thrust of the passage in Exodus 19 is about the promise of a divine grant, a great privilege which is being bestowed on Yhwh's treasured people, provided that they continue faithful to him. That grant is preeminently one of relationship with him. The other nations are not in view as objects of Israel's attention. The expression כי־לי כל־הארץ ('all the earth is mine', v. 5) will not serve this role of marking the nations as the beneficiaries of Israel's service. It is simply the backdrop for the divine election of Israel. The nearest reference to the nations in relation to Israel as an active agent in the wider cotext is at Exod. 17.14-16, which concerns the obliteration of the memory of the Amalekites! The Sinai pericope simply contains no direct reference to Israel's responsibilities towards the nations. We ought not to be looking then for a *functional* definition of

133. Dumbrell, *Covenant and Creation*, pp. 89-90.

134. Rowley (*Election*, pp. 45-49) strongly advocates the notion that 'election is for service' and uses Exod. 19.4-6 as his key passage.

priesthood, but for an *ontological* one. What is it that priests *are*, in their relation to God, and in the eyes of the community, which might serve as an analogy for expressing the status of the whole people?

This, again, is not to deny that there may be implications to be discerned in such priestly status, which other writers reflecting on the priestly character of Israel might draw out. Just as Isaiah, when confronted with the throne vision of God felt compelled to offer his services as a spokesperson for Yhwh (Isa. 6.8), so Israel may feel called upon to turn its face toward the world on behalf of God. But this is not the primary thrust of this chapter, which is the awesome event of the encounter of Israel with God. We will thus be looking for those features or perceptions of the priestly office which make it a suitable image for articulating the resultant relationship.

(3) *Priesthood as access to the divine presence*. It has frequently been overlooked that Exodus 19 itself provides a vital clue as to the significance of priesthood. Verse 22 reads: 'Even the priests, who approach (הנגשים) Yhwh, must consecrate themselves (יתקדשו), or Yhwh will break out against them'. As noted above, much of the attention devoted to this verse has concerned the identity of these 'priests' and their relationship with the Aaronic priests who are yet to be consecrated, and to the כהנים of v. 6. What tends to be missed is the virtual definition of what it is to be a priest. Priests are הנגשים אל־יהוה ('those who approach' [niphal participle] or 'draw near to Yhwh'). The articular present participle, in apposition with 'priests', here functions virtually as an occupational term, by analogy with הנגשים ('the slavedrivers' [qal participle of נגש], Exod. 5.6).

As noted earlier, central to any understanding of what a priest is, is the notion of his fitness to approach the deity and 'minister' in his presence like an attendant in the court of a king. The tabernacle cult depicted in Exodus 25–31 and 35–40 is a stylized replica of what, in the widespread ideology of the ancient world, took place within the divine realm of the heavenly temple. This notion of the heavenly cult with its earthly counterpart, and the place of the priest within it, will be taken up in Chapter 6.

Many interpreters affirm that the idea of access to the presence of Yhwh is central to the concept of priesthood in Exod. 19.6, albeit some of them only in passing, before moving on to notions of service and mission to the nations.[135] Baudissin, whose nineteenth-century study of the Old Testament

135. Driver, *Exodus*, p. 171; Haelvoet, 'La théophanie du Sinaï', p. 378; Kuntz, *Self-Revelation*, p. 79; Hyatt, *Exodus*, p. 200; McComiskey, *The Covenants of Promise*, p. 72; Blum, 'Israël à la montagne', p. 272.

priesthood is still useful, understands ממלכת כהנים by analogy with the priestly privilege of immediate proximity to Yhwh.[136] Mosis is among the most explicit in asserting the notion of privilege, not service, as the essence of the expression.[137] Nelson, whose discussion of priesthood in Israel is the most helpful of recent contributions, writes: 'The Hebrew Bible, therefore, defined priesthood by the issue of "access" (Lev. 10.3; Ezek. 44.15-16). Priests were those who could stand before Yahweh (Exod. 19.22), enter Yahweh's presence (Exod. 28.35), or go up to the altar (1 Sam. 2.28).'[138]

Like Kraus, Galling seeks to work from the meaning of קדוש, which is parallel with כהנים, to elucidate its meaning. He comes to very different conclusions, however, and denies that Israel's face is toward the world. He sees קדוש as having a negative force: separation from foreign cults, to which corresponds the positive notion of כהנים by way of antithesis. As 'priests' the people of Israel are 'Yhwh's adorers'.[139] Such worship or adoration is of course to be the attitude of those entering the presence of Yhwh (as Exod. 24.1), just as it is the occupation of those heavenly beings who more permanently enjoy that privilege (Isa. 6.3). Scott likewise rules out a mission to the nations on the basis of the notion of Israel's separation in the context.[140] The antithesis seen by Galling between כהנים and קדוש is an improbable reading, however, as it is based on an inadequate understanding of the meaning of קדוש. True, the idea of separation will at times be a connotation of the קדש group of words, and Israel was certainly conscious of its distinctiveness (Lev. 20.22-26; Num. 23.9).[141] However, its primary meaning has to do with the divine sphere to which the קדוש person or object relates, not the sphere from which it has thereby been separated. Persons or objects are holy to Yhwh, or in one case to Baal

136. 'Die Bezeichnung von ganz Israel als Priestvolk Ex. 19, 6, d.h. als ein Volk, welches unmittelbar seinem Gotte sich nahen darf, wäre in P kaum denkbar': Baudissin, *Geschichte*, p. 61. Whether this notion sits uncomfortably with the ('P') notion of special priestly access will be taken up in Chapter 6.

137. The priesthood envisaged in Exod. 19.6 is, according to Mosis ('Ex 19,5b.6a', p. 25), 'nicht ein Amt und eine Aufgabe, sondern einen Stand und eine Würde'. Ska ('Exode 19,3b-6', p. 301) is similarly unequivocal: 'Exod. 19.5-6 parle des privilèges d'Israël et non d'une mission universelle'.

138. Nelson, *Raising Up a Faithful Priest*, p. 61.

139. *Verehrer Jahwes*, Galling, *Erwählungstraditionen*, p. 27.

140. Scott, 'A Kingdom of Priests', p. 217.

141. For קדש see BDB, pp. 871-73; KB, pp. 825-28; H.-P. Müller, 'קדש', in *TLOT*, III, pp. 103-18; Jacobus A. Naudé, 'קדש', in *NIDOTE*, VI, pp. 877-87.

(2 Kgs 10.20).[142] They are fit to be associated with the one who is inherently קדוש, particularly when he is pictured as enthroned in his sanctuary (Isa. 6.3; Ps. 99.5, 9). It is no light matter to stand in the presence of Yhwh, the holy God, as the men of Beth Shemesh were aware (1 Sam. 6.20). The 'entrance liturgies' of Psalms 15 and 24 reinforce this demand for holiness on the part of the one who would approach God's dwelling place.

If we regard קדוש as being a guide to the understanding of כהנים, the character of Israel as כהנים will relate to their consecration or readiness to encounter Yhwh. This is the point of the preparations outlined in Exod. 19.14-15, including the washing of clothes, and the abstinence from sexual relations. It is also the point of the ritual in 24.3-8, as will be discussed in the following chapter. The preparations reach their fulfilment in the admission of Israel (through its representative elders) into the presence of God in his heavenly sanctuary in Exod. 24.9-11. This again will be taken up in the next chapter.

3. *The Meaning of* גוי קדוש

Finally, we consider briefly the expression גוי קדוש in Exod. 19.6. This phrase, and its development in the Hebrew Bible is the subject of a detailed study by Wells.[143] Israel is here a גוי ('nation'), not as the more common self-designation עם ('a people').[144] Much has been made of this unexpected choice of word in terms of source-critical discussions (for which see Chapter 2 above). We ought not to be surprised at the choice of word, however. עם is sometimes felt to be a kinship term, hence not an expected word for that which a group becomes. A group, or an individual progenitor may, however, become a גוי.[145] The background to its use in Exod. 19.6 is

142. Kraus, 'Das heilige Volk'.

143. Wells, *God's Holy People.*

144. Opinions differ on the degree of contrast between these two words. Speiser sees a sharp distinction: E.A. Speiser, '"People" and "Nation" of Israel', in J.J. Finkelstein and Moshe Greenberg (eds.), *Oriental and Biblical Studies: Collected Writings of E.A. Speiser* (Philadelphia: University of Pennsylvania Press, 1967), pp. 160-70. However, it is not clear that such a sharp distinction can be maintained. The LXX uses λαός and ἔθνος interchangeably for both. Cf. Perlitt, *Bundestheologie*, pp. 173-74.

145. The Deuteronomic preference for עם, particularly in the expression קדוש עם (7.6; 14.2, 21; 26.19; 28.9) may be a result of accommodation to the form of the 'covenant formula', where עם is used, perhaps because the expression is modelled on an adoption formula, whereby one becomes 'kin'. Cf. the 'father…son' language of 2 Sam. 7.14 and see Good, *The Sheep of his Pasture*, p. 66.

probably to be found in Gen. 12.2 where Abraham is promised that he would become לגוי גדול ('a great nation'), that is, a cohesive political entity (such as the tower builders of the preceding chapter sought for themselves) in contrast with the rest of humankind who are viewed as mere מִשְׁפחות ('families', Gen. 12.3).[146] Israel as a whole is to be a גוי קדוֹשׁ. As I have noted, קדוֹשׁ is a positive relational term. It is hard to imagine that Israel's Levitical priests are to be excluded from this designation, though that is the inference of the view of Moran and Fohrer, as discussed above. Sufficient has already been said on the meaning of קדוֹשׁ. Israel is to be a people who share a characteristic of God, and who are thus quailfied to approach him in his sanctuary (קֹדשׁ). This point will be taken up further when we come to consider what is probably an intertextual reflection of Exod. 19.6 in Ps. 114.2 (Chapter 10).

On this view, קדוֹשׁ functions as a virtual synonym of 'priestly', and it is to be noted that Hebrew lacks an adjectival form of the root כהן. The implications of what it means for the people to be 'holy' or 'priestly' in character are spelled out most particularly in Leviticus 17–26 (the Holiness Code), the characteristic feature of which is to broaden the priestly requirements and apply them to the whole people, or introduce requirements analogous to those applying to the priesthood, that they might be a people suited for a relationship with their God: 'Be holy because I, Yhwh your God, am holy' (Lev. 19.2; cf. 20.7, 26).[147] In Chapter 8 we will explore further the interplay of the words כהן and קדוֹשׁ in connection with a discussion on Numbers 16.

4. *Conclusion*

Though my discussion of Exod. 19.6 and more particularly the phrase ממלכת כהנים has been protracted, it is important not to lose sight of the movement of the unit (19.4-6a) in which it is set. The movement is that from redemptive activity—the bringing of Israel out of Egypt and to Yhwh himself—to the declaration of the highly privileged manner in which

146. Dumbrell, *Covenant and Creation*, p. 87.

147. The connection is also made by Ska, 'Exode 19,3b-6', p. 295; Erhard S. Gerstenberger, 'Er soll dir heilig sein: Priester und Gemeinde nach Lev 21,1–22,9', in Frank Crüsemann, Christof Hardmeier and Rainer Kessler (eds.), *Was ist der Mensch…? Beiträge zur Anthropologie des Alten Testaments* (Munich: Chr. Kaiser Verlag, 1992), pp. 194-210; Israel Knohl, *The Sanctuary of Silence: The Priestly Torah and the Holiness School* (Minneapolis, MN: Fortress Press, 1995), pp. 180-86.

Israel is to relate to God when thus brought into his presence, as a 'royal priesthood and holy nation'. Israel is not merely delivered from the hands of one king (Pharaoh), but is drawn to the heavenly court of the divine king. The attribution of a collective royal status to Israel (the 'active-corporate' interpretation) is a reading of ממלכת which enjoys widespread ancient support. It cannot be ruled out in favour of either of the two dominant contemporary interpretations, a purely passive understanding of 'kingdom', or an 'active-elite' reading where the referent is a priestly hierocracy. While the syntax may be deliberately ambivalent, the most natural reading of the expression ממלכת כהנים in its cotext is that it is addressed to Israel as a whole in an active sense. As I have interpreted the three designations of Israel in vv. 5b and 6a, all three are relational expressions and describe the perception Yhwh has of his chosen people and the relationship they are invited to have with him. It would be strange if the middle of these three expressions, ממלכת כהנים, referred not to Israel in relation to Yhwh, but to a particular form of administration the nation was to enjoy. As a nation, Israel is assured of the privilege of royal status, a royalty characterized by the essence of priesthood, namely, access to the divine presence. Israel's corporate priesthood is pre-eminently that which is exercised towards God, not other nations. Such a privilege is highly prized and is Israel's unique possession so long as the nation keeps the covenant. Chapter 6 will amplify on the observations made in this chapter on the ideology surrounding the exercise of the priestly office in Israel. In Chapter 7 I will explore more fully this nature of the Sinai covenant as the divine grant of this privilege to Israel. My more immediate task in the following chapter, however, is to set Exod. 19.6 and the divine speech of which it forms a part (19.4-6a) in their wider cotext in the book of Exodus to see to what extent our tentative understanding of the royal-priestly character of the declaration to Israel is borne out by the surrounding chapters and the book as a whole.

Chapter 5

The Royal Priesthood in the Exodus Narrative Framework: Exodus 1.1 to 24.11

1. *The Structure of Exodus*

If the phrase ממלכת כהנים is correctly understood as having as its referent the whole people, and as characterizing them as those who enjoy privileged royal and priestly status before Yhwh, we must then ask: Is this simply a passing metaphor, striking though it may be, which quickly gives way to other categories and modes of expression for the relationship between Yhwh and his people? Or does Exod. 19.4-6 have a greater structural significance for the Sinai complex than has generally been recognized? Are there other elements in the Sinai complex and the book of Exodus which can be directly related to the declaration contained in these verses, and elucidated by it?

It is not intended here to present a complete exegesis of Exodus 19–24, and it would be foolish to imagine that any one concept is likely to prove the 'key' which unlocks such a highly charged unit of text. Nevertheless, we may usefully consider aspects of these chapters in the light of our exegesis of 19.6. It is suggested here that the interpretation which sees royal and priestly imagery applied to the people as a whole is consistent with, and strengthened by the rest of these chapters in particular and the book of Exodus as a whole. We take up, then, a consideration of the implications of our exegesis of 19.4-6 within its wider cotext.

The book of Exodus divides into two parts. Chapters 1–18 deal with Israel in Egypt, the exodus and the journey to Mt Sinai. Chapters 19–40 deal with the encounter with Yhwh at Mt Sinai and the nature of the covenant Yhwh grants to Israel. Within this latter portion, chs. 19–24 deal more specifically with the theophany and covenantal constitution of Israel as the people of God, while chs. 25–40 deal with the provision of the tabernacle and its associated cult, with a narrative section in the middle of this unit dealing with the incident of the apostasy of the golden calf and its aftermath (chs. 32–34). A transitional unit linking the Sinai encounter with the cultic provisions is provided by 24.12-18. The Sinai pericope, in its most extended sense, continues through the book of Leviticus to Num. 10.10 when Israel breaks camp and moves on from Sinai. This extensive block of material contains a mixture of narrative and legal sections.[1]

Within this broader setting, 19.4-6 occupies a prominent place as the link between the account of the exodus experience and the Sinai narrative and laws. We may summarize the two sections for which 19.4-6 acts as a pivot point as anticipation and consummation of an encounter with Yhwh. Of course God has in a sense been present with Israel on the journey, yet it is paradoxically a journey which has God as its destination. The ideal set forth in both sections of the Sinai pericope is depicted in terms of dwelling in the presence of Yhwh. Thus for the first section, we may consider Exod. 15.13-18 as a statement of this ideal:

> (13) In your love you lead the people you have redeemed. In your strength you guide them to your holy dwelling. (14) The nations hear and tremble; anguish grips the people of Philistia. (15) The chiefs of Edom are terrified, the leaders of Moab are seized with trembling, the people of Canaan melt away; (16) terror and dread falls upon them. By the power of your arm they are as still as a stone—until your people pass by, Yhwh, until the people you bought pass by. (17) You will bring them in and plant them on the mountain of your inheritance—the place, Yhwh, you made for your dwelling, the sanctuary, O Lord, your hands established. (18) Yhwh reigns for ever and ever.

For the second section, we may cite Exod. 29.45-46:

> (45) Then I will dwell among the Israelites and be their God. (46) They will know that I am Yhwh their God, who brought them out of Egypt so that I might dwell among them. I am Yhwh their God.

Exodus 19.4, and in particular the clause ואבא אתכם אלי ('and I brought you to myself'), may then be understood as a retrospective summary of chs. 1–18. The past dealings of Yhwh with this people provide the basis for the undertaking of vv. 5-6. Considered in this light, the offer contained in vv. 5-6 may be seen as having paradigmatic force for the whole of the rest of the book of Exodus, or indeed, the whole of the Sinai pericope, to say nothing of the life of Israel in the land to which this section points.[2]

1. See John H. Sailhamer, 'The Mosaic Law and the Theology of the Pentateuch', *WTJ* 53 (1991), pp. 241-61.

2. For a more developed paradigmatic approach to these verses, see Kleinig, 'On Eagles' Wing'.

2. *The Preceding Cotext of Exodus 19.4-6*

The central event of Exodus 19 is the theophany, or awesome presence and voice of God manifested on the mountain (19.9, 16-19). The designation of the mountain at the foot of which Israel camped in the desert of Sinai simply as ההר ('the mountain', 19.2) points us back to the previous mention of this mountain in 18.5 where it is identified more fully as הר האלהים ('the mountain of God'), and so the reader anticipates some form of divine revelation in connection with this location. This in turn draws the reader's attention back to the earlier manifestation of God at this same 'mountain of God' (3.1). Here Moses experienced an encounter at the bush with the God who revealed himself through the strange fire as the God of the patriarchs, who had not forgotten his commitment to his people, and who was determined to rescue them and bring them into the land he had promised. To this end, Moses is commissioned to go to Pharaoh as the representative of the God who now reveals himself by the name (and character) of Yhwh.[3] While the narrative of Exodus 3 is often seen as belonging to the genre of the prophetic call,[4] and to be the paradigm of this standard feature of the prophetic experience, there are also elements of a *priestly* commissioning about the burning bush narrative. Moses is commanded not to approach any closer, then to remove his sandals, since the ground is holy (3.5). That is, the bush and the surrounding area are a sanctuary associated with the presence of God. For the parallelism מקדשי ('my sanctuary') and מקום רגלי ('place of my feet') see Isa. 60.13. Israelite priests, like some other priesthoods, ministered in bare feet.[5] Perhaps the removal of sandals (intended for a journey) indicates that this is 'home'. In Josh. 5.15, Joshua is similarly commanded to remove his shoes, again, because the ground is holy. There it is the holy ground of Eretz-Israel, the sanctuary land (cf. Exod. 15.17). Perhaps also to place one's foot over something is a symbol of sovereignty (Ps. 8.7 [ET 8.6]), and the unshod foot may draw

3. See the brief discussion on the divine name in the previous chapter and the references there.

4. E.g. N. Habel, 'The Form and Significance of the Call Narratives', *ZAW* NS 77 (1965), pp. 297-323 (301-305); Childs, *Exodus*, pp. 55-56; Fretheim, *Exodus*, p. 51.

5. For the evidence and some comparative material, see William Robertson Smith, *Lectures on the Religion of the Semites, Second and Third Series* (JSOTSup, 183; Sheffield: Sheffield Academic Press, 1995), p. 53; Ramban, *Exodus*, p. 27; Francis I. Andersen, 'Feet in Ancient Times', *Buried History* 35 (1999), pp. 9-20. No mention of footwear is included in the comprehensive priestly wardrobe in Exod. 28.

attention to this. When Moses is made aware of the presence of God, he responds by hiding his face, since he is fearful of the consequences of seeing God (Exod. 3.6). Moses is clearly portrayed to some degree in priestly terms. True, the designation כהן for Moses is not used in the Pentateuch, and only once in the Hebrew Bible (Ps. 99.6). Yet, for that matter, neither is Moses frequently described as a prophet, yet clearly he functions as the paradigm prophet (Deut. 18.15). It would be best to regard the portrayal of Moses as *sui generis*. But we will begin to see Moses exercising priestly or meta-priestly functions, not the least of which is the consecration of other priests (Exod. 28.41; 30.30; 40.13).[6]

At the bush, Moses is commissioned to go to Pharaoh and demand the release of the people whom Yhwh identifies by the relational term as עמי ('my people', 3.7, 10). The immediate goal of the divine rescue is stated to be a cultic gathering of the people at this same mountain, 'you (pl.) will worship (תעבדון) God on this mountain' (3.12; cf. 4.23; 7.16, 26 [ET 8.1]; 8.16 [ET 8.20]; 9.1; 10.3, 7-8, 11, 24, 26; 12.31). While there may be nothing more intended by the use of the word than a contrast with the hard 'service' (עבדה קשׁה) rendered to Pharaoh (1.14), it is noteworthy that at times the verb עבד and its cognate noun עבדה take on the specific cultic force of 'serve cultically as a priest' (Num. 18.7).[7]

By the clear geographical pointers, the readers of 19.1-2 are directed to connect the arrival of Israel at this mountain with the earlier theophany granted to Moses and to cast their minds back over the events which have transpired between Moses' initial encounter with God and the impending 'service' of the whole people. The people have left Egypt, as 19.1 reminds us, and have arrived at the mountain which has been the initial goal of the exodus. Thus there may be an expectation that Israel will now experience an encounter with God in a manner foreshadowed by that of Moses,[8] that is, a meeting which, at least in part, is conceived of as a priestly encounter.

The function of the plague narratives and the associated 'sonship' of Israel will be dealt with below in connection with the theophany of Exodus 19.

6. On the priestly role of Moses, see George Buchanan Gray, *Sacrifice in the Old Testament: Its Theory and Practice* (Oxford: Clarendon Press, 1925), pp. 194-210; C. Hauret, 'Moïse était-il prêtre?', *Bib* 40 (1959), pp. 509-21.

7. BDB, p. 713; KB, p. 671.

8. Noth regards the account of ch. 3 as J's prelude to the theophany of ch. 19 (*Exodus*, p. 40).

3. *The Following Cotext of Exodus 19.4-6 to Exodus 23*

If the preceding cotext, then, prepares the reader for a priestly encounter, what of the following cotext? How does the declaration of Exod. 19.4-6 relate to the theophany and its associated preparations, the promulgation of the divine law, and the sacrifice, the vision of God and the meal described in Exod. 24.1-11?

Following the response of the people to the declaration of their standing before God as a 'kingship of priests and a holy nation' and the relaying of that response to Yhwh (Exod. 19.7-8), we are provided with an initial proclamation of the impending theophany (v. 9). God says to Moses, 'I am coming to you in a dense cloud, so that people will hear me speaking with you and will always put their trust in you' (v. 9). This statement draws attention to the purpose of theophany accounts in ancient Near Eastern literature. Comparative studies of these accounts suggest that they are, in part, designed to enhance the status of the one receiving the theophany.[9] Mann in particular draws attention to the parallels to the exaltation theme in Exodus 19. The storm-theophany not only instils fear in the people, it also serves the purpose of exalting Moses in their eyes. In the same way, the *Tukulti-Ninurta Epic*,[10] a late second-millennium document, enhances the esteem of the Assyrian king Tukulti-Ninurta by reference to the divinely wrought cosmic upheavals: 'As when Addu bellows, the mountains tremble; As when Ninurta lifts his weapons, the quarters of the world are reduced to continual anguish' (column 1 lines 6-7).[11] The function of these hymnic elements is to exalt both the gods and the human king with whom the gods are associated. While the name of the king is lacking, the descriptions of column 1 lines 1-5 appear to refer to the king, while using epithets normally associated with deity, with which we might compare the use of the divine epithet קָדוֹשׁ to refer to Israel in Exod. 19.5):[12]

9. For the purpose of theophany accounts, see Kuntz, *Self-Revelation*; Thomas W. Mann, *Divine Presence and Guidance in Israelite Traditions: The Typology of Exaltation* (Near Eastern Studies [Johns Hopkins University]; Baltimore: The Johns Hopkins University Press, 1977); Niehaus, *God at Sinai*; Jörg Jeremias, *Theophanie: Die Geschichte einer alttestamentlichen Gattung* (WMANT, 10; Neukirchen–Vluyn: Neukirchener Verlag, 2nd edn, 1977).

10. Mann, *Divine Presence*, pp. 35-42.

11. Mann, *Divine Presence*, p. 37.

12. See also the discussion on holiness below in Chapter 6.

> Glorious is his might, it sco[rches] the [ir]reverent in front and behind;
> Blasting is his impetuosity, it burns the unsubmissive left and right;
> Fearful is his splendour, it overwhelms all his enemies.
> He who...the extremities of the four winds, all kings without exception live in dread of him.[13]

However, a further dimension to the exaltation motif in Exodus 19 may be suggested in the light of the honorific description of Israel in 19.5-6. Whereas all previous accounts of the self-manifestation of deity in Israel were granted to prominent individuals such as Abraham or Jacob, the theophany in Exodus 19 is granted not just to Moses (though he takes a leading role), but to all Israel. Perhaps this is to be seen as a visible indication of the enhanced status of the whole nation, conceived of as a collective royal entity, not merely that of Moses as an individual. One possible line of support for this perspective would be to note the designation, earlier in Exodus, of Israel as the 'firstborn' of Yhwh: 'Then say to Pharaoh, "This is what Yhwh says, 'Israel is my firstborn son', and I told you, 'Release my son, so he may worship me'. But you refused to release him; so I will kill your firstborn son"' (Exod. 4.22-23). It is to be noted that this designation of Israel as Yhwh's son is chiefly found in the Hebrew Bible in contexts dealing with the Sinai and exodus experience or with the return from exile in texts which may echo the exodus account (Jer. 3.19; 31.9, 20; Hos. 11.1).[14] It is also to be noted that this designation of Israel as Yhwh's firstborn is not found in the text of Exodus at the point where it might be expected, immediately prior to the relevant tenth plague (the death of Egypt's firstborn), but before all ten. This declaration regarding Israel's distinctive status thus takes on a more programmatic role and its prominent position fosters the idea that the divine intervention in the plagues has as one of its purposes the privileging of Yhwh's 'son' in relation to the Egyptians.

Similarly the honorific theophany accounts are found in close association with indications of the king's quasi-divine ancestry. The *Tukulti-Ninurta Epic* hymn includes the following designations of the king (column 1 lines 10-13):

> He is the eternal image of Enlil...
> Enlil, like a physical father, exalted him second to his first-born son.
> He is precious at his worth.[15]

13. Mann, *Divine Presence*, p. 37.
14. Cf. Hyatt, *Exodus*, p. 86.
15. Mann, *Divine Presence*, p. 38.

In *T. Levi* 4.2 priesthood and divine sonship are again closely associated, when Levi is addressed in these terms: 'The Most High has given heed to your prayer that you be delivered from wrongdoing, that you should become a son to him, as minister and priest in his presence'.[16] In the song which celebrates an earlier manifestation of the divine presence and power at the Reed Sea (Exod. 15), the exaltation of Yhwh (כי־גאה גאה, 'for he is highly exalted', v. 1) is bound up with reflection on the highly honoured position Israel occupies in the sight of the nations (vv. 13-16).

The Exodus 19 account then proceeds to recount instructions regarding the preparations which the people are to make in anticipation of the encounter with Yhwh. These involve a process of consecration (קדשׁ, piel, 19.10, 14), with Moses as the agent of consecration, and include or are closely associated with the washing of their clothes. The people are also to abstain from sexual relations during a three-day period of preparation. During this time, the mountain is declared to be decidedly off-limits, with the hiphil of גבל (v. 12 with the people as object, v. 23 with the mountain as object; cf. 3.5). There is to be no approach or transgression of the limits on pain of death.

The notion of a denial of access to Yhwh's place of abode, or place of manifestation (and both elements are present as complementary metaphors throughout the Sinai complex) may hardly seem suggestive of priestly prerogatives, of which access to Yhwh's spatial realm is a characteristic (19.22). Yet what we have in these restrictions bears some analogy to the rite of passage laid down in Leviticus 8 for the ordination of the Levitical priests (washing, v. 6; waiting, vv. 33, 35).

In Exodus 19 there are clear liminal markers—spatial (the limit at the base of the mountain), temporal (three days) and ceremonial (the washing, the sexual abstinence and the blast of the ram's horn (היבל, v. 13) or trumpet (השׁופר, v. 19) which are both associated with priestly prerogatives (Lev. 25.9; Num. 10.8; Josh. 6.1).[17] While the 'trumpet' has a number of uses, including liturgical and military, we may perhaps note in particular its use at 1 Kgs 1.39 for the proclamation of Solomon as king. The theophany of Exodus 19 is perhaps the supreme moment of the revelation of the kingship of Yhwh. We may not rule out also the possibility

16. *OTP*, I, p. 789.

17. Jacob Milgrom, 'The Priestly Consecration (Leviticus 8): A Rite of Passage', in Stanley F. Chyet and David H. Ellenson (eds.), *Bits of Honey: Essays for Samson H. Levey* (South Florida Studies in the History of Judaism, 74; Atlanta: Scholars Press, 1993), pp. 57-61.

that it marks the inauguration of the royal status of the people whose royalty is bound up with that of their God.

With the *limina* identified above, there is an expectation that in each of these categories the *limen* will be crossed at the appropriate juncture. Thus the period of three days of waiting must run its course, at the conclusion of which the people will be in a consecrated state (i.e. fit for the divine realm), the ram's horn will be sounded and the barrier separating the people from Yhwh may be safely crossed. The objective of the preparations is that Israel might 'meet with God' (לקראת האלהים, v. 17). In the only other usage of this phrase in the Hebrew Bible, it occurs in a context of impending doom, 'Prepare to meet your God' (Amos 4.12), yet clearly this is not the intention here. What makes the difference is the state of preparedness of the participants. Any default will result in death, whereas the expectation is here engendered that the result of the consecration will be an encounter with God which issues in life, not death, even though the people will both hear (v. 9) and see (v. 11) God.

Yet when the third day comes, and the divine manifestations are evident—thunder and lightning, the dense cloud, the blast of a very loud trumpet, billowing smoke and fire, and the violent trembling of the mountain (vv. 16-19)—what follows is not in fact the crossing of the threshold, but, surprisingly, a further reiteration of the warning (vv. 21-23). Instructively, those designated as כהנים ('priests') are to remain on the same side of the barrier as the rest of the people (v. 24). The identity of these 'priests', who clearly form a subset of Israelite society, is not particularly important for the moment,[18] but the reader might have assumed (apart from their explicit inclusion in the taboo) that their status as those who enjoy a more inherent degree of sanctity (v. 22) might have exempted them from the general prohibition. Only Moses and Aaron are to ascend at this point. There is thus a dramatic tension created by the lack of explanation of the apparent change of plan. This tension is further heightened by the introduction into the narrative of the Decalogue (20.1-17). This 'intrusion' of the Decalogue has long been felt to be an awkward dislocation of the theophany narrative.[19] From a literary standpoint, the introduction of

18. See below (Chapter 8) for discussion on the Korah incident (Num. 16), where it appears that the tribal chiefs exercised a priestly role prior to the designation of Aaron and his sons as priests for the whole community.

19. This has been noted from at least the time of Rashi. See Noth, *Exodus*, p. 154. For a treatment of the literary- and tradition-critical issues concerning the Decalogue, see Childs, *Exodus*, pp. 344-51, 388-401.

the Decalogue at this juncture serves to delay the resolution of the issue of access to the presence of Yhwh, besides giving content to the character of the God of the Sinai encounter, and in summary form, the content of his covenant requirements. The commandments spell out in moral and social terms the distinctions which are to mark those who are the beneficiaries of the redemptive activity of God (Exod. 20.2).

Only after the Decalogue is related is the narrative resumed and at least a partial resolution of the tension offered. One might have anticipated that the prospect of an encounter with the God of the exodus might instil a degree of fear as it had done with Moses (Exod. 3.6). There had been a brief indication of the response of the people to the theophany at 19.16, where we learn that 'Everyone in the camp trembled'. Now, at 20.18-19, this trembling is further elaborated, as we are apprised of the extent of the fear which produced such trembling. In a subtle play on the word ירא, the author turns the response of the people into an opportunity for stating an objective of the theophany from a divine perspective: 'Moses said to the people, "Do not be afraid (תיראו). God has come to test you, so that reverence (יראתו) for God will be with you to keep you from sinning"' (Exod. 20.20).

For the modern reader, who has only the verbal account of the dramatic theophany, and who cannot enter into the experience of the people at the foot of the mountain, the introduction of the Decalogue at 20.1, with its uncompromising demands of a jealous God, may serve to engender something of the same sense of awe and trembling.

Thus it seems that the narrator is working with ideals on two different orders of magnitude. At the highest level, the ideal would be for Israel to enjoy the privilege of unhindered access to Yhwh, to be able to approach him on his holy mountain in a state of priestly consecration, to catch a vision of his splendour and hear his words directly. This is what is held before Israel as the prized goal in its relationship with God—an outworking of what it means to be his priests. However, such an ideal is not possible in view of the fear which inevitably results from the thought of such an encounter with a holy God. The fear arises out of a sense of the disparity between the awesome nature of a God who exhibits such devastating signs of his presence—signs which carry in their very nature the threat of destruction—and the people's sense of inability to meet such a God directly. Hence the appeal to Moses for mediation (v. 19). Such mediation is to form a significant feature of the ensuing narratives and legislative sections of the remainder of Exodus and Leviticus. But the reader should not lose sight of the fact that mediation is a means to an end. It serves the interests of the higher and ultimate goal which is that Israel should be a people who as a whole should enjoy access to God in some form of priestly service.

What follows next is generally referred to as the Covenant Code (20.22–23.33).[20] This codification of law is in some ways an expansion of the provisions contained in the Decalogue. In contrast with the apodictic nature of the Decalogue ('You shall [not]...'), it is cast more in casuistic form ('If you...then...'), and contains a greater element than does the Decalogue of those provisions which we might describe as cultic rather than moral or social (e.g. offerings, 22.29; festivals, 23.14-19).

The Covenant Code begins and ends with a warning of the dangers of worshipping other gods, and this *inclusio* characterizes the function of the Code. It has presumably been inserted here in order to provide some content for the statement in 24.7 that Moses took the book of the covenant and read it to the people, and for the people's acquiescence in the provisions of the covenant, though there is no reason to restrict the meaning of ספר הברית to these stipulations.

The question of the function of the laws embedded in the Pentateuchal narrative framework has been a vexed one, and still lacks resolution.[21] Their present setting in a narrative matrix suggests that their primary function is not to serve as bodies of legislation as such, but to further the compositional strategy of the narrator. Thus far, the analysis of Sailhamer appears valid.[22] Sailhamer maintains, however, that the laws are included as examples of what he regards as a flawed basis for a relationship with God (lawkeeping), championed and exemplified in the narrative by Moses, who ultimately failed in this endeavour. This legalistic way of life was, according to Sailhamer's reading of the editorial agenda, not for Israel's good, and is given only as a foil for another principle—that of faith, which Sailhamer sees exemplified in the biography of Abraham. This antithesis between Abraham and Moses is rather contrived. The considerable space

20. For a study of these chapters which regards them as integral to the structure of the Pentateuch, see Joe M. Sprinkle, *'The Book of the Covenant': A Literary Approach* (JSOTSup, 174; Sheffield: JSOT Press, 1994).

21. The principal legal corpora of the Pentateuch may be identified as follows: the Decalogue (Exod. 20.1-17), the Covenant Code (Exod. 20.22–23.33), the Holiness Code (Lev. 17–26) and the Deuteronomic Laws (Deut. 12.1–26.19), together with the more specifically cultic material in Exodus and Leviticus which forms the substance of the following chapter.

22. John H. Sailhamer, 'The Mosaic Law', and *The Pentateuch as Narrative*, pp. 60-62.

devoted to the representation of Israel's laws in the Pentateuch seems out of all proportion if the purpose of their inclusion is simply to provide illustrative material for a life-principle the author wished his readers to avoid.

As an alternative explanation, I tentatively propose that the laws, while reflecting the actual legal principles and practice of Israelite society, serve the function in their present narrative setting of describing what life in the land, life lived 'before me [Yhwh]' (Exod. 20.3; 23.15) would be like as an ideal.[23] There are indications that this life is conceived in terms of a new creation. The Sabbath principle, for example (20.8-11; 23.10-12), points the reader of the Pentateuch back to Gen. 2.2-3 and the depiction there of an ideal state where the cosmos enjoys rest under God's blessing. If the land of Canaan is to be a new 'garden of Yhwh' (Gen. 13.10), then presumably the people of Israel, as God's 'special treasure', that is, his 'royal priesthood and holy nation'—are to take the place in that restored sanctuary of the primal man. We will see later how the Aaronide priest was thought of in just such terms as the primal man, enjoying access to God in his cosmic sanctuary (Chapter 6).

This is not to suggest that the legislation is hopelessly utopian. Clearly it contemplates and deals with the existence of evil, or that which has no place among a holy people. However, the provisions of the Sinai laws point the way forward to a society where such evil is curbed and dealt with in justice, and where there is a remedy for the breach of fellowship which infraction causes. The laws of the Decalogue and of the Covenant Code may thus be said to have an eschatological dimension.

4. *Exodus 24.1-11*

a. *The Literary Coherence of Exodus 24.1-11*

Following the itemization of the provisions of the Covenant Code, the narrative of events at Mt Sinai resumes once again. Exodus 24.1-11 contains an account of a cultic event performed by the Israelites at the base of the mountain, and an ascent of their representative leaders to its heights, who experience the extraordinary privilege of 'seeing God' and participate in a meal in the divine presence. These events are said to relate explicitly to the 'covenant' (ברית, vv. 7, 8) which Yhwh has made with Israel. We

23. This is not dissimilar to Schmitt's approach ('Redaktion des Pentateuch'), which is to see the theme of 'faith' as the structuring concept of the final redaction.

turn our attention to this unit, then, to see whether these actions, or more precisely, the literary record of them, sheds further light on the nature of this covenant. As indicated above, our primary focus is not on the historical issues which might be raised, for example the date at which a notion of covenant became a significant item of Israel's self-consciousness, but to deal with the literary and thematic issues of the text itself and, from this text, to elucidate something of the specific character of the Sinai covenant as the book of Exodus portrays it.

While a minority of scholars has observed a compositional unity to Exod. 24.1-11,[24] this section has been treated by most interpreters over the past century as a composite account, whose redactional seams are glaringly evident to the modern reader. A principal concern of the scholarly attention devoted to this chapter, then, has been directed to identifying the provenance of the strands, and to considering the relationship between either or both of the two major strands (or lack of any relationship) to the notion of covenant. Consequently, the narrative art of the final form and its place in the structure of the whole Sinai pericope have not always been adequately appreciated.

Verses 1 and 2, the summons to Moses and some associates to ascend and approach God, are frequently taken, from a source- or tradition-critical point of view, as belonging with vv. 9-11, which recount the anticipated ascent and the vision of God and the meal in his presence which follow.[25] An apparently unrelated scene at the base of the mountain, contained in vv. 3-8, is considered an intrusion which interrupts the flow of the ascent narrative. There is, however, no consensus on the date and provenance of such sources. The two strands are variously attributed to J and E, or E and J, or their redactors, or (for vv. 9-11) to Eissfeldt's L, or to early traditions independent of the major epic sources. While either or both units of text are frequently regarded as early (particularly vv. 9-11), vv. 3-8 have also been seen to have Deuteronomic influence, while vv. 9-11 have also been considered as the product of post-exilic concerns, and both have also been

24. Most notable in this regard among the commentators is Cassuto, *Exodus*, pp. 310-15. The monograph of Beyerlin (*Origins*, p. 36) sees vv. 1a, 9-11 and vv. 3-8, all of which he attributes to E, as being 'handed down in close connection'. Studies which see a literary integrity extending beyond this unit could also be mentioned at this point: Chirichigno, 'Narrative Structure'; John W. Hilber, 'Theology of Worship in Exodus 24', *JETS* 39 (1996), pp. 177-89; Alexander, 'Composition'.

25. Verse 1 is usually taken as introducing an abrupt change from 23.33, though Alexander has most recently argued for its continuity ('Composition', p. 6).

regarded as late scribal additions. 'So many men so many minds', as Vriezen expressed it.[26]

The only references to a ברית ('covenant') in Exod. 24.1-11 are contained in vv. 3-8. It would therefore be more easily open to the interpreter who does not seek to interpret the final form of the text, to reject any relationship between the vision scene (vv. 9-11) and the covenant. Perlitt goes further and by textual reconstruction finds no original connection with a covenant in the sacrifice of vv. 4-6.[27] On the other hand, there are those who see vv. 9-11 as early and yet as reflecting the notion of covenant.[28]

My approach will be to endeavour to understand the passage in its final form and in relation to its cotext. In doing this, it is here suggested, we will discover a greater degree of literary and thematic integrity in the passage than has often been observed. The resulting thematic coherence which emerges is congruent with and lends support to our interpretation of Exod. 19.4-6.

To some extent, the observation of a thematic continuity is not new. It has, of course, been the traditional Jewish understanding of the text.[29] Some scholars who recognize disparate sources and traditions underlying this unit nevertheless recognize at least an element of a redactional unity. It is sometimes a matter of emphasis. Vriezen, for example, notes the

26. Th.C. Vriezen, 'The Exegesis of Exodus XXIV 9-11', in M.A. Beek, S.P. Brock and F.F. Bruce (eds.), *The Witness of Tradition: Papers Read at the Joint British–Dutch Old Testament Conference Held at Woudschoten 1970* (OTS, 17; Leiden: E.J. Brill, 1972), pp. 100-33 (105). Vriezen gives a useful overview of the major source-critical approaches to this passage (pp. 102-105). Childs, in his discussion of the literary and traditio-historical issues (*Exodus*, pp. 499-502), comments on the 'arbitrariness' of much of the source analysis of this section (p. 500). See also Driver, *Exodus*, pp. 252-54; Haelvoet, 'La théophanie du Sinaï', pp. 386-89; Noth, *Exodus*, pp. 194-99; Eissfeldt, *Hexateuch-Synopse*, pp. 151-52; Perlitt, *Bundestheologie*, pp. 181-82, 190-91; Zenger, *Sinaitheophanie*, pp. 72-76, 215-17; Hyatt, *Exodus*, pp. 254-57; Ernest W. Nicholson, 'The Interpretation of Exodus xxiv 9-11', *VT* 24 (1974), pp. 77-97 (79); Eberhard Ruprecht, 'Exodus 24,9-11 als Beispiel lebendiger Erzähltradition aus der Zeit des babylonischen Exils', in Rainer Albertz (ed.), *Werden und Wirken des Alten Testaments* (Festschrift Claus Westermann; Neukirchen–Vluyn: Neukirchener Verlag, 1980), pp. 138-73 (138-39); Renaud, *La théophanie du Sinai*, p. 32; Jean Louis Ska, SJ, 'Le repas de Ex 24,11', *Bib* 74 (1993), pp. 305-27.

27. Perlitt, *Bundestheologie*, pp. 190-203.

28. E.g. Vriezen, 'Exegesis', p. 113; Dennis J. McCarthy, SJ, '*b^erît* in Old Testament History and Theology', *Bib* 53 (1972), pp. 111-21.

29. See, e.g., Targums *Onqelos*, *Pseudo-Jonathan* and *Neofiti* and the comments of Ibn Ezra *ad loc.*; Nicholson, 'Interpretation', p. 86.

'regular sequence' of the events on the surface of the text, but goes on to observe that on closer inspection 'the seeming unity of Ch. xxiv disintegrates completely'.[30] Nicholson, whose starting point for his several extensive treatments of this unit is the difference in terms of source between vv. 3-8 and 9-11,[31] concludes the latest of his treatments of the passage by noting its overall thematic cohesion, and allowing himself to find support for his exegesis of vv. 3-8 in vv. 9-11.[32]

In many ways Exod. 24.1-11 relates closely to the narrative of ch. 19, which it resumes after the suspension of movement by the recounting of the laws in chs. 20–23. Sarna has drawn attention to the perhaps deliberate use of דבר seven times in both chapters, and the sevenfold use of ירד ('descend') in ch. 19, matched by a sevenfold use of עלה ('ascend') in ch. 24. This is an extraordinary *inclusio* which would serve to bind the two chapters as anticipation and realization.[33] In particular a close link is sometimes observed between the units 19.3b-8 and 24.3-8, units where the covenant is first proposed, then consummated.[34]

Exodus 19 had laid foundations for an event of covenant making, but nowhere contained an explicit statement to the effect that such a covenant had been ratified and inaugurated. Rather, the overall impression we are left with from ch. 19 is a heightened sense of anticipation, mingled with an appreciation of the awesomeness of the God who initiates covenant with

30. Vriezen, 'Exegesis', p. 102. Others who, while accepting underlying sources of disparate provenance, observe a degree of redactional unity include Siegfried Mittmann, *Deuteronomium 1^1–6^3: Literarkritisch und traditionsgeschichtlich untersucht* (BZAW, 139; Berlin: W. de Gruyter, 1975), pp. 153-54; Childs, *Exodus*, pp. 497-507.

31. Nicholson, 'Interpretation', 'The Antiquity of the Tradition of Exodus xxiv 9-11', *VT* 25 (1975), pp. 69-79, 'The Origin of the Tradition in Exodus xxiv 9-11', *VT* 26 (1976), pp. 148-60, 'The Covenant Ritual in Exodus xxiv 3-8', *VT* 32 (1982), pp. 74-86. Much of this material was then incorporated into his monograph, *God and his People: Covenant and Theology in the Old Testament* (Oxford: Clarendon Press, 1986).

32. Nicholson, 'Covenant Ritual', pp. 84-85.

33. Nahum M. Sarna, *Exodus: The Traditional Hebrew Text with the New JPS Translation* (The JPS Torah Commentary; Philadelphia: Jewish Publication Society of America, 1991), p. 150.

34. Perlitt has well demonstrated the literary links between these sections of the Sinai pericope, attributing both to an exilic Deuteronomic source (*Bundestheologie*, pp. 190-92). Nicholson regards 24.3-8 as earlier than 19.3b-8, which he considers 'an anticipatory summary and interpretation of the nature and basis of the covenant' perhaps specifically of the ceremony of 24.3-8 ('Covenant Ritual', pp. 83-84); cf. Van Seters, '"Comparing Scripture with Scripture"', pp. 124-26.

Israel. Prominent are the warnings against any attempt to encroach upon the holy space associated with the presence of God. The intervening chapters have spelled out something of the character of this God, the relationships he designs for his people to enjoy with himself, and with each other, and the distinctiveness which is to mark off this holy people from the surrounding nations.

Moreover, the worship which has repeatedly been stated as the goal of the exodus has not yet taken place. Was the objective of worshipping God simply a cheap ruse, or do we still expect a significant cultic event to take place? In Exod. 24.1-2 we have an echo of the earlier invitation given by Yhwh to Moses and Aaron (19.24) to come up the mountain and approach him, though this time the invitation list of those who are to 'ascend to Yhwh' is widened to include Nadab and Abihu and seventy of the elders of Israel.[35] Nadab and Abihu are two of the sons of Aaron (Exod. 6.23) about whom we have heard nothing else in the narrative so far. The prominence given to representatives of the family soon to be designated as the priestly family may serve to point the reader to the priestly character of the event they are to participate in, as does the use of the verb נגשׁ ('approach', v. 2), frequently associated with cultic contexts. It has also been postulated that the seventy זקני־ישׂראל ('elders of Israel') are the same personnel referred to as הכהנים ('the priests') at 19.22, 24. Others, following Rashi and Ibn Ezra, would identify those priests with the young men (or firstborn) who perform the sacrifices in v. 5.[36] Perhaps, too, in the larger compositional strategy, the specific mention of Nadab and Abihu in ch. 24 (rather than a more general reference to 'the sons of Aaron') may anticipate their impending apostasy (Lev. 10.1; Num. 3.4), which in turn is symptomatic of the fickle response of the people as a whole. Thus the reader is forewarned that the event to be narrated in Exod. 24.1-11 is not to be seen as a point of finality in Israel's experience of God, as though Israel had 'arrived' once and for all. Rather, it is an ideal from which they were to fall far short through their own failures. However, there is no hint that the act of seeing God in vv. 10-11 is a high-handed sin, as it is treated by Rashi and some other Jewish exegetes.

35. The references to Nadab and Abihu in vv. 1 and 9 are unparallelled in the Sinai complex, and are sometimes regarded as secondary interpolations: Vriezen, 'Exegesis', p. 106. The Samaritan text includes also the names of Eleazar and Ithamar in vv. 1 and 9. Moses is also sometimes treated as a secondary addition to the text here: see, e.g., Nicholson, 'Interpretation', p. 79.

36. Hertz, *Pentateuch*, p. 294; Cassuto, *Exodus*, p. 311.

The elders appear to represent the people as do a similar group of seventy elders in Num. 11.16-17, 24 (cf. also Ezek. 8.11), where they are identified as זקני העם ('elders of the people').[37] There are further intertextual links between the Numbers passage and Exod. 24.1-11. Besides the theme of a divine meal common to both passages (see below), the elders are identified as אצילי בני ישראל (24.11). The word אציל is of uncertain origin, though clearly its referent is the leaders who are identified as elders of Israel in v. 1.[38] Regardless of its true etymology, there may be an intertextual connection with Num. 11.17, where the verb אצל is used to denote the action of God in 'taking, setting aside' some of the spirit that was on Moses and allocating it to the seventy elders. Ruprecht has identified the sometimes overlooked role of Israel's elders as representatives of all Israel, particularly in the context of significant cultic events.[39] Thus, for example, in 1 Kgs 8.1 (the bringing of the ark into the temple), Israel's elders and leaders (under various designations) are summoned. When the text says that 'all the men of Israel (כל־איש ישראל) came together', we are presumably to understand this to mean that their representatives mentioned in v. 1 physically came and all Israel was considered to be present in them (cf. Josh. 24.1, 2; 2 Kgs 23.1; Isa. 24.23). Perhaps the sequence 'the elders of the people...all the people' in Exod. 19.7-8 is then to be understood in the same way; that is, the response of the 'people' is conveyed through the representative voice of their elders. Thus, whatever conclusions we reach about the precise makeup of the group in Exod. 24.1, their function in the text seems to be a representative one. Will this group, perhaps, overcome the fears of the people, respond to the invitation and realize in some way the aspirations of Israel which were put on hold in ch. 19?

37. For the use of the numbers seven and seventy as inclusive round numbers, see Arvid S. Kapelrud, 'The Number Seven in Ugaritic Texts', *VT* 18 (1968), pp. 494-99; Nicholson, 'Antiquity', p. 78; Hilber, 'Theology of Worship', p. 180. The fact that there are 'seventy' elders here may strengthen the understanding that the number is representative of the totality of Israel. See further below for 'seventy' as the number of dinner guests in ancient sources. For elders generally see Hanoch Reviv, *The Elders in Ancient Israel: A Study of a Biblical Institution* (trans. Lucy Pitmann; Jerusalem: Magnes Press, 1989). Reviv regards the reference to elders here and in all pre-settlement traditions as a retrojection of a pan-national ideal (pp. 35-39).

38. See Nicholson, 'Interpretation', p. 83, for a discussion of its etymology and possible meaning 'noble'. If connected with the Hebrew verb אצל it might be a *qatil* form meaning 'designated one, set apart one' (cf. LXX τῶν ἐπιλέκτων τοῦ Ἰσραήλ and Vulgate *eos qui procul recesserant*).

39. Ruprecht, 'Exodus 24,9-11', p. 143.

b. *The Blood Rite as a Priestly Initiation: Exodus 24.3-8*

Nicholson draws attention to the problem created by the fact that the worship to which this representative group is summoned is to be 'from afar' (מרחק, v. 1) and they are not to 'come near' (יגשו, v. 2), whereas the apparent fulfilment of the summons in vv. 9-11 is one of the most intimate expressions of worship to be found in the Hebrew Bible. There are yet further degrees of intimacy in store for Moses in vv. 12-18 as he is summoned even higher, and consequently the other leaders might be thought of as somewhat 'distant' from God relative to Moses as they wait for his return. This observation cannot dispel, however, the remarkable reversal of expectations in vv. 9-11. We may observe a chiastic arrangement which draws attention to the reversal of the sequence of events from that of ch. 19, which is best represented diagrammatically:

A Expectation of nearness (19.1-19).
  B Unexpected warning to keep distance for fear of reprisal (19.20-25).
    C Revelation of the character expected of the people, their fear and plea for mediation (ch. 20).
  B′ Expectation of distance (24.1-2).
A′ Unexpected nearness without reprisal (24.9-11).

To what can we attribute this major turn of events? We look to vv. 3-8 for some clue. These verses introduce a further element of suspense into the narrative. In place of the anticipated ascent narrative, we find yet another scene change at 24.3. This suspense will not be resolved until v. 9.

The response of the people which had first been heard at 19.8, כל־אשר דבר יהוה נעשה, is echoed with minimal change at 24.3, כל־הדברים אשר דבר יהוה נעשה ('Everything Yhwh says, we will do'). These words then bracket the theophany and disclosure of the divine will for Israel contained in chs. 19–23. Moses then records in writing 'all the words of Yhwh' (v. 4). While this has sometimes been seen as confirmation that we are dealing with a close analogy with the suzerainty treaties with their documentary clause detailing the writing and preservation of the documents, and their stipulations imposed on and accepted by the vassal, we would be wise not to leap to conclusions, as numerous other legal and social arrangements were preserved in documentary form. While there has been a discernible compositional strategy in outlining the Covenant Code,[40] the narration at 24.3 has finally returned the reader to the point at which Israel willingly accepts the covenant.

40. For the relationship of the legal sections to the narratives, see Chirichigno, 'Narrative Structure'; Sprinkle, *'The Book of the Covenant'*, pp. 17-34.

Moses then rose early (seemingly a time favoured for important cultic events (Gen. 22.3; 28.18; Exod. 32.6; 34.4; Josh. 6.12; Judg. 21.4; 1 Sam. 1.19; 2 Chron. 29.20) and, now that instructions for building an altar have been given (20.24-26), built an altar at the foot of the mountain and set up twelve stone pillars representing the twelve tribes of Israel. Thereupon the 'young men of Israel' (נערי בני ישׂראל) offered up burnt offerings and sacrificed fellowship sacrifices to Yhwh (v. 5). The identity of these young men is a cause of much speculation. Are they to be identified with the 'priests' of 19.22, 24, or perhaps lower ranking cultic servants?[41] We simply do not know.

What we do know is something of the nature of the sacrifices they perform. They are עלת and זבחים שׁלמים, which are the very sacrifices identified at Exod. 20.24.[42] The rationale of the עלה or 'burnt offering' is described in the priestly legislation as being to render the worshipper (through the proxy of his sacrifice) 'acceptable to Yhwh', that is, 'to make atonement on his behalf' (Lev. 1.3-4). The verb כפר denotes the averting of anger (Gen. 32.21 [ET 32.20]; Prov. 16.14). The זבחים שׁלמים ('fellowship sacrifices') speak more positively of the resulting wholeness or well-being between the parties.[43] The שׁלמים are frequently associated with significant royal occasions, and specifically with the acknowledgment of kingship (e.g. 1 Sam. 10.8; 11.15; 13.9; 2 Sam. 6.17-18; 24.25; 1 Kgs 3.15; 8.63-64).[44] Taken together, these sacrifices have the characteristics of a rite for the removal of sin, that is, the movement from a state of unholiness to a state of holiness, the characteristic of God. They speak of reconciliation (atonement, Lev. 1.4), or the establishment of a communion with

41. Nicholson draws attention to a parallel in 1 Sam. 2.13-17 ('Covenant Ritual', p. 81).

42. These two passages are the first in the Pentateuch to bring these two sacrifices together. For the significance of this observation for the composition of Exodus, see Alexander, 'Composition', p. 6.

43. For discussions on the rituals and their rationale, see Gray, *Sacrifice*, pp. 1-95; Gordon J. Wenham, *The Book of Leviticus* (NICOT; Grand Rapids: Eerdmans, 1979), pp. 25-29; *idem*, 'The Theology of Old Testament Sacrifice', in Roger T. Beckwith and Martin J. Selman (eds.), *Sacrifice in the Bible* (Carlisle: Paternoster; Grand Rapids: Baker Book House, 1995), pp. 75-87; Philip P. Jenson, 'The Levitical Sacrificial System', pp. 25-40, in the same volume; Jacob Milgrom, *Leviticus 1–16: A New Translation with Introduction and Commentary* (AB, 3; New York: Doubleday, 1991), pp. 146-54;

44. Baruch A. Levine, *In the Presence of the Lord: A Study of Cult and Some Cultic Terms in Ancient Israel* (SJLA, 5; Leiden: E.J. Brill, 1974), pp. 29-32.

the deity, perhaps even a royal dignity, which would not otherwise be possible.[45]

There follows a blood manipulation rite in which Moses takes half of the blood and sprinkles it on the altar, while half is retained in bowls. The two aspects of the blood rite are then separated by the reading of the words of ספר הברית ('the covenant document', v. 7) before the people. Presumably, the intended referent is the document Moses is recorded as writing in v. 4. It makes little difference for our purposes whether by this is intended the Decalogue of 20.1-17 or the Covenant Code (20.23–23.33) or some other summary of the divine disposition towards Israel and the response appropriate to this. They are words which in some way spell out the nature of the commitment being undertaken in the ברית. The positioning of the reading of the document between the two halves of the blood rite is apparently designed to indicate the significance of the document as a hermeneutic for the rite.

The response of the people in v. 3 is then reiterated, this time strengthened by the addition of ונשמע ('and we will obey', v. 7). This is an explicit response to the conditional אם־שמוע תשמעו ('if you obey') of 19.5. The reader is thus prepared for whatever event is to be constitutive of the promised relationship. Now that the Israelites have solemnly undertaken to keep the covenant which they have had read to them, how will they understand that they have been constituted a 'royal priesthood and holy nation'?

There follows in the account an unparallelled event. The whole of the people of Israel are sprinkled with the remaining half of the blood which had been reserved after half had been applied to the altar. The declaration accompanying the sprinkling is: 'Behold the blood of the covenant (הברית) which Yhwh has made with you in accordance with all these words' (v. 8). Blood, containing life, belongs inherently to God, the giver of life, and is the appropriate medium therefore for use in consecration, or facilitating a symbolic transition from the side of unholiness and death to the side of holiness and life.[46] As we have been expecting some form of priestly inauguration of the whole congregation of Israel, it is difficult to

45. For a discussion of the nature of these sacrifices, see Hilber, 'Theology of Worship', pp. 181-83.

46. Note, for example, the closely analogous sacrifices and blood rites in the case of a diseased person needing to be declared restored to health (Lev. 14.1-20). See Hans Walter Wolff, *Anthropology of the Old Testament* (trans. Margaret Kohl; Philadelphia: Fortress Press, 1974), pp. 60-62.

escape the fact that the double application of blood to the altar (representing Yhwh)[47] and to the people constitutes such a rite. The people have in effect undergone something analogous to an 'ordination' to set them apart as belonging to Yhwh as his royal priesthood. Their life (blood) is bound up with his. As Nicholson rightly observes, there is no need to import (as does Kutsch)[48] the notion of a self-imprecatory rite by which Israel binds itself to fulfil certain obligations on the analogy of a rite in Aeschylus's *The Seven against Thebes*.[49] Such a view fails to account for the fact that it is clearly Yhwh who initiates or 'cuts' (כרת) the covenant (v. 8). How is this so, when he has not been a protagonist? The answer, according to Schenker, is to be found in understanding the cultic acts and their significance, rather than in a formal and purely semantic approach to the word ברית.[50] While it is Moses and the people of Israel who participate in the rite, their actions indicate that, far from taking on a set of burdensome obligations, they are responding willingly to an offer from God.

We can be even more specific than this, however, when we compare the rites of vv. 4-8 in the context of the structure of ch. 24 with an analogous event recorded in Leviticus 8.[51] We will leave until later a fuller discussion of the sign function of Israel's cult and priesthood. However, the ordination character of the rite of Exod. 24.4-8 is elucidated by a comparison with the sequence of events prescribed in Exodus 29 and executed in Leviticus 8. For the sake of clarity, the comparison will be based on the account of the fulfilment of the instructions. There is a ritual washing and donning of clothing (Lev. 8.6-9; cf. Exod. 19.10), sacrifices (Lev. 8.14-23; cf. Exod. 24.5), the application of blood to the altar (Lev. 8.15, 19, 24; cf. Exod. 24.6), the application of blood to the 'ordinands' (Lev. 8.23, 24, 30; cf. Exod. 24.8), followed by a meal before Yhwh (Lev. 8.31; cf. Exod. 24.11) and a period of time spent at the entrance to the tabernacle, that is, at the threshold of the replica of the heavenly sanctuary (Lev. 8.33, 35; cf. Exod. 24.10). There is the injunction ושׁמרתם את־משׁמרת יהוה ולא תמותו ('You are to keep Yhwh's charge, that you do not die', Lev. 8.35),

47. Driver, *Exodus*, p. 253; Noth, *Exodus*, p. 198.

48. Ernst Kutsch, 'Das sog. "Bundesblut" in Ex. xxiv 8 und Sach. ix 11', *VT* 23 (1973), pp. 25-30.

49. Nicholson, 'Covenant Ritual', pp. 79-80.

50. Adrian Schenker, OP, 'Les sacrifices d'alliance: Ex XXIV,3-8 dans leur portée narrative et religieuse: Contribution à l'étude de la *berît* dans l'Ancien Testament', *RB* 101 (1994), pp. 481-94 (485).

51. See Richard J. Sklba, 'The Redeemer of Israel', *CBQ* 34 (1972), pp. 1-18 (12); Milgrom, 'The Priestly Consecration'; Hilber, 'Theology of Worship'.

and the chapter concludes with the note that 'Aaron and his sons observed (ויעשׂ) all that Yhwh commanded through Moses' (Lev. 8.36; cf. Exod. 24.3, 7).

The Leviticus narrative continues in ch. 9 where Moses and Aaron and his sons and the elders of Israel (Lev. 9.1; cf. Exod. 24.1, 9) are again involved in a series of ritual acts which in many respects parallel those of ch. 8, acts which anticipate an appearance (נראה) of Yhwh to the whole congregation of Israel (Lev. 9.4). This appearance takes place after Moses and Aaron emerge from the tent of meeting and bless the people.[52] The effect of the appearance (וירא, niphal, vv. 6, 23) of the glory of Yhwh is that the people fall prostrate in joyful worship (Lev. 9.23-24; cf. Exod. 24.1).[53] Thus the people are beneficiaries of the priestly activity of Moses and Aaron. What is missing from Leviticus 9, however, is any indication that the people are all priests. There is no sprinkling of the people as the priests were sprinkled in ch. 8. However, on a reading of the Pentateuch which takes its compositional unity seriously, the people have already been sprinkled with blood in Exodus 24. It would therefore be both redundant and confusing to the reader to have them sprinkled again in Leviticus 9.

While there are of course some details unique to each account (the distinctive nature of the clothing in Lev. 8.7-9, the anointing, vv. 10-12, 30, and some details of the sacrifices), there are clear parallels with the overall sequence of events in the narrative of Exodus 19–24, and it seems that a deliberate typology is being established. What is declared to be ideally true for all Israel at one level is portrayed stylistically in Aaron and his sons at another level and linked through the mention of the same representative personnel (Exod. 24.1, 9; Lev. 9.1). It is difficult to avoid the conclusion that the sacrifices at the base of the mountain are the rites by which Israel is consecrated to be a 'royal priesthood' to Yhwh.[54]

52. Hossfeld has a valuable discussion of the analogy between the *Sinaitheophanie* (Exod. 19.1–24.11) and the *Kultgesetzgebung* (Exod. 24.12–Lev. 9.25) in which the culmination is the appearance of the glory of Yhwh to the whole people (Lev. 9.23-25), corresponding to the experience of the leaders on the mountain (Exod. 24.9-11): see Frank-Lothar Hossfeld, *Der Dekalog: Seine späten Fassungen, die originale Komposition und seine Vorstufen* (OBO, 45; Göttingen: Vandenhoeck & Ruprecht, 1982), pp. 203-204.

53. The verb והשׁתחויתם in Exod. 24.1 may have the meaning 'fall prostrate', or may indicate worship more generally.

54. Nicholson shares this conclusion, though with little elaboration. He understands this to mean Israel's 'status among the nations' ('Covenant Ritual', pp. 83-84).

We thus have an answer to the question posed above, as to why in the chiastic arrangement of the themes of distance and nearness, there is a reversal between Exod. 24.2 and 9. The answer appears to lie in the new sanctity which marks Israel as belonging to God, making the nation fit, through its representatives, to approach God without fear.

c. *Access to the Heavenly Court: Exodus 24.9-11*

If my understanding of the blood rite as a priestly initiation is correct, we might then expect the immediately following verses in Exodus 24 to signify what the newly confirmed status of priesthood would entail for all Israel. In accordance with the paradigm of the Aaronic ordination rite, we might expect a meal and access into the sanctuary presence of Yhwh, which is indeed what happens in vv. 9-11. It thus appears that the 'interruption' of vv. 3-8, as well as explaining the chiastic paradox, provides a framework for interpreting the nature of the ascent and encounter with Yhwh. Without vv. 3-8, the nature of the vision and meal would not be as clear. It would in any event be inconceivable to have drawn near to Yhwh, an inherently priestly prerogative, particularly for the degree of intimacy which is to follow, had there been no such sacrifice and consecration.

Hilber stresses the importance of the presence of God to an understanding of the covenant: 'God's presence is the benefit of the covenant (with all that his presence means for the worshipers' protection and subsistence). It is the glorious presence of YHWH that invokes the response of his people.'[55]

Worship (v. 1) has been the anticipated goal of the exodus, and is the appropriate response to the offer of covenant at Sinai, thus linking the two major elements of the book of Exodus which von Rad and Noth regard as independent traditions.[56] True worship can only meaningfully take place in the presence of the object of one's worship.

The climax of the section is then reached in vv. 9-11. With these verses we have a return to the *dramatis personae* of v. 1. It is these seventy or so persons who ascend the mountain. At the outset of this discussion on vv. 9-11 it is to be noted that here alone in these chapters of Exodus, God appears but is silent. There is no word of divine declaration which might aid our understanding of the event. Nicholson notes this silence, simply to

55. Hilber, 'Theology of Worship', p. 184.

56. Von Rad, 'The Form Critical Problem'; Noth, *Pentateuchal Traditions*, p. 59. For a critique of these views, see Weiser, *Introduction*, pp. 83-89; Beyerlin, *Origins*, pp. xv-xvii, 167-70.

draw the contrast with the theophany of ch. 19, an indication for him that 24.9-11 is an independent theophany tradition.[57] But this silence may be eloquent. The reader may be expected to infer the significance of the encounter from the totality of the cotext. The leaders ascend as the representatives of the whole people, a people who have now been consecrated as priests of Yhwh. The access the leaders gain is as the representatives of the priestly nation. All Israel is to be seen as participating in their experience.

Why then does not all Israel ascend the mountain? Would this not have made the point about the priestly status of all Israel more clearly? Apart from the obvious logistical difficulties inherent in such a scenario, the narrative effect of such an encounter may not have been as powerful as the one we have. What is designed to be a unique and privileged meeting may have come across as weakened in its effect. There is within the Hebrew Bible a great reticence about speaking glibly about access to the heavenly court, an experience sparingly granted to selected representatives and mediators. Certainly any large-scale visionary encounter other than that which is stylistically represented in cultic contexts (e.g. Lev. 9.23, where what Israel encounters is the 'glory of Yhwh') would be unlikely.

What, then, was the nature of the experience of this group? The interest in vv. 9-11 has sometimes centred on the meal of v. 11.[58] However, the activity of eating and drinking seems to be more by way of *dénouement* than climax. The feature given most prominence in the text (though still tantalizingly brief) is the *visio Dei*, the divine vision granted to Israel's representatives and its favourable outcome. Nicholson, who also notes this emphasis,[59] objects to the use of the term 'vision', with reference to the experience of the elders.[60] It is difficult, however, to contemplate what, for an Israelite, a non-visionary 'seeing' of God would mean. When El appears to mortals in the Ugaritic texts it is by means of a visionary or dream experience.[61] To emphasize the centrality of the vision, two words for seeing are used—ויראו (v. 10) and ויחזו (v. 11)—words which bracket a brief description of the scene in somewhat guarded terms, with a note as to the response of God to this act of seeing. It is possible that ויראו (v. 10) is to be understood in the sense of 'experience, consider, reflect, become

57. Nicholson, 'Interpretation', p. 96.

58. So, e.g., Vriezen, 'Exegesis', p. 114; Beyerlin, *Origins*, p. 33.

59. Nicholson, 'Interpretation', pp. 85-86.

60. Nicholson, 'Origin', pp. 158-59.

61. E.g. *Keret* (14) i, 35-37; (14) iii, 150-51; (14) vi, 296-97.

acquainted with' more generally, rather than as visual perception more specifically.[62] The translators of the LXX certainly had a problem with the boldness of the language at this point, paraphrasing the Hebrew text with καὶ εἶδον τὸν τόπον οὗ εἱστήκει ἐκεῖ ὁ θεὸς τοῦ Ισραηλ ('and they saw the place where the God of Israel stood', v. 10). The verb חזה ('behold', v. 11) is used of prophetic visionary experience (Num. 24.4, 16; Isa. 1.1; Amos 1.1; Mic. 1.1). It may also be used in the sense of 'gaze adoringly' (Song 7.1 [ET 6.13]). The LXX, again wishing to tone down the anthropomorphic language, renders ויחזו את־האלהים ('and they saw God') as καὶ ὤφθησαν ἐν τῷ τόπῳ τοῦ θεοῦ, ('and they were seen in the place of God', v. 11).[63] Another suggestion has been advanced by D. Or that the verb חזה here means 'to conclude a pact', by analogy with the noun forms חזה and חזות found in Isa. 28.15, 18 (each of which is parallel with ברית).[64] However, we should not seek to minimize the graphic element in order to accommodate a modern distaste for a degree of anthropomorphic language in the description of deity. The account here is restrained in comparison with that of Ezekiel 1, for example, though Ezekiel qualifies his language with such cautionary words as דמות ('likeness').[65] There may be a specific priestly flavour to the notion of seeing God in this passage in that the title 'He who Beholds the Great One' (later changed to 'The Greatest of Those Who Behold' appears to have been used for the Egyptian high priest of Re at Heliopolis.[66] An Egyptian priest says, 'It is the king who

62. Maimonides, *Guide* 1.4 (I, p. 26). These meanings are permissible though infrequent nuances of ראה. See BDB, pp. 906-909; KB, pp. 861-64.

63. Cf. Symmachus: καὶ εἶδον ὁράματι τὸν θεὸν Ἰσραήλ (v. 10), and *Targum Onqelos* וחזו ית יקר אלהא דישׂראל ותחות כרסא יקרא ('they saw the glory of the God of Israel and under his glorious throne…', v. 10), and ולרברבי בני ישׂראל לא הוה נזקא וחזו ית יקרא דיי והוו חדן בקרבניהון דאתקבלו כאלו אכלין ושתן ('and the great men among the children of Israel did not suffer loss, they saw the glory of Yhwh and rejoiced in the offerings that had been accepted, as if they ate and drank', v. 11). These readings, sensitive as they are to the unprecedented language, indirectly confirm the MT. The Samaritan text has ויאחזו ('and they took', i.e. partook of food) rather than ויחזו at 24.11, but this reading seems to be another form of avoidance of the anthropomorphic possibilities of the text.

64. Daniel Or, '"And they Behold God" (Exodus 24:11)', *Beth Mikra* 101 (1985), pp. 257-58 (Hebrew).

65. For other depictions of God's mountain-top/celestial throne-room in the Hebrew Bible, see Isa. 6; 14.13-14; Ezek. 28.13-15.

66. J. Bergman, Helmer Ringgren and W. Dommershausen, 'כהן', in *TDOT*, VII, p. 61.

sends me to look upon the deity'.[67] The fact that it is 'the God of Israel' (rather than 'Yhwh') whom the Israelite leaders see may point to the representative role of these men as standing in the place of Israel in the presence of God. The expression אלהי ישׂראל is surprisingly uncommon in the Pentateuch. The only previous reference to God by this designation in Exodus was at 5.1 where 'the God of Israel' says, 'Let my people (עמי) go, so that they may hold a festival to me in the desert'. The elders, then, are the עמי at this point in the celebrations.

An encounter with God at close quarters, particularly the act of 'seeing' God, while much to be desired (cf. Job 19.26; Mt. 5.8), could be expected to have dire consequences. The tension between the goal of nearness to God and the fear of death associated with this nearness has been stressed in the narrative to this point (19.12-13, 21-22; 20.19) and is a commonplace in the thought of the Hebrew Bible (Gen. 32.31 [ET 31.30]; Exod. 33.20; Judg. 6.22-23; 13.22; Isa. 6.5). Where then does this visionary encounter with God take place? We are clearly intended to regard this as an audience with God in his heavenly palace. The pavement under God's feet is made of ספיר ('lapis lazuli', rather than 'sapphire', v. 10), the semi-precious stone employed in ample quantities in ancient temples and palaces.[68] The use of the word טהר ('clarity, purity') is rich in cultic and ethical associations.[69] Here, the notion of clarity is explicitly brought into comparison with השׁמים ('the sky, heaven', cf. Job 37.21) which was by all ancients understood as a solid blue dome, not so far from the earth that it was inconceivable to approach it via the highest mountains.[70] For the

67. *The Ritual of Amon* 4.2, 5-6 (cited in Bergman, Ringgren and Dommershausen, 'כהן', p. 62).

68. For the associations of lapis lazuli with temples and particularly the cosmic temple see Beyerlin, *Origins*, pp. 31-32; Cassuto, *Exodus*, p. 314; Hyatt, *Exodus*, p. 257; Nicholson, 'Interpretation', p. 92; Ruprecht, 'Exodus 24,9-11', pp. 146-49; Peter Welten, 'Die Vernichtung des Todes und die Königsherrschaft Gottes: Eine traditionsgeschichtliche Studie zur Jes 25,6-8; 24,21-23 und Ex 24,9-11', *TZ* 38 (1982), pp. 129-46 (137-42); Dozeman, *God on the Mountain*, p. 113. Perhaps most notably, lapis lazuli is the medium used for conveying the pattern of the temple which Gudea of Lagaš is instructed to build: *Gudea Cylinder* A.6, line 4; see Thureau-Dangin, *Die sumerischen und akkadischen Königsinschriften*, pp. 94-95.

69. Wilfried Paschen, *Rein und Unrein* (SANT, 24; Munich: Kösel-Verlag, 1970), pp. 19-20; E. Maass, 'טהר', in *TLOT*, II, pp. 482-86. For the association of the root *ṭhr* with lapis lazuli at Ugarit, see *The Palace of Baal* (4), v 8; Gordon, *Ugaritic Textbook*, Glossary §1032, p. 406.

70. Paul H. Seely, 'The Firmament and the Water Above. I. The Meaning of *raqia'* in Gen 1.6-8', *WTJ* 53 (1991), pp. 227-40.

gods to live on the heights of the sacred mountain and in heaven are simply complementary ways of picturing the same truth. The gods are normally inaccessible to mortals. Yhwh is here pictured as having his rightful abode above this dome, since it constitutes the pavement under his feet.

It is highly likely, then, that we are intended, with *Targum Onqelos*, to understand this as a glimpse of the heavenly palace or temple, with its divine throne room, which will shortly form the basis of the model or pattern for the earthly tabernacle (Exod. 25.9).[71] Much is made of the throne vision in later Jewish literature. In these later visions, the heavenly throne is surrounded by angelic attendants, with just the occasional mortal granted the privilege of a heavenly journey (e.g. *1 En.* 71; *2 En.* 20; *T. Levi* 8; *Apocalypse of Zephaniah*; *Apocalypse of Abraham*; *Martyrdom of Isaiah*).[72] Here, however, there are no heavenly denizens. Rather it is the representatives of Israel who alone occupy the position of the heavenly courtiers or invited guests in God's palace. We might then compare this scene with the eschatological scene of Isaiah 24–27, where the triumphant God reigns in glory before his elders (זקניו, Isa. 24.23), prepares a feast for all nations on his holy mountain (25.6) and overcomes death (25.8).[73] On the strength of the connection with Isaiah 24–25, Uffenheimer even compares the event the elders experience to a 'coronation meal'.[74] The elders at Isa. 24.23 are members of the heavenly court, and may be compared with the phrase 'elders of the house of (a king)' (2 Sam. 12.17; cf. Gen. 24.2; 50.7), that is, the senior officials in the king's service, those with access to the king (vv. 16-23) and those who eat in the king's presence (vv. 17, 20).[75] (For other references to heavenly elders, see *2 Enoch* 4 and Rev. 4.4, 10; 5.5; 7.11.) The fact that in Exod. 24.11 the elders are the

71. Nicholson objects to seeing any allusion to a throne or to Yhwh as king at this point ('Origin', p. 156).

72. John J. Collins, 'The Jewish Apocalypses', *Semeia* 14 (1979), pp. 21-59; Martha Himmelfarb, 'Apocalyptic Ascent and the Heavenly Temple', in Kent Harold Richards (ed.), *Society of Biblical Literature 1987 Seminar Papers* (SBLSP, 26; Atlanta, GA: Scholars Press, 1987), pp. 210-17.

73. For the association of the meal of Exod. 24.11 with that of Isa. 25.6, see Welten, 'Die Vernichtung'.

74. Benjamin Uffenheimer, 'From Prophetic to Apocalyptic Eschatology', in Henning Graf Reventlow (ed.), *Eschatology in the Bible and in Jewish and Christian Tradition* (JSOTSup, 243; Sheffield: Sheffield Academic Press, 1997), pp. 200-17 (208).

75. See Timothy M. Willis, 'Yahweh's Elders (Isa 24,23): Senior Officials of the Divine Court', *ZAW* NS 103 (1991), pp. 375-85.

'elders of Israel' need not preclude them also being in some sense elders of the household of the heavenly king.

The tension which has built up in the narrative over what might happen in the event of a close encounter with the deity is then resolved. The vision of God does not result in any dreadful occurrence. It is clear from the fact that God 'did not raise his hand against these leaders' (v. 11) that they are not unwelcome intruders but are treated as truly belonging in that environment. Israel's representatives are welcome guests in God's presence. They have been granted free access to his throne room, just as priestly attendants on earth would alone enjoy access to the tabernacle replica of that throne room.

Comparison has been made between the seeing of God here and the prophetic call narratives where a vision of God in his throne room is a feature.[76] Such visions as are recounted in Isa. 6.1-11 and 1 Kgs 22.19-22 serve to authenticate the mission of the prophet. However, there is no hint in the cotext of Exodus 24 of a divinely mandated prophetic mission for the elders, or the people of Israel they represent. It would seem preferable to find a closer analogy in those passages where to 'see' royalty speaks of the privilege of access to and relationship with the king.[77] Though it is potentially dangerous to 'see the king' (Est. 4.11) and the king may deny access to his presence to those out of favour (Exod. 10.28), it is the privilege of those who attend the king and his invited guests to 'see' him (Jer. 52.25; Est. 1.14).

Moreover, the representatives of Israel join in a meal in the presence of God. We read simply that ויאכלו וישׁתו ('they ate and drank', v. 11), without further explanation as to the significance of this meal. While there is no justification in emending וישׁתו to וישׁתחו ('they worshipped') to echo v. 1,[78] the eating and drinking is clearly no ordinary meal,[79] but must, together with the 'seeing', be an expression of the nature of the relationship being granted by way of divine favour.

76. See Ska, 'Le repas', pp. 312-14; Habel, 'Form and Significance'; Klaus Baltzer, *Die Biographie der Propheten* (Neukirchen–Vluyn: Neukirchener Verlag, 1975), pp. 20-23.

77. Ska, 'Le repas', p. 316.

78. Beer, *Exodus*, p. 126.

79. *Contra* Harold Bloom, 'Exodus: From J to K, or the Uncanniness of the Yahwist', in David Rosenberg (ed.), *Congregation: Contemporary Writers Read the Jewish Bible* (San Diego: Harcourt Brace Jovanovich, 1987), pp. 9-26 (24), for whom it is simply a 'picnic'.

Regarded by most as an ancient tradition, the meal has been variously interpreted. Prominent among these is the understanding of the meal as a covenant ratification meal.[80] For some, the meal was linked with the establishment of an Israelite amphictyony after the Greek model of a confederacy of city-states around a common shrine, such as the one at Delphi.[81] It is beyond the scope of this work to interact with the amphictyonic theory as an historical model of Israel's origins.[82] Suffice it simply to point out that there is no hint here of an inter-tribal 'covenant'. Similarly any attempt to equate the meal of Exod. 24.11 with a Midianite–Israelite alliance, and to read the event narrated in Exodus 24 as a variant of the sacrificial meal of Exod. 18.12, when Jethro, Moses' father-in-law, ate a ceremonial meal with Aaron and all the elders of Israel 'in the presence of God', cannot be sustained. There God is witness to an alliance between two human parties. In Exodus 24, he is the host. This covenant is between God and Israel, and is one where God demonstrates his favour.

Those for whom any notion of covenant was late in making its appearance in Israel's thinking, and yet who believe this to be an early tradition, will of course see no covenantal associations to the meal.[83] It is simply a communal sacrifice or an act of worship, preserving a parallel cultic tradition to the one in vv. 3-8. Nicholson, for whom the reference to 'ate and drank' is too brief to refer to a covenant closure, at first regarded the phrase as simply equivalent to 'rejoiced' or 'worshipped' (citing Deut. 12.7; 14.26; 27.7; 1 Chron. 29.22; Exod. 18.12).[84] The relevance of the perceived difficulty regarding the brevity of the reference (as though a reference to a 'covenant meal' must conform to a particular word-length criterion) would be diminished on a reading of the text in relation to the preceding verses. Nicholson later revised his understanding of 'ate and drank' and in the

80. Among those who see here a covenant meal are Galling, *Erwählungstraditionen*, pp. 26-27; Newman, *The People of the Covenant*, p. 37; Noth, *Exodus*, p. 196; Beyerlin, *Origins*, p. 33; Vriezen, 'Exegesis', pp. 111-12; Childs, *Exodus*, p. 502; Rudolf Smend, 'Essen und Trinken: Ein Stück Weltlichkeit des Alten Testaments', in Donner, Hanhart and Smend (eds.), *Beiträge zur alttestamentlichen Theologie*, pp. 446-59 (456-57); McCarthy, *Treaty and Covenant*, pp. 264-66.

81. Mendenhall, *Law and Covenant*; Beyerlin, *Origins*, pp. 33-35.

82. For a critique of the amphictyony view see Vriezen, 'Exegesis', p. 115; Nicholson, 'Origin', pp. 150-51.

83. Welten, 'Die Vernichtung', pp. 137-42. For Perlitt it is a *Freudenmahl*, a celebratory meal, unrelated to any notion of covenant (*Bundestheologie*, pp. 181-90); cf. Dozeman, *God on the Mountain*, pp. 113-16.

84. Nicholson, 'Interpretation', pp. 93-94.

light of such parallels as 1 Kgs 4.20 and Eccl. 5.16 paraphrased it simply as 'they lived'.[85] Some of these are not necessarily mutually exclusive interpretative categories. However, our interpretation of this phrase should seek to be consistent with the thematic content of its cotext.

There are analogies, in varying degrees, with other meals—familial, royal and divine—of which we read in Hebrew and other ancient literature, which may to some degree fill out our understanding. A meal as a common social event speaks in the first instance of family solidarity and has frequently been used to symbolize the admission of those who are not natural members of a family or clan unit to such intimacy. In fact, given the plethora of covenant-types, the nearest we might come to a definition which best fits most is an understanding whereby non-kin are regarded and treated as though they are kin.[86] Hahn, who sees kinship as the common motif underlying all covenant types, sees in the meal of Exodus 24 the evidence that the Sinai covenant is primarily a celebration of the father–son relationship between Yhwh and Israel.[87]

Meals are then used in a range of human situations to mark or seal the establishing or reaffirmation of friendship or a bond. We see something of the role meals may play in the dynamics of human relationships in such passages as Gen. 26.26-31, where Isaac and Abimelech ratify a friendship pact with a meal, and again in Gen. 31.44-54, where Jacob and Laban sacrifice and share a meal, again as an indication of an amicable arrangement.[88] Viberg, who has made a study of symbolic actions in legal contexts, sees the symbolism of the meal as transparent: 'To share the fellowship at the table of someone's family would have been tantamount to being accepted into that fellowship... It was a clear way of displaying the mutual acceptance and agreement between the parties.'[89]

85. Nicholson, 'Origin', pp. 148-50.

86. Dennis J. McCarthy, SJ, 'Notes on the Love of God in Deuteronomy and the Father–Son Relationship between Yahweh and Israel', *CBQ* 27 (1965), pp. 144-47; Sklba, 'The Redeemer of Israel', p. 11; Gowan, *Theology in Exodus*, pp. 175-76.

87. Scott Walker Hahn, *Kinship by Covenant: A Biblical Theological Study of Covenant Types and Texts in the Old and New Testaments* (Marquette University PhD Thesis; Ann Arbor, MI: UMI Dissertation Services, 1995), pp. 41-53.

88. McCarthy discusses the social setting of these meals and their relationship with the meal in Exod. 24: Dennis J. McCarthy, SJ, 'Three Covenants in Genesis', *CBQ* 26 (1964), pp. 179-89. Nicholson rejects the comparison ('Interpretation', pp. 85-86).

89. Åke Viberg, *Symbols of Law: A Contextual Analysis of Legal Symbolic Acts in the Old Testament* (ConBOT, 34; Stockholm: Almqvist & Wiksell, 1992), p. 75.

Meals are not a common feature of international treaty texts, though we do have examples, such as the meal at the conclusion of the treaty between the kings of Amurru and Qadesh.[90] Such meals associated with treaties are more common in nomadic societies.[91] There is a Hittite text in which an individual householder makes a covenant with a god by means of sacrifice, the manipulation of blood, and a communal meal as in Exodus 24.[92] The householder, Zarpiya, makes a covenant with the god Sanda (who is associated by his logogram with Marduk) and the 'Violent Gods'. The purpose of this covenant seems simply to keep these undesirable gods at bay. It is instructive that following the slaughter of a sacrificial goat, its blood is smeared on a drinking tube from which Zarpiya drinks. He offers part of the goat to the gods, the raw liver and the heart, from which he then eats. The rest of the goat is cooked, which the householder and those associated with him then eat. While this text can usefully be compared (as Gurney observes) with the sequence of events in Exod. 24.1-11, and may support the coherence of that passage, the parallels should not be pressed too far. The nature and function of the covenant are of course very different.

The account of the Gibeonite ruse in Josh. 9.11-14, sometimes adduced as a parallel of a meal associated with a treaty, hardly fits.[93] The Israelites merely sample the food to verify its alleged age. Similarly the meal which David prepares for Abner and his men in 2 Sam. 3.20 occurs prior to any agreement, and may simply be regarded as a softening-up gesture. Both of these texts will serve, on the other hand, to illustrate the representative role that a few prominent men may have.

Are we perhaps to compare the scene in Exod. 24.11 with those accounts where guests ate 'before the king' or similar expressions (2 Sam. 11.13; 2 Kgs 25.29 [= Jer. 52.33]; Est. 1.3)?[94] Vriezen draws a distinction between this idiom and the expression 'to eat at the table of the king' (cf. 1 Sam. 20.29; 2 Sam. 9.7; 1 Kgs 2.7; 18.19; cf. Neh. 5.17), seeing the former expression as more appropriate for those invited to official occasions, while

90. EA 162, lines 22-23: J.A. Knudtzon, *Die El-Amarna-Tafeln mit Einleitung und Erläuterungen* (2 vols.; Leipzig: J.C. Hinrichs, 1915), I, pp. 654-55; Vriezen, 'Exegesis', p. 112.

91. Nicholson, 'Origin', p. 153; Ska, 'Le repas', p. 306; McCarthy, *Treaty and Covenant*, p. 254.

92. See O.R. Gurney, *Some Aspects of Hittite Religion* (Schweich Lectures, 1976; Oxford: Oxford University Press, 1977), pp. 29-30.

93. Vriezen, 'Exegesis', p. 112.

94. See Ska, 'Le repas', pp. 317-19.

the latter he sees as restricted to the inner family circle.[95] This distinction seems to be too artificial, and in any case does not help us in Exodus 24, where no adverbial phrase modifies the 'eating and drinking'. Perhaps for our purposes we may note in the passages referred to above, as is to be expected, the prominence of royalty and royal officials among those who dine with the king, whether on an occasional or a regular basis. Perhaps too, Ska has a point in noting that 'to eat at the table of the king' is virtually equivalent to 'to be part of the royal family' (2 Sam. 9.7-13).[96]

We do also have texts where a god is the host at a banquet. Both El and Baal in the Ugaritic texts fill this role of divine host. In one such text, Baal invites the seventy children of Asherah to a meal in his house (temple), just as there are seventy elders in Exod. 24.9-11.[97] There is a significant contrast, however, between the divine banquets in the mythological texts and the meal of Exod. 24.11. In Exodus, the guests invited to enter the divine abode are the people of Israel, filling the role occupied in the mythological texts by the other gods.

Vriezen's suggestion that the passage about the provision of manna in Numbers 11 is dependent on Exod. 24.11 has merit. There does seem to be an intertextual relationship. Note particularly the 'seventy elders' who appear again at Num. 11.16 in connection with this other divinely provided meal, in which all Israel, not simply its representatives, does participate. The manna tradition is sometimes elsewhere portrayed in terms of a divine banquet as in Pss. 78.19 and 23.5.[98]

The observations of Perlitt, Nicholson and others regarding the association of eating and drinking with rejoicing, worship and living in the presence of God, whether or not these are overtly linked with the idea of 'covenant' are no doubt all concomitant aspects of the meal.[99] Nor would

95. Vriezen, 'Exegesis', p. 113.

96. Ska, 'Le repas', pp. 317-18.

97. For divine banquets see Clifford, *The Cosmic Mountain*, p. 112. For the Ugaritic text, see *The Palace of Baal* (4) vi, 44-59. Similarly, an Egyptian text records that at a sacrificial meal in honour of the god Month, there were seventy invited guests: Vriezen, 'Exegesis', p. 107.

98. For the exodus background to Ps. 23, see David Noel Freedman, 'The Twenty-third Psalm', in *idem*, *Pottery, Poetry and Prophecy: Studies in Early Hebrew Poetry* (Winona Lake, IN: Eisenbrauns, 1980), pp. 275-302; Michael L. Barré, SS, and John S. Kselman, SS, 'New Exodus, Covenant, and Restoration in Psalm 23', in Meyers and O'Connor (eds.), *The Word of the Lord Shall Go Forth*, pp. 97-127 (98, 104).

99. For the association of eating and drinking with joyous celebration, cf. such passages as Deut. 12.7; 14.26; 27.7; 1 Chron. 29.22.

it be at all inconsistent with our understanding to see a close connection with the banquet scene in Isa. 25.6 where Yhwh of hosts prepares a victory feast of the finest foods for all peoples on his sacred mountain. What in Exodus 24 is a visionary event of Israel's past becomes for Isaiah a hope for an ideal future where the divine blessings will flow even beyond the limits of the people of Israel.

Little is to be gained by insisting that the meal of Exod. 24.11 in and of itself be taken as constituting the definitive act of formal ratification of a covenant. In its literary setting, however, we cannot escape the observation that the meal follows close behind the references to 'covenant' (vv. 7, 8) and more generally brings to a certain climax the whole section (from ch. 19) which has had this relationship with Yhwh as its undergirding theme. While the word ברית may be lacking in the text right at this point, this fact of course is not determinative,[100] as it is entirely lacking from 2 Samuel 7 as well, yet it is clear from such passages as Psalms 89 and 132 that the ברית or covenant of grant to David forms the substance of this chapter. Nicholson acknowledges that at a redactional level at least, the meal does function as a closure to a covenant pericope.[101] Some of the difficulty has been with some ill-founded assumptions about the nature of a covenant, and we must be wary of assuming that we have here something closely analogous to a suzerainty treaty (which is popularly regarded as the only viable covenant paradigm for the Sinai covenant). We must allow the text to speak for itself as to the nature of the 'covenant' with which this meal is associated, at least in the final form of the text.

In line with the understanding presented here of the entire Sinai event as a recognition and affirmation of Israel's royal-priestly character, and hence favoured access to the presence of God, the meal may be regarded as a further demonstration of the substance of the declaration already made regarding Israel. That is, whatever else the meal may suggest, it is above all a clear indication of the unconstrained access enjoyed by Israel to the domain of God as his royal attendants, or priests. The representatives of the royal company of priests, having been consecrated by the rites of vv. 3-8, take their favoured places in the presence of God himself at the divine banquet table and consummate their fearless enjoyment of him by eating at the king's table, that is, by becoming part of the royal family.

100. As Barr reminds us (*Semantics*), a concept, such as 'covenant', is not so bound to a particular word that the idea cannot be expressed without that particular word; cf. also his 'Some Semantic Notes'.

101. Nicholson, 'Covenant Ritual', p. 85.

A further observation by Polak has merit. Polak sees the 'meal' which Moses makes the Israelites eat from the pulverized 'calf' image in Exod. 32.20 as a parody of this meal. If intimacy and communion with God are central to the meal imagery, as suggested here, then the account of Exodus 32, which in many ways acts a foil to the theophany of Exodus 19–24, carries that intimacy to the point of absurdity.[102]

It seems rather beside the point to wonder whether the meal can really be an extension of the sacrifice or to point out that the participants on the heights of the mountain are a much smaller number than the participants at its base. The literary device of enfolding the one account within the other seems designed to link, at a literary level, the activity and the participants of vv. 3-8 with those of vv. 1-2 and 9-11. As an aspect of the tension between the fitness and the lack of fitness for access to Yhwh which we have identified as a theme of the complex, all the people cannot participate in person in the *visio Dei*, nor in the intimate encounter of the meal. However, the seventy elders stand in for the whole people in this divine encounter. The two events are complementary climaxes of the revelation of God, the one modelled on the pattern of a priestly ordination, the other on the model of a divine banquet in honour of his distinguished guests.

Perhaps there is even a veiled polemic against cruder notions of feeding the deity, which in some representations of Egyptian, Hittite, Mesopotamian and Canaanite religion was the responsibility of the priest. The priest (or king) gained access to the sanctuary for the purpose of feeding the god.[103] By way of marked contrast, the God of Exod. 24.11 needs no feeding. Rather, he himself feeds his worshippers.

Finally we note the somewhat parallel account to Exod. 24.1-11 appearing in Deut. 27.1-8. The Deuteronomic instructions for a covenant renewal ceremony to take place on Mt Gerizim and Mt Ebal contain the same essential elements as are found in Exodus 24: the recording of the divine stipulations, this time in a more permanent form suited to the location in the land (Deut. 27.2-4, 8), the construction of an altar and the performance

102. Frank Polak, 'Theophany and Mediator: The Unfolding of a Theme in the Book of Exodus', in Vervenne (ed.), *Studies in the Book of Exodus*, pp. 113-47 (139); cf. on the general nature of the calf episode in relation to the presence theme, Dale Ralph Davis, 'Rebellion, Presence and Covenant: A Study in Exodus 32–34', *WTJ* 44 (1982), pp. 71-87.

103. Othmar Keel, *The Symbolism of the Biblical World: Ancient Near Eastern Iconography and the Book of Psalms* (trans. Timothy J. Hallett; London: SPCK, 1978), p. 279.

of the same 'burnt offerings' and 'fellowship sacrifices' (vv. 5-7), and the enjoyment by the whole community of a meal 'in the presence of Yhwh your God' (v. 7). This instruction (we have a record of its enactment in Josh. 24) appears to echo the covenant ratification account of Exod. 24.1-11 and to add weight to its compositional integrity. In Deuteronomy, the setting down of these celebratory events is bracketed by a summons to 'obey' Yhwh (v. 1), and by the declaration, 'Then Moses and the Levite priests said to all Israel, "Be silent and listen, Israel! Today you have become the people of Yhwh your God"' (Deut. 27.9).[104]

5. *Conclusion*

To sum up this discussion of the cotext of Exod. 19.4-6, it is to be observed that there are features in the text of the book of Exodus, particularly the account of the burning bush, the plagues, and the expectations of a significant event of worship to take place at Mt Sinai, which lead us to anticipate an encounter between Yhwh and Israel which is priestly in character, one in which Israel is placed in a highly favoured position before God. This is borne out by the priestly preparations for the encounter, and by the subsequent privilege granted to Israel of a manifestation of God in a powerful and momentous event on the mountain. The clearest indications are in Exod. 24.1-11, where, contrary to most interpreters, we have observed a significant measure of coherence in the final form of the text.

There are some unexpected turns of event, notably the episode of the sacrifices and the rites involving blood at the foot of the mountain, which impede the expected ascent. On reflection, these events are seen as a necessary antecedent to the climax on the mountain and a valuable interpretative guide. Both the events at the foot of the mountain and those on its heights serve to explicate the nature of the covenant and represent its constitutive event. The blood rites, while *sui generis* in terms of their application to all Israel, find their closest analogy in the consecration of the Aaronic priesthood (Lev. 8). They may be understood as a form of 'ordination' of the nation Israel to the office and privileged status in relation to God promised at Exod. 19.6. The meal and the 'seeing' of God enjoyed by Israel's representatives are capable of a number of valid interpretations. A unified reading of Exodus suggests that this meal and the life-preserving access to the presence of God are to be seen as the consummation of royal-priestly intimacy in the court of the divine king. Without their connection

104. Alexander, 'Composition', p. 8.

with the sacrificial rites, the vision and meal would constitute an incomprehensible reversal of the expectations which have applied since the account of the Israelites' dread and their call for mediation. We are not forced to make a choice between an understanding of Exod. 24.1-11 as reflecting either a covenant ceremony, or a collective priestly ordination. Our understanding of the Sinai covenant is that it may be seen as a covenant of grant of royal-priestly status and prerogative.[105] Exodus 24.1-11 has depicted the constitutive covenant event as a complex episode consisting of a priestly ordination rite in which all Israelites participate directly, and a divine vision and banquet in the heavenly sanctuary, in which they again participate, but through the representation of their delegated leaders.

We ought not to imagine that all of the tensions in the text have been resolved by the above analysis. Exodus 19–24 remains among the most complex and mystifying of all biblical texts. Any depiction of relationship between deity and humanity must necessarily strain the limits of language, and any neat packaging of that relationship into formulas may do as much or more to obscure than to enlighten. The tension between God's hiddenness and his self-revelation remains, as does the tension between the objective of freedom of access and the need for mediation. Rather than having recourse, as has so often been the case, to source- or tradition-critical solutions (which are no solution with respect to the final form of the text), we would do better to be content with the dramatic tension of the text itself. Bloom aptly comments with respect to one aspect of this tension: 'That this uncanny festivity contradicts Yahweh's earlier warnings is not J's confusion, or something produced by his redactors, but is a dramatic confusion that J's Yahweh had to manifest if his blessing was to be extended from elite individuals to an entire people'.[106] There has been a dynamic movement, however, a 'rite of passage' of the entire congregation of Israel to a heightened awareness of who they are before the God who calls them 'my people'. While there is a level of symbolism operating in the language of Exodus 19–24, dealing as it does with events beyond the realm of normal human experience, it is a symbolism of a different order and operating under different rules from those which normally apply to the operation of Israel's sanctuary cult. The events of Exodus 19–24 seem to serve as a paradigm for that cult, or to put it another way, the sanctuary cult models what it means for Israel to be a royal priesthood. This will be the subject of the following chapter.

105. See Chapter 7 for the development of this understanding.

106. Bloom, 'Exodus: From J to K', p. 24.

Chapter 6

Modelling the Royal Priesthood: The Cultic Model of Exodus 24.12 to 40.38

1. *The Link between Exodus 19.6 and Exodus 25–40*

Fundamental to this thesis is the notion that the general portrayal of the Israelite priests by the biblical writers is relevant as background to a fuller understanding of the image of Israel as a 'royal priesthood' in Exod. 19.6. This affirmation is borne out by close observation of the macro-structure of the Sinai account. From Exod. 25.1 the movement of the narrative comes to a virtual standstill as an elaborate set of cultic regulations is given to Moses by God (25.1–31.18). In fact with very little narrative material interposed, the legislative material, much of it cultic in nature, continues until Lev. 27.34.

The relationship between the cultic material and the Sinai narrative proper is made clear by a transitional bridge (Exod. 24.12-18). Following the account of the vision and meal on Mt Sinai (24.1-11), Moses, accompanied in part by Joshua, ascends yet further up the slopes of the mountain and enters the cloud which represents the glory of God.[1] 'The glory of Yhwh settled on Mt Sinai. For six days the cloud covered the mountain, and on the seventh day Yhwh called to Moses from within the cloud' (Exod. 24.16).

It is easy for the reader to lose sight of the fact that the cultic provisions which ensue are, according to the compositional framework of the book of Exodus, very much a part of the ascending movements which begin in ch. 19 and which are prefaced by the designation of Israel as a 'royal priesthood' (19.6). They are in fact the pinnacle of that series of staged ascents.[2] At first glance, the instructions which commence at Exod. 25.2

1. For the notion of 'glory' in connection with the divine theophany, see Eichrodt, *Theology*, II, pp. 29-35.

2. J.H. McCrory, '"Up, Up, Up and Up": Exodus 24.9-18 as the Narrative Context for the Tabernacle Instructions of Exodus 25–31', in David J. Lull (ed.), *Society for*

might seem to be a sudden anticlimax—a movement away from the transcendent experience of the theophany to a mundane level, as God instructs Moses to have the Israelites bring offerings of everything from gold to goat's hair (25.2-7). The purpose of these offerings is explained, however: 'Then have them make a sanctuary for me, and I will dwell among them. Make this tabernacle and all its furnishings exactly like the model (תבנית) I will show you' (Exod. 25.8-9).

The importance of following the heavenly model or blueprint is stressed again at v. 40 (cf. also 26.30; 27.8; Num. 8.4; Ezek. 40.4; Wis. 9.8; Heb. 8.5). In 1 Chron. 28.11-12 the word תבנית is used of the plans David gave Solomon for the construction of the temple. Such divinely revealed patterns are a feature of ancient Near Eastern texts relating to the building of temples. The god Ningirsu, for example, shows Gudea of Lagaš in a vision a lapis lazuli tablet with the plan of the Eninnu temple which he is instructed to build for the god Enlil.[3] The model shown to Moses, then, is to serve as the basis for the construction of a stylized sanctuary. The issue being addressed is the significant one of how the unique and fleeting encounter at Sinai can in some sense be perpetuated. How can Israel continue to be assured of its special status before God and of his abiding presence with them? The apprehension about proceeding on their journey to the Promised Land without the accompanying divine presence is illustrated by the dialogue between God and Moses in Exod. 33.12-16. The answer is to take the form of a miniaturized and portable reproduction of God's heavenly sanctuary of which Israel has caught a glimpse at Exod. 24.9-11. The link between the tabernacle and the Sinai theophany account is made clear with the reference to the cloud which settles on and fills the tabernacle (Exod. 40.34-35). The tabernacle instructions and the account of its construction and setting up is thus bound to the earlier section of the Sinai pericope by an *inclusio* with the reference to the cloud which engulfs Moses on the mountain (Exod. 24.15-18).

Biblical Literature 1990 Seminar Papers (SBLSP, 29; Atlanta, GA: Scholars Press, 1990), pp. 570-82.

3. *Gudea Cylinder* A.5.12–6.4; see Thureau-Dangin (ed.), *Die sumerischen und akkadischen Königsinschriften*, pp. 94-95. For the ideology of royal sanctuary construction, see Henri Frankfort, *Kingship and the Gods: A Study of Ancient Near Eastern Religion as the Integration of Society and Nature* (Chicago: University of Chicago Press, 1948), pp. 255-57; Arvid S. Kapelrud, 'Temple Building: A Task for Gods and Kings', *Or* NS 32 (1963), pp. 56-62; Victor Hurowitz, *I Have Built you an Exalted House: Temple Building in the Bible in the Light of Mesopotamian and Northwest Semitic Writings* (JSOTSup, 115; Sheffield: Sheffield Academic Press, 1992).

2. *The Concept of Graded Holiness in Israel's Cult*

While our ultimate interest in this chapter will be on the cultic personnel, the priests, we cannot consider their role in isolation from the whole cultic system within which they operate. Priest and tabernacle are inseparable (Exod. 29.42-44). There are a number of comprehensive treatments of the Israelite cult, and it is not proposed to go over much of the ground covered in these works.[4] My concern will be to outline the fundamental conception of the cult, and to illustrate this with a few instances. Central to an understanding of the cult is the notion of sanctity or holiness as being the characteristic or realm associated with God, and the accompanying concept of gradation, or a series of concentric (or contiguous) areas of ascending orders of holiness. Cultic activity (such as washing, sacrificing, or merely waiting) consists largely in understanding the circumstances and giving effect to the means whereby transition may take place from one level of holiness to the next, the one nearer to God.[5]

While this gradation operates in ways other than spatial (such as temporal), it is perhaps more easily demonstrated in spatial terms. In the broadest sense, all Israel is, or is called upon to be holy (Lev. 19.2; 20.7, 8, 26). Visually this wider level of holiness may be discerned in the representation of Israel's wilderness camp (Num. 1.52–2.31), where the tabernacle is situated in the middle, and the tribes are arranged symmetrically around it. As one moves to the centre of the camp, one moves to higher levels of holiness where the tribe of Levi and the priests have their quarters. At the centre of this camp, the tabernacle or house of Yhwh is pitched.[6] This tabernacle area, in common with Canaanite and other sanctuaries, has three levels of holiness: the outer court, or 'entrance to the tent of meeting'

4. Menahem Haran, 'The Complex of Ritual Acts Performed inside the Tabernacle', *SH* 8 (1961), pp. 272-302; *idem*, 'The Priestly Image of the Tabernacle', *HUCA* 36 (1965), pp. 191-226; *idem*, *Temples and Temple Service*; de Vaux, *Ancient Israel*, II; Kraus, *Worship in Israel*; Rowley, *Worship in Ancient Israel*; Christopher J. Davey, 'Temples of the Levant and the Buildings of Solomon', *TB* 31 (1980), pp. 107-46.

5. Jenson, *Graded Holiness*; Nelson, *Raising Up a Faithful Priest*, pp. 17-38.

6. The tabernacle has often been considered a retrojection of the later temple back into a pre-monarchic era. This view has come under increasing scrutiny in the light of parallel tent shrines in the ancient world: see Frank Moore Cross, Jr, 'The Priestly Tabernacle: A Study from an Archaeological and Historical Approach', *BA* 10 (1947), pp. 45-68; Richard J. Clifford, 'The Tent of El and the Israelite Tent of Meeting', *CBQ* 33 (1971), pp. 221-27 (226); Joseph Blenkinsopp, 'The Structure of P', *CBQ* 38 (1976), pp. 275-92 (286).

(Exod. 29.4; 33.10), the holy place, the sphere of the daily priestly ministrations, and, beyond a dividing curtain, the most holy place (Exod. 26.33) in which the chest containing the tablets of the law is placed.[7] In the temple of Solomon it appears that these inner levels were stepped up from the surrounding courts, thus making the symbolism of ascent to the realm of God more obvious.[8] While there have been various counts of the total number of gradations in the system at different times, the overall ideology is sufficiently clear, with the *desideratum* being to move inwards and hence closer to God, while recognizing that there are obstacles and dangers inherent in such a movement.[9]

3. *Sanctuary Ideology in the Ancient Near East*

There are numerous points of correspondence between elements of the cult as described in Exodus and Leviticus, and the cultic buildings and practices of other peoples of the ancient Near East. Earlier studies drew mainly on pre-Islamic Arab or even classical Greek and Roman parallels, while more recent studies have had available a significantly more extensive basis for comparison in the literatures and epigraphic material of Egypt, Mesopotamia, Anatolia, Syria and Canaan.[10] Perhaps most pertinent in some

7. William Foxwell Albright, *Archeology and the Religion of Israel* (Baltimore: The Johns Hopkins University Press, 3rd edn, 1953), pp. 142-55.

8. André Parrot, *The Temple of Jerusalem* (trans. B.E. Hooke; Studies in Biblical Archaeology, 5; New York: Philosophical Library, 2nd edn, 1955), p. 33.

9. The standard Israelite or Canaanite sanctuary has three levels. *Kelim* 1.6 counts ten levels of holiness in the land: Herbert Danby, *The Mishnah, Translated from the Hebrew with Introduction and Brief Explanatory Notes* (London: Oxford University Press, 1933), p. 605. The *Temple Scroll* identifies eleven: Johann Maier, *The Temple Scroll: An Introduction, Translation and Commentary* (trans. Richard T. White; JSOTSup, 34; Sheffield: JSOT Press, 1985), pp. 5-6. See also Baruch M. Bokser, 'Approaching Sacred Space', *HTR* 78 (1985), pp. 279-99; Nelson, *Raising Up a Faithful Priest*, pp. 17-38, 83.

10. Julian Morgenstern, 'The Ark, the Ephod, and the "Tent of Meeting"', *HUCA* 17 (1942–43), pp. 153-266; W. Robertson Smith, *Lectures on the Religion of the Semites: The Fundamental Institutions* (London: A. & C. Black, 3rd edn, 1927); Albright, *Archeology and the Religion of Israel*; James, *Nature and Function*; Nelson, 'The Egyptian Temple', pp. 147-57; A. Leo Oppenheim, 'The Mesopotamian Temple', in Freedman and Wright (eds.), *The Biblical Archeologist Reader*, pp. 158-69, and G. Ernest Wright, 'The Temple in Palestine–Syria', pp. 169-84 of the same volume; H.W.F. Saggs, *The Greatness that Was Babylon: A Sketch of the Ancient Civilization of the Tigris–Euphrates Valley* (London: Sidgwick & Jackson, 1962), pp. 299-358;

respects, because closest in language and culture to the biblical texts, are the epic texts from Ras Shamra (Ugarit, fourteenth century BCE). In the Ugaritic texts, for example, we have references to the tent dwellings of the high god El and other gods of the pantheon. The tent of El, at least, appears to be situated at the top of a mountain. No permanent temple structure to El has been identified at Ras Shamra.[11] A common feature of ancient Near Eastern sanctuary ideology is the notion that a temple was an earthly replica of the heavenly abode of the god, or an idealized cosmos of heaven and earth, providing a point of contact for mortals with the realm of the gods. So, for example, the temple of Baal at Ras Shamra replicated the design of the mythical one on Mt Zaphon, known from the literary texts, including the detail of the window in the roof.[12] In Egyptian temples we find such features as a blue ceiling, with painted stars, an earthen floor, and marsh plants depicted on the walls in what 'becomes a microcosm of the universe'.[13] Expressions such as *'ꜣwy pt* ('doors of heaven') and *pt n kmt* ('Egypt's heaven') are a clear indication of how Egyptian shrines were conceived.[14] In Sumerian temple ideology it is the temple which serves as

B.G. Trigger *et al.*, *Ancient Egypt: A Social History* (Cambridge: Cambridge University Press, 1983); Samuel Noah Kramer, 'The Temple in Sumerian Literature', in Fox (ed.), *Temple in Society*, pp. 1-16; Wolfram von Soden, *The Ancient Orient: An Introduction to the Study of the Ancient Near East* (trans. Donald G. Schley; Grand Rapids: Eerdmans, 1994).

11. For the dwellings of El and the gods, see the Ugaritic texts *Baal and Yam* (2) iii, 4-6; *The Palace of Baal* (3) v, 13-17; (4) iv, 20-24; *Baal and Mot* (6) i, 32-36; *Keret* (15) iii, 18-19; *Aqhat* (17) v, 32-33; (17) vi, 46-49; (19), 212-13; and the fragmentary text [1] iii, 21-24 (Gibson, *Canaanite Myths*, p. 130). The text (15) iii, 18-19 uses two words for tent (*'hl* and *mškn*) which correspond to the two Hebrew words commonly used for the wilderness tabernacle of Yhwh, while a number of others (e.g. [4] iv, 24) use the word *qrš* which is related to the Hebrew קרשׁים (Exod. 26.15), used for the solid framing of the portable structure. See also Cross, 'The Priestly Tabernacle', pp. 45-68; Cassuto, *Exodus*, pp. 323-24; Clifford, 'The Tent of El', pp. 221-27; *idem*, *Cosmic Mountain*; John M. Lundquist, 'What Is a Temple? A Preliminary Typology', in Herbert B. Huffmon, F.A. Spina and A.R.W. Green (eds.), *The Quest for the Kingdom of God: Studies in Honor of George E. Mendenhall* (Winona Lake, IN: Eisenbrauns, 1983), pp. 205-19; E. Theodore Mullen, Jr, *The Divine Council in Canaanite and Early Hebrew Literature* (HSM, 24; Chico, CA: Scholars Press, 1980), pp. 168-75.

12. Clifford, 'The Tent of El', p. 225.

13. Clifford, *Cosmic Mountain*, p. 27; cf. Frank Moore Cross, Jr, and David Noel Freedman, 'The Song of Miriam', *JNES* 14 (1955), pp. 237-50.

14. Tryggve N.D. Mettinger, 'YHWH Sabaoth—the Heavenly King on the Cherubim Throne', in Tomoo Ishida (ed.), *Studies in the Period of David and*

the foundation of the universe, and the meeting point between heaven and earth.[15] A set of inscriptions by Tukulti-Ninurta, king of Assyria, describes his rebuilding of the temple of Ištar:

> I rebuilt Eme, 'Temple of Cultic Rubrics', her joyful dwelling, the shrine, her voluptuous dais, (and) the awesome sanctuary; I made them (lit. 'which were') more outstanding than before and made (the temple) as beautiful as a heavenly dwelling. I completed (it) from top to bottom and deposited my monumental inscriptions.[16]

Temples recreated the world with its three layers of heaven, earth and sea, hence to gain access to the innermost room, where the statue of the god stood, was like gaining access to heaven itself.[17]

One motif common throughout the ancient Near East is that the construction of a temple is a royal responsibility, undertaken at the behest of the gods, and is in continuity with their work of creation (cf. Ps. 78.69).[18] Following the overthrow of the forces of chaos, construction of a temple guarantees order to the cosmos. While a king may have the personal desire to build a temple for his god, or feel the expectations inherent in his office, the convention is that it is the prerogative of the gods to instruct kings to build and maintain temples for them, as Gudea was instructed in the text cited in the previous chapter (p. 127 n. 68).

Solomon and Other Essays: Papers Read at the International Symposium for Biblical Studies, Tokyo, 5-7 December, 1979 (Winona Lake, IN: Eisenbrauns, 1982), pp. 109-38 (121); cf. Jean Daniélou, 'La symbolique cosmique du temple de Jérusalem', in *Symbolisme cosmique et monuments religieux*. I. *Texte* (Paris: Editions des musées nationaux, 1953), pp. 61-64; Keel, *Symbolism*, p. 172.

15. G.W. Ahlström, 'Heaven on Earth—at Hazor and Arad', in Birger A. Pearson (ed.), *Religious Syncretism in Antiquity: Essays in Conversation with Geo Widengren* (AAR/Institute of Religious Studies, University of California. Series on Formative Contemporary Thinkers, 1; Missoula, MT: Scholars Press, 1975), pp. 67-83 (68).

16. A. Kirk Grayson, *Assyrian Rulers of the Third and Second Millennia* BC *(to 1115* BC*)* (The Royal Inscriptions of Mesopotamia—Assyrian Periods, 1; Toronto: University of Toronto Press, 1987), p. 254.

17. Blenkinsopp, 'The Structure of P', p. 286; *idem*, *Sage, Priest, Prophet: Religious and Intellectual Leadership in Ancient Israel* (Louisville, KY: Westminster/John Knox Press, 1995), p. 113; cf. Josephus, *Ant*. 3.123, 180.

18. See *Enuma Elish*, tablet 6 (*ANET*, pp. 68-69); Frankfort, *Kingship and the Gods*, pp. 267-74; Theodore M. Ludwig, 'The Traditions of the Establishing of the Earth in Deutero-Isaiah', *JBL* 92 (1973), pp. 345-57; Keel, *Symbolism*, p. 175; Kapelrud, 'Temple Building'; Helmut Utzschneider, *Das Heiligtum und das Gesetz: Studien zur Bedeutung der sinaitischen Heiligtumstexte (Ex 25–40; Lev 8–9)* (OBO, 77; Göttingen: Vandenhoeck & Ruprecht, 1988).

Within Israel, this same expectation is played out in the accounts of the commissioning and construction of the Jerusalem temple (2 Sam. 7.1-7; 1 Kgs 5.19 [ET 5.5]; 1 Chron. 28.10-12). Who, then, is the royal builder of the desert sanctuary of Yhwh? It might be assumed that Moses occupies the role of king to some extent in the accounts. However, a closer reading reveals that this is not so. Rather surprisingly, the emphasis is on the corporate role of Israel in this activity. Rather than being provided for out of the resources of a king, and hence designed to enhance his standing among the people, the materials for the construction of the tabernacle are all the voluntary contributions of the populace. Some prominence is given to this generosity of the people, and mention made of the fact that the supply of resources went beyond what was needed (Exod. 25.2-7; 35.4-29; 36.1-7). The initial commands of God to construct the tabernacle are cast in the third person plural, ועשׂו ('they are to make', Exod. 25.8), and second person plural forms, תעשׂו ('you are to make', Exod. 25.9). Some of the subsequent commands are addressed to Moses in the second person singular, and of course as coordinator, he has a major role. The framework has already been set, however, by the corporate references, and Moses functions not as king but as a member of the community of Israel. The conclusion seems inescapable that it is the people of Israel who corporately occupy the position normally occupied by the king in the paradigm of sanctuary construction.

4. *The Creational Associations of Israel's Tabernacle Cult*

What evidence is there that the Israelite shrines were based on such cosmic symbolism as suggested above? Our evidence is primarily the relevant texts of the Hebrew Bible, together with some later Second Temple Jewish sources. To this may perhaps be added the archaeological evidence from Israelite shrines, in particular the one at Arad, though again, caution is required, as material remains of themselves are inherently incapable of revealing a rationale (unless they were to contain inscriptions), though they invite comparison with the biblical texts and with Canaanite and other sanctuaries.[19]

There is no doubt that, in a later age, the sanctuary was interpreted as a cosmic symbol and such works as those of Philo and Josephus are valuable in suggesting understandings which, while perhaps speculative in part,

19. Yohanan Aharoni, 'Arad: Its Inscriptions and Temple', *BA* 31 (1968), pp. 1-32; Ahlström, 'Heaven on Earth'.

may well represent the general interpretative framework assumed within the biblical texts. Josephus writes:

> In fact, every one of these objects is intended to recall and represent the universe, as he will find it if he will but consent to examine them without prejudice, and with understanding. Thus, to take the tabernacle, thirty cubits long, by dividing this into three parts and giving up two of them to the priests, as a place approachable and open to all, Moses signifies the earth and the sea, since these too are accessible to all; but the third portion he reserved for God alone, because heaven also is inaccessible to men. (*Ant.* 3.180-81)[20]

Does such an interpretation reflect the intention of the biblical authors? Barker has no doubts that it does.[21] To some extent, her approach is a self-confessed over-reading of a later, more developed ideology back into the biblical texts, though there are good reasons to see the seeds of the developed sanctuary theology there in the Hebrew Bible itself.

The symbolism of the tabernacle has been a fruitful area for the more speculative and less controlled interpretations designed to serve the interests of religious piety.[22] There are nevertheless in the details of its design and contents clear indications of a cosmic symbolism, or to give it a cast more specific to Israelite thought, of a representation of an idyllic Eden or primal creation. This fact is acknowledged and has been developed (with different emphases) by numerous scholars.[23] We may note first the way in

20. Josephus, *Works* (LCL; 9 vols; London: Heinemann, 1956–65), IV, p. 403; cf. *Ant.* 3.123; *War* 5.212-13; Philo, *Vit. Mos.* 2.88, 117.

21. Margaret Barker, *The Gate of Heaven: The History and Symbolism of the Temple in Jerusalem* (London: SPCK, 1991), pp. 57-103.

22. One such is the monograph of Paul F. Kiene, *The Tabernacle of God in the Wilderness of Sinai* (trans. John S. Crandall; Grand Rapids: Zondervan, 1977).

23. See, e.g., Raphael Patai, *Man and Temple in Ancient Jewish Myth and Ritual* (London: Thomas Nelson, 1947); Cross, 'The Priestly Tabernacle'; Albright, *Archeology and the Religion of Israel*, pp. 147-55; Geo Widengren, 'Early Hebrew Myths and their Interpretation', in Hooke (ed.), *Myth, Ritual and Kingship*, pp. 49-203; Brevard S. Childs, *Myth and Reality in the Old Testament* (SBT, 27; London: SCM Press, 2nd edn, 1962); Ronald E. Clements, *God and Temple: The Presence of God in Israel's Worship* (Philadelphia: Fortress Press, 1965), pp. 64-68; Clifford, 'The Tent of El'; *idem*, *Cosmic Mountain*; Blenkinsopp, 'The Structure of P'; Michael Fishbane, *Text and Texture: Close Readings of Selected Biblical Texts* (New York: Schocken Books, 1979), pp. 12-13; Gordon J. Wenham, 'Sanctuary Symbolism in the Garden of Eden Story', in *Proceedings of the Ninth World Congress of Jewish Studies*. A. *The Period of the Bible* (Jerusalem: World Union of Jewish Studies, 1986), pp. 19-25; Margaret Barker, *The Older Testament: The Survival of Themes from the Ancient Royal Cult*

which the tabernacle account is structured. Kline draws attention to the parallel between the *fiat*–fulfilment structure of the tabernacle account and that of the creation narrative of Genesis 1.[24] Thus, with a combination of jussive (e.g. Exod. 25.2) and *weqatal* forms (e.g. Exod. 25.8), with the occasional imperative (e.g. Exod. 25.19), the divine *fiat* for the construction of the tabernacle echoes the *fiat* ('let there be...') of the creation narrative (e.g. Gen. 1.3). The principal *fiat* sections are Exodus 25–26 and 35.1-19, while the fulfilment sections, which repeat the substance of the divine *fiat* in narrative sequence (predominantly *wayyiqtol* forms, e.g. Exod. 35.21), are found at Exod. 35.20-29 and 36.8–38.31. Of course, such repetition is a not infrequent feature of Hebrew (and Ugaritic) epic style, and not too much weight can be attached to this factor in isolation.

A stronger point may be made of the use of the sabbatical structure, the six-days-plus-one cycle, which was used as the structuring device for the account of creation in Gen. 1.1–2.3. The pattern of six days plus a seventh forms an *inclusio* around the entire set of tabernacle instructions. The prelude to the tabernacle instructions is the account of Moses being taken up into the divine cloud on the mountain, where we read, 'For six days the cloud covered the mountain, and on the seventh day Yhwh called to Moses from within the cloud' (Exod. 24.16).

Further, just as the first section of the Genesis creation account concluded with the record of the divine rest (Gen. 2.2-3), so the whole *fiat* section of the tabernacle account (including the directives concerning the priesthood) concludes with a summons to its 'creators' to imitate the divine rest (Exod. 31.13-17). Batto remarks: 'There can be no doubt that the Priestly Writer intends this scene to parallel the opening scene in Genesis with six days of active creation and a seventh day in which God ceased his activity and "rested"'.[25] Kearney likewise draws attention to what he considers to be the framework of the P redactor, though in a somewhat more elaborate manner.[26] He detects in the wider framework of Exodus 25–40

in Sectarian Judaism and Early Christianity (London: SPCK, 1987), p. 25; Peter Weimar, 'Sinai und Schöpfung: Komposition und Theologie der priesterschriftlichen Sinaigeschichte', *RB* 95 (1988), pp. 337-85.

24. Meredith G. Kline, *Images of the Spirit* (Grand Rapids: Baker Book House, 1980), pp. 37-38; cf. Frank H. Gorman, Jr, *The Ideology of Ritual: Space, Time and Status in the Priestly Theology* (JSOTSup, 91; Sheffield: JSOT Press, 1990), pp. 39-45.

25. Bernard F. Batto, *Slaying the Dragon: Mythmaking in the Biblical Tradition* (Louisville, KY: Westminster/John Knox Press, 1992), p. 120.

26. Peter J. Kearney, 'Creation and Liturgy: The P Redaction of Exod. 25–40', *ZAW* NS 89 (1977), pp. 375-87; cf. Levenson, *Creation and the Persistence of Evil*, pp. 66-77.

a reflection of the thematic structure of creation (chs. 25–31), the fall (chs. 32–33) and the reconstruction (chs. 34–40). The seven separate divine speeches in the first section (commencing at 25.1; 30.11, 17, 22, 34; 31.1, 12) have a thematic correspondence in sequence to each of the seven creation days of Gen. 1.1–2.3. Not all of Kearney's parallels are equally convincing, though even the fact that there are seven speeches, of which the seventh is a summons to Sabbath rest is instructive. The sabbatical cycle of work and rest is also specifically enjoined on the people in connection with the work to be done in constructing the tabernacle (Exod. 35.2).

Then just as the divine spirit overshadowed the original creative enterprise (Gen. 1.2), so the mountain top is covered by the כבוד ('glory') of God (Exod. 24.16, 17).[27] This spirit endows gifted craftsmen (31.3; 35.31) for the creative work.[28]

It may be dangerous to extrapolate significance from the descriptions of the contents of the tabernacle, but there are some literary pointers to the function of these furnishings in depicting an ideal world, perhaps the prospect of a new beginning.[29] The lights in the heavens (Gen. 1.14-16) have their counterpart in the lampstand within the tabernacle (Exod. 25.6). In this case, it is the writer of Genesis 1 who seems deliberately to have chosen his word for 'lights' (מארה rather than אורים; cf. Ps. 136.7) in order to prepare the way for the coming tabernacle terminology.[30] The world, it seems, is a sanctuary on a cosmic scale.

The pomegranates which adorn the priestly vestments and later the temple (Exod. 28.33-34; 1 Kgs 7.18, 20, 42; 2 Kgs 25.17) are a symbol of fecundity (Song 4.13; 6.11; 7.12; 8.2), particularly the fertility of the Promised Land (Num. 13.23; 20.5; Deut. 8.8).[31] Similarly the palm trees, lotus flowers,[32] lions and bulls which decorate the panels or appurtenances

27. For the linking of רוח and כבוד see Ezek. 43.5; cf. Kline, *Images*, pp. 12-34.

28. Frequent comparison is made with the divine craftsmanship of the god Koshar wa-Khasis in the Ugaritic literary account of divine temple building, e.g. Clifford, 'The Tent of El', p. 226.

29. Cf. for the symbolism of the furnishings, Josephus, *Ant.* 3.180-87; Clifford, *Cosmic Mountain*, pp. 177-81; Blenkinsopp, 'The Structure of P', p. 286; *idem*, *Sage, Priest, Prophet*, p. 113.

30. In traditional source criticism, Gen. 1 is attributed to P, the same source (or redactional layer) as the tabernacle account.

31. For possible evidence of pomegranates in Ugaritic cultic furnishings, see Clifford, 'The Tent of El', p. 226.

32. See, for the identification of the flowers, J.F. Strange, 'The Idea of Afterlife in Ancient Israel: Some Remarks on the Iconography of Solomon's Temple', *PEQ* 117 (1985), pp. 35-40 (37-38).

of the Solomonic temple or the visionary temple of Ezekiel speak of a garden paradise (1 Kgs 6.29, 32, 35; 7.29, 36; Ezek. 40.16, 31, 34, 37; 41.18, 20, 25, 26). The gold and precious stones which lie under the ground in Genesis 2 reappear in the tabernacle and priestly adornments. It is to be noted that when one gem is singled out over the others (there are twelve different gems on the priestly breastpiece), it is the שֹׁהַם ('onyx'), the one gemstone also singled out for mention in the garden account in Gen. 2.12 (Exod. 25.7; 35.9, 27).

The כרובים ('cherubim'), sphinx-like creatures known also from Mesopotamia, are first encountered by the reader of the Pentateuch as the guardians of the Edenic sanctuary (Gen. 3.24).[33] These same beings also feature prominently in the tabernacle and temple designs (Exod. 25.18-20; 26.1; 1 Kgs 6.23, 29; Ezek. 10.14) and seem to encapsulate in one composite creature the diversity of life-forms in the world, while at the same time possibly avoiding the danger that any specific real creature so depicted in the sanctuary might become an object of worship. Cherubim are the only representational art forms found in the most holy place, where they are pictured as holding up the (normally unseen, except to the visionary eye) throne of God on their outstretched wings, and at times as providing the means of the throne's transportation (2 Sam. 6.2; Isa. 37.16; Ezek. 1.4-28; 10.1; 43.6-7; Pss. 80.2 [ET 80.1]; 99.1).

The completion of the work of constructing the tabernacle and its furnishings is marked by an inspection on the part of Moses who approves of the workmanship and imparts his blessing, in a close parallel with the action of God with reference to the original creation (Exod. 39.43; cf. Gen. 2.3). Finally, we note that the tabernacle is to be set up and dedicated on New Year's day, thus drawing attention to its role as marking a new beginning (Exod. 40.2; cf. Gen. 8.13).[34]

The tabernacle was a world where God could be conceived of as dwelling, as one of its names, מִשְׁכָּן (Exod. 25.9), implies, untrammelled by exposure to the defiled world of its surroundings. Yet the effect was at the same time to bring God near to Israel. The tabernacle was a meeting point between heaven and earth, hence another of its regular names, the אהל מועד ('tent of meeting', Exod. 27.21). The general understanding of the

33. Robert H. Pfeiffer, 'Cherubim', *JBL* 41 (1922), pp. 249-50; David Noel Freedman and M. O'Connor, 'כרוב', in *TDOT*, VII, pp. 307-19; Menahem Haran, 'The Ark and the Cherubim: Their Symbolic Significance in Biblical Ritual', *IEJ* 9 (1959), pp. 30-38, 89-94; Keel, *Symbolism*, pp. 167-71; Mettinger, 'YHWH Sabaoth'.

34. Blenkinsopp, 'The Structure of P', p. 283.

priestly theology is that it represents order and stability, or to put it a little more starkly, a static conception of the world, with no place for an 'eschatology'.[35] There is no scope in the present study to explore this notion, but it is suggested here that it is a notion which needs to be subjected to closer scrutiny. There may in fact be a future-oriented dimension built into the priestly ideology. The sabbatical cycle points to 'rest' or realization, and as Strange has shown, the visual symbolism of the sanctuary is capable of sustaining an interpretation which speaks of an afterlife.[36]

5. *The Priest as the Ideal Man in the Ideal World*

The picture is far from complete to this point. For while the ideology of the sanctuary is well enough understood, the implications of this for an understanding of the Levitical priesthood (and, on our view, by extension, the priesthood of Israel in Exod. 19.6) have not so often been considered. Much of the attention devoted to the priesthood over the past century or more has been concerned with reconstructing a history of its development, and with the attempt to unravel the struggles between rival priestly families or groups, and in particular the relationship between Aaronides and other Levites.[37] That discussion will not closely concern us here. What is

35. See Eichrodt, *Theology*, I, pp. 433-36; O. Plöger, *Theocracy and Eschatology* (trans. S. Rudman; Richmond, VA: John Knox Press, 1968), p. 32.

36. Strange, 'The Idea of Afterlife', pp. 35-40. Where I would differ with Strange is in placing less emphasis on the borrowing of basic ideas from Egypt, and in seeing the notion of an ideal world to which Israel may look forward as more deeply rooted in Israelite soil. For the more general notion that the Sinai pericope portrays things as they should be, see, for example, E. Theodore Mullen, Jr, *Ethnic Myths and Pentateuchal Foundations: A New Approach to the Formation of the Pentateuch* (SBLSS; Atlanta: Scholars Press, 1997), pp. 218-19.

37. Wellhausen, *Prolegomena*, pp. 121-55; Norman H. Snaith, 'The Priesthood and the Temple', in T.W. Manson (ed.), *A Companion to the Bible* (Edinburgh: T. & T. Clark, 1947), pp. 418-43; Francis Sparling North, 'Aaron's Rise in Prestige', *ZAW* NS 66 (1954), pp. 191-99; G. Ernest Wright, 'The Levites in Deuteronomy', *VT* 4 (1954), pp. 325-30; J.A. Emerton, 'Priests and Levites in Deuteronomy: An Examination of Dr G.E. Wright's Theory', *VT* 12 (1962), pp. 129-38; Elias Auerbach, 'Der Aufstieg der Priesterschaft zur Macht im Alten Israel', in *Congress Volume, Bonn 1962* (VTSup, 9; Leiden: E.J. Brill, 1963), pp. 236-49; de Vaux, *Ancient Israel*, II, p. 362; A.H.J. Gunneweg, *Leviten und Priester: Hauptlinien der Traditionsbildung und Geschichte des israelitisch–jüdischen Kultpersonals* (FRLANT, 89; Göttingen: Vandenhoeck & Ruprecht, 1965); Eichrodt, *Theology*, I, pp. 392-436; Fohrer, *History*, p. 163; Cross, *Canaanite Myth*, pp. 114-15; Raymond Abba, 'Priests and Levites

of interest is what is said in the texts concerning the priests, whatever their origin or party allegiance. What was the rationale for their existence as an office? What did they do? If the tabernacle had an overarching conceptual rationale along the lines sketched above, what role did the person of the priest play in that rationale? What impression was conveyed to the Israelite community as day by day they saw their priests, dressed in their finery, enter God's house to attend upon him and to enjoy his company in the surroundings of an ideal world?

a. *Israelite and Non-Israelite Priests*

First, the use by the biblical writers of the word כהן to denote non-Israelite cultic personnel (Gen. 41.45, 50; 46.20; 1 Sam. 5.5; 6.2; 2 Kgs 10.19; 11.18) indicates that they were conscious of the analogous status or role which such officials had for the devotees of those other religious cultures. This observation therefore invites us to set our discussion briefly within the wider context of what Israel knew, or can reasonably be expected to have known, of the rationale and practice of priesthood among its neighbours, just as the discussion above did with temple ideology generally.[38]

In the pre-monarchic settlement period and the early monarchy, Israel had its closest dealings with the Philistine cities. Of their priests, we learn in 1 Sam. 6.2 that their advice, together with that of the קסמים ('diviners'), was sought concerning what action it was best to take with regard to the Israelite sacred chest. In 1 Sam. 5.5 the priests of Dagon are singled out as one class of personnel who would customarily enter his temple at Ashdod, and in doing so would avoid stepping on the threshold.

In 2 Kgs 10.19 (cf. 2 Kgs 11.18; 2 Chron. 34.5) we read of priests of Baal who are among the 'attendants' or 'worshippers' of Baal whom Jehu summons by subterfuge in order to massacre them. Chemosh, Molech and the astral cults likewise have their priests (Jer. 48.7; 49.3; Zeph. 1.4). The

in Deuteronomy', *VT* 27 (1977), pp. 257-67; Haran, *Temples and Temple Service*, pp.58-111; Merlin D. Rehm, 'Levites and Priests', in *ABD*, IV, pp. 297-310; Nelson, *Raising Up a Faithful Priest*, pp. 1-15; Stephen L. Cook, 'Innerbiblical Interpretation in Ezekiel 44 and the History of Israel's Priesthood', *JBL* 114 (1995), pp. 193-208.

38. Meier sets the study of the Israelite priesthood against a comparative study of ancient Near Eastern priesthood and notes the 'highly privileged status' of first temple priests and Levites: Johann Maier, 'Self-Definition, Prestige, and Status of Priests Towards the End of the Second Temple Period', *BTB* 23 (1993), pp. 139-50 (139-40). See also Leopold Sabourin, SJ, *Priesthood: A Comparative Study* (Leiden: E.J. Brill, 1973).

word כמר occurs three times to denote a foreign priest (never an Israelite priest), once in association with כהן (2 Kgs 23.5; Hos. 10.5; Zeph. 1.4).

In Gen. 47.22-26 we catch a glimpse of the privileged life of the Egyptian priesthood as perceived by the Hebrews. Being on the payroll of the Pharaoh, their situation is singled out as the exception to the general distress of the population due to the famine. From Egyptian texts, we know that priests were known as 'servants' of the god, as was also the Pharaoh, and they acted as his deputies in the care of the god and the god's shrine. Priests underwent rituals of purification which included abstinence from sexual intercourse, lustration, shaving and being reclothed in fine linen. Among other things, they attended to the needs of the god by bathing, dressing and feeding the image which stood in the temple. As with the professions generally, those professions which involved a priestly component were hereditary, at least from the 19th Dynasty.[39]

In Mesopotamia, as in Egypt, there is no single word to correspond to the Hebrew כהן, but a considerable number of specialized religious functionaries exercised the roles of temple attendant, sacrificial expert, diviner and other priestly functions. At least some priestly positions were hereditary.[40]

The city of Ugarit maintained a sizable professional priestly class consisting of a *rb khnm* ('high priest') and twelve families of *khnm*, as well as *qdšm*,[41] singers and various craftsmen. The priest at Ugarit held a prominent position in society,[42] as he did in Phoenicia, the Punic colonies and Palmyra.[43]

39. On the Egyptian priesthood and cult generally see Nelson, 'The Egyptian Temple'; Haran, 'The Complex of Ritual Acts', pp. 293-94; de Vaux, *Ancient Israel*, II, p. 359; A. Rosalie David, *The Ancient Egyptians: Religious Beliefs and Practices* (London: Routledge & Kegan Paul, 1982), pp. 135-37; Keel, *Symbolism*, pp. 277-80.

40. Oppenheim, 'The Mesopotamian Temple'; Saggs, *The Greatness that Was Babylon*, pp. 345-51; de Vaux, *Ancient Israel*, II, p. 359; J. Renger, 'Untersuchungen zum Priestertum in der altbabylonischen Zeit', *Zeitschrift der Assyrologie* 58 (1966), pp. 110-88, and 59 (1969), pp. 104-239; Cody, *History*, pp. 23-25; Kramer, 'The Temple in Sumerian Literature'; W. von Soden, *The Ancient Orient*, pp. 194-97.

41. See Wolfram von Soden, 'Zur Stellung des "Geweihten" (*qdš*) in Ugarit', *UF* 2 (1970), pp. 329-30.

42. John Gray, *The Legacy of Canaan: The Ras Shamra Texts and their Relevance to the Old Testament* (VTSup, 5; Leiden: E.J. Brill, 2nd edn, 1965), pp. 209-17; Henshaw, *Female and Male*, pp. 68-69.

43. De Vaux, *Ancient Israel*, II, p. 359; Cody, *History*, pp. 18-23.

There were priestesses in Assyria, and Phoenicia, but, so far as our evidence goes, only males might serve as priests in Egypt, Ugarit and Israel.[44]

b. *Priesthood, Royalty and Nobility: The Social Status of Priests*

A common feature of much of the evidence regarding priesthood in the early period of these cultures is that the priesthood was originally and fundamentally the prerogative and responsibility of the king. In the Memphite theology of Egypt, the Pharaoh was divine—the incarnation of Horus and the earthly representation of Re, the Sun. At the same time, he was in principle the priest of every god. Temple scenes show him as the officiant, even in a prostrate position before the image of the god,[45] though for practical purposes, in historical times his duties were largely fulfilled by the professional priests on his behalf.[46]

The kings of Mesopotamia, though never truly considered divine (apart from a ceremonial representation of deity in some ritual events), were the principal point of contact between the divine and human spheres. The Sumerian *en* or ruler originally lived in the temple. Later, the priestly functions of the Assyrians and Babylonians devolved increasingly onto specialist classes of cultic officials, though Gadd would caution against minimizing the participation of the king in the cult even in later periods.[47]

The legends of *Aqhat* and *Keret* suggest that the priesthood at Ugarit was also inherently the prerogative of the king.[48] In historical times, the role of the king in the Ugaritic cult appears to have been minor, as the more routine religious responsibilities were fulfilled by the professional priestly class.

The Midianite priesthood, exemplified in the figure of Jethro (Exod. 2.16; 3.1; 4.18; 18.1-27), has been held out as a significant influence on Israelite religious belief and practice.[49] Rather than being 'a priest of

44. Saggs, *The Greatness that Was Babylon*, pp. 349-51; de Vaux, *Ancient Israel*, II, p. 383; David, *The Ancient Egyptians*, p. 135.

45. See Keel, *Symbolism*, p. 127.

46. Frankfort, *Kingship and the Gods*, pp. 15-212; James, *Nature and Function*, pp. 107-21; Ivan Engnell, *Studies in Divine Kingship in the Ancient Near East* (Oxford: Basil Blackwell, 1967), pp. 4-15.

47. C.J. Gadd, *Ideas of Divine Rule in the Ancient East* (London: Oxford University Press, 1948), pp. 33-62; cf. Frankfort, *Kingship and the Gods*, pp. 215-333; Saggs, *The Greatness that Was Babylon*, p. 345; Engnell, *Divine Kingship*, pp. 16-51; Henshaw, *Female and Male*, pp. 67-68.

48. E.g. *Keret* (14), 156-70; cf. Henshaw, *Female and Male*, pp. 68-69.

49. H.H. Rowley, *From Joseph to Joshua: Biblical Traditions in the Light of Archaeology* (Schweich Lectures of the British Academy, 1948; London: Oxford University Press, 1950), pp. 149-56; Vriezen, *Old Testament Theology*, p. 264; Roland

Midian' (Exod. 2.16 NIV), the construction (construct state followed by proper noun) requires that he be *the* priest of Midian, and he appears to enjoy something like the general authority, civil and religious, in his community that the Israelite patriarchs, as portrayed in Genesis, did in theirs. While there is no evidence to suggest that Israel was so devoid of its own religious heritage or so susceptible of influence by a desert encounter as to derive much of its theology and cultic practice from this episode, as has sometimes been held, the biblical characterization of the priest-king of Midian does add another facet to the broad portrayal of the status of priests in the world familiar to the Israelites.

The Israelite tradition regarding Melchizedek, the priest-king of the high god El Elyon of Salem (Gen. 14.18; Ps. 110.4) gives some indication of how Israel understood that the roles of מלך and כהן could be bound up in one figure and this Melchizedek serves in some sense as an exemplar for the Davidic kings.[50] The king embodied the people in their standing before the god. If in Israel the people were a priestly nation, then the king embodied that role, and though his cultic functions were circumscribed, he was nevertheless appropriately described as a 'priest'.[51] Speaking of the priestly nature of the Jerusalem kingship, Dumbrell writes, 'The person of the king embodies the expectations of Exodus 19.6 that Israel itself would become a priestly royalty'.[52] Through the occupant of the throne of Israel, Davidic kingship is to reflect the values that the Sinai covenant requires of the nation. So bound up were king and cult that to lack a king implied (in a pre-exilic Israelite context) the cessation of the cult (Hos. 3.4-5). In the world with which Israel was familiar, the temple was in part a royal shrine, and the priests within it were royal appointees and delegates, as became true in Israel (1 Kgs 2.27, 35; 4.2).

Another line of approach to determine the perception of priesthood in Israel might be to consider the contexts and tone of the references to priests, and in particular the parallel and associated terms with which the word כהן is linked in biblical texts. Priests are frequently listed together

de Vaux, OP, *The Early History of Israel to the Exodus and Covenant of Sinai* (trans. David Smith; London: Darton, Longman & Todd, 1978), pp. 330-38.

50. See Fred L. Horton, Jr, *The Melchizedek Tradition: A Critical Examination of the Sources to the Fifth Century A.D. and in the Epistle to the Hebrews* (London: Cambridge University Press, 1976), pp. 12-53; de Vaux, *Ancient Israel*, I, p. 114. The view of R. Tournay ('Le Psaume 110', *RB* 67 [1960], pp. 5-41 [38]) that Ps. 110 is addressed not to a Davidic king but a post-exilic high priest has received little support.

51. De Vaux, *Ancient Israel*, I, pp. 113-14.

52. Dumbrell, *The Search for Order*, p. 72.

with kings, princes, nobles and other persons of high social status (Jer. 1.18; 2.26; 4.9; 8.1; 13.13; 18.18; 32.32; 34.19; Mic. 3.11; Lam. 1.19; 2.6; 4.15; Neh. 2.16). As noted earlier, Haran stresses the aristocratic nature of priesthood. While the prophetic movement, with its literary and theological contribution, may take pride of place in the modern mind, whenever priests and prophets are mentioned together, it is regularly the priest who is listed first (e.g. 1 Kgs 1.32-38; Isa. 28.7; Jer. 4.9).[53] When Joshua, the civil and military leader is listed together with the high priest, it is always Eleazar the priest whose name is given first (Num. 34.17; Josh. 14.1; 17.4; 19.51; 21.1). In Job 12, as evidence of God's 'wisdom and power, counsel and understanding' (v. 13), we read among other things in v. 19, 'He leads priests (כהנים) away stripped and overthrows the establishment (אתנים)', where the word אתנים seems to refer to a body of eminent persons whose position in society (apart from God's intervention) appears to be permanent. Others in the list are counsellors, judges, kings, advisors, elders, nobles and the mighty (vv. 17-21). A similar association is to be observed in the case of the priests of Chemosh and Molech (Jer. 48.7; 49.3).

The incident of the Levite being engaged to serve as a priest in Micah's household (Judg. 17.7-13) is also instructive. Though young enough to be Micah's son (v. 11), the priest is dignified with the title 'father' (v. 10). The retention of a Levite priest within his household had great prestige value for a wealthy landholder like Micah.

Perhaps the most honorific of the expressions referring to the priests is the designation עבדי־יהוה ('servants of Yhwh', Pss. 134.1; 135.1). While not a title exclusive to priests (it is shared by prophets: 2 Kgs 9.7; Jer. 26.5), it is far from being a menial description. The expression 'servant of X' takes its significance not from the general meaning of the word 'servant' but from the status of the king or deity or other official named.[54] A designation with a similar meaning is the participial form of the piel of שׁרת used in what Haran calls a 'fossilized' way to refer to the priestly 'servants' of Yhwh (Jer. 33.21; Ezek. 45.4; Joel 1.9, 13; 2.17; Neh. 10.37

53. Haran, 'Temple and Community', p. 19.

54. Keret is *'bd 'il* in an honorific context where El makes a gracious commitment to the king: *Keret* (14), 153; cf. Isa. 41.8-9. A seal, probably belonging to a priest of the first half of the eighth century BCE, bears the inscription למקניו עבד יהוה: Frank Moore Cross, Jr, 'The Seal of Miqnêyaw, Servant of Yahweh', in Leonard Gorelick and Elizabeth Williams-Forte (eds.), *Ancient Seals and the Bible* (Monographic Journals of the Near East. Occasional Papers on the Near East, 2.1; Los Angeles: Undena Publications, 1983), pp. 55-63.

[ET 10.36]; 2 Chron 13.10).[55] With these passages may be compared Ps. 103.21, where מְשָׁרְתָיו is parallel to צְבָאָיו ('his [heavenly] host'), that is, the army of heavenly beings who attend upon God,[56] and Isa. 61.6, where the priesthood in view is corporate Israel (as in Exod. 19.6).

Finally, notice should be taken of the point to which Olyan draws attention, namely that much of the biblical material on priesthood, making use of the binary oppositions of holy/common, clean/unclean, Israelite/alien, serves the social function of privileging the Israelite priesthood. Priestly rights such as sanctuary access, the performance of sacrifice, the right to holy foods and the control of Urim and Thummim all serve to enhance the prestige of the priesthood in the eyes of the community.[57] The accounts of rival priestly claims to 'holiness', such as those of Korah (Num. 16) reinforce this perception that the priesthood is a privileged elite and that in part the notion of holiness serves a sociological function.

c. *The Levitical Priesthood: Qualifications for Participation*

For the writers of the Pentateuch and much of the rest of the Hebrew Bible, the preponderance of the usage of כֹּהֵן is to denote Aaron and his descendants (or at least those presented by the writers as his descendants),[58] members of the tribe of Levi, who were chosen by God and set apart to the priestly office within Israel. The *sine qua non* of priesthood is that the priest be chosen by God (1 Sam. 2.28). Priesthood, like royalty, is a matter of divine grant or choice (Num. 16.5, 7; 17.20; 18.7; Ps. 105.26; *Jub*. 30.18; *T. Levi* 5.2), and as the writer to the Hebrews remarks, 'No-one takes this honour upon himself' (Heb. 5.4). When Jeroboam appointed as priests of the high places 'all sorts of people, even though they were not Levites', this is the exception to prove the rule, as it is considered part of his 'evil way' (1 Kgs 12.31; 13.33). Thus priesthood and election are closely intertwined concepts.[59] Maier even claims: 'The general concept of the election

55. Haran, 'Temple and Community', p. 17.

56. See Mettinger, 'YHWH Sabaoth'.

57. Olyan, *Rites and Rank*, esp. pp. 27-37; Olyan then finds it difficult to correlate this with the designation of the whole people as holy in such texts as Exod. 19.6 and the Holiness Code (pp. 121-22), for which this work is suggesting a rationale.

58. It is sometimes assumed that the Aaronide genealogy of Zadok is fictitious and that he has a Jebusite ancestry. See, e.g., de Vaux, *Ancient Israel*, II, pp. 373-74. Some sections of the Hebrew Bible (e.g. 1 and 2 Samuel) are silent as to any necessary Aaronic ancestry of Israelite priests.

59. Preuss, *Old Testament Theology*, II, p. 52.

of Israel as a whole seems to have been derived from such older special concepts of election'.[60]

The texts describe Yhwh's choice of Levi, both as an individual (though this is given minimal attention within the Hebrew Bible),[61] and as the tribe from which priests may come. There is considerable discussion on whether this means that at one stage, or in the judgment of some groups, all males from the tribe of Levi were priests or potentially priests. The Deuteronomic references to הכהנים הלוים (Deut. 17.9, 18; 18.1; 24.8; 27.9) might suggest this, as proposed by Wellhausen[62] and supported among others by Kaufmann[63] and Emerton.[64] Others, such as Wright,[65] Abba[66] and Duke,[67] see a distinction between priests and other Levites even in Deuteronomy. The references in the rest of the Pentateuch clearly restrict the priesthood to the family of Aaron. Yet other texts only envisage priests from the line of Zadok, a priest in Jerusalem at the time of Solomon (2 Sam. 8.17; 1 Kgs 1.39; Ezek. 40.46). Subsidiary to this hereditary principle, it is also Yhwh's prerogative to lay down stringent physical requirements. If, as we shall see, the priest is to serve as a visual model of what ideal humanity is to look like, humankind in their original created dignity

60. Maier, 'Self-Definition', pp. 145-46. For Koch, it is one of several influences: Klaus Koch, 'Zur Geschichte der Erwählungsvorstellung in Israel', *ZAW* NS 67 (1955), pp. 205-26 (212-13).

61. See Deut. 33.8-13 and Mal. 2.4-7 and the discussion in the following chapter. Levi's priestly role is much expanded upon in *Aramaic Levi*, *Jub*. 30.1–32.9 and *T. Levi*; cf. André Caquot, 'La double investiture de Lévi (brèves remarques sur Testament de Lévi, VIII)', in C.J. Bleeker, S.G.F. Brandon and M. Simon (eds.), *Ex orbe religionum: Studia Geo Widengren* (Studies in the History of Religions, 21-22; 2 vols.; Leiden: E.J. Brill, 1972), I, pp. 156-61; James Kugel, 'Levi's Elevation to the Priesthood in Second Temple Writings', *HTR* 86 (1993), pp. 1-64; Robert A. Kugler, *From Patriarch to Priest: The Levi-Priestly Tradition from* Aramaic Levi *to* Testament of Levi (Atlanta: Scholars Press, 1996). The royal colouring of the description of Levi is particularly noted by Geo Widengren, 'Royal Ideology and the Testaments of the Twelve Patriarchs', in F.F. Bruce (ed.), *Promise and Fulfilment: Essays Presented to Professor S.H. Hooke in Celebration of his Ninetieth Birthday* (Edinburgh: T. & T. Clark, 1963), pp. 202-12; and Jonas C. Greenfield and Michael E. Stone, 'Remarks on the Aramaic Testament of Levi from the Geniza', *RB* 86 (1979), pp. 214-30.

62. Wellhausen, *Prolegomena*.

63. Kaufmann, *The Religion of Israel*, pp. 193-200.

64. Emerton, 'Priests and Levites'.

65. Wright, 'The Levites in Deuteronomy'.

66. Abba, 'Priests and Levites in Deuteronomy'.

67. R.K. Duke, 'The Portion of the Levite: Another Reading of Deuteronomy 18.6-8', *JBL* 106 (1987), pp. 193-201.

and honour in relation to God and the world around them, then to have an evident disability will send the wrong signals (Lev. 21.17-23).

A priest is to be associated with החיים והשלום ('life and wellbeing', Mal. 2.5), not death, disease and dysfunction. Hence the restrictions placed on the priest in connection with mourning (Lev. 10.6; 21.1-5), and the necessity for there being no obvious impediment to procreation (Lev. 21.20). Priestly marriages must also be examples of probity (Lev. 21.7, 14). The life of a priest is to exhibit purity in every respect—moral as well as cultic.[68]

d. *The Priestly Regal Vestments*

The depiction of the priest in his vestments can only be described as regal in character. As with the tabernacle and its furnishings, the priestly vestments have also proved a fruitful area for fertile imaginations, but there are a number of good sober treatments of both the physical descriptions and the significance these descriptions seem designed to convey, and it is not proposed to cover this ground again in any detail.[69] A few instances will suffice to demonstrate that such garments and such materials of which they were made were otherwise associated with royalty, or at the least with the wealthy and influential aristocracy, or were restricted to special occasions such as weddings, when a bridegroom may perhaps be 'king (or priest) for a day' (Isa. 61.10).

The breastpiece, for example (Exod. 28.15-30), appears to reflect those worn by the Pharaohs and the Syrian kings who imitated the Pharaohs. The king of Tyre, portrayed as the primal man in Ezek. 28.12-14, is bedecked with an array of precious stones. The MT only lists nine, though there are twelve (plus silver and gold) in the LXX. However, all nine are found on the high priest's breastpiece in Exod. 28.17-20, and there is substantial correspondence in the order of the stones.[70] The מצנפת ('turban',

68. For the close association of cultic and moral purity in Hebrew law, see David P. Wright, 'The Spectrum of Priestly Impurity', in Gary A. Anderson and Saul M. Olyon (eds.), *Priesthood and Cult in Ancient Israel* (JSOTSup, 125; Sheffield: JSOT Press, 1991), pp. 150-81; Jacob Neusner, *The Idea of Purity in Ancient Judaism* (The Haskell Lectures, 1972–73; Leiden: E.J. Brill, 1973).

69. See C.F. Keil, *Manual of Biblical Archaeology* (trans. P. Christie; 2 vols.; Edinburgh: T. & T. Clark, 1887–88), I, pp. 230-36; Haran, 'The Priestly Image of the Tabernacle'; Fohrer, *History*, p. 381.

70. De Vaux believes it quite likely that the kings of Israel also wore a similar breastpiece (*Ancient Israel*, II, p. 400); cf. Pierre Montet, *Byblos et l'Egypte: Quatre campagnes de fouilles à Gebeil 1921–1922–1923–1924* (3 vols.; Paris: Libraire

Exod. 28.4) or צניף ('turban', Zech. 3.5), with its attached ציץ ('rosette') or נזר ('diadem', Exod. 29.6; 39.30; Lev. 8.9) was likewise, apart from its use by the priests, restricted to kings, or the aristocracy (2 Sam. 1.10; 2 Kgs 11.12; Isa. 3.23; Isa. 62.3; Ezek. 21.31 [ET 21.26]; Ps. 132.18). Philo understood this diadem as a symbol of vice-regency.[71] Kaufmann observes: 'the priestly diadem (*ṣiṣ* "rosette", called *nēzer* "crown" in Lev. 8.9) and anointing are genuine points of contact between the priesthood and the monarchy. But these symbols are not in themselves signs of authority, but of sanctity and importance.'[72] The פאר ('cap') worn by the priests other than the high priest is associated with a verb which has to do with bestowing honour or adorning (Isa. 44.23; 49.3; 61.3, 10; Ps. 149.4; Ezra 7.27).

The overall effect of the accounts of the priestly regalia (Exod. 28–29; 39; Lev. 8) with their fine materials, their gold and their precious stones is to provide the reader with a mental image of the 'glory and honour' (Exod. 28.2, 40) such clothing represented. Ben Sira speaks of the garments as σκεύεσιν ἰσχύος ('symbols of authority') and their effect as εὐκοσμία ('stateliness', 45.7-8).

More significantly, not only was it in general terms the clothing of royalty, but there is a close correspondence between the priestly clothing and the materials of the sanctuary as they would appear from within, such that the priest was appropriately attired to enter a renewed cosmos and stand in the presence of the divine resident of this cosmic temple.[73] The terms כבוד ('glory') and תפארת ('honour') which form an *inclusio* around the account of the vestments in Exodus 28 (vv. 2, 40) are both also used of the glory theophany of Yhwh himself (for כבוד see Exod. 24.16-17; Isa. 4.5; Ps. 57.6 [ET 57.5]; for תפארת [root פאר] see Isa. 63.15; Pss. 71.8; 96.6; 1 Chron. 29.11; note especially Isa. 46.13 where God grants his תפארת to Israel).

Orientaliste Paul Geuthner, 1929), Plate 94; cf. Widengren, 'Early Hebrew Myths', pp. 149-203 (165-69).

71. Philo, *Fug*. 111. For Philo's understanding of the meaning of the priestly garments in general, see *Migr. Abr*. 102; *Spec. Leg*. 1.97.

72. Kaufmann, *The Religion of Israel*, p. 186. Fohrer similarly notes the connection between priestly and royal garments (*History*, p. 380).

73. Kline, *Images*, pp. 42-47; Haran, 'The Complex of Ritual Acts', pp. 279-98. The Wisdom of Solomon (probably a first-century BCE work) seems to be aware of this correspondence between the cosmic sanctuary symbolism and the priestly garments: 'For on his long robe the whole world was depicted, and the glories of the ancestors were engraved on the four rows of stones, and your majesty was on the diadem upon his head' (18.24).

Dressed in such glorious raiment, the priest could portray humankind in their original created dignity (cf. the similar portrayal of the king of Tyre as the primal man in Ezek. 28.12-15)—a royal figure in a world where the besetting problems which lead to the separation of God and humanity are unknown.[74] This problem of human rebellion is represented in Genesis 3 as causing the expulsion of humankind from the paradise garden. We might compare this with the depiction of humanity in Ps. 8.6 (ET 8.5): 'You made them a little lower than the heavenly beings (אלהים) and crowned them with glory (כבוד) and honour (הדר)', where the words used for the regal splendour of humankind are again reflective of words used for the divine majesty (for הדר see Isa. 2.10, 19, 21; 35.2; Pss. 29.4; 104.1; 1 Chron. 16.27).

Perhaps most clearly of all, the high priest is pre-eminently a 'holy' person. He is not holy in the abstract, but קדש ליהוה ('holy to Yhwh', Exod. 28.36) as the inscription on his headband proclaims. Such a declaration speaks not so much of that from which the priest is separated, as Gammie maintains,[75] as it does of the one with whom he is made fit to have a relationship and whose presence he is able to enjoy without fear or impediment. The popular notion that קדש has as its core meaning 'separation' is, as Mettinger rightly demonstrates, 'hardly tenable'.[76]

Clothing imagery is also used generally in a metaphorical way for the restoration of such qualities of an ideal or pristine world as ישע (Ps. 132.16), תשועה (2 Chron. 6.41), ישועה (Ps. 149.4 where the verb יפאר echoes the פאר,'cap', of the priests; cf. Isa. 61.10), all meaning 'salvation', צדקה ('righteousness', Ps. 132.9; cf. Isa. 61.10), צדק ('righteousness') or משפט ('justice', Job 29.14).[77] The donning of special clothing is

74. For the image of man as king in the garden, see Hans Wildberger, 'Das Abbild Gottes: Gen. 1,26-30', *TZ* 21 (1965), pp. 245-59, 481-501; Levenson, *Creation and the Persistence of Evil*, pp. 114-15; Barker, *The Gate of Heaven*, pp. 57-103.

75. John G. Gammie, *Holiness in Israel* (Minneapolis, MN: Fortress Press, 1989), pp. 9-70.

76. Mettinger, *In Search of God*, p. 154. קדש is never followed by מן *separationis*, for example, as might be expected of any word whose basic meaning is alleged to be 'to be separate'. For more on the nature of holiness, see Mary Douglas, *Purity and Danger: An Analysis of the Concepts of Pollution and Taboo* (London: Ark Paperbacks, 1984); Kraus, 'Das heilige Volk'; James Kugel, 'The Holiness of Israel and the Land in Second Temple Times', in Fox *et al.* (eds.), *Texts, Temples and Traditions*, pp. 21-32; David P. Wright, 'Holiness: Old Testament', in *ABD*, III, pp. 237-49; Wells, *God's Holy People*, esp. pp. 16-26

77. Kline, *Images*, pp. 42-50.

a widely recognized ritual act of transformation, or of gaining rights of access where one might otherwise be denied them. In *The Martyrdom and Ascension of Isaiah*, for example, the granting of a special robe makes the wearer become like the angels and hence permitted to enter the seventh heaven (8.14-15; 9.9).

When the high priest entered the most holy place, that is, the throne room of Yhwh, he was dressed differently from when he ministered daily in the holy place. For this most intimate of encounters with God, the high priest wore garments of בד ('linen', Lev. 16.4), which according to *Yom.* 3.6 were white in colour.[78] The plain linen seems to mark a degree of holiness greater even than the royal finery of the regular vestments. The Egyptian priesthood also considered linen garments to be particularly sacred (cf. Gen. 41.42; 2 Sam. 6.14).[79] Linen garments or white garments are the characteristic attire of angels, the heavenly counterparts to earthly priests when they make their appearances as divine envoys and when they are pictured as attending upon the heavenly throne (Ezek. 9.2-3, 11; 10.2; Dan. 10.5; 12.6-7; *1 En.* 87.2; 90.22; *2 En.* 22.8-10; Rev. 15.6). Haran writes of the high priestly linen garments: 'These garments serve to indicate a kind of dialectical elevation into that sphere which is beyond even the material, contagious holiness characterizing the tabernacle and its accessories'.[80] De Vaux writes, 'The priest, therefore, had quitted the profane world, and entered into a sacred realm'.[81]

The Enochic literature depicts the angelic 'Watchers' as heavenly priests (e.g. *1 En.* 14.22-23), and the identification of priests as 'other-worldly' is in fact widespread in Second Temple Judaism.[82] The Jewish group responsible for some liturgical texts found at Qumran shared the viewpoint that angels and earthly priests have closely corresponding roles.[83] While the

78. Danby, *Mishnah*, p. 165.

79. Haran, 'The Priestly Image of the Tabernacle', p. 215.

80. Haran, 'The Priestly Image of the Tabernacle', pp. 215-16.

81. De Vaux, *Ancient Israel*, II, p. 348.

82. *Jub.* 30.18; 31.14; Philo, *Spec. Leg.* 1.116. See also Maier, 'Self-Definition'; Joseph M. Baumgarten, 'The Duodecimal Courts of Qumran, Revelation and the Sanhedrin', *JBL* 95 (1976), pp. 59-78.

83. Carol A. Newsom, 'He Has Established for Himself Priests: Human and Angelic Priesthood in the Qumran Sabbath *Shirot*', in Lawrence H. Schiffman (ed.), *Archaeology and History in the Dead Sea Scrolls: The New York University Conference in Memory of Yigael Yadin* (JSPSup, 8; Sheffield: JSOT Press, 1990), pp. 101-20; cf. Barker, *The Gate of Heaven*, pp. 113-18.

Qumran material represents a later and more developed stage of this tradition, there may be a continuity with the ideology which informs the biblical texts at this point and an explicit link is possibly to be seen in the reference to the priest as מלאך יהוה־צבאות in Mal. 2.7. While מלאך may simply mean 'messenger', its conjunction with יהוה־צבאות, which generally refers to Yhwh's heavenly army, suggests 'angel' as a more appropriate translation.[84]

e. *Priestly Consecration*

Priests are to be consecrated (קדשׁ, piel), sometimes by a human agent, sometimes with God as subject (Exod. 28.3, 41; 29.11, 44; Lev. 22.9; 1 Sam. 7.1), and are subsequently reminded of the need to maintain holiness (קדשׁ, Lev. 21.6-7). The consecration of priests involved an elaborate ritual which included components of washing, investiture and anointing (Exod. 29.4-7; Lev. 8.6-12). In common with kings (1 Sam. 10.1; 16.13; 2 Sam. 2.4; 1 Kgs 1.39; 2 Kgs 11.12), priests are said to be anointed with oil (Exod. 29.7; 40.12-15; Lev. 4.3, 5, 16; 8.12; Num. 3.3).[85] Such anointing is attested as a royal initiation rite among the Canaanites and Hittites at least and possibly further afield.[86] Niditch comments: 'The ceremony of anointing in olive oil makes [the priest], like a king, a liminal being, that is, a human on the boundary between this world and the other world, a man with the touch of the divine upon him'.[87]

84. See J.P. Fokkelman, 'Exodus', in Alter and Kermode (eds.), *The Literary Guide to the Bible*, pp. 50-65 (64).

85. The anointing of priests is sometimes seen as a post-exilic development, and as a practice restricted to the high priest at a time when the high priest exercised real political power: de Vaux, *Ancient Israel*, II, p. 347; Blenkinsopp, *Sage, Priest, Prophet*, p. 80. If, however, such regal indicators as are seen in the priestly vestments and ceremonies were, as is suggested here, a symbolic exhibition of the *ideal* or *image* of royalty rather than its actual exercise, then there is no reason to set aside the evidence of the references to pre-exilic and general priestly anointing. For relevant ancient Near Eastern background on the anointing of priests, and support for the pre-exilic anointing of Israelite priests, see Daniel Fleming, 'The Biblical Tradition of Anointing Priests', *JBL* 117 (1998), pp. 401-14.

86. Judg. 9.15 points to the existence of the rite among the Canaanites and 1 Kgs 19.15 is evidence of the fact that the Israelites, at least, would not have considered the practice out of place in a Syrian context. See de Fraine, *L'aspect religieux*, pp. 315-20; de Vaux, *Ancient Israel*, I, pp. 103-106.

87. Susan Niditch, *The Symbolic Vision in Biblical Tradition* (HSM, 30; Chico, CA: Scholars Press, 1980), p. 110.

f. *The Paramount Priestly Prerogative*

The essence of the priestly prerogative consisted in access to the presence of God, particularly the presence of God associated with the altar, and above all the sanctuary. Among the varied vocabulary used for such access are forms of קרב, נגשׁ and עמד, and phrases with the prepositional form לפני in relation to Yhwh. To 'draw near' or 'be brought near' to God is a remarkable privilege. At one level, as we have seen, it is true of all Israel (Exod. 19.4). At another level, it is true of the Levites generally (Num. 16.9-10), and at yet another level in the graded system of holiness, it is the exclusive prerogative of the priests (Num. 16.5; Ezek. 40.46; 42.13; 43.19; 44.15). Such access took place on a daily basis at the central shrine.

Priests are defined as הנגשׁים אל־יהוה ('the ones who draw near to Yhwh', Exod. 19.22), or קרובים ליהוה ('those who approach Yhwh', Ezek. 42.13; cf. 43.19; Lev. 10.3). Certainly it was a circumscribed access, subject to certain levels of restriction. The most intimate of the representations of access took place only once a year on the Day of Atonement, and after the most elaborate preparations (Lev. 16.2-17). If the holy of holies was at the centre of sacred space, then the Day of Atonement, or purgation of the tabernacle, was the focus of Israel's cultic calendar.[88] This day was marked by rituals which represented the removal of guilt and defilement from the community. A corollary of the right of access is that the privilege had to be guarded, and no unauthorized approach permitted or other infringement of the sanctity provisions countenanced. Together with the Levites, the priests had charge of all aspects of maintaining and guarding the holiness of the sanctuary (Num. 1.53; 3.32; 18.5; 2 Kgs 12.11; Ezek. 40.45; 44.15).

g. *The Priestly Duties*

The priest's duties at the altar (which may or may not be associated with a sanctuary) did not necessarily include the performance of all sacrifices, though increasingly he took on this role. In part, the priest's function was to be an expert on the sacrificial requirements and a facilitator of the approach of others (Lev. 1.5; Deut. 33.10).[89]

88. On the Day of Atonement, see Vriezen, *Old Testament Theology*, pp. 286-87; H. Wheeler Robinson, cited by Vriezen, aptly describes atonement as 'renewal of the relation'. See also James, *Nature and Function*, pp. 161-65; Wenham, *Leviticus*, pp. 225-38; Milgrom, *Leviticus 1–16*, pp. 1009-84; David P. Wright, 'Day of Atonement', in *ABD*, II, pp. 72-76.

89 See, e.g. de Vaux, *Ancient Israel*, II, p. 356.

The roles of the priest extended to those of teacher, interpreter of the law and judge, particularly, but not exclusively on matters to do with the cult (Lev. 10.11; Deut. 17.8-9; 21.5; 31.9-11; 33.9-10; Jer. 2.8; 18.18; Ezek. 7.26; 44.23-24; Mic. 3.11; Hag. 2.11-12; Zech. 7.3; Mal. 2.7; 2 Chron. 15.3; 19.8).[90] If it were not simply a matter of applying the statutes or precedents of the body of traditional legal material, the priest had direct access to the divine oracle, the Urim and Thummim associated with the priestly ephod (Exod. 28.30; Num. 27.21; Deut. 33.8).[91]

The priest functioned as an intermediary between God and people. This is most clearly seen in his role as one who declares or imparts divine blessing and as one who intercedes with God on behalf of the people. The priestly blessing found in Num. 6.23-27 (cf. Deut. 10.8) is also reflected in the text on two amulets found in Jerusalem.[92] To invoke the divine blessing on Israel is to place the name of God on them (Num. 6.27), that is, Israel is to have a privilege analogous to that of the high priest, who physically displays the divine name on his person. Blessing is thus to grant an assurance of the relationship, the divine good intent and the prospect of the wellbeing of the world and one's place in it in terms of the creation account (Gen. 1.22, 28; 2.3).[93] Israel is not to wear that name in such a way that it comes into disrepute (Exod. 20.7).[94] Intercession is the plea before God on behalf of others that they might enjoy the restoration of that good order, beginning with their exclusive relationship with Yhwh (1 Sam. 7.5; Joel 2.17; Mal. 1.9; 2 Chron. 34.20-28; Ezra 9.5-15). It is a role not restricted

90. Eichrodt, *Theology*, 1, p. 87; Cody, *History*, pp. 120-23; Nelson, *Raising Up a Faithful Priest*, pp. 39-49. For the judicial role of priests in a later period, see Jonathan A. Draper, 'The Twelve Apostles as Foundation Stones of the Heavenly Jerusalem and the Foundation of the Qumran Community', *Neotestamentica* 22 (1988), pp. 41-63. We may compare the action of Pharaoh Horemheb (fourteenth century), who appointed priests as judges with the action of Jehoshaphat in 2 Chron. 19.8: cf. de Vaux, *Ancient Israel*, I, p. 154.

91. De Vaux, *Ancient Israel*, II, pp. 349-53.

92. Ada Yardeni, 'Remarks on the Priestly Blessing on Two Ancient Amulets from Jerusalem', *VT* 41 (1991), pp. 176-85. For priestly blessing, see Nelson, *Raising Up a Faithful Priest*, pp. 4-46.

93. On the significance of blessing generally, see Preuss, *Old Testament Theology*, I, pp. 179-93.

94. Walter C. Kaiser, Jr, *Toward Old Testament Ethics* (Grand Rapids: Academie Books, 1983), pp. 87-88; Allan Harman, 'The Interpretation of the Third Commandment', *RTR* 47 (1988), pp. 1-7; Meir Bar-Ilan, 'They Shall Put My Name Upon the People of Israel', *HUCA* 60 (1989), pp. *19-*31 (Hebrew).

to priests, but shared by kings (2 Sam. 24.17; Isa. 37.15-20; 1 Chron. 21.17; 29.10-19; 2 Chron. 6.14-42; 14.11; 30.18) and prophets (1 Sam. 7.5-6; 1 Kgs 18.36-37), all of whom appear to be acting in their official capacities.[95]

h. *A Unifying Rationale of Priesthood in Israel*

It remains to attempt to discern a unifying rationale for this portrayal of Israel's priesthood. Is there a common thread to the various aspects of priestly qualification, initiation and function outlined above?

If the sanctuary is בית יהוה ('the home of Yhwh', Exod. 23.19), then the priest is at least a regular visitor to that divine abode, a welcome and honoured beneficiary of the divine hospitality. The priest belongs in two worlds. While his everyday life is among his fellow Israelites, when he dons his vestments and crosses the threshold he becomes a participant in the heavenly or ideal world.

Just as the original creation of the cosmos, according to Genesis 1, is incomplete until humanity as the image or visual representation of God is placed in the world as its custodian and vice-regent (Gen. 1.26), so the recreated or restored world represented by the tabernacle is not finished when the last inert furnishing is in place. The sanctuary is robbed of much of its meaning apart from the presence in it of its priests. It may still speak of the glory of God who sits enthroned in its inner room, but this God is not left in solitary splendour. It is only when his priests are invested and consecrated for access to the tabernacle and service within it that the purpose for which it is designed is accomplished (Exod. 28–29; Lev. 8–10). Appropriately, when the tabernacle is spoken of in association with Aaron and his sons (consistently from Exod. 27.21 to 31.7), it is אהל מועד ('the tent of meeting'), that is, the place where God meets humankind, rather than משכן ('the dwelling') of Yhwh in the abstract (which is consistently used prior to that point).[96] People could not easily be described by the word תבנית, the word used for the template of the tabernacle, for this is a word more suited to buildings and inert artefacts (from the root בנה, 'build'). Yet in Gen. 1.26, humanity is described as being the צלם and דמות of God himself. The words דמות and תבנית are used as synonyms

95. This is not at all to deny that other individuals also intercede on behalf of others with a variety of motivations.

96. This use of the word מועד is possibly a deliberate echo of its use in polytheistic contexts where it refers to the assembly of the gods; cf. Clifford, 'The Tent of El', pp. 224-25; Mullen, *The Divine Council*, pp. 168-75.

in 2 Kgs 16.10. The priest of the tabernacle cult may be said to form a vital part of the elaborate representation in a stylized and symbolic form of a heavenly or ideal prototype. Here is the prospect of Eden restored, and a restored humanity to dwell in it in security and in harmony with God and with the world around them. Describing the scene in the temple with the priests dressed in their splendid vestments and going about their duties the *Letter of Aristeas* (dated some time from c. 250 BCE to c. 100 CE) makes the comment: 'A man would think he had come out of this world into another one' (v. 99).[97] This captures the essence of what I understand to be the rationale of the priestly attendance and ministration in the sanctuary.

The priest represents the community. One indication of this fact is that the priest and the community are to be regarded as being of equivalent value. When the value of the priest is being assessed for the purposes of the offering for unintended sin, the priest, in distinction from the נשׂיא ('leader'), or any other individual, is to bring a young bull for sacrifice, the same sacrifice as is prescribed for the unintended sin of the whole community (Lev. 4.1–5.13). More obviously, the priest bears the names of all the tribes inscribed on the gemstones on his shoulders representing the whole community 'before Yhwh as a memorial' (Exod. 28.12; 39.6). A rabbinic tradition draws the inference that this is an expression of the priesthood of all Israel as declared in Exod. 19.6.[98]

6. *The Aaronic Priesthood and the Royal Priesthood*

What then does the portrayal of the priest say to Israel about the 'royal priesthood' which they corporately enjoy? Or is there no relationship between the two concepts? Writing in *The Interpreter's Bible*, Park comments on Exod. 19.6: 'This verse was written either before the rise of the professional priesthood in Israel, or by one who believed that sacred officialdom represents a stage in religious growth which should be outgrown'.[99] For Blum, the account of the selection of the Levites (Exod. 32.25-29), coming after the account of the apostasy of the golden calf, is

97. *OTP*, II, p. 19; cf. the glowing description of the priestly vestments in Philo, *Vit. Mos*. 2.109-35; Josephus, *Ant*. 3.151-78.

98. *Ag. Ber*. 79 (R. Acha [c. 320 CE]); cf. Strack and Billerbeck, *Kommentar*, III, p. 390.

99. J. Edgar Park, 'Exodus', in George Arthur Buttrick *et al*. (eds.), *The Interpreter's Bible: The Holy Scriptures in the King James and Revised Standard Versions with General Articles and Introduction, Exegesis, Exposition for Each Book of the Bible* (12 vols.; New York: Abingdon Press, 1952–57), I, pp. 831-1099 (972).

proof that the 'general priesthood' is finished, and from that point Israel no longer enjoys the status it once had.[100] This can hardly be the compositional intention, as provision for the priesthood of Aaron and his sons has been made since 27.21, and the presence of some form of dedicated priesthood is integral to the sanctuary which has been the focus since 25.1. Nicholson is surely correct when he asks: 'is it not more likely that the high vocation [Exod. 19.6] declared to be Israel's is a promise that points beyond the events of Sinai, notwithstanding Israel's apostasy, just as for example, the promise of the blessing for the nations in Genesis points beyond the immediate events being narrated?'[101] Dumbrell sees the cultic provision as guaranteeing and giving meaning to the notion of Israel's corporate royal-priestly position.[102] All Israel has access, and is able to focus its worship, at some graded level, in relation to the dwelling-place of God in its midst.

The priest appears to represent a people restored to pristine perfection. He is a visible prospect of a glorious condition and acceptability to God such as might once again become a wider reality, rather than a limited and stylized experience of a privileged few.[103] When the priest enters the divine presence in the sanctuary, the community enters through him. He exists and functions within the cult, then, to hold up the ideal and affirm the prospect to Israel of a royal and priestly dignity which is in principle the possession of the whole community.

At this point it is necessary to be reminded that the edifice which is identified as the priestly ideology is but a representation, a drama. It makes no claim to be the reality. Inner contrition, love and longing for God and personal integrity are essential dimensions accompanying the outward ritual. In particular, Israel's psalms, many of which were designed for temple use, or found an appropriate place within the temple liturgy, fill out the inner dimensions of the cult (e.g. Pss. 26; 27.4; 43.4; 48.10 [ET 48.9]; 51.19; 118).[104] The tension which has sometimes been seen between

100. Blum, *Komposition des Pentateuch*, p. 56; cf. Hahn, *Kinship by Covenant*, pp. 226-304.

101. Ernest Nicholson, *The Pentateuch in the Twentieth Century: The Legacy of Julius Wellhausen* (Oxford: Clarendon Press, 1998), p. 191.

102. Dumbrell, *The Search for Order*, pp. 47-48.

103. Schenker ('Besonderes und allgemeines Priestertum', p. 115) expresses it most succinctly: 'Dic Institution des Priestertums in Israel ist ein Zeichen der Auserwählung dieses Volkes und seiner Berüfung zur Heiligkeit'.

104. Vriezen, *Old Testament Theology*, pp. 128-47; Eichrodt, *Theology*, I, p. 160; II, p. 446; Rowley, *Worship in Ancient Israel*, pp. 246-71.

priestly and prophetic conceptions of religious experience in Israel has been overplayed, and the idea that the prophets advocated a religion devoid of sacrifice and all other cultic activity has been largely abandoned.[105] Far from being incompatible notions, the account of the designated priesthood of Aaron and his sons along with the whole cultic apparatus is designed to present a graphic image and reminder of the character of the priesthood to which the whole community is called.

As noted above, the Pentateuch, through its structure, suggests that the cultic system is designed to enhance Israel's perception of the privileged standing granted to the whole community on Mt Sinai. Further, if Exodus and Leviticus are seen as components of a larger compositional whole, the pattern becomes clearer. While the focus from Exod. 25.1 to Lev. 16.34 with regard to holiness is on the Levitical priesthood and all that pertains to the priesthood, from Lev. 17.1 (the Holiness Code) there is more frequent reference made to the holiness which ought to characterize the whole community (Lev. 19.2; 20.7, 8, 26; 22.16). This quasi-priestly language may be seen as forming an *inclusio* with the designation in Exod. 19.6 of the holiness of all Israel. In a similar vein, references to Israel as עבדי ('my servants' or 'my worshippers', Lev. 25.42, 55) may have a priestly overtone without there being an overt reference to Israel as 'priests' here or indeed in any Pentateuchal passage beyond Exod. 19.6. The result then would be an enfolding of the special priestly legislation within a framework which exhibits a wider conception of Israel's holiness and special status before Yhwh. It would appear that the purpose of the writer is to draw attention to the paradigmatic nature of the Levitical priesthood. Aaron and his sons are representational models of what Israel's holiness in relation to God should be.[106]

Of course the Holiness Code does not depict Israel as holy without regard to compliance with the holiness provisions, just as Exod. 19.6 was predicated on the conditional 'if you obey me...' (v. 5). The promised

105. Eichrodt, *Theology*, I, pp. 364-69; S. Dawes, 'Walking Humbly: Micah 6.8 Revisited', *SJT* 41 (1988), pp. 331-39; Meir Weiss, 'Concerning Amos' Repudiation of the Cult', in David P. Wright, David Noel Freedman and Avi Hurvitz (eds.), *Pomegranates and Golden Bells: Studies in Biblical, Jewish and Near Eastern Ritual, Law, and Literature in Honor of Jacob Milgrom* (Winona Lake, IN: Eisenbrauns, 1995), pp. 199-214.

106. Knohl would regard the redactional layer he identifies as HS (closely identified with the Holiness Code) as providing the final editorial framework for the priestly legislation (PT): Knohl, *The Sanctuary of Silence*; cf. Mullen, *Ethnic Myths*, p. 217; Nicholson, *The Pentateuch in the Twentieth Century*, pp. 18, 46.

status of renewal and recreation is ultimately true only as it is worked out in the life of obedience in the idealistic terms portrayed in the lawcode. The fickleness of the people's response subsequent to the Sinai theophany is a feature of the narrative portions of the Pentateuch, not the least of which is the apostasy of the golden calf (Exod. 32), which is positioned between the *fiat* and the fulfilment of the tabernacle and priestly provisions. The people do not fully appropriate the promised blessing and fall far short of the ideal. The priesthood and tabernacle constitute a constant reminder of the goal and prospect of holiness and acceptability to God. In the cult the people have a visible representation of what it would mean were they all to live in priestly holiness. Similarly, the glory and honour which characterize the Aaronic priests serve as a visible reminder of the glory and honour to which God has called the whole people (Deut. 26.19; Isa. 17.3; 62.2; Jer. 13.11).

The anointing of priests and kings would serve to illustrate what is meant at a more metaphorical level by the 'anointing' of the people of Israel generally (Ps. 105.15), a passage which Kraus regards as a 'democratized' reference under the influence of Exod. 19.6.[107]

From this framework, it is not difficult, then, to see the rationale for much of the remainder of the priestly duties. As the one who moves between heaven and earth, the priest is ideally placed to be a mediator of divine blessing and an imparter of divine truth. Even his role as a certifier of that which is healthy or free from agents of decay finds ready explanation (Lev. 13–14). The priest is the living symbol of blessing and wellbeing, of life to the full, of all that humanity should be and could become in relation to God.[108]

7. *Conclusion*

The account of Israel's tabernacle cult and consecrated priesthood has strong structural links with the preceding section of the Sinai pericope in which the priesthood of the whole people is proclaimed. The notion of the corporate royal priesthood of Israel is not inherently in tension with the notion of a restricted institutional (Aaronic or Levitical) priesthood any

107. Hans-Joachim Kraus, *Psalms 60–150: A Commentary* (trans. Hilton C. Oswald; Continental Commentaries; Minneapolis, MN: Augsburg, 1989), p. 311.

108. This future-oriented aspect of the portrayal of the priest is demonstrated by Alex T.M. Cheung, 'The Priest as the Redeemed Man: A Biblical-Theological Study of the Priesthood', *JETS* 29 (1986), pp. 265-75.

more than it is with the notion of the Davidic monarchy. Rather, the corporate royal priesthood of Israel has a priority over the Levitical priesthood, perhaps historically, but more demonstrably at a literary level within the book of Exodus. The notion of Israel's corporate priesthood is the frame of reference for understanding the significance of the cult and, within the book of Exodus, is never seen to be in competition with the cultic priesthood. Rather, the Aaronic priesthood is presented as both modelling and facilitating (in the cultic drama) the nearness to God which is the objective of Israel's covenantal relationship with Yhwh.

Israel's cult shares some common features with the sanctuary ideology of the ancient world. The tabernacle is a representation of an ideal or restored cosmos, where God and man meet in an environment which transcends the limitations of the mundane world. The priest, granted access to the sacred space, is a model of the ideal held out to Israel of the meaning of its collective priesthood and the access to the presence of God of which it speaks. The priests are the chosen and privileged ones who are granted a royal dignity and the right of access to this realm, even, in the case of the high priest, to that sacred space which is regarded as the throne-room of heaven, the innermost sanctum of an ideal cosmos.

Priests share characteristics of royalty in the prevailing ideology of priesthood in the ancient Near East. Israel had a collective memory of ancient priest-kings, and the descriptions of the garb of the Israelite priests preserve something of these royal associations. In their priests, the Israelites had a perpetual reminder of their own royal-priestly standing and privilege. The detailed literary portrayal of the priesthood of Aaron and his sons serves to flesh out for the reader something of what is meant by the image of Israel's corporate royal priesthood.

In keeping with the expectation that sanctuary-building is the work of a chosen king, acting on instructions of a god and according to a divinely revealed pattern, it is suggested that Israel corporately functions as the royal sanctuary builder according to Exodus, in keeping with the designation of Israel as a 'royal priesthood'.

Chapter 7

The Sinai Covenant as Grant of Royal Priesthood

1. *The Sinai Covenant and the Ancient Treaties*

Durham describes Exod. 19.4-6 as 'a poetic summary of covenant theology'.[1] If this is the case (and Durham would not be alone in expressing such sentiments), what is the character of that 'covenant theology'? How has it been understood in discussions of this unit of text, the wider Sinai pericope and the Hebrew Bible generally?

Our discussion so far has observed some points of contact between Yhwh's declaration of the royal-priestly status of Israel and the ברית ('covenant') between Yhwh and Israel (Exod. 19.5-6; 24.7-8). Yet much of the discussion on the nature of the Mosaic or Sinai 'covenant' over the past half century has not taken sufficient cognizance of this association. As Rendtorff observes, Exod. 19.5-6 has been marginalized in treatments of the covenant.[2] This chapter will briefly outline the main contours of the discussion on the Sinai covenant and its relation to other biblical covenants, and the parallel which is frequently drawn with the diplomatic suzerainty (or vassal) treaties of the second and first millenniums BCE. It will be suggested that a more instructive analogy for understanding the Sinai covenant, at least as presented in Exodus, is the covenanted grant of royal favour to individuals, particularly the favour of royal or priestly office.

Following the work of Korošec on the Hittite diplomatic treaties,[3] texts which spell out the formal relations between the Hittite kingdom and its neighbouring (particularly client) states in the fourteenth and thirteenth centuries, Mendenhall in his famous 1954 article in the *Biblical Archaeologist* applied the pattern to the divine covenants of the Hebrew Bible.[4]

1. Durham, *Exodus*, p. 261.
2. Rendtorff, *The Covenant Formula*, p. 3.
3. V. Korošec, *Hethitische Staatsverträge* (Leipziger Rechtswissenschaftliche Studien; Leipzig: T. Weicher, 1931).
4. George E. Mendenhall, 'Covenant Forms in Israelite Tradition', in Campbell and Freedman (eds.), *The Biblical Archaeologist Reader 3*, pp. 25-53.

He identified the following elements in a typical treaty or covenant document: (1) preamble, (2) historical prologue, (3) stipulations, (4) provisions for deposit in the temple and periodic public reading, (5) list of gods as witnesses and (6) curses and blessings formula.[5] For Mendenhall, the Sinai covenant is undoubtedly a reflection of the suzerainty treaty.[6]

Some subsequent studies have tended to draw a closer link with the Assyrian treaties of the first millennium, and to note the formal contrasts between the Hittite and the Assyrian models, particularly the lack of the historical prologue and blessings in the Assyrian exemplars.[7] While Hatti and Assyria are the two dominant cultures whose treaty texts are studied in parallel with the biblical data, treaty forms are known (whether from extant examples or from literary references) throughout the ancient world generally (including the Greek sphere) from the third millennium to the late first millennium.[8]

Instruments of statecraft such as the diplomatic treaty are by definition trans-cultural to some degree, and the assumption is that there was a widespread and relatively stable convention for spelling out the relations between states.[9] The chief function of the treaties was the attempt to shore up the interests of the suzerain with cogent arguments from history, and oath-bound affirmations of loyalty on the part of the vassal states, and the sanction of the gods lying behind the oaths. In an unpublished manuscript,

5. Mendenhall, 'Covenant Forms in Israelite Tradition', pp. 32-36; cf. Hillers, *Covenant*, pp. 25-45.

6. See also George E. Mendenhall and Gary A. Herion, 'Covenant', in *ABD*, I, p. 1183.

7. See, e.g., R. Frankena, 'The Vassal-Treaties of Esarhaddon and the Dating of Deuteronomy', *OTS* 14 (1965), pp. 122-54. Kitchen, on the other hand, draws attention to the contrast in order to defend the Hittite analogy: K.A. Kitchen, 'The Fall and Rise of Covenant, Law and Treaty', *TynBul* 40 (1989), pp. 118-35.

8. For surveys of the treaty and covenant discussion, see Hillers, *Covenant*; McCarthy, *Old Testament Covenant*; Ernest W. Nicholson, 'Covenant in a Century of Study Since Wellhausen', *OTS* 24 (1986), pp. 54-69; *idem*, *God and his People*, pp. 3-117; Robert A. Oden, Jr, 'The Place of Covenant in the Religion of Israel', in Patrick D. Miller, Jr, Paul D. Hanson and S. Dean McBride (eds.), *Ancient Israelite Religion: Essays in Honor of Frank Moore Cross* (Philadelphia: Fortress Press, 1987), pp. 429-47; Rendtorff, *The Covenant Formula*.

9. See, e.g., McCarthy, *Treaty and Covenant*, pp. 122-40; Moshe Weinfeld, 'The Common Heritage of Covenantal Traditions in the Ancient World', in Luciano Canfora, Mario Liverani and Carlo Zaccagnini (eds.), *I trattati nel mondo antico: Forma, ideologia, funzione* (Saggi di storia antica, 2; Rome: L'Erma di Bretschneider, 1990), pp. 175-91.

Weeks has taken issue with some underlying assumptions of what has been the dominant position on the commonality of treaty conventions, and has demonstrated a greater degree of diversity among the ideologies of the treaty-making states, particularly with regard to their treatment of history, in the representations of treaties from the major geographical regions and epochs of the ancient Near East.[10]

While the Hittite and later the Assyrian analogies have served as catalysts for discussion of the Hebrew covenants since the 1950s, it ought not to be imagined that only then did biblical covenants become the object of serious scholarly attention. Some notion of covenant had always been a factor in discussions of Israel's understanding of its relationship with Yhwh. Most prominently in the last century, Eichrodt's *Theology of the Old Testament*, which appeared in its original German edition in the years 1933–39, is a work structured upon the covenant concept. However, it is since Mendenhall's article that there has been a considerable amount of attention devoted to drawing out the parallels in form and terminology between the treaties and the biblical covenants, particularly the Sinai covenant. The passages most frequently cited as bearing the stamp of the treaty form are the Decalogue and Joshua 24, but other units of the Sinai and Deuteronomic material have been compared with the treaty texts.

Beyerlin's monograph on the Sinai traditions traces the origins of the units of the Sinai complex in cultic celebrations, and the development of the material, making extensive use of the analogy between Israel's covenant formulations and the Hittite state-treaties.[11] In particular, Exod. 19.3b-8

> is closely connected with the same covenant that is embodied in contractual form in the Decalogue and the ratification and cultic observance of which is attested especially in Exod. 24.3-8. This connection is apparent from the fact that within this unit of tradition several of the elements which are characteristic of the Decalogue and its formal model, the covenant-form well-known from the Hittite vassal-treaties, recur.[12]

Beyerlin notes the 'historical prologue' in the I–thou style (v. 4), a summary reference to the stipulations (v. 5a), and above all, the exclusive claim on the vassal (v. 5b), followed by the people's response (v. 8). While

10. I am indebted to Noel K. Weeks of the Department of History at the University of Sydney for allowing me to read his monograph-length 'Admonition and Curse' (1999) in its unpublished form.

11. Beyerlin, *Origins*.

12. Beyerlin, *Origins*, p. 69.

some elements of the treaty-form are sometimes felt to be lacking from Exodus 19—the taking of an oath, the reference to witnesses, the curses and the recording of the covenant in written form—this analysis has been widely echoed.[13]

The acceptance of the Hittite parallels to the Sinai covenant generally went hand in hand with an acceptance of the historical core of the covenant tradition. Thus Beyerlin observes, 'It was God's activity in *history* that gave the impulse to the formation of this tradition and had a decisive influence on its content and character'.[14]

Not all scholars have shared the enthusiasm for seeing the covenant as an echo of international treaties, or as being an early and formative factor in Israel's sense of identity as a nation. Kraus considers that 'some essential features of this covenant are obscured or completely displaced by the introduction of the treaty pattern'.[15] Particularly influential has been the contribution of Perlitt. In his *Bundestheologie im Alten Testament* he mounts a significant critique of the prevailing emphasis on the role that the cult had come to occupy in discussions of the Sinai material, and the closely associated notion that the covenant formulation, modelled on the Hittite suzerainty treaties, is integral to the shaping of the Sinai complex.[16] For example, there is no real equivalent to the historical prologue in the accounts of Israel's encounter with God. Moreover, God is not portrayed as a suzerain, or even a partner to the covenant, but is simply present at the covenant renewal in Joshua 24. Where a covenant is recognized, it is one defined not in terms of mutual relationship (*Verhältnis*) but of obligation (*Verpflichtung*) of one or other party. Such covenant formulations as can be found in the Old Testament are a late theological innovation, attributable to the Deuteronomic redaction, or to writers influenced by the Deuteronomic literature, and form no part of the older heritage of Israel's Sinai beliefs. The introduction of the covenant idea, with its emphasis on conditionality, constitutes a response to the strain which the relationship between Yhwh and Israel was undergoing at the time of the decline of the monarchy. Like Wellhausen, Perlitt takes the perceived silence of the eighth-century prophets on the covenant as a confirmation that no such

13. Baltzer, *The Covenant Formulary*, pp. 28-29; Thompson, *The Ancient Near Eastern Treaties*, p. 22; Hillers, *Covenant*, p. 64; Vogels, *God's Universal Covenant*, pp. 46-50.

14. Beyerlin, *Origins*, p. 169.

15. Kraus, *Worship in Israel*, p. 139.

16. Perlitt, *Bundestheologie*, pp. 163-67.

notion can be found at that time in Israel's thinking.[17] Thus, as indicated above, Perlitt has revived Wellhausen's notion that Exod. 19.3b-8 is attributable to the Deuteronomic redactor.[18]

McCarthy, who has undertaken a major study of treaty and covenant forms, concludes that Exodus 19–24 bears only a remote relationship to the covenant form.[19] History and parenesis are hardly to be found, whereas the theophany account (not an expected element in covenant accounts) assumes a prominent place in the Exodus narrative. The one possible candidate for a historical prologue in the Sinai narrative material is Exod. 19.4, which is virtually lost sight of in the surrounding dramatic events. Moreover, v. 4 'is part of a literary unity, 3b-8, which stands apart from the rest' as an overture, 'a complete narration of the Sinai events by itself'.[20] With regard to the Decalogue, while it does have a brief historical prologue, it lacks the expected curse and blessing formulae.[21] McCarthy sees in the Sinai pericope a combination of historical resumé and a conditional blessing, but sees this as falling short of the complete covenant formula.

Nicholson has also given a considerable amount of attention to the Sinai complex in a series of monographs and articles.[22] Like Perlitt, Nicholson takes issue with the view that the idea of covenant, rather than being a later religious construct, derives from a historic event which bound Israel to Yhwh, on the analogy of the second-millennium Hittite treaties. The only covenant influence on the Sinai complex which Nicholson is prepared to entertain is that of late Assyrian models, which might have had some effect on the shaping of Deuteronomic modes of expression.[23] Like Perlitt, he gives a significant role to the hand of D in shaping the Pentateuchal materials. The notion of covenant is not integral to the Decalogue or to the structure of Exodus 19–24. Unlike Perlitt, Nicholson does see the beginnings of a notion of covenant in the eighth-century prophets.[24]

17. Perlitt, *Bundestheologie*, pp. 129-55. This results in some strained exegesis at times as Nicholson demonstrates (*God and his People*, pp. 183-86).

18. Perlitt, *Bundestheologie*, pp. 167-81.

19. McCarthy, *Treaty and Covenant*, pp. 245-76.

20. McCarthy, *Treaty and Covenant*, p. 247.

21. McCarthy, *Old Testament Covenant*, pp. 15-21.

22. Nicholson, *Exodus and Sinai*; 'Interpretation'; 'Antiquity'; 'Origin'; 'Covenant Ritual'; *God and his People*; 'Covenant in a Century of Study Since Wellhausen'.

23. Nicholson, *Exodus and Sinai*, p. 76.

24. Nicholson, *God and his People*, pp. 179-88.

Two general observations on this discussion need to be made. First, it has not always been made clear whether what is being claimed is a conscious analogy with the state-treaties at the level of the form of the texts themselves—that is, should one look for all of the elements to be present—or whether the texts, while alluding to the notion of the treaty as an analogy, are secondary free literary adaptations of the treaty genre—epic or historical or hymnodic accounts of the relationship. Is Exodus 19–24 or any of its component parts consciously aiming to be a treaty document as such? The position of Knutson that it is better seen as a *proposal* of a covenant is at least preferable to forcing it to fit the mould of the treaty *Gattung per se*.[25]

Secondly, in much of the literature on covenant since Mendenhall, the discussion of the Sinai covenant has been too narrowly focussed on the parallels with the suzerainty (vassal) treaties, both among those who support and those who deny the relevance of extra-biblical models. There is no doubt that the treaties have been a fruitful and instructive parallel. However, it is unduly restricting and ultimately misleading if it is imagined that this is the only possible parallel, or even the best one for capturing the essence of the biblical covenants. There is a danger of losing sight of the fact that it is an analogy, and any analogy of divine–human relationships is likely to obscure as much as it explains. A moment's reflection will reveal, for example, that Yhwh has not subjugated Israel, a situation frequently presupposed in the suzerainty treaties. Further, whereas the diplomatic treaties are universally designed for the benefit of the suzerain, the benefit to the vassal consists largely in not being annihilated, which would be the price of rebellion. The biblical covenants on the other hand are not cast in terms of the benefit to Yhwh, and clearly the benefit to Israel under these covenants is more far-reaching.

2. *The Semantic Domain of* ברית

The etymology and meaning of ברית have generated considerable discussion.[26] The principal debate centres upon whether ברית can denote a

25. F. Brent Knutson, 'Literary Genres in *PRU* 4', in Fisher (ed.), *Ras Shamra Parallels*, II, pp. 155-214 (190-93); cf. Muilenburg, 'Form and Structure', pp. 351-52; Baltzer, *The Covenant Formulary*, pp. 28-29.

26. On the etymology of ברית see Alfred Jepsen, '*Berith*: Ein Beitrag zur Theologie der Exilszeit', in Arnulf Kuschke (ed.), *Verbannung und Heimkehr: Beitrage zur Geschichte und Theologie Israels im 6 und 5. Jahrhundert v. Chr.* (Festschrift Wilhelm Rudolph; Tübingen: J.C.B. Mohr, 1961), pp. 161-79; O. Loretz, 'ברית—"Band—

relationship between parties, or simply the obligation one party takes upon himself. Kutsch has been prominent in advocating the latter position,[27] while the former is defended among others by Weinfeld,[28] Kalluveettil[29] and Kapelrud.[30] For our purposes, it is not necessary to come down on one side of this divide, but merely to observe something of the range of its uses within the Hebrew Bible and beyond. Some form of synthesis, whereby ברית is understood to mean the instrument whereby parties are committed to a particular social arrangement, involving formal and perhaps implied commitments on at least one party, may suffice as a reasonable working definition.

The West Semitic term ברית is attested from texts of the late second millennium,[31] and defines a broad range of relationships or commitments, such as contracted labour, an oath of loyalty, a grant of land or of a privileged position, as well as treaties of parity and suzerainty. It is attested in a Hurrian hymn from Ugarit in the form *il brt.il.dn.* which may be compared (and perhaps equated) with the biblical references to the god(s) El Berith/ Baal Berith of Shechem (Judg. 8.33; 9.4, 46).[32] While the significance of these divine names is disputed, it is at least a strong possibility that they refer to a god or gods bound by covenantal ties to the Shechemites rather than simply witnessing treaties as a third party.[33] A seventh-century

Bund"', *VT* 16 (1966), pp. 239-41; Moshe Weinfeld, 'ברית', in *TDOT*, I, pp. 253-79; Frank Moore Cross, 'The Ideologies of Kingship in the Era of the Empire: Conditional Covenant and Eternal Decree', in *idem*, *Canaanite Myth and Hebrew Epic*, pp. 219-73. Barr correctly cautions against an etymologizing approach to semantics in relation to covenant: James Barr, 'Some Semantic Notes on the Covenant', in Donner, Hanhart and Smend (eds.), *Beiträge zur alttestamentlichen Theologie*, pp. 23-38.

27. Kutsch, *Verheissung und Gesetz*; cf. Fohrer, *History*, pp. 80-81.

28. Moshe Weinfeld, '*B^{e}rît:* Covenant vs. Obligation', *Bib* 55 (1975), pp. 120-28.

29. Kalluveettil, *Declaration and Covenant*, p. 91.

30. Arvid S. Kapelrud, 'The Prophets and the Covenant', in W. Boyd Barrick and John R. Spencer (eds.), *In the Shelter of Elyon: Essays on Ancient Palestinian Life and Literature in Honor of G.W. Ahlström* (JSOTSup, 31; Sheffield: JSOT Press, 1984), pp. 175-83.

31. The forms *brt* and *bryt* are both found as loanwords in Egyptian texts from the 19th and 20th Dynasties (1300–1170); see K.A. Kitchen, 'Egypt, Ugarit, Qatna and Covenant', *UF* 11 (1979), pp. 453-64.

32. Text 1.128, lines 14-16 in Dietrich, Loretz and Sanmartín, *Die keilalphabetischen Texte*, pp. 126-27; Kitchen, 'Egypt, Ugarit, Qatna and Covenant', p. 458.

33. See Ronald E. Clements, 'Baal-Berith of Shechem', *JSS* 13 (1968), pp. 21-32; Theodore J. Lewis, 'The Identity and Function of El/Baal Berith', *JBL* 115 (1996), pp. 401-23.

Phoenician magical text from Arslan Tash is also relevant.[34] If the authenticity of this text is accepted (and Van Dijk[35] argues convincingly against Teixidor[36] that it should be), it appears to speak of an 'eternal covenant' (אלת עלם) which is established ('cut') by Aššur in association with other deities with the owners of the amulet.[37]

The notion of a relationship between a people and a god expressed in covenantal terms, despite repeated assertions,[38] is not unique to Israel, though it does appear to have been most developed in an Israelite context.[39]

It would appear that the fundamental image behind each of the applications of ברית is the use of familial categories for those who are not bound by ties of natural kinship. By legal or quasi-legal process, people become 'father', 'son' or 'brother' to one another for a range of purposes.[40] The

34. R. du Mesnil du Buisson, 'Une tablette magique de la région du Moyen Euphrate', in *Mélanges syriens offerts à Monsieur René Dussaud* (Bibliotheque archéologique et historique, 30; 2 vols.; Paris: Librairie Orientaliste Paul Geuthner, 1939), I, pp. 421-34; William Foxwell Albright, 'An Aramaean Magical Text in Hebrew from the Seventh Century BC', *BASOR* 76 (1939), pp. 5-11; Frank Moore Cross, Jr, and Richard J. Saley, 'Phoenician Incantations on a Plaque of the Seventh Century BC from Arslan Tash in Upper Syria', *BASOR* 197 (1970), pp. 42-49; Ziony Zevit, 'A Phoenician Inscription and Biblical Covenant Terminology', *IEJ* 27 (1977), pp. 110-18; S. David Sperling, 'An Arslan Tash Incantation: Interpretations and Implications', *HUCA* 53 (1982), pp. 1-10; Lewis, 'The Identity and Function of El/Baal Berith', pp. 408-10.

35. Jacobus Van Dijk, 'The Authenticity of the Arslan Tash Amulets', *Iraq* 54 (1992), pp. 65-68. This opinion is supported by Cross in a personal letter to T. Lewis ('The Identity and Function of El/Baal Berith', p. 409).

36. J. Teixidor, 'Les tablettes d'Arslan Tash au Musée d'Alep', *Aula Orientalis* 1 (1983), pp. 105-108.

37. Zevit, 'A Phoenician Inscription'.

38. Friedrich Nötscher, 'Bundesformular und "Amtsschimmel": Ein kritischer Überblick', *BZ* 9 (1965), pp. 181-214 (193); D.J. Wiseman, 'Archaeology and Scripture', *WTJ* 33 (1971), pp. 133-52 (143); Weinfeld, 'ברית', p. 278; Gene M. Tucker, 'Covenant Forms and Contract Forms', *VT* 15 (1965), pp. 487-503 (502).

39. For a further example of a divine–human covenant, see Chapter 5 for Zarpiya's covenant with the god Sanda and the Violent Gods.

40. See J.M. Munn-Rankin, 'Diplomacy in Western Asia in the Early Second Millennium BC', *Iraq* 18 (1956), pp. 76-84; Sklba, 'The Redeemer of Israel', p. 11; F. Charles Fensham, 'Father and Son as Terminology for Treaty and Covenant', in Hans Goedicke (ed.), *Near Eastern Studies in Honor of W.F. Albright* (Baltimore: The Johns Hopkins University Press, 1971), pp. 121-35; Hahn, *Kinship by Covenant*. Hahn recognizes the 'covenant of kinship' as one of three distinct covenant types, but then

Israelite covenant formula 'I will be your God and you shall be my people' (Lev. 26.12; Jer. 7.23) appears to be closely analogous to an adoption formula, and perhaps a marriage formula, both of which are instruments of declaration of kinship.[41]

3. *The Covenant of Grant*

While such familial terms as 'father', 'son' and 'brother' are used in diplomatic language, Weinfeld has drawn attention to their use also in the legal form he identifies as a 'covenant of grant' in Hittite, neo-Assyrian and other texts.[42] In these, lands or houses are given as a reward for devoted service and as an incentive for future loyalty. The record of these land-grants is preserved in *kudurru*-inscriptions, or stone boundary markers.[43] 'The grant *par excellence* is an act of royal benevolence arising from the king's desire to reward his loyal servant.'[44]

Grant treaties of the ancient Near East, while they are initiated as acts of royal favour, usually as a reward for loyal and devoted service, are also not lacking in references to the expectations of continued loyalty.[45] The treaties of grant of land (or house) are of course a suggestive parallel for the biblical covenants, particularly the Abrahamic covenant with its focus on the land (Gen. 15.7, 18; 17.8; 26.4-5) and the Davidic covenant, where 'house' (in the sense of dynasty) is the key promise (2 Sam. 7.11).[46] Weinfeld identifies both of these covenants as belonging to the grant or

sees kinship as an undergirding concept for his remaining two categories—treaty and grant.

41. See Knight, *A Christian Theology of the Old Testament*, p. 219; Samuel Greengus, 'The Old Babylonian Marriage Contract', *JAOS* 89 (1969), pp. 505-32; Mordechai A. Friedman, 'Israel's Response in Hosea 2.17b: "You are my husband"', *JBL* 99 (1980), pp. 199-204; Sohn, *The Divine Election of Israel*, p. 64.

42. Weinfeld, 'The Covenant of Grant', *JAOS* 90 (1970), pp. 184-203 (191); cf. J.N. Postgate, *Neo-Assyrian Royal Grants and Decrees* (Studia Pohl Series Maior, 1; Rome: Pontifical Biblical Institute Press, 1969); Hahn, *Kinship by Covenant*, pp. 145-67.

43. Weinfeld, 'The Covenant of Grant', p. 185.

44. Moshe Weinfeld, *Deuteronomy and the Deuteronomic School* (Winona Lake, IN: Eisenbrauns, 1992), p. 77.

45. Weinfeld, 'The Covenant of Grant', p. 193.

46. For an extended treatment of the Davidic 'house' theme, see Robert M. Polzin, *David and the Deuteronomist: A Literary Study of the Deuteronomic History*. III. *2 Samuel* (Indiana Studies in Biblical Literature; Bloomington, IN: Indiana University Press, 1993), pp. 54-87.

promissory category of covenant (ברית) and this is a widely shared understanding.[47] The land is an important component of the Abrahamic promise, but it would be too restricting to limit the boon to Abraham to that of territory. The prospect of a 'great name', a 'great nation', a 'blessing' which flows through him to all the families of the earth and a relationship with God must also be considered as important elements of what is promised to Abraham (Gen. 12.2-3; 17.4-8, 16, 20; 18.18; 22.17-18). The commitment to David of a perpetual dynasty is an extended use of the word 'house', and again, does not exhaust the extent of the commitment, which includes an ongoing relationship between the deity and the monarch, and a sovereignty over the nations which in some sense includes a charter with implications for all humankind (Ps. 2.8; 2 Sam. 7.19).[48]

By way of contrast with the Abrahamic and Davidic covenants, Weinfeld considers the Sinai covenant to be of the suzerainty or 'obligatory' type.[49] Whereas the emphasis in the grant covenant is on the divine commitment, the emphasis in the Sinai covenant is on the obligations imposed on the vassal, as in the suzerainty treaties. Another way of expressing this is to say that the grant, while based on loyal service, is generally understood to be unconditional (the Abrahamic and Davidic covenants), while the suzerainty type of treaty (Sinai) is conditional upon fulfilment of the stipulations. Weinfeld notes a distinction in terminology between הברית והחסד ('the gracious covenant') in Deuteronomic texts which refer to the Abrahamic and Davidic covenants (e.g. Deut. 7.9-12; 1 Kgs 8.23), whereas simply ברית ('covenant') is used for the Sinai covenant (e.g. Deut. 5.2; 9.9, 11).[50] This sharp contrast between the conditionality of the Sinai covenant (with its obligations) and the unconditionality of the Abrahamic and Davidic covenants (with their lack of obligations) is widely held.[51]

47. Weinfeld, 'The Covenant of Grant', p. 184; cf. Hillers, *Covenant*, p. 105; Ronald E. Clements, *Abraham and David: Genesis 15 and its Meaning for Israelite Tradition* (SBT, 2.5; London: SCM Press, 1967); James Plastaras, *Creation and Covenant* (Milwaukee: Bruce Publishing Co., 1968); John Bright, *Covenant and Promise* (London: SCM Press, 1977); McComiskey, *The Covenants of Promise*; E. Theodore Mullen, Jr, 'The Divine Witness and the Davidic Royal Grant: Ps 89.37-38', *JBL* 102 (1983), pp. 207-18; Hahn, *Kinship by Covenant*, pp. 168-211.

48. Walter C. Kaiser, Jr, *Toward an Old Theology Theology* (Grand Rapids: Zondervan, 1978), pp. 152-55.

49. Weinfeld, 'The Covenant of Grant', p. 184.

50. Weinfeld, 'The Covenant of Grant', p. 188.

51. See Mendenhall, 'Covenant Forms in Israelite Tradition', p. 37; Freedman, 'Divine Commitment and Human Obligation'; Kuntz, *Self-Revelation*, pp. 76-80;

The strong contrast which is often maintained between the Abrahamic and the Sinai covenants would elicit a bewildered response from the intended readers of the book of Exodus. The reader is introduced to the 'covenant' at 2.24 where the basis for God's taking notice of the plight of his people is 'his covenant with Abraham, with Isaac and with Jacob'. This reference, in turn, would alert the reader of the unified Pentateuch to make a connection with the references to God's covenantal dealings with the patriarchs in Genesis. The Abrahamic covenant with its grant of land, its promise of nationhood and above all a relationship with God is very much in view as providing the framework for the exodus and Sinai covenant (Exod. 2.24; 3.6, 16; 4.5; 6.3-8; cf. Lev. 26.42-43; Deut. 4.31; 8.18; 29.9-12 [ET 29.10-13]). The ultimate objective of the Exodus and wilderness narratives—which are closely linked with the Sinai material[52]— and the projected setting of much of the Sinai legislative material ('when you enter the land', Lev. 14.34; 19.9, 23; 23.10, 23; 25.2; Num. 10.9; 15.18; Deut. 17.14; 18.9) is the land promised to Abraham.[53]

Then the covenant with David offers an analogy of a covenant with perpetual kingship and the divine sonship of the Davidic line as its core commitments (2 Sam. 7; Pss. 89.4-5 [ET 89.3-4]; 132.11-12), which, on my exegesis, may be considered as a particularization of the 'sonship' and 'kingship' of the nation as a whole (Exod. 4.23; Hos. 11.1; Isa. 63.8; Exod. 19.6). Divine election is of course a common motif in ancient Near Eastern kingship ideology. Thus Nabû-aplu-iddina is 'the king of Babylon, the elect of Marduk'.[54] While the root בחר ('choose') is not found in Exodus 19, the concept of election is far from being absent. It is implicit in the description of the unique divine patronage Israel has enjoyed in its pilgrimage. The word סגלה ('special treasure') is closely associated with divine election (Deut. 7.6; 14.2). In the Qumran text 4Q504 4.10-11 the phrase [ממלכת] כוהנים וגוי קדוש is followed by the words [א]שר בחרת ('whom you chose').[55] What was in the Sinai material presented as a

Cleon L. Rogers, Jr, 'The Covenant with Abraham and its Historical Setting', *BSac* 127 (1970), pp. 241-56; Jon D. Levenson, 'The Davidic Covenant and its Modern Interpreters', *CBQ* 41 (1979), pp. 205-19.

52. Whatever view one takes of the pre-literary form of the traditions, they are closely linked in the text of Exodus.

53. Perlitt, *Bundestheologie*, pp. 32-35.

54. Text 36 column 2 lines 19-20 in L.W. King (ed.), *Babylonian Boundary-Stones and Memorial-Tablets in the British Museum* (London: British Museum, 1912), p. 122.

55. Martínez and Tigchelaar, *Dead Sea Scrolls*, II, p. 1010.

corporate royal status is in the Davidic covenant personified in the king, who in a sense *is* the nation. The royal election language used with reference to Israel (Exod. 19.5-6; Deut. 7.6; 10.15) becomes focussed on one elect king (Ps. 78.70).[56]

Close scrutiny of Weinfeld's observations on the differentiation in terminology between biblical promise covenants and the Sinai obligatory covenant indicates that it is not as simple as Weinfeld maintains. The compound expression הברית והחסד (Deut. 7.9), which Weinfeld sees as referring exclusively to the Abrahamic promise, has a dual reference, on the one hand arising out of God's commitment to the patriarchs (v. 8), and on the other hand serving as the underpinning of and motivation for continued faithfulness under the Sinai provisions (vv. 11-12). Further, the word חסד alone may be used for the commitment of God to those who keep his (Sinaitic) commandments (Deut. 5.10). This positive assessment of the function of the gracious provision of the commandments is reflected generally in the Hebrew Bible. For Israel to possess the laws is in itself a blessing, not a burden—a privilege no other nation enjoys (Deut. 4.8; 30.11-14; Pss. 19.8-12 [ET 19.7-11]; 119; 147.20).

The contrast between conditional and unconditional covenants has frequently been too starkly drawn. As Weinfeld acknowledges, the Abrahamic covenant is not without its element of expectation of continued faithful service (Gen. 17.1, 9-14; 18.19). The recourse to a source-critical solution (attributing the conditional emphasis to P) will not satisfy the reader of the final form of the text.[57] The Davidic covenant similarly has an inbuilt expectation of obedience (1 Sam. 7.14; Ps. 132.12). The tensions which result may not be the result of careless redaction, but the necessary tensions in an account of a relationship which attempts to grapple with the conundrum of a persistent divine commitment and a meaningful human responsibility.

By the same token it is also simplistic to see in the Sinai covenant purely a conditional covenant. This would imply that once the covenant is

56. The psalm is the *locus classicus* for Israelite reflection on the transition from the Sinai to the Davidic covenant. For the election of David in relation to the election of Israel, see Kraus, *Worship in Israel*, pp. 179-81.

57. Weinfeld, 'The Covenant of Grant', p. 195; cf. also Arvid S. Kapelrud, 'The Covenant as Agreement', *SJOT* 1 (1988), pp. 30-38 (33); Ronald Youngblood, 'The Abrahamic Covenant: Conditional or Unconditional?', in Morris Inch and Ronald Youngblood (eds.), *The Living and Active Word of God: Studies in Honor of Samuel J. Schultz* (Winona Lake, IN: Eisenbrauns, 1983), pp. 31-46.

in force, it would be annulled by a breach on the part of Israel. Clearly such is not the case, and even the major breach of faith in the incident of the golden calf (Exod. 32–33) does not lead to the covenant being annulled. This suggests that my exegesis (following Patrick)[58] of the conditional clause in Exod. 19.5-6 (see Chapter 3) is correct, and that the protasis is to be understood in a definitional sense. The resultant declaration is then more of a promise or commitment on Yhwh's part than it is a contingent demand laid upon Israel.[59] This is not to deny that there are stipulations as part of the Sinai covenant, of course, nor that they can be expressed at times as conditions for the continuance of the covenant (Deut. 28).[60] The ברית may be identified, by way of a short-hand expression, with the 'ten words' (Exod. 34.28), which summarize the stipulations. Just as valid, however, are the statements to the effect that the covenant will never be abrogated:

> Yet in spite of this, when they are in the land of their enemies, I will not reject them or despise them so as to destroy them, breaking my covenant with them. I am Yhwh their God. But I will remember for their sake the covenant with their ancestors whom I brought out of Egypt in the sight of the nations to be their God. I am Yhwh. (Lev. 26.44-45)

The Sinai covenant cannot be reduced to a set of conditional obligations laid on Israel. The framework within which the stipulations are set is consistently one of the awesome and gracious activity of Yhwh, which not only enhances his prestige, but honours his people in the sight of the nations: 'Behold, I am making a covenant before all your people. I will perform wonders never before created (ברא) in all the world and in all nations. The people you live among will see how awesome is the work that I, Yhwh, will do for you' (Exod. 34.10).

It would thus appear just as valid to speak of unconditionality with respect to the Sinai covenant as it is with the Abrahamic or Davidic, if by this is meant the certainty that God will abide by his commitments.[61] Waltke introduces a refinement into Weinfeld's scheme (while maintaining some level of distinction between the treaty and promissory types of

58. Patrick, 'The Covenant Code Source', p. 149.

59. This is acknowledged by Weinfeld, though he maintains the distinction and does not see the Sinai covenant as corresponding to the grant ('The Covenant of Grant', p. 195).

60. This is not necessarily to identify the formal features of this chapter with the treaty curses, however; see Nicholson, *God and his People*, pp. 73-78.

61. See Dumbrell, 'The Prospect of Unconditionality', pp. 141-55.

covenant), observing elements of 'conditionality' in what are nevertheless substantially 'unconditional covenants'.[62] Freedman, while still sharply distinguishing two covenant types, grapples with the tensions inherent in the dual covenantal tradition and sees a resolution in the prophetic concept of a 'new covenant' in which there is engendered a new spirit of willingness to comply with the terms of the covenant.[63]

a. *Covenant as Grant of Honoured Position*

In addition to the grant of property, the royal grant may take the form of a grant of privileged position. Thus, kingship is granted by the imperial king to lesser monarchs, who owe their throne to the emperor's good grace. The grant of the Hittite king Muršiliš II to Abiraddaš consists of a guarantee of throne, house and land to his son, on condition that he remain loyal.[64] This grant may seem indistinguishable from the suzerainty treaty, since both of course expect continued loyalty on the part of a client king in return for patronage and protection. If a difference is to be observed, it will be in terms of the fact that a suzerainty treaty places the emphasis on the interstate relationships (expressed in terms of the monarchs' personal dealings), while the grant treaty has its focus more on the interpersonal relationships, and the favour of the greater king to the lesser. We might then prefer to see the two treaty types as expressing differing emphases of the same relationship, on a continuum rather than being polar opposites (suzerainty and grant).

This royal grant has its divine counterpart in texts where the high god grants kingship to other deities, or the gods grant kingship to mortal kings. The Sumerian King List speaks of kingship being lowered from heaven.[65] Mesopotamian kings generally regarded themselves as the objects of divine election for their task, or as the offspring of the gods.[66] The mid-third millennium Sumerian king Uru'inimgina appears to have enjoyed something like the benefit of a covenant with his god Ningirsu. He was granted the

62. Bruce K. Waltke, 'The Phenomenon of Conditionality within Unconditional Covenants', in Avraham Gileadi (ed.), *Israel's Apostasy and Restoration*, pp. 123-39.

63. David Noel Freedman, 'Divine Commitment and Human Obligation'; cf. Cross, 'The Ideologies of Kingship', pp. 236-37.

64. Weinfeld, 'The Covenant of Grant', p. 193, and references cited there.

65. *ANET*, p. 265; cf. Frankfort, *Kingship and the Gods*, pp. 237-38; Niehaus, *God at Sinai*, pp. 92-107.

66. Frankfort, *Kingship and the Gods*, pp. 238-40, 299-301; Daniel Isaac Block, *Gods of the Nations: Studies in Ancient Near Eastern National Theology* (ETSMS, 2; Jackson, MS: Evangelical Theological Society, 1988), pp. 92-96.

kingship of Lagaš by divine election and affirmed his commitment to keep the commands of the god.[67] King Pabil of Udm received his kingdom as 'the gift of El and present from the Father of humankind'.[68] A late second millennium text *The Prophetic Speech of Marduk* speaks of Marduk establishing a covenant (employing the verb *salāmu*, used in alliances and in prayers for reconciliation with the gods) with a future human king, who will do as Marduk commands.[69] While the evidence is not plentiful, it is sufficient to set the biblical grants of kingship and covenants between God and king in a wider context.

The Abrahamic promises contained the promise of a grant of kingship, albeit to future generations (Gen. 17.6, 16; cf. 35.11), while the Davidic covenant may simply particularize this aspect of the Abrahamic covenant (and cf. also the 'great name' promised to David [2 Sam. 7.9; cf. Gen. 12.2]). Could it be that the Sinai covenant is intended to occupy a position mid-way between these and that the grant of dynasty to David might be considered as a close parallel with the grant of a collective royal status to the nation as a 'royal priesthood', the nation described as the 'firstborn son' of Yhwh (Exod. 4.22; cf. 2 Sam. 7.14; Ps. 2.7)? This then raises the question of who the 'kings' are in the promise to Abraham (Gen. 17.6, 16; 35.11). While מלכים is generally taken as a proleptic reference to the Israelite and Judaean monarchs from Saul and David onwards, we ought not so quickly rule out the possibility that even in Genesis the referent may be the Israelites collectively, a nation of kings. This would appear to have been the understanding adopted by the writer of *Jub.* 16.18, a passage which links the divine commitment to Abraham with the 'kingdom of priests' (Exod. 19.6). The most likely biblical passages to have triggered this association between Abraham's progeny and the root מלך are Gen. 17.6, 16 and 35.11.

b. *Covenant as Grant of Priesthood*

In addition to the grant of kingship, the office of priesthood (closely associated with kingship) is considered the donation of kings or deities. The

67. This king's name is otherwise read as Urukagina. See McCarthy, *Treaty and Covenant*, p. 31; Niehaus, *God at Sinai*, p. 98; Lewis, 'The Identity and Function of El/Baal Berith', p. 405.

68. *Keret* (14) iii, 135-36.

69. Column 3 line 22; see Block, *Gods of the Nations*, p. 175; Sperling, 'An Arslan Tash Incantation', p. 10; Niehaus, *God at Sinai*, p. 99; Lewis, 'The Identity and Function of El/Baal Berith', p. 406. See also Chapter 5 for the mention of the covenant between Zarpiya and Sanda and the Violent Gods.

language of 'grant' is prominent in accounts of the privilege of priestly service in the ancient Near East. A seal inscription of Niqmepa grants a certain Qabia and his family in perpetuity the priesthood of Enlil.[70] Similarly the king Marduk-zâkir-šumi grants or confirms the priestly office with all that pertains to it to Ibni-Ištar,[71] while another text attributes to the gods Nanâ and Mâr-bîti the grant to a priest.[72] Thureau-Dangin makes the point that a royal grant may confirm an already existing privilege as well as bestow a fresh one.[73]

An analogous understanding applies to the grant of priesthood in Israel, where Yhwh declares of Aaron and his sons, 'I am giving you your priestly service (כהנתכם) as a grant (מתנה)' (Num. 18.7). This grant of an honoured position has its material benefits in the grant of the perquisites of the priestly office (vv. 8-9; cf. 1 Sam. 23.28). Philo, in a passage which alludes to Exod. 19.6, reflects on Abraham's progeny as 'the nation dearest of all to God, which, as I hold, has received priesthood and prophecy on behalf of all mankind'.[74]

The grant of priesthood to Levi, to Phinehas and to the Levites and Aaronides is expressed in terms of a covenant.[75] The covenant with Levi is most clearly represented in Mal. 2.4-7, which is an arraignment of the priesthood for their breach of covenant in language which may reflect the language of Deut. 33.8-13 and Num. 25.6-13.[76] Central to Malachi's exposé of the priests is v. 5: 'My covenant (בריתי) was with him, [a covenant of] life and wellbeing, and I granted (ואתנם) them to him'. The priests have

70. ATT.8.49 in Sidney Smith, 'A Preliminary Account of the Tablets from Atchana', *The Antiquaries Journal* 19 (1939), pp. 40-48 (43).

71. F. Thureau-Dangin, 'Un acte de donation de Marduk-zâkir-šumi', *Revue d'Assyriologie et d'Archéologie Orientale* 16 (1919), pp. 117-56 (127-30).

72. Thureau-Dangin, 'Un acte de donation', pp. 141-44.

73. Thureau-Dangin, 'Un acte de donation', p. 118.

74. Philo, *Abr*. 98.

75. The Levitical or priestly covenant has been rather neglected in covenantal discussions. Hahn devotes a sizeable section of his thesis to a consideration of the Levitical covenant, recognizing it as a manifestation of the grant-type covenant (*Kinship by Covenant*, pp. 212-304). Levenson treats Ezekiel's programme for the Zadokites as an instance of the covenant of grant: Jon D. Levenson, *Theology of the Program of Restoration of Ezekiel 40–48* (HSM, 10; Atlanta: Scholars Press, 1986), pp. 145-51.

76. Steven L. McKenzie and Howard N. Wallace, 'Covenant Themes in Malachi', *CBQ* 45 (1983), pp. 549-63; Beth Glazier-McDonald, *Malachi: The Divine Messenger* (SBLDS, 98; Atlanta: Scholars Press, 1987), pp. 73-80; Julia M. O'Brien, *Priest and Levite in Malachi* (SBLDS, 121; Atlanta: Scholars Press, 1990).

failed to 'listen' (תשמעו, v. 2; cf. Exod. 19.5) to God. As a consequence, the essential quality or 'blessings' (ברכותיכם, v. 2) of the grant of priesthood will be turned into a curse. Opinions differ on what these blessings are. Some see them as the material perquisites of the priestly office,[77] though it may be better to see in the 'life and wellbeing' a more general equivalent to the blessings, that is, the idyllic life lived in relation to God discussed in the previous chapter. Yet we should note that the object of the admonition (מצוה, vv. 1, 4) is not the annulment of the covenant, but its preservation. It is 'that my covenant with Levi might continue' (v. 4). This, then, is no contingent covenant.

The account of Moses' testamentary blessing on Levi (Deut. 33.8-13) also presents Levi's position as priest in relation to a 'covenant' (v. 9). While other Pentateuchal references to Levi emphasize his zeal for purity and honour (Gen. 34; Exod. 32.25-29), Deut. 33.8-13 moves from singular to plural forms in a manner designed to identify the patriarch Levi with the tribe to which the priestly office was entrusted, and thus to depict the patriarch himself in priestly terms.[78] In the account of the covenant of priesthood with Phinehas (Num. 25.6-13), Phinehas's uncompromising zeal is again mentioned as background to the divine grant (נתן) of 'my covenant of wellbeing' (v. 12). Verse 13 describes this covenant as ברית כהנת עולם ('a covenant of eternal priesthood'). In other references to the covenant with the priestly tribe, Jeremiah reasserts the irrevocability of this covenant, associating it with the Davidic—it is as sure as night follows day (Jer. 33.21)—and Nehemiah prays that God would 'remember' (in vengeance) the defilement of 'the covenant of the priesthood and the Levites' (Neh. 13.29). Ben Sira likewise presents the grant of priesthood to Aaron in terms of an eternal covenant (45.7). Yet the possibility remained that individuals who defaulted on the expected loyalty might forfeit their priestly status, as is said of Eli (1 Sam. 2.30).

Such texts present a unified picture of a covenant as a grant of an honoured position of service, where faithfulness is expected and disloyalty will be punished, but where the primary emphasis is not on the imposition of terms, but of the high honour bestowed on the favoured recipient of the grant. In the first instance, the grant or covenant is with an individual

77. So, e.g., Hitzig, as cited by Glazier-McDonald, *Malachi*, p. 65.

78. The manuscript 4QDeut^{h} has singular forms in vv. 9-10 where MT has plurals. For later depictions of Levi as a priest, see *T. Levi* 2.10; 4.2; 5.2; 8.2-10; *Aramaic Levi*; *Jub.* 30.1–32.9; and for discussion on these, see Kugel, 'Levi's Elevation to the Priesthood'; Kugler, *From Patriarch to Priest*.

(whether Levi, Aaron or Phinehas), but is extended to include a body of those who enjoy priestly status and the privilege of priestly service. Though there are clear expectations of the priests to live up to the high ideals, the priestly covenant is an 'eternal' covenant.

c. *The Sinai Covenant as Grant of Collective Royal Priesthood*

We ought not to press the analogy too far and attempt to see every subsequent reference to the Sinai covenant as being closely linked with the grant of kingship or of priesthood. Nevertheless, the grants of kingship and of priesthood to individuals are certainly suggestive parallels for the references to the community covenant which God grants to Israel in Exodus 19–24 and which the exegesis in previous chapters demonstrates is to be seen depicted in royal and priestly terms.[79] Such an understanding of the Sinai covenant as fundamentally one of grant, rather than fundamentally one of imposed obligation, is also essential to an understanding of those passages which reflect on the divine beneficence in its bestowal (e.g. Exod. 34.10; Deut. 4.6-8; Ps. 111.9). Here it is the whole people, the divine 'son', who has been made a grant of royal priesthood. As with some royal or divine grants to individuals, there is a call for continued loyalty as the expectation of the circumstances under which the grant will be enjoyed.

Perhaps the greatest difference between the royal grants to individuals and the Sinai covenant is to be found not in the conditional nature of the Sinai covenant, as is sometimes supposed, but in the fact that there is no stress on the prior loyalty or zeal of the grantee. Rather, the emphasis is on the divine grace in bringing Israel to this point (Exod. 19.4). The consistent treatment of the Sinai covenant is that it is a privilege, bestowed on an elect people for their benefit.

4. *Conclusion*

The covenants with individuals recorded in the Hebrew Bible, and through them, with the people of Israel, constitute an extended metaphor of divine–human relationships expressed in terms which are elsewhere employed to express human patterns of relationship. These relationships may be quite varied in nature, but a common thread appears to be the legal or quasi-legal treatment of those who are not naturally kin as though they were, for

79. See de Moor, *The Rise of Yahwism*, p. 254. De Moor observes that there may be a connection between the covenant with Phinehas and Exod. 19.6 but does not develop his observation, noting simply that 'this matter requires further study'.

the purpose of exercising certain prerogatives, bestowing certain privileges or eliciting certain responses.[80] The suzerainty treaty, much canvassed as a parallel for the divine covenants, is one prominent use of the covenant or treaty instrument. It is not suggested here that there are no possible parallels with this form in relation to the divine covenants. There are, however, some obvious dissimilarities which are sometimes overlooked and a more fruitful area of parallels is suggested. The grant treaties, where property or a privileged position is granted by the king, or god, constitute a general parallel which, while it has been explored in relation to the Abrahamic and Davidic covenants, has been all but ignored so far as the Sinai covenant is concerned. The strong contrast which is sometimes drawn between conditional and unconditional covenantal commitments is seen to be untenable and the Sinai covenant shares many features with those covenants which are regarded as belonging to the 'grant' type. In particular the covenant of eternal priesthood granted to the tribe of Levi and its representative leaders constitutes a very close analogy for the Sinai covenant as this is presented in Exodus 19–24.

80. Erhard S. Gerstenberger, 'Covenant and Commandment', *JBL* 84 (1965), pp. 38-51; Cross, 'The Epic Traditions of Early Israel', p. 35.

Chapter 8

THE TESTING OF THE ROYAL PRIESTHOOD: NUMBERS 16

1. *Universal Priesthood and Priestly Aspirations*

The declaration of Israel to be in some sense a corporate royal priesthood (Exod. 19.6) and the establishment of the Levitical priesthood were seen in Chapter 6 to be related in terms of the structure of the book of Exodus as corporate ideal to symbolic representation. But is there not a potential for tension and misunderstanding? Are there any texts which bring these dual aspects of Israel's priesthood—the general priesthood of the community and the elite Levitical priesthood—into sharper focus? McNamara writes, 'How this universal priesthood of all Israel was related to the ministering priesthood of the sons of Aaron was a matter that did not exercise the Jewish mind'.[1] The Korah pericope in Num. 16.1-35 may provide a counter-example to this assessment.

In the interweaving of legal and narrative sections which structure the book of Numbers, the account of the rebellion of Korah introduces a fresh narrative cycle. It is the first of three episodes which seem designed to affirm the legitimacy of the Aaronic priesthood. The second of these episodes involves further unrest in the Israelite camp (Num. 17.1-15 [ET 16.36-50]). Moses and Aaron were being held responsible for the deaths of the Israelite leaders and Yhwh's displeasure at the people is expressed in the form of a deadly plague. It is then Aaron's highly visible intervention when he 'stood between the living and the dead' (Num. 17.13 [ET 16.48]) and offered incense and made atonement that is effective in stopping the plague. Any suggestion that the people of God are immune from divine displeasure as a consequence of their 'consecrated' status is quickly dispelled, and the need for mediation, clearly evident in the Sinai pericope, is reinforced.

In the third incident (Num. 17.16-28 [ET 17.1-13]) the issue is to settle which of the ancestral tribes, represented by their tribal chiefs, is to ex-

1. McNamara, *Targum and Testament*, p. 155.

ercise the priestly office. Aaron, it is assumed, is the tribal chief of Levi. It may have been such tribal leaders who were in view in Exod. 19.22, 24, as together exercising a priestly office for their tribes prior to the appointment of Aaron and his sons in the narrative. If this is so, it is not difficult to understand the measure of resentment at the singling out of one of their number to exercise such prerogatives on behalf of the whole people. What is at issue is why it should be the tribe of Levi which receives this honour.

The effect of the three episodes is to reinforce the understanding that the discontent is widespread and deeply entrenched. There is 'ongoing grumbling' (מלינם, present participle) against Moses and Aaron (note the plural suffix, Num. 17.20 [ET 17.5]). In a test involving the placing of the twelve tribal totems in Yhwh's tent, it is Aaron's which receives divine authentication. His staff alone produces signs of fresh growth and life overnight (17.23 [ET 17.8]). The response of the people is dismay and an unwillingness to approach Yhwh's tent. Once again the need for mediation is established and the priestly prerogatives of the Aaronides vindicated.

These three narrative episodes then serve to introduce a section which deals with the responsibilities and prerogatives of the Aaronic priesthood (ch. 18).[2] The major issue in the complex of stories is the need for a priesthood to deal with the threat of annihilation at the hands of God and confirmation of the choice of Aaron of the tribe of Levi to be that priest over against rival claims, either from within the tribe of Levi or from other tribes.

2. *Narrative Tension in the Korah Incident*

The account of the Korah insurrection, the first of these episodes, follows immediately after the instruction to the Israelites regarding the wearing of tassels on the corners of their garments (Num. 15.37-41). Such tassels are

2. It is commonly held that these narratives have been constructed as a polemic related to the rival priestly ambitions within the post-exilic community, e.g. Driver, *Introduction to the Literature of the Old Testament*, pp. 63-65; George Buchanan Gray, *A Critical and Exegetical Commentary on Numbers* (ICC; Edinburgh: T. & T. Clark, 1903), pp. 186-96; Newman, *The People of the Covenant*, p. 96; Philip J. Budd, *Numbers* (WBC, 5; Waco, TX: Word Books, 1984), pp. 189-91. While this issue is beyond the scope of our immediate concerns, there is no evidence to suggest that there would be any need by post-exilic times to counter *non-Levitical* claims on the priesthood as distinct from rival Levitical claims. There does not seem to be any good reason to doubt that Numbers preserves much older traditions which deal with genuine concerns of the wilderness period.

to be a reminder to them of their commitment to keep all of Yhwh's requirements and a sign that they are to be consecrated (קדשים) to their God (v. 40). There are hints of a royal-priestly status for all Israel in this provision. The ornamental ציצת ('tassels') echo the priestly ציץ while the פתיל תכלת ('blue cord') which is to be fastened to them is also part of the priestly vestments (Exod. 28.28, 37; 39.21). The expensive blue dye involved is associated with royalty.[3]

The narrative commences with the verb ויקח (16.1) without object, which is unusual if it is from לקח ('take') and it is consequently sometimes regarded as a form of a root קחה or יקח ('murmur, become insolent').[4] I do not wish to rule out a possible connection with such a root (cf. Job 15.12). There may nevertheless be a play on the idea of 'take, usurp', the antonym of 'grant', which, as we have seen, is fundamental to legitimate priestly office (18.7). The use of ויקח is to be noted, again strangely without object, at 17.12 (ET 16.47), where it is used of Aaron's taking of his censer, which resulted in the arrest of the plague. This legitimating act of 'taking' is thus probably intended as an antithesis to Korah's illegitimate activity of 16.1.

Korah, a Levite, is joined in part or all of his charges against Moses and Aaron by certain named Reubenites, together with 250 community leaders, members of the מועד ('council', 16.1-2). There appear to be two aspects to the insurrection. First, Korah and his associates seek either to join Moses and Aaron or to replace them altogether in the exercise of their office. Secondly, there is a more general complaint regarding the hardships of the wilderness and Moses' failure to deliver on the promise of the good life in the promised land (vv. 13-14).

Because of its complexity, the account is often treated as a conflation of two originally separate traditions, one dealing with a Reubenite-led uprising (with its more general complaint) and the other a Korahite rebellion regarding the restriction of priestly prerogatives.[5]

3. Baruch A. Levine, *Numbers 1–20* (AB, 4; New York: Doubleday, 1993), pp. 400-402; Knohl, *The Sanctuary of Silence*, pp. 90, 186.

4. G. Richter, 'Die Einheitlichkeit der Geschichte von der Rotte Korah', *ZAW* 39 (1921), pp. 128-37 (129); Budd, *Numbers*, p. 180.

5. There is a widely accepted view that an older JE tradition of a Reubenite rebellion has been transformed by the later priestly writer so as to include an account of Levitical claims on the priesthood in order to address the rival claims of different priestly houses of a later era, perhaps the early Second Temple period. For a detailed discussion on the source analysis of the text into two separate accounts, see Gray, *Numbers*, pp. 187-93; cf. Martin Noth, *Numbers: A Commentary* (trans. James D.

Whatever sources may underlie the text (and it is difficult to justify the confidence placed in some of the reconstructions), our concern is with the form we encounter in Numbers 16. Despite some complexity, the account as we have it is more coherent than some imagine. The words of Moses in vv. 8-11 specifically accuse only Korah and the Levites of seeking for themselves the priestly office (כהנה, v. 10; cf. Exod. 29.9; Ezra 2.62; Neh. 7.64) and aspects of Moses' speech can apply directly only to the Levites. Yet we cannot so easily restrict the wider claim upon priestly prerogatives to a Levitical faction. As the narrative stands, Moses' response of vv. 8-11 follows immediately upon his instruction to Korah regarding an ordeal to test the legitimacy of their claims before Yhwh (vv. 5-7)—an ordeal in which all 250 rebel leaders eventually take part. The words of vv. 5-7 in turn are the first response to the general accusation against Moses and Aaron which is given in v. 3: 'They banded together against Moses and Aaron and said to them, "You have gone too far! The whole community is holy, every one of them, and Yhwh is in their midst. Why then do you exalt yourselves above Yhwh's assembly?"'

The charge of laying claim (בקש, v. 10) to priesthood can only be understood as a response to the complaint against Moses and Aaron of v. 3. Yet in vv. 1-3 Korah and the Levites are joined by Dathan, Abiram and On (Reubenites) and the whole company of 250 leaders of unspecified tribal origins in appealing to the notion of the holiness of the whole community.[6] These non-Levite leaders are again bracketed with Korah at

Martin; OTL; London: SCM Press, 1968), pp. 120-22; Coats, *Rebellion in the Wilderness*, pp. 156-84; Buber, *Moses*, pp. 182-90; Jacob Milgrom, 'Korah's Rebellion: A Study in Redaction', in Maurice Carrez, Joseph Doré and Pierre Grelot (eds.), *De la Tôra au Messie: Etudes d'exégèse et d'herméneutique bibliques offertes à Henri Cazelles pour ses 25 années d'enseignement à l'Institut Catholique de Paris (Octobre 1979)* (Paris: Desclée, 1981), pp. 135-46; Budd, *Numbers*, pp. 181-86; Levine, *Numbers 1–20*, pp. 405-407. Jacob Liver's approach, though not based on the documentary sources, similarly involves a complex combination of accounts: 'Korah, Dathan and Abiram', in Chaim Rabin (ed.), *Studies in the Bible* (SH, 8; Jerusalem: Magnes Press, 1961), pp. 189-217. Those who see in the account a greater level of literary coherence include Richter, 'Einheitlichkeit'; Johannes Pedersen, *Israel, its Life and Culture* (4 vols. in 2; London: Oxford University, 1926–40), II, pp. 283-86; Greta Hort, 'The Death of Qorah', *AusBR* 7 (1959), pp. 2-26; Jonathan Magonet, 'The Korah Rebellion', *JSOT* 24 (1982), pp. 3-25; R.K. Harrison, *Numbers* (Wycliffe Exegetical Commentary; Chicago: Moody Press, 1990); Timothy R. Ashley, *The Book of Numbers* (NICOT; Grand Rapids: Eerdmans, 1993), pp. 298-321.

6. The reference to On is generally regarded as a textual corruption. He disappears from view in the remainder of the account and in the traditions preserved elsewhere,

the conclusion of the episode in v. 27. Considerable emphasis is placed on the holy status of the entire congregation. Note the repetition of 'all' in כל and כלם (v. 3). The appeal of the insurrectionists to the holiness (קדשים) of the whole people is intended as a telling argument against what they regard as an unacceptable restriction of their privileges. The word קדש, then, in the minds of the insurrectionists, is virtually a synonym for כהן and their designs for some form of wider exercise of priestly office is transparent, as Moses recognizes. This would appear then to be an echo of Exod. 19.6, the only biblical passage where כהנים and קדוש are brought into close correlation and where these terms refer to the whole Israelite community.[7]

Several further expressions serve to fill out what is understood by this claimed status as קדשים. In the mouth of the insurrectionists, the holy state of the community means that 'Yhwh is in their midst' (Num. 16.3). Moses' response contains the expressions את אשר לו ('those who belong to him', v. 5) and את אשר יבחר־בו ('the one he chooses', v. 5; cf. v. 7) and finally והקריב אליו...יקריב אליו ('he draws near to him', v. 5). These phrases all seem to be expressions, acceptable to both parties to the dispute, which are used to denote the group which may legitimately exercise priesthood before Yhwh. We will return to a consideration of these phrases shortly.

The word the insurrectionists use for what they consider the arrogant behaviour of Moses and Aaron is תתנשאו (v. 5), a hithpael of נשא with a reflexive denominative force: 'to establish oneself in the role of נשיא ("leader")' (cf. 1 Kgs 1.5 where it is used of Adonijah's presumption).[8] Given that the 250 rebels are introduced as נשיאי עדה ('community leaders', v. 2), it is not difficult to see the cause of their dissatisfaction. They have been deprived of a prerogative which they perceive to be theirs by right as 'leaders'. A term closely associated with נשיא is נגיד which is used both for 'prince' or secular ruler, or member of the royal family and in a more specific sense for the high priest (1 Chron. 9.11; 2 Chron. 31.13; Neh. 11.11).[9]

It is probably quite deliberate, however, that despite the apparent echo of Exod. 19.6, it is not the insurrectionists who employ the term כהן. To

which mention only Korah (Num. 26.10) or Dathan and Abiram (Num. 26.9; Deut. 11.6; Ps. 106.17).

7. Ashley, *Numbers*, p. 305.

8. See GKC, §54[e], pp. 149-50, for this use of the hithpael.

9. KB, p. 592.

have done so would have obscured the point they wished to make. We should probably not see Korah and his associates as seeking כהנה for every Israelite. Theirs is not a democratizing movement aimed at the restoration of the priestly 'prerogative of the whole community',[10] but a distinctly aristocratic one. Rather, they are taking advantage of a tenet which was agreed by all parties—the vocation of all of Israel to a special state of holiness and intimacy in relation to Yhwh—in order to further their own claims at the expense of Moses and Aaron.

The fact that specifically cultic prerogatives are among the personal ambitions of the whole group of insurrectionists (not merely the Levites) is also suggested by the form of the ordeal which Moses sets up, the offering of incense in the courtyard of the tent of meeting—clearly a priestly activity (cf. 1 Sam. 2.28). An expectation of the danger involved in such an activity, if undertaken contrary to Yhwh's appointment, has been set up by the narrative of Lev. 10.1-3, in which Nadab and Abihu are consumed by fire for offering incense contrary to Yhwh's authorization. All 250 insurrectionists (albeit with some reluctance) participate in this activity, which they can hardly fail to do if increased cultic prerogatives form part of their claim. The disasters which then befall Korah and his men and all 250 leaders are portrayed by the author as Yhwh's endorsement of the leadership of Moses and Aaron.

There is considerable artistry in the use of irony in the account, for example, in the turning of the rebels' רב־לכם ('you have gone too far', v. 3) back on their own heads (v. 7). It is the insurrectionists who are shown to be those who seek something for themselves (ובקשתם, v. 10), and who 'rise up' (v. 2), whereas Moses and Aaron are shown in a posture of humility and supplication for the wellbeing of Israel (vv. 4, 22). Far from the usurpation of authority of which Moses and Aaron are accused (תתנשאו, v. 3), Moses has not even 'taken' (נשׂאתי) a donkey (v. 15). In an anticipation of their final fate, rather than being vindicated in their claims to priesthood, they are excluded from the community (עדה, vv. 24, 26), ironically the same word which is used throughout for the rebellious company (vv. 5, 6, 11, 16, 19, 40).[11] It is as though the insurrectionists are a self-

10. Eastwood, *The Royal Priesthood of the Faithful*, p. 18.

11. On the political associations of this word, see Robert Gordis, 'Democratic Origins in Ancient Israel: The Biblical *'edah*', in *Alexander Marx Jubilee Volume on the Occasion of his Seventieth Birthday* (New York: Jewish Theological Seminary of America, 1950), English section, pp. 369-88; Jacob Milgrom, 'Priestly Terminology and the Political and Social Structures of Pre-monarchic Israel', *JQR* 69 (1978), pp. 65-81.

styled rival 'Israel'. Yet, by means of the ordeal and its judgment (by the opening up of the earth and by fire), they are declared not to be holy, not to belong to Yhwh, not to be his chosen intimates, in short, not to be Israel.

What is important for our purpose is first to note that the wider and narrower understanding of priesthood can be brought together in the same discussion, albeit somewhat obliquely. We may further note the elements which are singled out for consideration in this context as being the correlates of the claim of כהנה ('priesthood') as these are brought out in vv. 3 and 5. Most instructively, each of the expressions may be used in both a wider and a narrower sense.

The use of the word קדשים/קדוש ('holy, vv. 3, 5, 7) is central to the dynamics of the narrative, as it has a usefully ambiguous set of referents for the purpose of the plot. Within Israel's graded system of holiness (see Chapter 6) there are not separate terms to mark the inner and outer levels of sanctity, or nearness to God. Thus the city of Jerusalem is holy (Isa. 52.1; Neh. 11.1) and the temple within it is holy (Ps. 79.1; 1 Chron. 29.3), and God's throne is holy (Ps. 47.9 [ET 47.8]), without it being implied that there is the same degree of holiness pertaining to each. The only 'superlative' used is in the expression קדש הקדשים for the innermost room of the tabernacle or temple (Exod. 26.33; 1 Kgs 6.16), otherwise called the דביר (1 Kgs 6.16).[12] Thus it is true, as Korah cleverly asserts, that the whole community is holy (Num. 16.3; Exod. 19.6), just as it is true that the priesthood is holy (Lev. 21.7; 22.9). There would of course be a flaw in the syllogism to deduce that the whole community has all of the prerogatives of the Levitical priesthood.[13]

Secondly, the notion of belonging to Yhwh, using the preposition ל with pronominal suffix in the expression את אשר לו ('those who belong to him', Num. 16.5) may be used generally of Israel (as Exod. 19.5-6) or more specifically it may be used for the distinctive relationship of the Levites to Yhwh (והיו לי הלוים, 'and the Levites will belong to me', Num. 8.14).[14] Further, the election motif in the words את אשר יבחר־בו ('the one he chooses', Num. 16.5; cf. v. 7) is commonly used for the divine choice of Israel (Deut. 4.37; 10.15; Isa. 14.1; Ps. 33.12), but may be used

12. Even this distinction is not consistently maintained: see Exod. 20.29 and *Temple Scroll* 35.9, where קדש קדשים refers to areas and objects beyond the temple proper.

13. A.B. Davidson, *The Theology of the Old Testament* (ed. S.D.F. Salmond; Edinburgh: T. & T. Clark, 1904), p. 153.

14. The notions of holiness and belonging to Yhwh are to be regarded as a hendiadys, with Levine, *Numbers 1–20*, p. 412.

in a more specific way to refer to the election of the priests or Levites (Deut. 18.5; 21.5; 1 Sam. 2.28; Ps. 105.26).

Then the expression בתוכם יהוה ('Yhwh is in their midst', v. 3) characteristically encompasses the whole Israelite community, while at the same time being closely associated with the tent-sanctuary in the middle of the Israelite camp which visually represents Yhwh's presence with his people in the Pentateuchal narrative from Exod. 25.8. This presence of Yhwh in the sanctuary is of course closely tied to the priesthood of the Aaronides who mediate that presence by their tabernacle ministry:

> I will consecrate the tent of meeting and the altar and will consecrate Aaron and his sons to serve me as priests. Then I will dwell among the Israelites and be their God. They will know that I am Yhwh their God, who brought them out of Egypt so that I might dwell among them. I am Yhwh their God. (Exod. 29.44-46)

Similarly Lev. 26.12 (part of the Holiness Code, a characteristic of which is to broaden the holiness requirements of the priesthood to the whole community) brings the dwelling of Yhwh in the midst of Israel into close relationship with the full covenant formula: 'I will walk in your midst and be your God, and you will be my people'.

Finally, we consider the use of קרב in the expression ...והקריב אליו יקריב אליו (Num. 16.5). Levine suggests that rather than 'draws... near' (transitive), the hiphil should be translated as a declarative: 'he declares intimate', and sees in it a reflection of court language (cf. Gen. 45.10; Est. 1.14, where the king grants intimacy as a favour).[15] Such favour is again granted to both a wider and a narrower group. In the Deuteronomic theology, Yhwh is 'near' the whole people through prayer, a privilege not granted to any other people by their god (Deut. 4.7), though this 'nearness' could be taken for granted and abused (Jer. 23.23). Following the deaths by divine judgment of Nadab and Abihu, Yhwh declares through Moses: 'Among my intimates (בקרבי) I will be declared holy and before all the people I will be honoured' (Lev. 10.3). It is open to debate whether בקרבי should here be understood extensively (as a synonymous parallel to כל־העם, 'all the people') or whether it is a reference to the illegitimate approach of Nadab and Abihu and hence carries a more restricted reference to the cultic activity of the priests. Ezekiel also uses the expression אשׁר קרובים ליהוה ('who are intimate with Yhwh', 42.13) as an epithet for the priests. Psalm 65.5 (ET 65.4) brings together the notions of divine

15. Levine, *Numbers 1–20*, p. 413.

choice and being brought near to the sanctuary of God as tokens of the divine favour and blessing on the whole people: 'Blessed is the one you choose (תבחר) and draw near (ותקרב, piel) to dwell in your courts'.

Thus, the whole episode in Numbers 16 hinges on the ambiguity inherent in the words כהנה, קדש and each of the broadly synonymous expressions used. There is a sense in which Korah and his company have a valid point, in that the whole community is holy and does enjoy intimacy with Yhwh. There is an equally valid sense in which, from the narrator's point of view, their claim is invalid, in that there is also a more restricted sense in which these expressions are to be understood when applied to the Levitical priesthood. The text does not enter into any explicit discussion of how the ideal of the universal priestly status of Israel relates to the need for the Aaronic priesthood. The former is simply presupposed and the latter is simply affirmed by this pericope. The ideal of the holy status of the whole people, while accepted as being true in principle, is not regarded by the narrator as an alternative but as complementary to the Aaronic priesthood. If we may discern a positive connection between the dual aspects of priesthood in Numbers 16–18, then it may be expressed in these terms: the Aaronic priesthood has been initiated by Yhwh as a means to the end of preserving and fostering the holiness of the community as a whole. The remark of Chadwick is apposite: 'It was because the function belonged to all, that no man might arrogate it who was not commissioned to act on behalf of all'.[16] However, this is left subtly unstated and it would have laboured the point and marred the narrative artistry to spell this out.

3. *Conclusion*

The narrative of the rebellion of Korah and his associates is something of a test case for the understanding of a notion of a priesthood which is wider than the priestly clan of Levi. By its positioning after an allusion to the royal-priestly character of all Israel in the mention of the tassels, and at the head of a series of narratives which lead into a description of the duties of the Aaronic priesthood, this account seems designed to bring into focus the relationship between these inclusive and restrictive notions of priesthood. There is no direct assertion of universal priesthood on Korah's part (which would have proved too much) and no direct denial by Moses and Aaron of the validity of Korah's claims of sanctity and divine choice of

16. Chadwick, *Exodus*, p. 274.

and intimacy with the whole community. The use of the roots קדשׁ and כהן in close proximity as virtual synonyms, where קדשׁ is specifically applied to the whole people, is best understood when seen as an echo of Exod. 19.6, the only other passage where both roots are used of the status of all Israel. The nuanced interplay of the notions of sanctity, divine proximity, divine possession and election, all of which are explicative of the notion of priesthood, suggests that the narrator is aware of the dynamics, indeed the tensions, latent in the dual aspects of priesthood in Israel. The narrator's message would seem to be that Israel needs both forms of priesthood, and that they are not mutually incompatible. In fact, the Aaronic priesthood has a vital role in preserving the very existence of Israel and facilitating the intimacy with God to which the nation is called. Priesthood is again seen as a matter of divine grant, and one arrogates priesthood to himself at his peril.

Chapter 9

The Royal Priesthood in Jeopardy: Hosea 4.4-9

1. *Priestly Language in Hosea 4.4-9*

A much overlooked passage in discussions of Exod. 19.6 and its intertextual links is Hos. 4.6: 'My people are destroyed from lack of knowledge. Because you have rejected knowledge, I have rejected you from serving as my priest (מכהן, piel); because you have ignored the law of your God, I, even I, will ignore your children.' Opinions differ as to whether v. 4 commences a fresh oracle, discontinuous with the preceding verses,[1] or whether it follows closely vv. 1-3, which are addressed to the Israelites generally (4.1),[2] and constitute a ריב ('lawsuit') against them for a breach of the covenant (cf. Mic. 6.1-8).[3] The attributes which ought to characterize this people, but which are alleged in the charge to be lacking, are אמת ('integrity'), חסד ('loyalty') and דעת אלהים ('knowledge of God'). What has taken their place is a catena of sins such as cursing, lying, murder, theft and adultery (v. 2), which summarize and in part reflect the wording of the Decalogue (Exod. 20.13-15; cf. Jer. 7.9). In consequence, the land or earth is in mourning and life is being extinguished. Creation is becoming uncreation as the animals and birds and fish disappear (cf. Jer. 4.22-26). The setting for what follows may then be described as *cosmic*.[4] The idyllic world of Genesis 1 and 2, with humankind at its centre as its guardian priest-king, is no more to be seen.

1. So, e.g., J.L. Mays, *Hosea: A Commentary* (OTL; London: SCM Press, 1969), pp. 60-79; Hans Walter Wolff, *A Commentary on the Book of the Prophet Hosea* (ed. Paul D. Hanson; trans. Gary Stansell; Hermeneia; Philadelphia: Fortress Press, 1974), pp. 70-93; Francis I. Andersen and David Noel Freedman, *Hosea: A New Translation with Introduction and Commentary* (AB, 24; Garden City, NY: Doubleday, 1980), pp. 343-79.

2. So, e.g., Keil and Delitzsch, *Commentary on the Old Testament*, X, pp. 74-84.

3. For an outline of the structure of this section see Andersen and Freedman, *Hosea*, p. 332.

4. Cf. Andersen and Freedman, *Hosea*, p. 334.

With v. 4, we begin at least a new sub-unit (אך) which throws up for us a number of grammatical enigmas. The identity of the speakers and those addressed or spoken of is not at all clear. In the absence of markers to the contrary, however, the reader of the final form can be expected to assume continuity of both speaker and addressee from the previous section. If Yhwh is the speaker of the prohibition on disputation (v. 4), it may be a way of saying 'the matter is beyond dispute; there is no defence'. Andersen and Freedman envisage a fresh speaker at this point, a chief priest, and see more of a dramatic dialogue in these verses.[5] As it stands in the MT, the following line ועמך כמריבי כהן (v. 4b) would mean 'your people are like those who contend against a priest' (reading מריבי as a hiphil construct plural participle). If the MT is followed, the simile would appear to be a reference to the notion expressed in Deut. 17.12, where lack of respect for the office of priest is deserving of death. However, this reading has been felt to be difficult and a large number of variant readings has been suggested. Most of these involve greater or lesser alterations to the consonantal text and will be ignored here.[6] The reading proposed by Kuhnigk simply involves a different word division and pointing וְעִמְּךָ כָּם רִיבִי כֹּהֵן, which would translate as 'With you, indeed, is my contention, O priest'.[7] This must be viewed with some caution, as the evidence for a deictic particle כָּם (or כִּים) is not strong. We will return to the question of the identity of the 'priest' in v. 4 shortly.

The crux, for our purposes, is to determine the referent of the second person singular address in v. 6. The initial clause of v. 6 is clear, נדמו עמי מבלי הדעת ('My people are destroyed for lack of knowledge'). That is, the present predicament of the people is brought about through the neglect of the relationship with God (understanding דעת in a relational sense and assuming אלהים from v. 1), which entails a neglect of the commandments. There follows a reversion to a second person singular form of address begun in v. 4 in עמך. Who, then, is the unidentified singular 'you' in the passage? It is a person with a mother (v. 5) and children (v. 6) who are also subject to condemnation. A commonly accepted reading is that this is an address to the (Levitical) priests, or one priest in particular, who, along with the prophet (נביא, v. 5), is to blame for the neglect of instruction. This is a possible reading, and is in part suggested by the occurrence

5. Andersen and Freedman, *Hosea*, pp. 342-46.

6. See Andersen and Freedman, *Hosea*, pp. 347-48.

7. Willibald Kuhnigk, OSB, *Nordwestsemitische Studien zum Hoseabuch* (BibOr, 27; Rome: Pontifical Biblical Institute Press, 1974), p. 30; cf. Mays, *Hosea*, p. 65.

of כהן in v. 4. However, as we are not sure if the priest in v. 4 is being addressed, or spoken of allusively in the third person, it would be unsafe to assume that the 'you' is the high priest or the priesthood corporately. If considering the latter, one needs to bear in mind that the use of a singular form of address for a body of priests who are not normally spoken of or to in the singular by a collective name such as 'Levi' or 'Aaron' would be unusual. Where the collective expression 'house of Aaron' is used in poetic contexts in Pss. 115.10, 12; 118.3; 135.9, the verbs are all plural. The reference to a collective 'mother' for the priesthood would also be awkward.

While there are difficulties on any reading, it is at least possible to take the second person singular as the direct address to the accused in court and to understand this to be the same as the accused identified in v. 1, that is, the Israelites generally.[8] It is not unusual to switch from plural to singular when addressing the nation of Israel (e.g. Exod. 22.20-26 [ET 22.21-27], 28-30 [ET 22.29-31]; 32.4; Deut. 6.1-2). The reference to Israel's 'mother' and 'children', while still difficult, would seem on this reading to refer back to the mother and children of 2.2, 4 (and cf. Isa. 50.1 for a similar metaphor), who are part of the extended and at times elusive metaphorical *dramatis personae* of Hosea's message.[9]

On this reading, the judgment is that Israel is to be rejected from serving as Yhwh's corporate priest (כהן, piel infinitive construct), in what appears to amount to an annulment of the promise of Exod. 19.6. This reading would be a colourful way of representing the breach of relationship Hosea has expressed elsewhere through the name לא עמי ('Not My People', 1.9; 2.1 [ET 1.10]). Adopting this understanding, we might then consider further the identity of the 'priest' in v. 4. It is possible that there, too, the sin of contempt for a 'priest' is the sin of the Israelites' collective mutual contempt for one another, as DeRoche understands it.[10] Verse 7 then switches to third person plural forms, though appears to continue the arraignment of v. 6, while v. 8 introduces a distinction between 'my people' and the third person plural group who in some sense 'devour' (יאכלו) the people's sin (חטאת). DeRoche is surely correct in arguing that חטאת cannot mean 'sin

8. For this view see Keil and Delitzsch, *Commentary on the Old Testament*, X, pp. 77-78; Baudissin, *Geschichte*, p. 237; Michael DeRoche, 'Structure, Rhetoric and Meaning in Hosea iv 4-10', *VT* 33 (1983), pp. 185-98.

9. Thomas Edward McComiskey, 'Hosea', in Thomas Edward McComiskey (ed.), *The Minor Prophets: An Exegetical and Expository Commentary* (3 vols.; Grand Rapids: Baker Book House, 1992), I, pp. 1-237 (60).

10. DeRoche, 'Structure, Rhetoric and Meaning', pp. 189-90.

offerings' here (a reference to priestly avarice), since Hosea uses חטאת as a parallel to עון elsewhere only in the sense of the people's 'sin' (8.13; 9.9; 13.12). In this case, יאכלו would need to have a more metaphorical reference, such as 'enjoy'.[11] Thus DeRoche adopts a coherent interpretation of vv. 4-10 which does not involve any reference to a (Levitical) priest, other than in the expression כעם ככהן (v. 9) which he understands simply to refer to the totality of the population, priests and people alike (to which may be added prophets, v. 5; cf. 2 Kgs 23.2).[12] There may be more of a programmatic note in the expression 'like people like priest' than DeRoche realizes. The use of the identical maxim in Isa. 24.2 suggests that the expression was not original to either prophet but was already proverbial. While it has been cleverly appropriated for a judgment context in each case, that is, a common fate awaits both priest and people, as a standalone expression it could hardly have meant that, but would presumably have meant something along the lines that there is or should be a correlation (in character or status) between the priesthood and the whole people. Such an expression would then seem to owe its genesis to Exod. 19.6 or at least to the notion of a corporate priesthood of Israel exhibited in this verse. Now, however, both people and priest have exemplified the same *corrupt* behaviour and both will be subject to the same fate. The maxim has been turned on its head. The priestly community of Israel ought to portray all that is ideal about humanity and its relationship with God and the world, as in the sanctuary-garden of Genesis 2, though, as in that garden, the reality fails to measure up to the ideal.

This understanding might lend support to the unfashionable reading 'like Adam' (Vulgate, RV, NASB, NIV) for כאדם at 6.7. If Hosea has as part of his shared presupposition pool with his readers the story of Genesis 2, with Adam as the idyllic priest-king (cf. Ezek. 28.12-15; *Jub*. 4.23-26), together with the notion that Israel at Sinai was constituted as the new humanity, the true successors to Adam (cf. *4 Ezra* 3.3-36; 6.53-59; *2 Bar*. 14.17-19), then it makes sense to compare the breach of the Sinai covenant (e.g. Hos. 4.1, 2) with the rebellion in the garden (Gen. 3; cf. Ezek. 28.16-17).[13] The LXX ὡς ἄνθρωπος understands the reference to be to a man. An alternative is to read כאדם as a place reference (cf. שׁם, 'there', which seems to call for a place reference), though why the preposition

11. DeRoche, 'Structure, Rhetoric and Meaning', p. 196.

12. DeRoche, 'Structure, Rhetoric and Meaning', pp. 193-98.

13. For recent support for the 'Adam' reading, see McComiskey, 'Hosea', p. 95.

כ should have been chosen (it is usually emended to ב on this understanding), and why the notion of 'covenant' should be introduced in connection with the place Adam (RSV, JB, NRSV) or Admah (NEB) is unclear.[14]

Finally, it should be noted that the apparent rejection of Israel from 'priestly service' at 4.6 may not be final. While there is no corresponding affirmation of a specific restoration of priestly service, if my understanding is correct that the rejection from priesthood is another way of expressing the rejection of Israel as God's people, then the message of Hosea is clear that there is the prospect of a way back (e.g. 1.10; 2.23).

2. *Conclusion*

My conclusion on Hos. 4.4-9 and in particular v. 6 must be tentative, due to the difficulty of understanding the very compressed language and in particular the abrupt changes of person and number. The interpretation offered here observes a greater coherence in the chapter than is generally accepted. These verses are best regarded as continuing the arraignment of Israel begun in v. 1. The people are said to have exercised a corporate priestly role, or to have enjoyed priestly status. Hosea indicates that this role or status is to be denied them as a judgment for their breach of the terms under which the privilege was granted (identified at 6.7 as the covenant). In particular they have been guilty of a lack of mutual respect and of rejecting the relationship with God and submission to his law which are the essence of the covenant. Hosea is aware of a tradition which closely associates Israel with the notion of priesthood and makes artful use of a proverbial expression which he turns on its head in the arraignment. The maxim 'like people like priest' is reminiscent of the sentiment, if not the language, of Exod. 19.6. There may be the prospect, however, of a restoration of Israel's priestly role or status if, as suggested, the ascription to Israel of a corporate priesthood is one image of what it means to be the elect people of God, for Hosea does not depict Israel's rejection as ultimate. Our interpretation has lent support to the reading 'like Adam' at Hos. 6.7 as being consistent with the ideology of Adam as the archetypal priest-king in the primal paradise-garden.

14. For support for the locational reading, see Andersen and Freedman, *Hosea*, p. 436; Kuhnigk (*Nordwestsemitische Studien*, p. 82) reads כאדם as 'wie den Erdboden', that is, אדם = אדמה, which is also possible, though not compelling; cf. Nicholson, *God and his People*, pp. 183-86.

Chapter 10

Reassurance of Royal Priesthood: Two Intertextual Studies

1. *Micah 4.8*

In Micah's prophetic portrayal of the restoration of fallen Judah after the foreshadowed calamity of exile in Babylon, there may be heard echoes of Exod. 19.6. In particular v. 8 contains the words: 'As for you, watchtower of the flock, stronghold of daughter Zion, upon you it is coming; the foremost dominion (הממשלה), the royalty (ממלכת) belonging to daughter Jerusalem will come'.

As is so often the case in prophetic material, it is difficult to define the limits of the pericope with any precision. Shaw mounts a case for treating 3.1–4.8 as a literary unity, thus making our verse the climax of an oracle.[1] There does not seem to be a major discourse break at 4.9, however, and it may be better to see an even more extensive literary unity, whatever the original setting of the constituent oracles may have been. Before we look closely at v. 8, we should note that the cotext contains at least one other indication that the exodus experience colours Micah's choice of language. The image of daughter Jerusalem leaving the city and camping in the open *en route* to Babylon (v. 10) is perhaps to be taken as an ironic reversal of the exodus from Egypt and the encampment in the wilderness *en route* to Canaan.[2]

The word order of v. 8 is striking, commencing with a vocative, ואתה (resumed by עדיך), followed by two noun phrases in apposition which are poetic descriptions of Jerusalem.[3] Then follows in chiastic arrangement a

1. Charles S. Shaw, *The Speeches of Micah: A Rhetorical-Historical Analysis* (JSOTSup, 145; Sheffield: JSOT Press, 1993), pp. 97-127.

2. Ralph L. Smith, *Micah–Malachi* (WBC, 32; Waco, TX: Word Books, 1984), p. 40.

3. For alternative explanations, see William McKane, *The Book of Micah: Introduction and Commentary* (Edinburgh: T. & T. Clark, 1998), pp. 131-33.

prepositional phrase (+ subject) + verb, balanced by verb + subject + prepositional phrase. The gapping of the subject in the first stich is unusual and has led to a number of suggested emendations.[4] However, it would be better to see the structure with two synonymous verbs, followed by two synonymous nouns as creating suspense: 'It's coming, yes it's on its way, (but what is it?)'.[5]

What then is the meaning of the ממשׁלה ('sovereignty, dominion') and ממלכת ('kingship, royalty') which are the subjects of the verbs, or perhaps more strictly the second verb? As a compound subject, the words may be expected to be mutually explanatory. Both verbal nouns are indisputably used here in an active sense. Daughter Jerusalem (rather than the daughter of Jerusalem),[6] that is, the people of God corporately, is promised its rightful regal status and hegemony after a projected period of distress and humiliation (v. 9). The adjective הראשׁנה which qualifies הממשׁלה is generally understood in the sense of 'former', that is, that Jerusalem is promised a restoration of the hegemony the city once enjoyed (presumably under David and Solomon), and this is certainly possible. It is also possible, however, to understand הראשׁנה in the sense of 'principal, chief', that is, that Israel's dominion is to be as a 'world-empire'.[7] The corresponding noun ראשׁ has been used in v. 1 and is particularly used in contexts of exaltation and triumph over enemies (e.g. Pss. 27.6; 110.6 [ET 110.7]). Israel is assured of becoming a strong nation (גוי, v. 7). The word גוי is not the usual word for the people of Israel, which is עם. The use, then, of both גוי and ממלכת in close proximity to refer to the people of Israel is highly suggestive of a link with Exod. 19.6. This impression is strengthened by the fact that the word ממלכת is somewhat unexpectedly in this form, rather than the absolute form ממלכה. It may either be understood as a Phoenician-type absolute form (as has also been suggested for Exod. 19.6), or a rare use of the construct before a preposition.[8] On either view, it is at least

4. See, for discussion, Bruce K. Waltke, 'Micah', in Thomas Edward McComiskey (ed.), *The Minor Prophets: An Exegetical and Expository Commentary* (3 vols.; Grand Rapids: Baker Book House, 1992), II, pp. 591-764 (690-91).

5. Shaw, *The Speeches of Micah*, p. 122.

6. W.F. Stinespring, 'No Daughter of Zion: A Study in the Appositional Genitive in Hebrew Grammar', *Encounter* 26 (1965), pp. 133-41.

7. John Merlin Powis Smith, William Hayes Ward and Julius A. Bewer, *A Critical and Exegetical Commentary on Micah, Zephaniah, Nahum, Habakkuk, Obadiah and Joel* (ICC; Edinburgh: T. & T. Clark, 1912), p. 95.

8. See GKC, §130a, p. 421. The editors of *BHS* felt some awkwardness about this form, proposing the emendation מַמְלֶכֶת.

possible that the form of the word is a deliberate echo of its form in Exod. 19.6. The notion that Israel is to be a 'strong' nation is not explicitly present in Exod. 19.6, though interestingly it is found in one form of the *Samaritan Targum*,[9] and reflects the probable connection with the Abrahamic promise of Gen. 12.2 to be seen in the choice of גוי rather than עם in Exod. 19.6.[10]

The sovereignty promised to Israel is closely coordinated with the sovereignty of Yhwh which is asserted in v. 7 (ומלך יהוה), in language which reflects that of the 'enthronement psalms' (Pss. 93; 95; 97; 99). Jerusalem is promised by divine grant the symbols of dominion in the form of horns of iron with which to 'thresh' the nations and is summoned to exercise that dominion by breaking them in pieces (v. 13). This divine summons presupposes that the nations are Yhwh's to do with as he sees fit (cf. 'all the earth is mine', Exod. 19.5).

Clearly the royal prerogative and dominion are to be the possession of the whole people, or at least such as constitute the 'remnant' (v. 7) after their period of affliction. There can be no doubt as to the active nature of this dominion. Yet it is at the same time a submissive dominion, in that they are to devote the ill-gotten wealth of the nations which they plunder to 'the lord of all the earth' (v. 13). Their dominion is not to be seen as in any way antithetical to God's, but as an expression of it.

Are there also echoes of the 'priestly' character of Israel in this oracle of hope? In answer to this, we look at the choice of words to describe the state of the afflicted nation. They are הצלעה ('the lame') and הנהלאה (v. 7). This latter word is of uncertain meaning. It appears to be a niphal participle of הלא, an otherwise unattested root. Given its pairing with החלעה, this word may be a by-form of (or error for) הנחלא ('sick').[11] Whatever the precise meaning, the words may be intended as a summary of the extended list in Lev. 21.16-23 of disabilities which preclude one from serving as a priest. It is otherwise difficult to account for physical deformity being singled out as characterizing the deprivations of exile. These are the ones God has banished from his presence (הנדחה, v. 6) as being unfit to approach him just as priests with any of the itemized defects were to be excluded from sanctuary service.[12] It is God who has afflicted them

9. *Samaritan Targum* A reads for גוי קדש (the text form of the Samaritan Pentateuch) עמה רבה קדיש (Tal, *The Samaritan Targum*, p. 299 [Hebrew]).

10. This point is well argued by Dumbrell, *Covenant and Creation*, p. 87.

11. R.L. Smith, *Micah–Malachi*, p. 38. KB (p. 231) suggests either a form from חלה ('fall ill') or לאה ('be weary').

12. R.L. Smith, *Micah–Malachi*, p. 39.

thus (ואשׁר הרעתי, v. 6) and it is God who will restore them to their rightful place (אספה and אקבצה, v. 7). This then may be an echo of the priestly character of all Israel proclaimed in Exod. 19.6.

We may make one further observation on this passage. This concerns the questions in v. 9 which are generally translated along the following lines: 'Now why do you cry aloud (רע)? Is there no king (המלך) among you? Has your counsellor (יועצך) perished, that pain seizes you like that of a woman in labour?' The word רע is generally taken as being רֵעַ I ('shouting, roar'), which is a rare word and not found elsewhere as a cognate accusative after the verb רוע with adverbial force.[13] Is it possible that we have here a further reference to the office of רע המלך ('friend of the king'), that is, minister of state, advisor (from רֵעַ II)? For the use of this expression as a parallel to יועץ ('counsellor'), as here, cf. 1 Chron. 27.33. Rudolph feels the need to repoint מֶלֶךְ as מֹלֵךְ, understood in the sense of 'counsellor' as in some other Semitic languages.[14] This explanation assumes a meaning for מלך which is only otherwise attested once in Classical Hebrew (in the niphal, Neh. 5.7) and still has the difficulty of what to do with רע. On the reading suggested here, הֲמֶלֶךְ would need to be repointed as הַמֶּלֶךְ and the words רע המלך אין־בך still read as a (now unmarked) question: 'Is there no royal adviser among you?' Such a reading might even hint at a 'democratized' understanding of the royalty of Israel, as it is Israel who needs counsel, not some king who would otherwise be absent from view on this reading. On the other hand, if the word רֵעַ I is accepted, there is no particular difficulty with the pairing of 'king' and counsellor' as the text stands (cf. Job 3.14; Ezra 7.28; 8.25) and no compelling case for a fresh interpretation is advanced at this point, merely a suggestion to be considered. One factor which might suggest 'friend of the king' as a preferable reading is that if, as seems likely, the writer has Exod. 19.6 and its reference to כהנים on his mind, then by association of ideas he may move readily to an expression for which כהן may serve as a synonym (as in 1 Kgs 4.5).[15]

13. KB (p. 897) lists only three other occurrences of the word: Exod. 32.17; Job 36.33; Ps. 49.6. The last of these, however, is based on a conjecture and the consonantal MT makes sense as it is: בימי רע ('in time of evil' [רע = רעה]). BDB (p. 929) regards the word as doubtful.

14. Rudolph, cited by Delbert R. Hillers, *A Commentary on the Book of the Prophet Micah* (Hermeneia; Philadelphia: Fortress Press, 1984), p. 58. See KB, pp. 529-30.

15. For priests as royal advisers see also 2 Kgs 12.2 and *Temple Scroll* 57.12-15.

2. *Psalm 114.2*

The connections between Psalm 114 and Exodus 19 have been observed by not a few commentators.[16] Weiss has made a study of these intertextual links, with a particular focus on Exod. 19.6 and Ps. 114.2.[17] Psalm 114.2 reads: 'Judah became his sanctuary (לקדשו), Israel his sovereignty (ממשלותיו)'. Ibn Ezra and Radak had already drawn attention to the connection whereby the words לקדשו and ממשלותיו (Ps. 114.2) stand in relation to one another as do קדוש and ממלכת in Exod. 19.6. The reversal of word order is to be noted, which, according to Weiss, is a consistent feature of such allusive treatments of passages of Scripture. The difference of the verbal noun (ממשלה from משל rather than ממלכה from מלך) is also to be noted. Weiss draws attention to a number of linguistic features which serve to link Exodus 19 and Psalm 114. These include the distinctive manner of describing the exodus event (Exod. 19.1; Ps. 114.1), and the particular form of the double appellation of Israel–Jacob (Exod. 19.3; Ps. 114.1). He then proceeds to interpret the Psalm in the light of the wider cotext of Exodus 19 and in doing so sheds light on the unusual expression עם לעז ('a people of foreign speech') used to describe the Egyptians in v. 1. This he does by means of a further intertextual connection from the eagle image in Exod. 19.4 to the eagle image in Deut. 28.49 and the reference there to 'a nation whose language you do not understand' (Israel's future captors in the event of covenant unfaithfulness).

Accepting that there is an intertextual connection, our interest is in reversing the pathway and elucidating Exod. 19.6 by reference to the Psalm. In doing so I draw attention to the use of ממשלה and ממלכה as synonyms in Mic. 4.8 (discussed above) and suggest that these passages (Exod. 19.6; Ps. 114.2; Mic. 4.8) may form another three-way intertextual link, similar to Weiss's three-way link of Exod. 19.6, Ps. 114.2 and Deut. 28.49.

If the word ממשלה (Ps. 114.2) represents an interpretation of ממלכה (Exod. 19.6), it should help us to determine in which sense the Psalmist, at

16. John Calvin, *Commentary on the Book of Psalms* (trans. James Anderson; 5 vols.; Grand Rapids: Eerdmans, 1948–49), IV, p. 337; J.J. Stewart Perowne, *The Book of Psalms: A New Translation, with Introduction and Notes Explanatory and Critical* (Grand Rapids: Zondervan, 1966), p. 326; Wildberger, *Jahwes Eigentumsvolk*, pp. 20-21; Allen, *Psalms 101–150*, p. 103. The connection is denied by Lipiński, *La royauté de Yahwé*, p. 251; Sarna, *Exodus: The Traditional Hebrew Text*, p. 104.

17. Meir Weiss, *The Bible from Within: The Method of Total Interpretation* (Hebrew University of Jerusalem. Perry Foundation for Biblical Research Publications; Jerusalem: Magnes Press, 1984), pp. 93-100.

least, understood the Exodus passage. On a first reading, the impression the reader has is that it is Yhwh's dominion over Israel which is spoken of.[18] That is, that Israel is the domain over which God rules, or the body of people who are pre-eminently his subjects. The Psalm does not speak explicitly of Yhwh as king (as Mic. 4.7, above, had done) in close association with Israel's dominion. Rather it uses powerful allusive references to the great events of the exodus and entry into Canaan traditions. Those who experienced subjection were not Israel so much as Egypt (v. 1) and the natural world of the sea, the river and the mountains which respond submissively to the advance of Israel (vv. 3-6). Of course their response is ultimately to the awesome presence of Yhwh with his people, which is the focal point of the psalm (v. 7) just as it is in Exodus 19. But could it be that the dominion is something God exercises *through* rather than over Israel? That is, is Israel the active agent of the verbal noun ממשלותיו? A possible objection is that generally where ממשלה has a suffixed pronoun, the pronoun is a subjective genitive (e.g. in Isa. 22.21 ממשלתך is 'the dominion you exercise'),[19] and it could not on any account be an objective genitive (they do not have dominion over God!). However, an alternative to both of these is a simple possessive genitive: Israel is *his* body of people (note the plural) who exercise dominion. Plumer glosses ממשלתיו by 'an instance of his power'.[20] This would provide a good parallel to לקדשו where the suffix is also possessive. Wellhausen likewise lends his support to an active understanding of the sovereignty with respect to Israel: 'The convulsion amid which the Theocracy arose in the days of Moses and Joshua is depicted in these vivid colours because something similar is now happening: Israel's dominion in Palestine is now founded afresh by the casting off of a foreign yoke.'[21]

18. William Rainey Harper, *A Critical and Exegetical Commentary on Amos and Hosea* (ICC; Edinburgh: T. & T. Clark, 1936), p. 391.

19. Though there is no antecedent to the third person suffixes of v. 2, they are surely references to God. The LXX may make this slightly more explicit by including as a heading the ascription Ἀλληλουια (from the previous Psalm), which contains the divine name. Weiser is probably correct, however, in seeing the lack of direct reference to Yhwh until v. 7 as a deliberate device to heighten tension: Artur Weiser, *The Psalms: A Commentary* (trans. Herbert Hartwell; OTL; London: SCM Press, 1962), p. 701.

20. William S. Plumer, *Psalms: A Critical and Expository Commentary with Doctrinal and Practical Remarks* (Edinburgh: Banner of Truth Trust, 1975), p. 992.

21. Julius Wellhausen, *The Book of Psalms: A New English Translation with Explanatory Notes* (trans. Horace Howard Furness; The Polychrome Bible; London: James Clarke, 1898), p. 208.

It would appear, then, that in Psalm 114, where exodus and Sinai language are employed in describing Yhwh's relationship with Israel, the image may also be one of Yhwh's dominion being exercised through Israel. However, what is clearer than whether ממשׁלה has an active or passive force in Ps. 114.2 is the fact that it applies to the whole of Israel. It makes little difference for our purposes whether 'Judah' and 'Israel' in this verse are considered as two distinct components of the total national entity,[22] or, as is more likely, they are co-referential, which would mean the psalm need not assume the separate existence of the Northern Kingdom.[23] Thepoint is that it is the people of God as a whole, not an elite ruling body which has as its complement the word for sovereignty or dominion. If the intertextual link with Exod. 19.6 is accepted, then the case for reading ממלכת in that verse as a reference to all Israel is strengthened.

What then of the word לקדשׁו in Ps. 114.2? If it echoes קדושׁ in Exod. 19.6, what interpretative light does it shed? Here it is a noun form, not an adjective as its counterpart in Exod. 19.6. One of the frequent uses of the noun is to denote the place associated with the presence of God—the 'sanctuary', and this is the English translation tradition for this verse (RV, RSV, NEB, JB, NIV, NASB, NRSV).[24] The adjective קדושׁ in Exod. 19.6 is not restricted to qualifying that which pertains to the sanctuary as such. It may, as may also the noun, denote anything or any person who is 'holy' or

22. See Hermann Gunkel, *Die Psalmen* (Göttingen: Vandenhoeck & Ruprecht, 6th edn, 1986), p. 494; Weiser, *Psalms*, p. 709; Kraus, *Psalms 60–150*, p. 374.

23. See Mitchell Dahood, SJ, *Psalms: Introduction, Translation and Notes* (AB, 16-17A; 3 vols.; Garden City, NY: Doubleday, 1965–70), III, p. 134; A.A. Anderson, *The Book of Psalms*. II. *Psalms 73–150* (NCB; London: Oliphants, 1972), pp. 783-84; Allen, *Psalms 101–150*, p. 103.

24. It may be this passage, in conjunction with Exod. 15.17, which is reflected in the notion of the community as temple, which is one reading of *4QFlorilegium* line 6, for example: see Menachem Ben-Yashar, 'Noch zum *miqdaš 'ādām* in 4QFlorilegium', *RevQ* 10 (1981), pp. 587-88; M.O. Wise, '*4QFlorilegium* and the Temple of Adam', *RevQ* 15 (1991), pp. 103-132; John A. Davies, 'The *Temple Scroll* from Qumran and the Ultimate Temple', *RTR* 57 (1998), pp. 1-21 (17). For the notion of community as temple generally, see Bertil Gärtner, *The Temple and the Community in Qumran and the New Testament: A Comparative Study in the Temple Symbolism of the Qumran Texts and the New Testament* (SNTSMS, 1; Cambridge: Cambridge University, 1965). The concept takes on a greater prominence in the thinking of the apostle Paul (1 Cor. 3.16-17): see J.C. Coppens, 'The Spiritual Temple in the Pauline Letters and its Background', *Studia Evangelica* 6 (1969), pp. 53-66.

fit for a close association with deity. But Ps. 114.2 may suggest a nuanced reading of גוי קדוש in Exod. 19.6: 'a nation fit to serve as the sanctuary presence of Yhwh'. In Exod. 15.17, the land where Israel is to settle is described as a מקדש ('sanctuary'). It is a short step from there to seeing the people who dwell in that land as a metaphorical sanctuary. The nation Israel is that entity within which Yhwh chooses to dwell. Wherever they are, God is there with them and they have the privilege of access to him.

3. *Conclusion*

The evidence afforded by verbal echoes is at the least highly suggestive of the fact that we have in Mic. 4.8 and Ps. 114.2 two intertextual links with Exod. 19.6. The echo is stronger in the case of Mic. 4.8 with its unexpected use of the construct (or northern absolute) form ממלכת. Both passages point to an interpretation of Exod. 19.6 in which Judah–Israel or Zion collectively (rather than a subset of it) is the possessor of regal dominion. The cotext of Mic. 4.8 may also suggest that a priestly image of Israel underlies Micah's language. Psalm 114.2, by bringing ממשלתיו into close association with לקדשו, may also be dependent on Mic. 4.8 where ממשלה is parallel with ממלכת. These two passages may also in different ways help to fill out what holiness means. In the case of the Micah passage this is expressed negatively, in terms which see Israel for a time deprived of the credentials for priestly access and hence banished from God's presence, followed by the prospect of restoration. The psalm expresses it positively in terms of daughter Jerusalem possessing the quality of a sanctuary, or at least the qualification which would render one fit for access to the sanctuary, that is, to the presence of God.

Chapter 11

The Prospect of the Royal Priesthood: Isaiah 61.6

1. *Royal–Priestly Imagery in Isaiah's Restoration Agenda*

The verse most widely recognized as relating intertextually to Exod. 19.6 within the Hebrew Bible is Isa. 61.6: 'You will be called priests of Yhwh, you will be named attendants of our God. You will consume the wealth of nations and in their riches you will boast.' Noting the link with Exod. 19.6, McKenzie remarks on this corporate priestly role: 'The Israelites shall mediate between Yahweh and the nations'.[1] In the intertextual study which follows, we will be interested to see whether this understanding of Israel's priesthood predominantly in terms of a mission to the nations is borne out by the evidence.

After a description of the lamentable situation of Zion in Isa. 59.1-15, the result of separation from God through the people's sins and offences (59.2), a turning point is reached at v. 16, where the arm of Yhwh intervenes on his people's behalf. There follows a sustained depiction of a glorious restoration of Zion, once again to be graced with the divine presence and glory. This depiction continues without interruption through to the end of ch. 62.

The key to the restoration is Yhwh's return to Zion in zealous pursuit of the interests of his people and his glorious presence there (59.17-20), together with his declared 'covenant' (v. 21) or commitment to remain forever with his people through his spirit and his words. Chapters 60–62 then draw on a rich store of imagery to portray the implications of this restoration of Zion (the remnant of Israel) to an exalted status. One strand of this, not confined to 61.6, is the imagery of the priestly office, though royal aspects of the status of Zion are also present through these chapters.

1. John L. McKenzie, SJ, *Second Isaiah: Introduction, Translation and Notes* (AB, 20; Garden City, NY: Doubleday, 1968), p. 181; cf. Eichrodt, *Theology*, II, p. 343.

The image of Yhwh himself in 59.17 as one 'clothed in righteousness (צדקה) like armour, and the helmet of salvation (ישועה) on his head' is predominantly military; the restoration of צדקה ('a correct state of affairs') and ישועה ('deliverance') can be military objectives. There may be, however, a further association with priestly terminology, for the combination of items of clothing with these abstract nouns is not otherwise associated with the soldier's outfit, whereas it is a commonplace with respect to priestly garb (Isa. 61.10; Ps. 132.9, 16; 2 Chron. 6.41; perhaps Ps. 149.4—noting the verb פאר and its suggestion of the priestly פאר cap). Similarly the קנאה ('zeal') with which Yhwh is clad is a priestly virtue (Num. 25.11).[2]

Yhwh's glory will be upon Zion (60.2) and he will adorn (פאר, piel) his temple (60.7), which will be a focal attraction for the nations. The nations bring their wealth and come to serve both Zion's God and the people whom Yhwh adorns and honours (60.3-16). Zion's royal status is affirmed in the image of sucking at royal breasts (שד מלכים, v. 16). We might compare this with a similar image of royal parentage or guardianship in Isa. 49.23, a verse which in rabbinic discussion is connected with Exod. 19.6: 'Kings will be your foster fathers, and their queens your nursing mothers'.[3]

At 60.21 'all your people' (עמך כלם) will be 'righteous' (צדיקים), and are identified as the נצר ('shoot') of Yhwh's planting. This image of the 'shoot' is used of the future Davidic king envisaged in 11.1. If these images are related, it matters little for our purpose whether the figure of the individual royal 'shoot' is a particularization of the image of Zion as a whole, or whether the application of the terminology in Isa. 60.21 is a 'democratization' of the royal image, designed to convey something of the royal status of the whole people.

At 61.1 a messenger or agent of Yhwh speaks in the first person. This is a spirit-endowed and anointed figure and one who, from his role not only as proclaiming but as effecting the consolations spoken of, may have affinities with the 'servant' of earlier chapters. He speaks in the third person of those for whom a 'jubilee' restoration is imminent (61.1-4). The anointed figure quickly recedes, however, and the people of Zion are addressed directly in the second person in vv. 5-6. The central declaration of these verses concerns the designation of the people as 'priests of Yhwh'. This

2. For the relationship of the zeal of Phinehas and Levi to their grant of priesthood, see Kugler, *From Patriarch to Priest*, pp. 9-22.

3. Strack and Billerbeck, *Kommentar*, IV, p. 897.

declaration is flanked by references to the service which the nations will render to Zion (v. 5) and the wealth they will bring to Zion (v. 6), which resume the general tenor of 60.3-16. The 'inheritance (a 'double portion', that is, the right of the firstborn son) and the joy the people of Zion experience in this scenario are the subject of v. 7.

Verse 8 then speaks of the ideal state which is being depicted in terms of a promise to 'grant their reward' (ונתתי פעלתם) which is in parallel with a commitment to 'make (cut) an everlasting covenant with them'. This association of the grant of priestly office with a covenant is of course reminiscent of Exod. 19.5-6 and of the 'eternal' Levitical priesthood covenants described above (Chapter 6). The cotext in Isaiah 61 makes no reference to a conditional basis for the divine action, unless this is felt to be implicit in פעלתם (and the idea of wages or that which is due, while frequently a concomitant idea, is not inherent in the word פעל).[4] The whole emphasis of the surrounding chapters is on the divine initiative and decisive action on behalf of his otherwise hapless people, not on what Israel has come to deserve. If, then, this intertextual link with Exod. 19.5-6 is accepted, it constitutes evidence for how the Sinai covenant was understood by the writer of Isaiah 61 at least. The covenant of which he knows is an eternal covenant, not one subject to automatic annulment upon its breach by Israel.

Then the clothing imagery, representing the same abstract qualities of ישע and צדקה with which Yhwh himself was clad in 59.17, is applied by a first person speaker to himself. Whether this is the anointed one of v. 1, the prophet, or a personification of Zion speaking in response to the declarations is hard to determine. In any event, the speaker seems to embody that which has been said of Zion. The mention of being clothed in such qualities as 'salvation' and 'righteousness' would be sufficient to suggest a priestly image (as noted above). However, Isa. 61.10 makes use of the verb כהן (piel) normally meaning 'to serve as a priest', though apparently used here in the sense of 'to adorn oneself as a priest' as a bridegroom might do.[5]

4. BDB, p. 821; KB, p. 771.

5. There is considerable reluctance to accept the reading יכהן here. KB (p. 424) proposes an emendation to יכונן. *BHS* and Westermann propose the reading יכין ('decks himself'): Claus Westermann, *Isaiah 40 66: A Commentary* (trans. David M.G. Stalker; OTL; London: SCM Press, 1969), p. 369. These emendations are not necessary. The verb כהן would be suggested by the noun כהנים in v. 6 as readily to the author as to a copyist.

The royal-priestly imagery continues in 62.3: 'You (feminine singular) will be a crown of splendour (עטרת תפארת) in Yhwh's hand, a royal diadem (צנוף [*qere* צניף] מלוכה) in the hand of your God'. Both expressions used to describe Zion have priestly as well as royal overtones, as a priest is said to wear 'crowns' (עטרות, Zech. 6.11), while the roots פאר and צנף, as noted earlier, are both associated with the priestly headdress. The image shifts in vv. 4-5 to that of a bride. The combination of priestly and wedding imagery found here has already been suggested by 61.10 and may also lie behind the mixing of priestly with bridal imagery when the prophet John envisages the new Jerusalem (Rev. 20.6; 21.2).[6] Yhwh makes a commitment to establish Jerusalem as תהלה בארץ ('an object of praise throughout the earth', v. 7).

The 'highway', which had been proclaimed in 40.3 as a highway for God to return to Zion, once more comes into focus. Over this highway the people of Zion may return from what appears to be a period of exile and God himself is to come into the city with his 'reward' in hand (vv. 10-11). The chapter ends on the note that the people of Jerusalem will be called 'the holy people, redeemed by Yhwh...sought after, the city no longer deserted' (v. 12). The designation 'holy people' (עם הקדש) in this section which has used priestly imagery is also possibly suggestive of an allusion to Exod. 19.6, though it is closer in wording to the more common Deuteronomic variant (Deut. 7.6; 14.2, 21; 26.19; 28.9). In any event, it is the only instance in Isaiah of קדש being brought into relation with any word for 'people' or 'nation', the majority of instances of קדש having Yhwh as their referent.

The exodus and entry into Canaan have long been recognized as forming a backdrop for much of the language of Isaiah 40–66.[7] The use of the covenant formula עמי המה ('they are my people') and the reference to Israel as Yhwh's 'sons' (63.8) are highly suggestive of the exodus and Sinai traditions, and this is made explicit in vv. 11-14. This makes it almost certain that the reference in v. 9 to Yhwh 'lifting up' and 'carrying' Israel 'as in days of old' is an allusion to Exod. 19.4, the 'eagle' image. Finally Isa. 63.19–64.3 may contain an allusion to the Exodus–Sinai tradition complex, with its reference to fire and mountains trembling, and God coming down to intervene on behalf of his people.[8]

6. Kline, *Images*, pp. 47-56.
7. See Westermann, *Isaiah 40–66*, pp. 21-22.
8. J.L. McKenzie, *Second Isaiah*, p. 192.

2. *The Meaning of 'Priests of Yhwh'*

Having set Isa. 61.6 in its general cotext, we turn to consider more closely the referent and significance of the phrases כהני יהוה and משרתי יהוה. These are clearly intended to be honorific designations, as the whole cotext demonstrates. They call to mind the Levitical priesthood (1 Sam. 22.17, 21; Jer. 33.21; Joel 1.13; 1 Chron. 16.4; 2 Chron. 13.9; 23.6; Ezra 8.17), or their counterpart in the unseen heavenly host (Ps. 103.21; cf. Ps. 104.4 where משרתיו is parallel with מלאכיו, 'messengers, angels'). While משרת alone may refer to other non-cultic attendants (such as Joshua: Exod. 24.13; 33.11) the use of the words כהן and משרת together is only otherwise associated with cultic contexts, and some extended cultic metaphor seems unavoidable. That is, Zion as a whole occupies in some idealized sense, or will come to occupy, an analogous relationship to Yhwh to that enjoyed by the Levitical priests. The emphasis, however, is not on that which they might *do* by way of actual cultic service (שרת), for the term has become somewhat fossilized as Haran notes.[9] Rather, it is on the contrast between the humiliation of the fortunes of the foreigners and the newfound esteem with which Zion is now to be regarded. It is the position of God's people in the eyes of the observer which is paramount, not what functions they may fulfil. This is made clear by the use of the niphal forms תקראו ('you will be known as') and יאמר ('it shall be said').[10] The only person in view with whom the priestly service has anything directly to do is Yhwh Elohim (the composite divine title being split over two hemistichs). Such 'priesthood' is to be seen as a corollary of the fact that Yhwh's presence has been restored to his people and city after an apparent absence. Far from being engaged in a mission, or a service role in relation to the nations, Israel is rather to be held in honour and to have the riches of the nations placed at its disposal.

It is not until ch. 66 that there is explicit mention of an active mission to the nations.[11] Certainly there it forms part of the eschatological picture

9. Haran, 'Temple and Community', p. 19.

10. Schenker ('Besonderes und allgemeines Priestertum', p. 115) identifies the speaker as the nations, who will address these words to Israel in the eschatological time.

11. The references to Israel, or the servant, being a 'light to the nations' (42.6; 60.1-3) hardly qualify as indicators of active service to the nations and are not brought into close correlation with Israel's priesthood. On the other hand, the role of Israel in declaring the praise of Yhwh (43.21), also cited by Elliott (*The Elect and the Holy*, p. 61) in support of a mediatorial implication of Isa. 61.6, does not speak of a declaration before the nations. The context is cultic (43.22-24) and seems to refer rather to a

(66.19). The nations are then to be included in the sphere of those where God's glory is known. They will flock to Jerusalem, and will have a share in the benefits of Israel's relation to Yhwh in that he 'will select some of them to be priests and Levites' (66.20-21).

While it seems clear that the referent of Isa. 61.6 is the whole remnant people of Zion, there are those, like Cazelles, who understand it as a restricted reference to the special priesthood within Israel.[12] Cazelles takes his cue from Isa. 59.21, where he understands that the reference to the one who possesses the Spirit of God and his words must be the high priest, the anointed one of 61.1, who speaks of and to his priestly colleagues. The whole cotext, however, is against this reading and it seems rather to be influenced by the desire to read a special priesthood back into Exod. 19.6.

Elliott recognizes that Isa. 61.6 speaks of Israel's 'position of privilege' but because he has rejected this understanding at Exod. 19.6, denies that there is any intertextual link between the two passages.[13] The understanding adopted here is rather that the interpretation of Exod. 19.6 set out in Chapter 4 is one shared, in outline at least, by this prophet.

3. *Conclusion*

Isaiah 59–62 contains a number of allusions to the exodus and the Sinai encounter and employs the imagery of Israel as a royal and priestly nation. In particular Isa. 61.6 contains a clear reference to the priestly designation of the remnant of Israel. It would be perfectly feasible for Isa. 61.6 to have taken the image of the Israelite priest in his finery and in his privileged position with respect to access to God and to have recast the image along a 'democratizing' line as his own original contribution. Had he wished to do this, there would have been any number of intertextual references he might have chosen. The fact that it appears he has chosen Exod. 19.6, and to have done so with an awareness of its cotext, suggests that the image of the people of Yhwh as a collective royal priesthood was not original to the writer of Isaiah 61, but drawn from Exodus itself. Isaiah 61.6 confirms our understanding that Israel's priesthood is not, in the first instance, exercised towards the nations as a form of service, but consists in their being 'attendants' of God in an image drawn from Israel's rich sanctuary ideology.

declaration of praise before Yhwh himself, an activity most closely associated with the priesthood (2 Chron. 31.2; Ps. 99.6).

12. Cazelles, 'Alliance du Sinai', p. 77.

13. Elliott, *The Elect and the Holy*, pp. 61-62.

Chapter 12

The Pinnacle of Royal Priesthood—Access to the Heavenly Court: Zechariah 3

1. *The Setting of Zechariah 3*

In our investigation of possible echoes of the theme of the royal-priestly status of all Israel, we turn our attention finally to the sixth-century restoration prophet Zechariah. From such genealogical information as we have, it seems that Zechariah was probably a priest as well as a prophet, who was active in Jerusalem around 520–518 BCE.[1] Zechariah's subject matter and imagery reflect his interest in and concern for the re-establishment of the Jerusalem cult after the exile and the desolation of the temple. Yet it would be doing the prophet a disservice to limit his concerns to the rebuilding of the physical temple with its associated priestly prerogatives. Marinkovic observes that Zechariah has at times been read rather narrowly through the lens of the references to his (and Haggai's) work in Ezra 4.24–5.2 and 6.14, whereas it is predominantly the status of the relationship between Yhwh and the returnees which occupies his attention.[2]

The opening section (1.1-6) provides the framework for the message of the book as a whole and particularly prepares the reader for the visions which follow. These verses describe a covenant, broken though not annulled. There is the prospect of a restoration following repentance: '"Return to me", oracle of Yhwh of hosts, "and I will return to you", says Yhwh of hosts' (Zech. 1.3).

The sequence of 'night visions' with their associated oracles makes up the first section of the work (1.7–6.15).[3] The eight visions are arranged in

1. T.M. Mauch, 'Zechariah', in *IDB*, IV, pp. 941-43 (942).

2. Peter Marinkovic, 'What Does Zechariah 1–8 Tell Us about the Second Temple?', in Tamara C. Eskenazi and Kent R. Richards (eds.), *Second Temple Studies*. II. *Temple and Community in the Persian Period* (JSOTSup, 175; Sheffield: JSOT Press, 1994), pp. 88-103.

3. I am not here concerned to address the overall unity of Zechariah. For my purposes, it is sufficient to focus on the first portion of the final work often known as

an envelope fashion such that there is a thematic correspondence between the outer visions, numbers one (1.7-17) and eight (6.1-15). These concern the divine patrols which roam the whole earth, and set Yhwh's concern for Jerusalem and Judah in the widest possible context. In Zech. 1.14-16, Yhwh's anger with the excesses of the nations forms the backdrop for a declaration of his jealous passion (קנאתי, v. 14; cf. 8.2) and mercy (רחמים, v. 16; cf. 10.6) towards his people. While the remainder of the structure of the visions is less clear, the innermost pair, visions four (3.1-10) and five (4.1-14), both relate either to the earthly temple or its heavenly counterpart and the resources provided for the high priest Joshua and the royal scion Zerubbabel. The structure has been represented as a series of concentric rings which move from the widest sphere of God's interest (the world), through his dealings with Judah and Jerusalem, to the most intimate *locus* of his relationships as we move towards the centre of the vision complex.[4]

Our interest in this chapter is particularly in the vision of ch. 3, which forms one of the central units of this envelope pattern. It is clearly linked with the following vision of the lampstands (4.1-14). It makes little difference whether (as proposed above) it is regarded as one of eight visions,[5] or whether it is regarded as an interruption to a sequence of seven visions, though closely associated with the following vision.[6] This vision does present some degree of variation from the structure of the visions which

'Proto-Zechariah'. For the unity of this section see Baruch Halpern, 'The Ritual Background of Zechariah's Temple Song', *CBQ* 40 (1978), pp. 167-90.

4. Joyce G. Baldwin, *Haggai, Zechariah, Malachi: An Introduction and Commentary* (TOTC; London: Tyndale Press, 1972), p. 85; Carol L. Meyers and Eric M. Meyers, *Haggai, Zechariah 1–8: A New Translation with Introduction and Commentary* (AB, 25B; Garden City, NY: Doubleday, 1987), pp. liii-lx.

5. Hinckley G. Mitchell, John Merlin Powis Smith and Julius A. Bewer, *A Critical and Exegetical Commentary on Haggai, Zechariah, Malachi and Jonah* (ICC; Edinburgh: T. & T. Clark, 1912), p. 115; Baldwin, *Haggai, Zechariah, Malachi*, p. 85.

6. See Christian Jeremias, *Die Nachtgesichte des Sacharjah: Untersuchungen zu ihrer Stellung im Zusammenhang der Visionsberichte im Alten Testament und zu ihrem Bildmaterial* (FRLANT, 117; Göttingen: Vandenhoeck & Ruprecht, 1977), pp. 12-13; Meyers and Meyers, *Haggai, Zechariah 1–8*, p. liv; *idem*, 'Jerusalem and Zion after the Exile: The Evidence of First Zechariah', in Michael Fishbane and Emanuel Tov (eds.), *'Sha'arei Talmon': Studies in the Bible, Qumran and the Ancient Near East, Presented to Shemaryahu Talmon* (Winona Lake, IN: Eisenbrauns, 1992), pp. 121-35 (128). For a treatment of the structure which sees 6.9-15 as pivotal to the macrostructure of the book, with the thematically related oracles 3.1-10 and 11.1-17 constituting the pivotal points of the two resulting halves of the diptych, see Meredith G. Kline, 'The Structure of the Book of Zechariah', *JETS* 34 (1991), pp. 179-93.

surround it, lacking for example the introductory formula of seeing, the questioning of the interpreting angel and consequently the helpful explanations of visionary elements. While noting these differences, our concern is with the basic contours of the text with its existing structure. We will not take up issues of the possible diachronic development of this chapter or seek interpretative solutions which are inconsistent with its literary coherence.[7]

2. *The Vision: Zechariah 3.1-7*

The chapter recounts a vision which begins with Joshua, the high priest, being accused before an angelic tribunal (3.1-7). There follows a related oracle (vv. 8-10), which brings out something of the significance of the preceding vision.[8] In the vision we are apparently observing a heavenly court scene,[9] with the angel of Yhwh officiating as judge. The angel is possibly to be identified with the interpreting angel of the other visions, though he here appears in a different role. It is also difficult (as in the

7. Verses 8-10 are frequently regarded as a late addition, and held to support a different point of view from vv. 1-7. See Petitjean, *Les oracles du Proto-Zacharie*, pp. 161-206; Mike Butterworth, *Structure and the Book of Zechariah* (JSOTSup, 120; Sheffield: JSOT, 1992), p. 111. Many scholars would query the legitimacy of various elements of the chapter; for example, Mitchell (Mitchell, Powis Smith and Bewer, *Haggai, Zechariah, Malachi and Jonah*, p. 156) would excise v. 8b as an erroneous gloss. Beuken does not regard vv. 6-7 as original: W.A.M. Beuken, SJ, *Haggai–Sacharja 1–8: Studien zur Überlieferungsgeschichte frühnachexilischen Prophetie* (Assen: Van Gorcum, n.d.), pp. 282-303.

8. This division is disputed, as the divine declaration in v. 8 may be regarded as a seamless continuation with that of v. 7. For an alternative division whereby vv. 1-5 and 6-10 are taken as the primary units, see Keil and Delitzsch, *Commentary on the Old Testament*, X (part 2), pp. 256-62; cf. Mitchell, Powis Smith and Bewer, *Haggai, Zechariah, Malachi and Jonah*, pp. 154-56; David Petersen, *Haggai and Zechariah 1–8: A Commentary* (OTL; Philadelphia: Westminster Press, 1984), p. 202; Paul L. Redditt, 'Zerubbabel, Joshua and the Night Visions of Zechariah', *CBQ* 54 (1992), pp. 249-59 (254). See the discussion below on the oracle (vv. 8-10) for further comment on the structure of the chapter.

9. It has been questioned whether this vision is in fact intended to portray a scene in heaven; for example, Mitchell, Powis Smith and Bewer, *Haggai, Zechariah, Malachi and Jonah*, pp. 147-48. In view of the close parallel with the scene in Job 1–2 (cf. 1 Kgs 22.19-22), an earthly setting seems difficult to sustain. See Baldwin, *Haggai, Zechariah, Malachi*, p. 113; Petersen, *Haggai and Zechariah 1–8*, p. 191; R.L. Smith, *Micah–Malachi*, p. 198; Allan J. McNicol, 'The Heavenly Sanctuary in Judaism: A Model for Tracing the Origin of an Apocalypse', *JRS* 13 (1987), pp. 66-94 (78-82).

Pentateuchal traditions of Genesis and Exodus) clearly to distinguish this angel from Yhwh himself (v. 2). The prosecutor of the divine council (השטן, cf. Job 1.6)[10] apparently intends to challenge the credentials of Joshua, the historical high priest of the returnees from Babylon. In particular it is his 'standing' in the heavenly court which is at issue. The participle עמד ('standing', with different subjects) functions as a *leitmotif* throughout the vision (vv. 1, 3, 4, 5, 7).[11] Perhaps the experience of exile and the desecration of Jerusalem have compromised both Joshua and the cult he represents. Perhaps the objection runs deeper and challenges the right of any mortal agent to be in the privileged position of access to Yhwh's temple. Perhaps the prosecution even challenges the wisdom of Yhwh in choosing an earthly habitation and thus exposing himself to unworthy approaches.[12] Before the prosecutor has opportunity to present his case against Joshua, however, Yhwh intervenes and rebukes the prosecutor. First, it is worth noting the epithet of Yhwh at this point. He is יהוה...הבחר בירושלם ('Yhwh who chooses Jerusalem', 3.2; cf. 1.17; 2.16 [ET 2.12]). Thus, while the immediate focus is on the figure of Joshua, and perhaps with real historical issues of his acceptability as the background, Joshua seems to some extent to have a representative role in the vision. As Ackroyd puts it, 'the expressive phrase is pointless unless it contains the main emphasis of the vision'.[13] The language of the vision exhibits a 'merging of historical and suprahistorical reality'.[14] The deeper concern of the vision is with the destiny of the people of God as a whole.

Yhwh then identifies Joshua as 'a burning stick (אוד) snatched (מצל) from the fire' (3.2). This image, too, draws attention to his representative function, for it is the same language which had earlier been used of the remnant people of God (Amos 4.11).[15] The fire of exile may have charred the remnant,[16] but the fire image also leaves open the possibility that it has

10. See Marvin E. Tate, 'Satan in the Old Testament', *RevExp* 89 (1992), pp. 461-74.

11. The editors of *BHS* have failed to notice this and have deleted it from v. 3.

12. Petersen, *Haggai and Zechariah 1 8*, p. 192.

13. P.R. Ackroyd, *Exile and Restoration: A Study of Hebrew Thought of the Sixth Century BC* (London: SCM Press, 1968), p. 184.

14. Meyers and Meyers, 'Jerusalem and Zion', p. 133.

15. Mitchell, Powis Smith and Bewer, *Haggai, Zechariah, Malachi and Jonah*, p. 150; Janet E. Tollington, *Tradition and Innovation in Haggai and Zechariah 1–8* (JSOTSup, 150; Sheffield: JSOT, 1993), p. 155.

16. See Deut. 4.20; Jer. 11.4 for the use of fire as a metaphor of the experience of Israel in the exodus.

been a purifying experience rather than one for which Joshua (and the people) are inevitably to be rejected.[17]

The angel then instructs those standing before him (presumably other angelic attendants of the heavenly court) to remove Joshua's filthy clothing. The word for 'filthy' (צואים, v. 3, or צאים, v. 4) may signify ritual impurity generally (e.g. Prov. 30.12 where it is antithetical to טהור, 'clean, pure'), or may refer more specifically to bodily excrement (e.g. Deut. 23.14 [ET 23.13]; Ezek. 4.12). It is also possible that here the prophet is playing on the root יצא (infinitive צאת) as a reference to the exiles, those who had 'gone out' and lived among foreigners and hence defiled themselves. As Ackroyd shows, the defilement is less likely to refer to any personal defilement of Joshua than it is to the exiled community generally.[18]

The removal of Joshua's defiled clothing is tantamount to a removal of עון (vv. 4, 9). This word may refer to sin, or to the guilt it entails, or again to the punishment it deserves. The removal of sin is of course essential before any access to the divine presence is possible. Petersen takes it in the sense of punishment and sees here an allusion to the vicarious role of the priest in Exod. 28.36-38 and Num. 18.1.[19] Perhaps the closest parallel to this removal of defilement is found in Isa. 4.3-4:

> Those left in Zion, those who remain in Jerusalem, will be called holy, all who are recorded among the living in Jerusalem, when the Lord washes away the filth (צאת) of the daughters of Zion, and cleanses the bloodstains of Jerusalem from its midst by a spirit of judgment (משפט) and a spirit of fire (בער).

The filthy garments are to be replaced by מחלצות ('rich garments', 3.4), a word used of the fine apparel of the wealthy (Isa. 3.22, the only other occurrence).[20] These would be garments fit for entering the presence of a king. While the word מחלצות does not have intrinsic cultic associations in Israel, it has been connected with Assyrian *ḥalaṣu* ('to purify') and the notion of purity may have been a connotation of the word in Hebrew as well.[21] It would certainly not be inappropriate as a reference to the priestly regalia, though the emphasis here is not on the technical cultic vestments

17. Petersen, *Haggai and Zechariah 1–8*, pp. 192-93.
18. Ackroyd, *Exile and Restoration*, p. 184.
19. Petersen, *Haggai and Zechariah 1–8*, p. 194.
20. D. Winton Thomas, 'A Note on מחלצות in Zech. 3.4', *JTS* 34 (1932), pp. 279-80.
21. *CAD*, VI, p. 40.

of the priest. Rather the text creates an impression of Joshua's newly bestowed or confirmed legitimate standing in the heavenly court.

Then someone remarks specifically on the lack of a צניף ('turban', v. 5). Whether it is the prophet himself speaking or perhaps the angel is unclear, due to a diverse textual tradition. For a parallel to MT's use of the first person in a divine council scene, see Isa. 6.5, 8. However Petersen, following the Vulgate and Syriac versions, mounts a case for adopting the third person reading.[22] It might seem presumptuous for the prophetic observer to interject with advice, which is quite different from Isaiah's confession of unworthiness and his volunteering for service in response to the divine invitation.

A clean (טהור) turban is then placed on the high priest's head. Unlike the ritual texts relating to the priestly investiture (e.g. Exod. 29.5-6; Lev. 8.7-9), this text does not itemize the priestly vestments with the exception of this turban. Even here, Zechariah does not use the regular technical word for this item, which is מצנפת (Exod. 28.4, 39; 29.6; 39.28-31; Lev. 8.9). The term צניף might again be compared with its use in Isa. 3.23 as one of the items of *haute couture*, the clothing of royalty and the upper classes.[23] The word צניף also has non-literal connotations. We find it used in a metaphorical expression in Job 29.14 where it is linked with משׁפט ('justice, rightness'). In Isa. 62.3, restored Zion is promised the splendour of מלוכה [*qere* צניף] צנוף ('a royal turban'//עטרה, 'crown'). There may be no great significance in the choice of צניף over מצנפת here. They are of course closely related forms, and מצנפת may also be used for the royal turban (Ezek. 21.31 [ET 21.26]), but the choice of צניף may make these royal and metaphorical associations clearer and diminish the focus on its specifically cultic associations.

The effect of the turban imagery is then to strengthen the reader's apprehension of the regal-priestly standing of restored Zion represented in its high priest. Perhaps the reason for singling out the turban here is simply that as the last item of the investiture ritual before the anointing, it could stand for the whole (Exod. 29.6; Lev. 8.9; 16.4). Or it may be because, according to Exod. 28.36-38, it is this item which exhibited most clearly

22. Petersen, *Haggai and Zechariah 1 8*, p. 197. The LXX omits the verb of speaking and hence assumes continuity with the third person speaker of v. 4.

23. Petersen, *Haggai and Zechariah 1–8*, p. 196; Meyers and Meyers, *Haggai, Zechariah 1–8*, p. 198. Halpern ('The Ritual Background', p. 173) sees in צניף a mixture of royal and priestly garb.

the acceptability (רצון, v. 38) of Israel before God, particularly symbolized by the inscription it bore: קדש ליהוה ('holy to Yhwh', v. 36).

As noted in Chapter 6, it is the priestly clothing which distinguishes its wearer as one possessed of 'dignity and honour' (Exod. 28.2, 40) and fit to minister in the presence of God. Psalm 132.9 characterizes the clothing of the priests as צדק ('righteousness, rightness, that which is fitting'). The donning of acceptable clothing upon a heavenly initiative is thus symbolic of the divine favour of Yhwh and the bestowal of an acceptability before him which one cannot achieve by any other means.

Though the clothing Joshua is given is undoubtedly intended to refer to the priestly vestments,[24] it does not seem that we have here a description of a priestly consecration or rite of passage, nor are there present any of the customary rites which might normally follow upon ritual defilement (washing, sacrifice and manipulation of blood). Rather we have a divine vindication of an existing priestly status. It might seem that the experience of exile had forever cut off Israel (represented here in its priest) from access to God, but Zechariah brings a word of consolation from the highest source that this is not the case. Despite past events and present appearances, the honorific designation of the high priest, and through him, of the people of God, is to continue.

Verse 7 provides the content of Yhwh's declaration delivered by his angel to the newly resplendent high priest. This declaration is in the form of a conditional promise, where the protasis commences, 'If you walk in my ways, and if you keep my charge…' The requirement to 'walk in my ways' is a general duty on all Israelites (e.g. Deut. 8.6). It may be that the parallel 'keep my charge', where מִשְׁמֶרֶת is cognate object of the verb שׁמר, is likewise to be understood as a general requirement: 'Keep (guard) that which I have required you to keep (guard)'.[25] In Gen. 26.5 מִשְׁמַרְתִּי occurs at the head of a list of objects after שׁמר followed by מצותי חקותי ותורתי ('my commands, statutes and laws'). It might therefore be regarded as a semantic equivalent to 'keep (observe) my covenant' (as Exod. 19.5). On the other hand, the word מִשְׁמֶרֶת is used as a more technical term to indicate the responsibility of the priests (and Levites) in cultic matters (e.g. Lev. 22.9; Num. 1.53).[26] In Ezek. 44.8 (again as object of שׁמר), מִשְׁמֶרֶת refers to the collective responsibility of Israel to guard

24. Petersen, *Haggai and Zechariah 1–8*, p. 199.
25. So Tollington, *Tradition and Innovation*, p. 158.
26. KB, p. 578; Milgrom, *Leviticus 1–16*, p. 7.

access to the sanctuary so as to prevent the unauthorized entry of foreigners. If understood this way in Zech. 3.7, the clause would anticipate the more clearly identifiable sanctuary responsibilities/privileges of the following וגם clauses and may, with its connotation of restricting access, act as a foil for the introduction of the positive notion of access contained in the apodosis to follow. We may then detect a further indication that thc responsibilities entrusted to Joshua operate on a symbolic level, since elsewhere it is the Levites rather than the high priest who, in practice, are depicted as acting as the actual custodians of the sanctuary (Num. 1.53; Ezek. 44.14).

The apodosis is in the nature of a divine grant (ונתתי, v. 7) and contains the promise, 'then I will grant you מהלכים among these who stand'. Besides the meaning of מהלכים, to which we will return, what remains unclear about this sentence is the syntactic role of the intervening clauses introduced by וגם...וגם. Are they part of the protasis or the beginning of the apodosis? It is possible to take both וגם clauses as continuing the conditions of the protasis: 'and if you exercise authority over my house and take charge of my courts...'[27] This would mean that the duties expected of Joshua are already understood to be included in the priestly mandate (cf. Lev. 8.35; Num. 3.32) rather than a new privilege and there is much to be said for this. On the other hand, the first וגם is awkward as a continuation of the protasis after there has already been a second ואם clause. While some interpreters overemphasize the newness of the privilege granted to the post-exilic high priesthood to exercise 'rule' (תדין) in the courts of God,[28] this expression seems merely to be a synonymous expression for the oversight (תשמר) of the parallel hemistich, which is resumptive of the משמרת of the protasis. It may be preferable, then, to take the וגם clauses as part of the apodosis, which would then mean that the actions of 'governing my house and taking charge or my courts' would be part of the boon to be granted.[29] On this view the reward is cut from the same cloth as the responsibilities and closely echoes our understanding of the structure

27. So Beuken, *Haggai–Sacharja 1–8*, pp. 292-93; Petersen, *Haggai and Zechariah 1–8*, pp. 206-207.

28. Ackroyd, *Exile and Restoration*, p. 187; Meyers and Meyers, *Haggai, Zechariah 1–8*, pp. 194-96.

29. So RSV; NIV; NEB; NRSV; Baldwin, *Haggai, Zechariah, Malachi*, p. 115; C. Jeremias, *Die Nachtgesichte*, p. 212; R.L. Smith, *Micah–Malachi*, p. 200; Meyers and Meyers, *Haggai, Zechariah 1–8*, p. 194. The LXX understands the first וגם clause as the apodosis to a preceding protasis and the second וגם clause as introducing a new parallel protasis, the apodosis of which is the ונתתי clause.

of Exod. 19.5-6.[30] On either syntactic analysis (as protasis or apodosis), it must be the earthly courts of the (yet to be rebuilt) Jerusalem temple which are in view in the וגם clauses. An earthly high priest, though he might be portrayed as being granted access to the heavenly temple, could hardly be conceived of as exercising authority or taking charge of it while he lived on earth.[31]

The apodosis continues with the clause beginning ונתתי, the object of which is the enigmatic מהלכים. The first thing to note about this word is that, coming from the root הלך, it too (as תשמר...משמרתי) ties the apodosis to the protasis, where הלך was the verb of the first clause and hence the promise to Joshua appears in some way a fitting reward for 'walking' in God's ways. There is thus a chiastic structure to the conditional sentence of v. 7: שמר...הלך//הלך...שמר. What precisely does the word in the apodosis mean? Most modern commentators take מהלכים as a plural noun, either of מַהֲלָךְ in the abstract sense of 'access' or perhaps an unattested מַהֲלֵךְ.[32] The MT would need to be repointed to מַהֲלָכִים for the former of these, which in any case does not quite mean the right of access, but rather 'passageway, journey' (Ezek. 42.4; Jon. 3.3, 4; Neh. 2.6). Understood thus, the reference would be to a personal privilege granted to Joshua of access to the heavenly court. 'These standing here' are presumably the angelic creatures as in v. 4 (cf. Targum 'seraphim'). Thus Mitchell understands it as 'the privilege of direct and immediate communion with Yahweh'.[33] While this is possible, there seems little point in such a grant. Joshua has already clearly gained access to the heavenly court and been vindicated in doing so in the face of his heavenly detractor. How then can the access already granted be made conditional on a further probation?

30. See Chapter 3.

31. Melchizedek would later be regarded by some Jewish groups as exercising considerable authority in the heavenly sanctuary. See 11QMelch; A.S. van der Woude, 'Melchisedek als himmlische Erlösergestalt in den neugefunden eschatologischen Midraschim aus Qumran Höhle xi', *OTS* 14 (1965), pp. 354-73; J.T. Milik, '*Milkî-ṣedeq* et *Milkî-reša'* dans les anciens écrits juifs et chrétiens', *JJS* 23 (1972), pp. 95-144; Émile Puech, 'Notes sur le manuscrit de *XIQMelkîsédeq*', *RevQ* 12 (1987), pp. 483-513.

32. See BDB, p. 237; KB, p. 499. GKC (§53o, p. 147) would treat the MT as a dialectal form of the hiphil participle, though queries the Masoretic pointing and prefers to read the word as a noun.

33. Mitchell, Powis Smith and Bewer, *Haggai, Zechariah, Malachi and Jonah*, p. 155; cf. C. Jeremias, *Die Nachtgesichte*, p. 217; Petersen, *Haggai and Zechariah 1–8*, p. 207; Meyers and Meyers, *Haggai, Zechariah 1–8*, p. 196.

A better solution, and one with strong versional support, is to take מהלכים as a masculine plural piel participle of הלך in the sense of 'those who come and go, have access'. This reading is supported by LXX ἀναστρεφομένους ('those who walk, conduct themselves') and the Vulgate *ambulantes*.[34] Whereas the qal of הלך, when used of literal motion, most commonly means movement in a single direction, the piel may be used to express the idea of movement more generally, of coming and going, going about one's daily business (1 Kgs 21.27; Isa. 59.9; Ps. 38.6; Job 24.10; 30.28; Eccl. 4.15). We may also compare the Aramaic מהלכין (a pael form, with identical pointing) in Dan. 3.25 and 4.34 (ET 4.37), also in the sense of 'walking to and fro', once literally and once metaphorically 'conducting themselves'.

A more specialized use, however, is to denote the activity of coming and going with respect to the temple. Thus Ps. 55.15 (ET 55.14): 'with whom I once enjoyed sweet fellowship as we came and went (נהלך, piel) at the house of God with the throng'; and Eccl. 8.10: 'those who used to come and go (יהלכו, piel) from the holy place'. Meyers and Meyers object that this understanding assumes a comparison: 'I will make you *like* those who…',[35] but this is to misunderstand the nature of the grant and assumes that the access is being granted to Joshua himself. On the reading proposed here, however, Joshua, through his faithful service, is being granted a body of others who may join him in such heavenly access.

This participial reading, with the cultic associations observed in Ps. 55.15 and Eccl. 8.10, would admirably suit the cotext of Zech. 3.7, with the proviso that the 'temple' in question would not be the earthly temple, but the heavenly sanctuary of the visionary setting. That is, through the representative role of the high priest, others may be considered as gaining freedom of access to the heavenly court—access of the sort normally regarded (in the standard cosmic imagery of the ancient Near East) as the prerogative of the priest or priest-king. The identity of this group is as yet unspecified. It may be Joshua's fellow priests, or it may be the members of the temple community generally, the remnant of Judah. Because of the clear indications of the scope of Zechariah's concerns already mentioned (the returned exiles), this latter interpretation commends itself. It is

34. Beuken (*Haggai–Sacharja 1–8*, p. 295) has 'Männer, die gehen'; cf. C. Jeremias, *Die Nachtgesichte*, pp. 224-25; Wilhelm Rudolph, *Haggai, Sacharja 1–8; Sacharja 9–14; Maleachi, mit einer Zeittafel von Alfred Jepsen* (Gütersloh: Gütersloher Verlagshaus, 1976), p. 93.

35. Meyers and Meyers, *Haggai, Zechariah 1–8*, p. 196 (emphasis added).

possible that the use of ביתי ('my house') in the immediately preceding cotext has prepared the reader for this, for while ביתי (//חצרי) may have the temple and its associated cult as its immediate referent, there may also be a connotation of the 'house' of Israel over which Joshua is to exercise his priestly ministry.[36] However, there is insufficient evidence to be certain as to the identity of those granted access at this point. On either reading of מהלכים (as abstract noun or as piel participle), there is both an element of high priestly mediation and at least a hint, if not a more explicit indication, of the privileged position of the community which is pictured as somehow gaining access to the courts of Yhwh, either as represented in, or as benefiting from the faithful service of its high priest.

We may observe at this stage some formal similarities between Zech. 3.7 and Exod. 19.5-6. As we have seen above, the Exodus passage constitutes a divine grant of royal-priestly prerogative, related to the fulfilment of certain conditions. In both Zechariah and Exodus we find the root שׁמר ('keep, take charge') as a key element of the protasis. Analogous with my observations at Exod. 19.5-6, it probably makes surprisingly little difference whether the וגם clauses are part of the protasis or apodosis, for in either case, they simply fill out what is entrusted to the high priestly office, both by way of responsibility and privilege. As with Exod. 19.5-6, the fulfilment of the responsibility is in itself a blessing, as the conditions are another way of stating the end to be enjoyed—the privilege of serving God.

3. *The Oracle: Zechariah 3.8-10*

Verses 8-10 contain an oracle which appears to provide a divine word of explanation following the vision proper, though for the modern reader, it raises at least as many questions as the earlier verses. At a structural level, we may note the correspondence between the full formal references to 'Joshua the high priest' in v. 1 and v. 8, which serve to mark vv. 8-10 off as a new section, and the *inclusio* formed by the repetition לרעיך (v. 8) and לרעהו (v. 10). Who or what is the 'shoot' (RSV, NRSV) or 'branch' (NIV v. 8)? Who or what is the stone (v. 9) and what are its 'eyes', or are they perhaps 'fountains'?

The angel, it appears, is still speaking and he quotes the words of Yhwh of Hosts once again (v. 9). Where the quoted speech of Yhwh begins is not

36. Jeremias (*Die Nachtgesichte*, p. 214) likewise sees a dual aspect to the use of בית here.

clear. It may be best to take it as commencing with the כי הנני of v. 8b, though it is possible that the divine speech has continued without interruption from v. 7 and incorporates the summons in v. 8a (as NIV). The section commences with a summons to Joshua and his associates (רעיך) to pay attention to the oracle. But who are these associates, who are initially linked with him in the vocative address (v. 8a), then immediately referred to in the third person (המה)? They are depicted as being seated, as distinct from those standing and those granted access privileges in v. 7. They have an entirely passive role here, their only function being to serve as 'human signs' (אנשי מופת). Consistent with their more political interpretation of the chapter as championing the rise to power of the post-exilic priesthood, Meyers and Meyers understand אנשי מופת as 'men of portent' in the sense of priests who have now assumed responsibilities formerly the prerogative of the prophets.[37] This would be an unparallelled usage. The word מופת serves to point beyond itself to something else, particularly something manifesting the powerful action of God. It occurs as a parallel to נפלאות ('wonders', Ps. 105.5; 1 Chron. 16.12), and is particularly used to express the gracious activity of God on behalf of Israel in association with the exodus (Exod. 4.21; 7.3, 9; 11.9, 10; Deut. 4.34; 6.22; 7.19; 26.8; 29.3; 34.11; Jer. 32.20, 21; Pss. 78.43; 105.27; 135.9; Neh. 9.10). For other examples of individuals being designated by God as 'signs' see Isa. 8.18; Ezek. 12.6, 11; 24.24, 27.

The word מופת in Zech. 3.8 is frequently understood as a reference to the future, as NIV: 'men symbolic of things to come'.[38] A predictive interpretation of the 'sign' might then lead into a messianic-age understanding of the following section, with its references to the 'shoot', and the 'stone' understood as messianic symbols. There is undoubtedly some future orientation in vv. 8-10. The *weqatal* form ומשתי in v. 9, and the *yiqtol* form תקראו following the eschatological formula ביום ההוא ('on that day', v. 10) are future indicators. However the participles מביא (v. 8) and מפתח (v. 9), though commonly translated as futures (NEB, NIV, NRSV), could just

37. Meyers and Meyers, *Haggai, Zechariah 1–8*, pp. 199-201; cf. Petitjean, *Les oracles du Proto-Zacharie*, pp. 168-70.

38. So also NEB; NRSV: 'an omen of things to come'; cf. S.R. Driver, *The Minor Prophets Nahum, Habakkuk, Zephaniah, Haggai, Zechariah, Malachi, Introductions: Revised Version with Notes, Index and Map* (Century Bible, 2; Edinburgh: T.C. & E.C. Jack, 1906), p. 197: 'The restored priesthood is a pledge of the approach of the Messianic kingdom'; Ackroyd, *Exile and Restoration*, pp. 189-90; Butterworth, *Structure and the Book of Zechariah*, p. 111.

as well be timeless presents, while the *qatal* form נתתי ('I have set', v. 9; cf. the similar divine grant form ונתתי in v. 7) refers back to a past action. Moreover, an exclusively future understanding of the sign function of Joshua's associates does not seem to explain the preceding declaration regarding access to the heavenly court (v. 7), which was the climax of the vision scene. There was no hint there that the privilege was some way off in the future such that it needed a sign to keep the hope alive.

Since Joshua is specifically identified (for the second time) as high priest, we may be reasonably confident that his associates are his colleagues in the priesthood.[39] The heavenly vision appears to have faded. Had Joshua's associates been observers of the divine council, we might expect them to have been standing rather than sitting and to have been facing the angelic judge rather than Joshua. We may thus have here a glimpse of a convocation of priests under the presidency of their high priest, though we lack an explicit parallel for this in the Hebrew Bible.

We will then want to know the relationship between this body of priests and the heavenly vision. The simplest and to my mind most compelling approach is that the priesthood is a living symbolic pointer (מופת) to the full reality of the access just mentioned. That is, their presence in the environs of the earthly sanctuary is to be understood as an indicator and reassurance of a reality which lies beyond the visual realm. This understanding of the sign function of the priesthood would in turn strengthen my understanding of the meaning of מהלכים (v. 7). That is, the heavenly 'priestly' access gained by a body of people is the unseen reality of which this body of priests in a more limited and stylized way serves as a reminder and a reassurance. There are future dimensions to this reality and the oracle hints at these. However, we would not be warranted in restricting the scope of the sign function to a future age, but should see it as an indication of a present reality of a different order, a sphere with which the priesthood in Israel (and beyond Israel) had long been associated—the cosmic realm of divine–human interaction. Thus the very existence of the priestly order is a divinely granted sign of the favour which God shows and will continue to show his people.

What, then, is the import of the oracle? The oracle begins with the enigmatic clause כי־הנני מביא את־עבדי צמח (v. 8). This is frequently

39. Baldwin, *Haggai, Zechariah, Malachi*, p. 116; Rudolph, *Haggai, Sacharja 1–8; Sacharja 9–14; Maleachi*, p. 99; R.L. Smith, *Micah–Malachi*, p. 200; Meyers and Meyers, *Haggai, Zechariah 1–8*, p. 198. The main dissenting voice is Petersen (*Haggai and Zechariah 1–8*, pp. 208-209), who argues for a wider gathering of leading citizens.

translated along the lines of NRSV: 'I am going to bring my servant the branch'. The focal role of this clause is signalled by the discourse markers כי־הנני which alert the reader to the significance of what is to follow. One whom Yhwh identifies as 'my servant' (עבדי) is also designated as a 'branch' or better a 'shoot' (צמח). We will defer discussion of the more general word 'servant' until we have considered the word 'shoot'. The referent intended by these terms is generally understood to be a Davidide ruler (cf. the Davidic 'shoot' of Jer. 23.5 and the royal 'shoot' of Isa. 11.1 where, however, the word is נצר). Zechariah will again make reference to a 'shoot' (6.12), who is more clearly an individual (אִישׁ) and who is usually identified with Zerubbabel.[40] The identification of Zerubbabel in 6.12 has very much influenced the interpretation of 3.8.[41] However, if Zerubbabel were intended at 3.8, why is he not named just as Joshua is named throughout the chapter? There is no hesitation about naming Zerubbabel in the following vision (4.1-14), so fear of Persian reprisal seems an unlikely motivation. If any Davidide is intended, he disappears from view almost before he is introduced and his role is left totally unexplained in the vision or the oracle, which goes on rather to speak of Joshua once again.[42] Could Zechariah have used the same word to refer to two different individuals? Or is the first reference not to an individual?

The term צמח may be used for any vegetation as in Gen. 19.25, where it refers to the lush greenery of the Jordan plain (which is likened to 'Yhwh's garden', Gen. 13.10). Its most common metaphorical use is to refer to Israel, or to the remnant of Judah, or to the quality of righteousness which should characterize this people. In Isa. 4.2-3, for example, צמח יהוה ('Yhwh's vegetation') is parallel with פרי הארץ ('the fruit of the land') and is symbolic of the blessing of the holy remnant of Zion. More explicit as a reference to the people of God is its use in Ezek. 16.7 where Yhwh says of Jerusalem, 'I made you grow like a plant (צמח) of the field'. As Yhwh's plant, Israel can be expected to produce the fruit of righteousness.

40. Baldwin, *Haggai, Zechariah, Malachi*, p. 134; Meyers and Meyers, *Haggai, Zechariah 1–8*, pp. 355-56.

41. See, e.g., Petersen, *Haggai and Zechariah 1–8*, pp. 210-11. Meyers and Meyers (*Haggai, Zechariah 1–8*, pp. 202-203) are representative of those who see a less specific reference to the ideal of future restoration of kingship.

42. Mitchell, for example (Mitchell, Powis Smith and Bewer, *Haggai, Zechariah, Malachi and Jonah*, p. 156), recognizes the awkwardness here, yet because of his assumption that the 'shoot' must refer to Zerubbabel, excises it from the text as the gloss of a later hand who did not understand the context.

In the same passage, which links the clothing imagery and even the priestly headdress with the righteousness of God's people, Isaiah makes use of the green shoot image:

> I delight greatly in Yhwh; my soul rejoices in my God. For he has clothed me with garments of salvation and covered me in a robe of righteousness, as a bridegroom adorns his head like a priest, and as a bride adorns herself with her jewels. For as the earth makes the shoot come up and a garden causes seeds to grow, so the Lord, Yhwh, will make righteousness and praise spring up before all nations. (Isa. 61.10-11)

The use of botanical imagery to refer to the people of God is not infrequent in the Hebrew Bible. God 'planted' Israel on his mountain (Exod. 15.17; cf. 2 Sam. 7.10; Jer. 2.21; 24.6; 32.41; 42.10; Amos 9.15; Pss. 80.9, 16 [ET 80.8], 15; 1 Chron. 17.9). Among the more extended applications of the green imagery to Israel, we may include Isaiah's vineyard song (Isa. 5.1-7) and Ezekiel's parable of the trees and the eagles (Ezek. 17.1-24). In this parable the greenery which is plucked away by the eagles is variously interpreted by the prophet himself as being 'the king and the nobles' (17.12), or 'a member of the royal family', or 'the leading men of the land' (v. 13), or simply 'the king' (v. 15). If Ezekiel is permitted some flexibility in his application of vegetation imagery, could not Zechariah be allowed the same flexibility with his use of the word 'shoot'? An image which is appropriate for the remnant population at 3.8 may be given a more specific referent in its leader at 6.12, since the people's welfare is summed up in their leader. If there is any necessary connotation of royalty in the image of the צמח,[43] then this would comport well with our understanding of the royal status granted to all Israel under the Sinai covenant. There is no need to import a specific reference to a Davidic ruler into Zechariah 3.

The word 'shoot' in Zech. 3.8 is in apposition with עבדי ('my servant'). The word עבד has a wide range of referents. Besides its use to denote a menial household slave, it is an honorific term used to refer *inter alios* to various court officials, prophets and priests of God and Israel collectively (e.g. Isa. 41.8; 44.1, 21; 45.4; 49.3; Jer. 30.10; 46.27; Ps. 136.22; 1 Chron. 16.13). There would thus be no problem in understanding the phrase 'my servant, a shoot' as a reference to the remnant people of Judah and this best suits the cotext.

If the 'shoot' is the people of God, what is God announcing that he is doing with them? The כי־הנני with which the divine declaration begins

43. For Ackroyd (*Exile and Restoration*, p. 190), the term 'indicates royal dignity'.

could be expected to draw the reader's focus to the central concern of the pericope. What then is the force of the hiphil participle מביא with God (the pronominal suffix on הנני) as agent? A search of those passages where God 'brings' a personal object to a location reveals that the majority are concerned with bringing Israel to the land of Canaan, or Judah, or Zion, particularly after the experiences of the exodus or the exile in Babylon (Exod. 6.8; Lev. 18.3; 20.22; Num. 14.24, 31; 15.18; Deut. 31.20, 21; Josh. 24.8; Judg. 2.1; Isa. 43.5; 56.7; Jer. 3.14; 31.8; Ezek. 20.10, 28; 34.13; 36.24; 37.21; Zeph. 3.20; Zech. 8.8; 10.10; Neh. 1.9). In these cases, God is frequently pictured as leading or accompanying his people, hence 'bring' rather than 'send' (שׁלח or perhaps the hiphil of הלך) is appropriate. However, such a meaning will hardly suit here, for the inhabitants of Judah have already returned to the land.

For God to 'bring' or 'cause to enter' may have overtones of intimacy and close association with God himself. Once, God makes a commitment that those foreigners who submit to his covenant: 'I will bring to my holy mountain, and make them joyful in my house of prayer' (Isa. 56.7). Similarly, the Psalmist appeals to God that the personified divine attributes might be sent forth to 'bring' (יביאוני) the worshipper into the cultic presence of God (Ps. 43.3 [ET 43.4]).[44] There is also a smaller number of passages where the goal of the bringing is expressed more abstractly. In Ezek. 20.37, God says, 'I will bring you into the bond of the covenant'.

So to where could God be 'bringing' or 'causing to enter' his people? Since there is no adverbial modifier (such as a prepositional phrase of place) to define the destination, we have little option but to understand the goal of the 'bringing' to be the speaker himself. That is, in accordance with the normal referential point of בוא, God is drawing, or inviting them to come into his own presence. There is some analogy with the idioms of Isa. 56.7 and Ezek. 20.37, though the image is bolder. It is not to an abstract 'covenant', nor to an earthly temple, but it is to the heavenly court that Yhwh invites this servant of his. We may well then have here an intertextual echo of Exod. 19.4 where God 'brought' (hiphil of בוא) Israel to himself, for while בוא is of course an extremely common root, its use in the sense of God granting Israel an audience directly with himself is not.

This understanding of the access to God which is granted to God's servant, or 'shoot', would provide within the oracle a close point of correspondence with מהלכים (v. 7) in the vision and serve to expound it. The high point of the privilege bestowed through Joshua is that the people he

44. See Preuss, 'בוא', pp. 22-25.

represents might be granted access, that is, that as they 'go' from their own referential standpoint, they are 'brought to' or 'invited to enter' the divine presence from Yhwh's referential standpoint.

The unusual repetition of the arresting כי הנה (v. 9) which had just been used in v. 8 draws attention to an equally significant statement to that which we have just encountered.[45] The parallelism thus set up by the כי הנה//כי הנני clauses suggests that the granting of access to the citizens of Judah and the setting of the stone may also be mutually explanatory. The stone which is set לפני ('before', or perhaps more literally 'on the face [forehead] of') Joshua has been variously interpreted. It is not our place here to canvass all of the possibilities.[46] One prominent interpretation is that the stone is a foundation stone of the restored temple,[47] or in what is essentially a variant of this, that the stone is the primaeval stone or mountain on which the temple rests.[48] This interpretation is linked with a perception that these verses (8-10) have been dislocated from their original setting in connection with the following vision. Petitjean is quite explicit that the supposed original independence of the oracles from the visions constitutes for him a decisive interpretative framework.[49] Whatever the merits of the case may be for the existence of an oracles source, this approach does not deal with the coherence of the text we have and the presumably deliberate arrangement of material by an author or editor. This interpretation also suffers from the problem identified by Marinkovic of reading Zechariah predominantly through the grid of the temple rebuilding programme, whereas we have observed that Zechariah's agenda is wider than this.[50] The rebuilding of the temple is not the specific thrust of this section of the prophecy and a foundation stone makes little sense at this point.

45. Petersen (*Haggai and Zechariah 1–8*, p. 211) notes the 'anomalous' nature of this repetition and treats the arrangement of the text as suspect.

46. See Petersen, *Haggai and Zechariah 1–8*, pp. 211-12. Petitjean (*Les oracles du Proto-Zacharie*, pp. 170-85) has a detailed treatment of the interpretations of the stone. For an interpretation which treats the expression על־אבן אחת as an idiom meaning 'at the same time' (cf. Judg. 9.5, 18), see E. Lipiński, 'Recherches sur le livre de Zacharie', *VT* 20 (1970), pp. 25-55 (25-30). The evidence for this idiom seems tenuous.

47. So Petitjean, *Les oracles du Proto-Zacharie*, pp. 170-85; Halpern, 'The Ritual Background', pp. 167-90.

48. A.S. van der Woude, 'Zion as Primeval Stone in Zechariah 3 and 4', in W. Claassen (ed.), *Text and Context: Old Testament and Semitic Studies for F.C. Fensham* (JSOTSup, 48; Sheffield: JSOT Press, 1988), pp. 237-48.

49. Petitjean, *Les oracles du Proto-Zacharie*, p. 179.

50. Marinkovic, 'What Does Zechariah 1–8 Tell Us?'.

The understanding of the stone favoured by such commentators as Mitchell,[51] Petersen,[52] Tollington,[53] de Vaux[54] and Ackroyd[55] is that it is a reference to the gold ornament (ציץ, Exod. 28.36) which forms part of the tiara attached to the high priestly turban. Meyers and Meyers see a possible intentional ambiguity, with the stone being pivotal in a transition from the investiture scene of ch. 3 and the following vision where it may anticipate the two references to a stone in 4.7, 10.[56] The mention of the 'eyes' of the stone has prompted some to suggest the facets of a cut gemstone. The parallel reference to an inscription on the stone inclines one to think of the inscription which the high priest bore on his headdress according to Exod. 28.36—'Holy to Yhwh'. Beuken suggests that if this were written in its hypocoristic form קדש ליהו we may have an explanation for the seven 'eyes' in the form of the seven letters which make up this inscription.[57] Against this, it must be said that apart from its use in names, we have no evidence for this spelling of the divine name, and our earliest evidence has it in the familiar tetragrammaton form.[58] Alternatively, the 'eyes' have been taken to represent the all-seeing presence of Yhwh, whose seven eyes range throughout the earth (cf. 4.10),[59] eyes which above all take into their purview the people who are the 'apple of his eye' (בבת עינו, 2.12 [ET 2.8]).[60]

More satisfying is the explanation given by VanderKam,[61] who takes the stone with its seven *pairs* of eyes (dual עינים) as a reference to the *fourteen* individual stones mentioned in Exodus 28—the two onyx stones

51. Mitchell, Powis Smith and Bewer, *Haggai, Zechariah, Malachi and Jonah*, pp. 157-59.

52. Petersen, *Haggai and Zechariah 1–8*, pp. 211-12.

53. Tollington, *Tradition and Innovation*, p. 164.

54. De Vaux, *Ancient Israel*, II, p. 399.

55. Peter R. Ackroyd, 'Zechariah', in Matthew Black and H.H. Rowley (eds.), *Peake's Commentary on the Bible* (London: Thomas Nelson, 1962), pp. 646-55 (648); *idem*, *Exile and Restoration*, p. 191.

56. Meyers and Meyers, *Haggai, Zechariah 1–8*, pp. 204-11.

57. Beuken, *Haggai–Sacharja 1–8*, p. 285.

58. Yardeni, 'Remarks on the Priestly Blessing'. Philo speaks of the divine name as τετραγράμματον: *Vit. Mos*. 2.115.

59. For further possible links with the eyes of ch. 4, see Meyers and Meyers, *Haggai, Zechariah 1–8*, pp. 208-209.

60. For the possible meaning of עינים here as 'fountains', see Lipiński, 'Recherches sur le livre de Zacharie', pp. 25-30; Baldwin, *Haggai, Zechariah, Malachi*, p. 117.

61. James C. VanderKam, 'Joshua the High Priest and the Interpretation of Zechariah 3', *CBQ* 53 (1991), pp. 553-70.

on the shoulder pieces of the high priestly ephod (vv. 9-12) and the twelve gems on the breastpiece (vv. 17-21). The use of the singular אבן is still difficult, though VanderKam notes the circumstance of the use of the singular in the syntax of Exod. 28.10 and 17 as a possible reason for its use here.[62] These stones are all inscribed (פתח, Exod. 28.9, 11) with the names of the tribes—six on each of the two shoulder stones and one on each of the breastpiece stones.

We may be best not seeking too close an identification with any one image, but should perhaps be prepared to accept the multifaceted and allusive nature of the description. Thus Meyers and Meyers see a conflation of the various stones mentioned in connection with the high priestly garb and the adornment to the headdress.[63] What is clear, though not always made central to the interpretation of the symbolism, is that the stone speaks of the definitive ('on a single day') removal of the guilt (עון) of the land. From Exod. 28.36-38 we learn that the removal of guilt is associated with the head adornment. However, not too much weight can be placed on this, as a similar association is said to be true of the linen undergarments (Exod. 28.42-43), so the mention of one item may stand for the whole outfit. The removal of guilt is of course presupposed by the access to Yhwh which the high priest enjoys as he wears the stones of the breastpiece or shoulder pieces of the ephod (Exod. 28.12, 29).

This removal of guilt in v. 8 clearly ties the oracle back into the preceding vision (v. 4) where the removal of guilt was central to an understanding of the symbolism of the reclothing of the high priest. What was there spoken of as the removal of Joshua's guilt, has now been shown to be a removal of the guilt of the whole land. The divine action of removing the guilt of the 'land' is an indication that any barrier to fellowship with God on the part of the returned citizens of Jerusalem–Judah is being removed in the same way that the guilt of the high priest was removed in the vision.

In the concluding verse (v. 10), we see a stylized idyllic picture of what this removal of guilt and restored access to God will entail in terms of interpersonal relationships. In the vine and fig-tree image we have a classic portrayal of the security, prosperity and harmony which characterize life in the land under the covenant blessing of God—blessing which flows from a right relationship with him (cf. 1 Kgs 5.5 [ET 4.25]; Mic. 4.4). The intimacy and invitation to fellowship which characterize Yhwh's attitudes and actions towards his people are to spill over into everyday human relationships.

62. VanderKam, 'Joshua the High Priest', p. 568.

63. Meyers and Meyers, *Haggai, Zechariah 1–8*, pp. 225-26.

The oracle (vv. 8-10) then supports my tentative conclusions regarding the vision (vv. 1-7), and particularly its climax in the declaration of v. 7. The subject of both is a relationship which Yhwh confirms with his people—a relationship which has its visionary expression in the form of heavenly access or approach to the presence of God, and has as its perpetual reminder and guarantee the earthly priesthood with its stylized and representative form of access, and has its outworking in terms of harmony and security in the land.

4. *Conclusion*

Zechariah's fourth vision depicts a royal grant in which Joshua (as the representative high priest of the returned exiles) is observed as a participant in the visionary world which lies beyond normal human perception. As with other heavenly visions, there is a degree of reverential reserve in the description. Yhwh is not visually depicted, but is represented by his 'angel', though seemingly is to be closely identified with that angel. There, in the face of potential objection, Joshua is assured, by means of the reclothing scene, of the privilege of access to the divine realm. More than this, the wider community he represents is promised a share in such access through the continued faithful service of their priest. This grant is against the backdrop of the wider context of the restoration of a people to their city and land and their privileged position as Yhwh's chosen ones. This understanding is confirmed by the accompanying oracle which portrays the same notion from a divine point of view. Among other tokens of the divine favour, the servant nation or 'shoot' is invited to enter or is drawn into the divine presence, the paramount priestly prerogative.

There are thus significant points of contact with the promise of a universal priestly access for the people of God in Exod. 19.6 and its cotext. In both places, the blessing promised is closely related to (and is tantamount to) the condition of continued covenant faithfulness. In both places the privilege is related to the issue of access to God's sanctuary, whether that be conceived of as the heights of Mt Sinai, or the heavenly court. In both cases, the privilege of priestly service takes on regal overtones. In both cases, the wider cotext links the divine declaration to an ensuing programme of construction of an earthly sanctuary which replicates the heavenly one. Finally, in both cases, the global dimensions of the grant are in view as the nations observe the attitude and actions of Yhwh towards his chosen people.

Chapter 13

CONCLUSION

Through a literary analysis of Exod. 19.4-6a, with particular reference to v. 6a and the phrase ממלכת כהנים, this study has called into question the two prevailing analyses of this unit as being inadequate to do full justice to the text as we have it. The covenant which God established with his people, Israel, at Mt Sinai, according to the book of Exodus, has as one of its central elements a declaration of the honoured standing this people is to have in his sight. In distinction from the nations, Israel as a whole (rather than a subset of Israel) is to be a 'royal priesthood and a holy nation', words which spell out the uniquely favoured position Israel occupies as a result of divine grant. Through divine favour, Israel is said to enjoy an affinity, or fitness for access to the divine dwelling place, the presence of God. The words of the declaration denote primarily how the nation is to relate to God, rather than how it is to relate to the other nations as is often supposed, though it is not denied that there may be implications for human relationships of what it means to be the chosen and treasured people of God.

The declaration involves the attribution to Israel of both royal and priestly characteristics by way of an explanatory expansion on the otherwise somewhat cryptic word סגלה. This royal-priestly designation of Israel draws on a rich world of ideology and symbolism, much of it common to the ancient Near East, where access to the divine realm is the prerogative of kings or their priests who acted as their surrogates. This rich symbolism has generally been all but overlooked, and occasionally explicitly denied, when it comes to elucidating the meaning of the phrase ממלכת כהנים in Exod. 19.6. It is the discerning of this symbolism in the cotext of Exod. 19.6, and in some of its intertextual links, which constitutes one of the central contributions of this work.

Attempts to make the Sinai covenant, particularly as summarized in Exod. 19.4-6, fit the suzerainty treaty pattern have not been altogether convincing and this has led to an overly hasty rejection by some of any form of covenant as a useful category for expressing the nature of the divine relationship with Israel. Among the diverse forms of legal or quasi-legal instruments collectively known as 'treaties' or 'covenants', one form, the 'treaty of grant', offers to some extent an instructive parallel with the offer of covenant to Israel at Mt Sinai. This covenant is in substantial continuity with the covenant granted to the patriarchs, but develops more fully the character of Israel as the 'nation' descended from Abraham, the one from whom 'kings' would come. The covenant only has meaning and validity as Israel conforms to the character and requirements of Yhwh, that is, to the extent that they are 'holy'. There is one major respect in which the analogy with grant treaties is deficient. Unlike the secular grant texts and some biblical texts which ascribe the grant of priesthood to individuals or a tribe in Israel, the emphasis in the corporate grant falls not on the devotion or loyal service on the part of Israel as the ground of the grant, but on Yhwh's own actions in delivering Israel from Egypt and bringing the nation to himself.

It is this notion of the status of Israel as a royal company of priests which undergirds much of the rest of the book of Exodus. The burning bush episode is seen to be a precursor to the experience of the whole people at Sinai, and a pointer to the priestly character of their encounter with God. The theophany, or manifestation of God on the mountain serves a number of functions. It demonstrates the awesome nature of God, it enhances the prestige of the people who witness the event and it heightens the dramatic tension as the people, through fear, keep their distance and plead for mediation. A turning point is reached in Exod. 24.1-11, which depicts what is essentially a priestly ordination rite, at which point the people are symbolically prepared for an intimate encounter with the deity. The people's representatives then ascend God's mountain abode and are granted a vision of God and a meal in his heavenly temple. The expected ancient Near Eastern ideology is reversed as God feeds his worshippers or heavenly attendants rather than being fed by them.

Provision is made for the perpetuation of the experience and a regular graphic portrayal in an elaborate drama of the honorific estimation this people enjoys in relation to their God. The close structural links between the cultic material of Exodus and the Sinai encounter are to be noted. The tabernacle cult is seen to reflect aspects of the original good created order, an ideal world in which God resides, free from the corruption, disorder and death which characterize the world outside the sanctuary, as in the paradise garden depicted in Genesis 2. Into this symbolically recreated world God invites his priests, men chosen by his appointment and consecrated by rites of passage for access to the divine realm. Priests, by their splendid attire, are a visual representation of regal dignity, and all that is said of them points to their being associated with life and wellbeing.

The Levitical priesthood as portrayed in Exodus is seen not as diminishing or supplanting the collective royal priesthood, but as providing a visual model of that vocation, and secondly as facilitating it. Priests, like angels, their heavenly counterparts, demonstrate what it means to gain access to the presence of God, to worship and serve him in an environment where the restrictions to access have been removed. They and the world they frequent are pointers to the potential for the repristination of the cosmos.

In considering aspects of the Sinai pericope, we have observed a greater degree of coherence than has frequently been acknowledged, and suggested a rationale for the interweaving of law and narrative which is consistent with the declaration of Israel as a 'royal priesthood'. The laws establish a pattern of life for the priestly nation as this is to be lived in the sanctuary land of Israel.

By some, the 'kingdom of priests' is treated as a passing metaphor, with little or no subsequent reflection on it in the Hebrew Bible. This study has suggested otherwise. Even if not all of the intertextual links adduced are regarded as equally convincing examples of inner biblical exegesis or direct allusion, there should be sufficient to indicate that Exod. 19.4-6 is a unit of text, and in particular, the designation of the people of God as a royal priesthood is a concept to which the biblical writers (and those who followed them in intertestamental and New Testament writings) returned as a passage and a theme which informed their own thought. Their readings of the passage support (at least in general terms) the understanding of it presented above.

The narrative of the rebellion of Korah in Numbers 16 is a carefully crafted narrative which makes little sense if the collective priesthood of Israel is not assumed as part of the presupposition pool of the *dramatis personae*, the author and the reader. By bringing the semantic domains כהן and קדש into close relationship with each other and applying at least the latter (and by inference the former) to the whole congregation of Israel, the writer would appear to be echoing the use of these roots in Exod. 19.6. Through subtle narrative artistry, the tensions which are potentially inherent in holding together the notion of the royal priesthood of all Israel and the dedicated Aaronic priesthood are played out. Both the restricted priestly consecration of Aaron and his sons and the wider consecrated status of the people as a whole are upheld. The former is necessary, in fact, for the preservation of the latter.

Hosea 4 contains an arraignment of Israel for unfaithfulness. While the syntax is not clear, a viable reading of v. 6 is to see in it an address to Israel as God's corporate priest, a role from which the nation is being rejected in judgment. The analogy which ought to operate between priest and people, the analogy of which Exod. 19.6 is an expression, appears to be the subject of a proverbial maxim—'like people, like priest'—which is quoted and given an ironic twist in v. 9.

A number of passages in the Hebrew Bible affirm the royalty or sovereignty of Israel, at least as a future projection. Two which do so in language which appears to reflect Exod. 19.6 and demonstrate an awareness of its cotext are Mic. 4.8 and Ps. 114.2. By its choice of language, the psalm may be a two-way intertextual link with the Micah passage and with Exod. 19.6. The psalm relates this sovereignty to the quality of holiness or the sanctuary character of Israel, while the cotext of the Micah passage may more allusively suggest a relationship with the notion of priesthood.

Isaiah contains a number of passages which appear to reflect upon the declaration of the royal and priestly character of Israel. In particular I have noted Isa. 61.6 and its immediate cotext (including v. 10) where that priesthood is presented in an eschatologically oriented context as the ideal prospect in store for the people of God. Verse 10 makes use of the symbolic value of the priestly regalia to provide a metaphor for the righteous and glorious standing the people will come to enjoy in relation to God. The rejection announced in Hosea 4 is not ultimate, it seems, in the prophetic portrayal. Israel's priesthood consists not so much in its service to the nations, as in the privilege of attending on God.

Finally, Zechariah 3 presents a visionary vindication of Joshua, the high priest, who in reality stands for the whole of the population of restored Zion or Judah after the exile. The assurance of his privilege of access to the heavenly court in the face of opposition is not given for his benefit alone, but for the community hc represents. This restoration, involving the removal of sin, is symbolized in the royal-priestly reclothing image and the 'stone' which characterizes the removal of sin, which would otherwise constitute a barrier to fellowship with God. In supporting a reading of מהלכים as 'those who gain access' (v. 7), and by demonstrating that the 'shoot' (v. 8) is the nation of Israel which is being brought to God himself, I have demonstrated the link between the newly authenticated priesthood of the high priest, and the royal-priestly character of the nation. This priestly character is expressed above all in Israel's privilege of access to and enjoyment of the presence of God, an enjoyment which spills over to an idyllic relationship with one's neighbours. There are structural, verbal and thematic echoes of Exod. 19.4-6 in this chapter.

We have thus seen at least two passages, Isa. 61.6-10 and Zechariah 3 which appear both to relate intertextually to Exod. 19.6 and to draw on the royal priestly clothing imagery of the Aaronic priesthood in their portrayal of Israel in royal-priestly terms. This relationship is that of corporate ideal to its symbolic representation, the pattern we have observed in the structure of the book of Exodus.

It perhaps needs to be stressed that no single analysis is likely to do justice to such a rich and complex unit of Scripture as the Sinai pericope. The encounter of the divine with the human sphere will strain the limits of any narrative artistry. However, the source-critical solutions to the tensions in the narrative which in the past have generally been invoked have not proved satisfying, and the way forward is likely to lie in further application of methodologies which are sensitive to the integrity of the text of Scripture which has come down to us. What has been offered here is not so much the 'key' to interpreting the Sinai pericope, but a perspective from which to view it. It is to be hoped that this study prompts further reflection along these lines. In particular, the last word has not been said regarding the extent to which secular treaty models have influenced the categories in which Israel's consciousness of its relationship with God find expression, and which models might have greater relevance in this discussion. It is also to be hoped that the present study might stimulate further reflection on the passages in the New Testament which draw upon the strand of imagery which has been the subject of this book, as well as on the broader themes of election, grace and covenant which the New Testament writers see as finding their fulfilment in Jesus Christ, and that our perceptions of the inestimable divine favour granted to all the people of God might be enriched.

Bibliography

Abba, Raymond, 'Priests and Levites in Deuteronomy', *VT* 27 (1977), pp. 257-67.

Ackroyd, Peter R., 'The Book of Haggai and Zechariah 1–8', *JJS* 3 (1952), pp. 151-56.

—'Zechariah', in Matthew Black and H.H. Rowley (eds.), *Peake's Commentary on the Bible* (London: Thomas Nelson, 1962), pp. 646-55.

Aharoni, Yohanan, 'Arad: Its Inscriptions and Temple', *BA* 31 (1968), pp. 1-32.

Ahlström, G.W., 'Heaven on Earth—at Hazor and Arad', in Birger A. Pearson (ed.), *Religious Syncretism in Antiquity: Essays in Conversation with Geo Widengren* (AAR/Institute of Religious Studies, University of California. Series on Formative Contemporary Thinkers, 1; Missoula, MT: Scholars Press, 1975), pp. 67-83.

Albright, William Foxwell, 'An Aramaean Magical Text in Hebrew from the Seventh Century BC', *BASOR* 76 (1939), pp. 5-11.

—*Archeology and the Religion of Israel* (Baltimore: The Johns Hopkins University Press, 3rd edn, 1953).

Alexander, T.D., 'The Composition of the Sinai Narrative in Exodus xix 1–xxiv 11', *VT* 49 (1999), pp. 2-20.

Allen, Leslie C., *The Books of Joel, Obadiah, Jonah and Micah* (NICOT; Grand Rapids: Eerdmans, 1976).

—*Psalms 101–150* (WBC, 21; Waco, TX: Word Books, 1987).

Alt, Albrecht, 'Gedanken über das Königtum Jahwes', in Albrecht Alt, *Kleine Schriften zur Geschichte des Volkes Israel* (2 vols.; Munich: Beck, 1953), I, pp. 345-57.

Alter, Robert, *The Art of Biblical Narrative* (New York: Basic Books, 1981).

—*The Art of Biblical Poetry* (New York: Basic Books, 1985).

Alter, Robert, and Frank Kermode (eds.), *The Literary Guide to the Bible* (Glasgow: Fontana, 1989).

Altmann, Peter, *Erwählungstheologie und Universalismus im Alten Testament* (BZAW, 92; Berlin: Alfred Töpelmann, 1964).

Andersen, Francis I., 'Feet in Ancient Times', *Buried History* 35 (1999), pp. 9-20.

Andersen, Francis I., and A. Dean Forbes, '"Prose Particle" Counts in the Hebrew Bible', in Meyers and O'Connor (eds.), *The Word of the Lord Shall Go Forth*, pp. 165-83.

Andersen, Francis I., and David Noel Freedman, *Hosea: A New Translation with Introduction and Commentary* (AB, 24; Garden City, NY: Doubleday, 1980).

Anderson, A.A., *The Book of Psalms*. II. *Psalms 73–150* (NCB; London: Oliphants, 1972).

Arichea, Daniel C., Jr, 'The Ups and Downs of Moses: Locating Moses in Exodus 19–33', *BT* 40 (1989), pp. 244-46.

Armerding, Carl Edward, 'Were David's Sons Really Priests?' in Gerald F. Hawthorne (ed.), *Current Issues in Biblical and Patristic Interpretation: Studies in Honor of Merrill C. Tenney Presented by his Former Students* (Grand Rapids: Eerdmans, 1975), pp. 75-86.

Ashley, Timothy R., *The Book of Numbers* (NICOT; Grand Rapids: Eerdmans, 1993).

Auerbach, Elias, 'Der Aufstieg der Priesterschaft zur Macht im Alten Israel', in *Congress Volume, Bonn 1962* (VTSup, 9; Leiden: E.J. Brill, 1963), pp. 236-49.

Auzou, Georges, *De la servitude au service: Etude du livre de l'Exode* (Connaissance de la Bible, 3; Paris: Editions de l'Orante, 1961).

Baldwin, Joyce G., *Haggai, Zechariah, Malachi: An Introduction and Commentary* (TOTC; London: Tyndale Press, 1972).

Baltzer, Klaus, *Die Biographie der Propheten* (Neukirchen–Vluyn: Neukirchener Verlag, 1975).

—*The Covenant Formulary in Old Testament, Jewish and Early Christian Writings* (trans. David E. Green; Oxford: Basil Blackwell, 1971).

Barbiero, Gianni, '*Mamleket kohanîm*: (Es 19,6a): I sacerdoti al potere?', *Rivista Biblica* 37 (1989), pp. 427-46.

Bar-Ilan, Meir, 'They Shall Put My Name Upon the People of Israel', *HUCA* 60 (1989), pp. *19-*31 (Hebrew).

Barker, Margaret, *The Gate of Heaven: The History and Symbolism of the Temple in Jerusalem* (London: SPCK, 1991).

—*The Older Testament: The Survival of Themes from the Ancient Royal Cult in Sectarian Judaism and Early Christianity* (London: SPCK, 1987).

Barr, James, *Comparative Philology and the Text of the Old Testament* (London: SCM Press, 1983).

—*The Semantics of Biblical Language* (London: Oxford University Press, 1961).

—'Some Semantic Notes on the Covenant', in Donner, Hanhart and Smend (eds.), *Beiträge zur alttestamentlichen Theologie*, pp. 23-38.

—'Theophany and Anthropomorphism in the Old Testament', in *Congress Volume, Oxford 1959* (VTSup, 7; Leiden: E.J.Brill, 1960), pp. 31-38.

Barré, Michael L., SS, and John S. Kselman, SS, 'New Exodus, Covenant, and Restoration in Psalm 23', in Meyers and O'Connor (eds.), *The Word of the Lord Shall Go Forth*, pp. 97-127.

Barthélemy, D., OP, and J.T. Milik, *Qumran Cave 1* (DJD, 1; Oxford: Clarendon Press, 1955).

Batto, Bernard F., *Slaying the Dragon: Mythmaking in the Biblical Tradition* (Louisville, KY: Westminster/John Knox Press, 1992).

Baudissin, Wolf Wilhelm Grafen, *Die Geschichte des alttestamentlichen Priesterthums* (Osnabrück: Otto Zeller, 1967).

Bauer, J.B., 'Könige und Priester, ein heiliges Volk (Ex 19,6)', *BZ* 2 (1958), pp. 283-86.

Baumgarten, Joseph M., 'The Duodecimal Courts of Qumran, Revelation and the Sanhedrin', *JBL* 95 (1976), pp. 59-78.

Beale, G.K., *John's Use of the Old Testament in Revelation* (JSNTSup, 166; Sheffield: Sheffield Academic Press, 1998).

Beckwith, Roger T., and Martin J. Selman (eds.), *Sacrifice in the Bible* (Carlisle: Paternoster; Grand Rapids: Baker Book House, 1995).

Beer, Georg, *Exodus, mit einem Beitrag von K. Galling* (HAT, 3; Tübingen: J.C.B. Mohr, 1939).

Beitzel, Barry J., 'Exodus 3:14 and the Divine Name: A Case of Paronomasia', *Trinity Journal* NS 1 (1980), pp. 5-20.

Bennett, W.H. (ed.), *Exodus, Introduction: Revised Version with Notes, Giving an Analysis Showing from which of the Original Documents Each Portion of the Text Is Taken* (Century Bible; Edinburgh: T.C. & E.C. Jack, 1910).

Ben-Yashar, Menachem, 'Noch zum *miqdaṣ 'ādām* in 4QFlorilegium', *RevQ* 10 (1981), pp. 587-88.

Bergman, J., Helmer Ringgren and W. Dommershausen, 'כהן', in *TDOT*, VII, pp. 60-75.

Berlin, Adele, *Poetics and Interpretation of Biblical Narrative* (Bible and Literature Series, 9; Sheffield: Almond Press, 1983).

—'A Search for a New Biblical Hermeneutics: Preliminary Observations', in Jerrold S. Cooper and Glenn M. Schwartz (eds.), *The Study of the Ancient Near East in the Twenty-First Century: The William Foxwell Albright Centennial Conference* (Winona Lake, IN: Eisenbrauns, 1996), pp. 195-207.

Beuken, W.A.M., SJ, *Haggai–Sacharja 1–8: Studien zur Überlieferungsgeschichte früh-nachexilischen Prophetie* (Assen: Van Gorcum, n.d.).

Beyerlin, Walter, *Origins and History of the Oldest Sinaitic Traditions* (trans. S. Rudman; Oxford: Basil Blackwell, 1965).

Biran, Avraham (ed.), *Temples and High Places in Biblical Times: Proceedings of the Colloquium in Honor of the Centennial of Hebrew Union College—Jewish Institute of Religion* (Jerusalem: Hebrew Union College Press/Jewish Institute of Religion, 1981).

Blenkinsopp, Joseph, *Sage, Priest, Prophet: Religious and Intellectual Leadership in Ancient Israel* (Louisville, KY: Westminster/John Knox Press, 1995).

—'The Structure of P', *CBQ* 38 (1976), pp. 275-92.

Block, Daniel Isaac, *Gods of the Nations: Studies in Ancient Near Eastern National Theology* (ETSMS, 2; Jackson, MS: Evangelical Theological Society, 1988).

Bloom, Harold, 'Exodus: From J to K, or the Uncanniness of the Yahwist', in David Rosenberg (ed.), *Congregation: Contemporary Writers Read the Jewish Bible* (San Diego: Harcourt Brace Jovanovich, 1987), pp. 9-26.

Bloom, Harold (ed.), *Exodus* (New York: Chelsea House, 1987).

Blum, Erhard, 'Israël à la montagne de Dieu: Remarques sur Ex 19–24, 32–34 et sur le contexte littéraire et historique de sa composition', in de Pury (ed.), *Le Pentateuque en question*, pp. 271-95.

—*Studien zur Komposition des Pentateuch* (BZAW, 189; Berlin: W. de Gruyter, 1990).

Bokser, Baruch M., 'Approaching Sacred Space', *HTR* 78 (1985), pp. 279-99.

Bousset, Wilhelm, *Die Offenbarung Johannis* (Göttingen: Vandenhoeck & Ruprecht, rev. edn, 1906).

Boyd Barrick, W., and John R. Spencer (eds.), *In the Shelter of Elyon: Essays on Ancient Palestinian Life and Literature in honor of G.W. Ahlström* (JSOTSup, 31; Sheffield: JSOT Press, 1984).

Briggs, Charles A., *Messianic Prophecy: The Prediction of the Fulfillment of Redemption through the Messiah* (New York: Charles Scribner's Sons, 1886).

Bright, John, *Covenant and Promise* (London: SCM Press, 1977).

Brinkman, John A., *et al.*, *The Assyrian Dictionary of the Oriental Institute of the University of Chicago* (21 vols.; Chicago: Oriental Institute, 1956–92).

Brockelmann, Carl, *Hebräische Syntax* (Neukirchen: Buchhandlung des Erziehungsvereins, 1956).

Brooke, Alan England, and Norman McLean (eds.), *The Old Testament in Greek* (3 vols. in 9 parts; London: Cambridge University Press, 1906–40).

Brueggemann, Walter, *Theology of the Old Testament: Testimony, Dispute, Advocacy* (Minneapolis: Fortress Press, 1997).

Buber, Martin, 'Holy Event (Exodus 19–27)', in Harold Bloom (ed.), *Exodus*, pp. 45-58.

—*Kingship of God* (trans. Richard Scheimann; London: George Allen & Unwin, 3rd edn, 1967).

—*Moses: The Revelation and the Covenant* (Atlantic Highlands, NJ: Humanities Press International, 1989).

Budd, Philip J., *Numbers* (WBC, 5; Waco, TX: Word Books, 1984).
Bush, George, *Notes on Exodus* (2 vols.; New York: Newman & Ivison, 1852).
Butterworth, Mike, *Structure and the Book of Zechariah* (JSOTSup, 130; Sheffield: JSOT Press, 1992).
Calvin, John, *Commentary on the Book of Psalms* (trans. James Anderson; 5 vols.; Grand Rapids: Eerdmans, 1948–49).
—*Commentaries on the Last Four Books of Moses Arranged in the Form of a Harmony* (trans. Charles William Bingham; 4 vols.; repr. Grand Rapids: Eerdmans, 1979).
Campbell, E.F., 'Sovereign God', *McCormick Quarterly* 20 (1967), pp. 173-86.
Campbell, Edward F. and David Noel Freedman (eds.), *The Biblical Archaeologist Reader* 3 (Garden City, NY: Doubleday, 1970).
Caquot, André, 'La double investiture de Lévi (brèves remarques sur Testament de Lévi, VIII)', in C.J. Bleeker, S.G.F. Brandon and M. Simon (eds.), *Ex orbe religionum: Studia Geo Widengren* (Studies in the History of Religions, 21-22; 2 vols.; Leiden: E.J. Brill, 1972), I, pp. 156-61.
Carpenter, J. Estlin, and George Harford, *The Composition of the Hexateuch: An Introduction with Select Lists of Words and Phrases* (London: Longmans, Green & Co., 1902).
Caspari, Wilhelm, 'Das priesterliche Königreich', *Theologische Blätter* 8 (1929), cols. 105-10.
Cassuto, U., *A Commentary on the Book of Exodus* (trans. I. Abrahams; Perry Foundation for Biblical Research Publications; Jerusalem: Magnes Press, 1967).
Cazelles, Henri, PSS, 'Alliance du Sinai, alliance de l'Horeb et renouvellement de l'alliance', in Donner, Hanhart and Smend (eds.), *Beiträge zur alttestamentlichen Theologie*, pp. 69-79.
—'L'alliance du Sinaï en Ex. 34,10-27', in A. Caquot, S. Légasse and M. Tardieu (eds.), *Melanges bibliques et orientaux* (Festschrift M. Mathias Delcor; AOAT, 215; Neukirchen–Vluyn: Neukirchener Verlag, 1985), pp. 57-68.
—'"Royaume de prêtres et nation consacrée" (Exode XIX,6)', in Henri Cazelles, PSS, *Autour de l'Exode (Etudes)* (Sources bibliques; Paris: J. Gabalda, 1987), pp. 289-94.
Cerfaux, Lucien, 'Regale sacerdotium', in *Recueil Lucien Cerfaux: Etudes d'exegèsezet d'histoire religieuse* (BETL, 6-7, 18; 3 vols.; Gembloux: Duculot, 1954–62), pp. 283-315.
Chadwick, G.A., *The Book of Exodus* (The Expositors Bible; London: Hodder & Stoughton, 1903).
Charles, R.H., *A Critical and Exegetical Commentary on the Revelation of St. John* (ICC; Edinburgh: T. & T. Clark, 1920).
—*The Greek Versions of the Testaments of the Twelve Patriarchs* (Oxford: Clarendon Press, 1908).
Cheung, Alex T.M., 'The Priest as the Redeemed Man: A Biblical-Theological Study of the Priesthood', *JETS* 29 (1986), pp. 265-75.
Childs, Brevard S., *Exodus: A Commentary* (OTL; Philadelphia: Westminster Press, 1974).
—*Introduction to the Old Testament as Scripture* (Philadelphia: Fortress Press, 1979).
—*Myth and Reality in the Old Testament* (SBT, 27; London: SCM Press, 2nd edn, 1962).
Chirichigno, G.C., 'The Narrative Structure of Exod 19–24', *Bib* 68 (1987), pp. 457-79.
Clements, Ronald E., *Abraham and David: Genesis 15 and its Meaning for Israelite Tradition* (SBT, 2.5; London: SCM Press, 1967).
—'Baal-Berith of Shechem', *JSS* 13 (1968), pp. 21-32.
—*Exodus: Commentary* (Cambridge Bible Commentary; Cambridge: Cambridge University Press, 1972).

—*God and Temple: The Presence of God in Israel's Worship* (Philadelphia: Fortress Press, 1965).

—*Old Testament Theology: A Fresh Approach* (Marshall's Theological Library; London: Marshall, Morgan & Scott, 1978).

—*Prophecy and Covenant* (London: SCM Press, 1965).

Clifford, Richard J., *The Cosmic Mountain in Canaan and the Old Testament* (HSM, 4; Cambridge, MA: Harvard University Press, 1972).

—'The Tent of El and the Israelite Tent of Meeting', *CBQ* 33 (1971), pp. 221-27.

Clines, David J.A., *The Theme of the Pentateuch* (JSOTSup, 10; Sheffield: JSOT Press, 1978).

Coats, George W., *Rebellion in the Wilderness: The Murmuring Motif in the Wilderness Traditions of the Old Testament* (Nashville: Abingdon Press, 1968).

—'The Yahwist as Theologian? A Critical Reflection', *JSOT* 3 (1977), pp. 28-32.

Cody, Aelred, OSB, 'Exodus 18,12—Jethro Accepts a Covenant with the Israelites', *Bib* 49 (1968), pp. 153-66.

—*Ezekiel: With a History of Old Testament Priesthood* (Wilmington, DE: Michael Glazier, 1984).

—*A History of Old Testament Priesthood* (AnBib, 35; Rome: Pontifical Biblical Institute Press, 1969).

—'When Is the Chosen People Called a *gôy*?', *VT* 14 (1964), pp. 1-6.

Collins, John J., 'The Jewish Apocalypses', *Semeia* 14 (1979), pp. 21-59.

Collins, John J., and Michael Fishbane (eds.), *Death, Ecstasy and Otherworldly Journeys* (Albany: State University of New York Press, 1995).

Colson, F.H. (ed)., *Philo, with an English Translation by F.H. Colson* (LCL; 12 vols.; London: Loeb Classics, 1929–53).

Coppens, J.C., 'The Spiritual Temple in the Pauline Letters and its Background', *Studia Evangelica* 6 (1969), pp. 53-66.

Cotterell, Peter, and Max Turner, *Linguistics and Biblical Interpretation* (London: SPCK, 1989).

Cross, Frank Moore, Jr, *Canaanite Myth and Hebrew Epic: Essays in the History of the Religion of Israel* (Cambridge, MA: Harvard University Press, 1973).

—'The Epic Traditions of Early Israel: Epic Narrative and the Reconstruction of Early Israelite Institutions', in Richard Elliott Friedman (ed.), *The Poet and the Historian: Essays in Literary and Historical Biblical Criticism* (HSS, 26; Chico, CA: Scholars Press, 1983), pp. 13-39.

—*From Epic to Canon: History and Literature in Ancient Israel* (Baltimore: The Johns Hopkins University Press, 1998).

—'The Ideologies of Kingship in the Era of the Empire: Conditional Covenant and Eternal Decree', in Frank Moore Cross, Jr, *Canaanite Myth and Hebrew Epic: Essays in the History of the Religion of Israel* (Cambridge, MA: Harvard University Press, 1973), pp. 219-73.

—'The Priestly Tabernacle: A Study from an Archaeological and Historical Approach', *BA* 10 (1947), pp. 45-68.

—'The Priestly Tabernacle in the Light of Recent Research', in Avraham Biran (ed.), *Temples and High Places in Biblical Times*, pp. 169-81.

—'The Priestly Work', in Frank Moore Cross, Jr, *Canaanite Myth and Hebrew Epic: Essays in the History of the Religion of Israel* (Cambridge, MA: Harvard University Press, 1973), pp. 293-325.

—'The Seal of Miqnêyaw, Servant of Yahweh', in Leonard Gorelick and Elizabeth Williams-Forte (eds.), *Ancient Seals and the Bible* (Monographic Journals of the Near East. Occasional Papers on the Near East, 2.1; Los Angeles: Undena Publications, 1983), pp. 55-63.

Cross, Frank Moore, Jr, and David Noel Freedman, 'The Song of Miriam', *JNES* 14 (1955), pp. 237-50.

Cross, Frank Moore, Jr, and Richard J. Saley, 'Phoenician Incantations on a Plaque of the Seventh Century BC from Arslan Tash in Upper Syria', *BASOR* 197 (1970), pp. 42-49.

Dabin, Paul, SJ, *Le sacerdoce royale des fidèles dans la tradition ancienne et moderne* (Museum Lessianum. Section Théologique; Brussels: Desclée, 1950).

Dahood, Mitchell, SJ, *Psalms: Introduction, Translation and Notes* (AB, 16-17A; 3 vols.; Garden City, NY: Doubleday, 1965–70).

—'Ugaritic Hebrew Parallel Pairs', in Fisher (ed.), *Ras Shamra Parallels*, II, pp. 1-33.

Damrosch, David, *The Narrative Covenant: Transformations of Genre in the Growth of Biblical Literature* (San Francisco: Harper & Row, 1987).

Danby, Herbert, *The Mishnah, Translated from the Hebrew with Introduction and Brief Explanatory Notes* (London: Oxford University Press, 1933).

Daniélou, Jean, 'La symbolique cosmique du temple de Jérusalem', in *Symbolisme cosmique et monuments religieux*. I. *Texte* (Paris: Editions des musées nationaux, 1953), pp. 61-64.

Davey, Christopher J., 'Temples of the Levant and the Buildings of Solomon', *TB* 31 (1980), pp. 107-46.

David, A. Rosalie, *The Ancient Egyptians: Religious Beliefs and Practices* (London: Routledge & Kegan Paul, 1982).

Davidson, A.B., *The Theology of the Old Testament* (ed. S.D.F. Salmond; Edinburgh: T. & T. Clark, 1904).

Davies, G.I., 'The Composition of the Book of Exodus: Reflections on the Theses of Erhard Blum', in Fox *et al.* (eds.), *Texts, Temples and Traditions*, pp. 71-85.

Davies, John A., 'The *Temple Scroll* from Qumran and the Ultimate Temple', *RTR* 57 (1998), pp. 1-21.

Davis, Dale Ralph, 'Rebellion, Presence and Covenant: A Study in Exodus 32–34', *WTJ* 44 (1982), pp. 71-87.

Dawes, S., 'Walking Humbly: Micah 6.8 Revisited', *SJT* 41 (1988), pp. 331-39.

DeRoche, Michael, 'Jeremiah 2:2-3 and Israel's Love for God during the Wilderness Wanderings', *CBQ* 45 (1983), pp. 364-76.

—'Structure, Rhetoric and Meaning in Hosea iv 4-10', *VT* 33 (1983), pp. 185-98.

Dietrich M., and O. Loretz, 'Zur ugaritischen Lexikographie (II)', *OLZ* 62 (1967), cols. 533-52.

Dietrich, M., O. Loretz and J. Sanmartín, *Die keilalphabetischen Texte aus Ugarit: Einschließlich der keilalphabetischen Texte außerhalb Ugarits*. I. *Transkription* (AOAT, 24; Neukirchen–Vluyn: Neukirchener Verlag, 1976).

Donner, Herbert, 'Der "Freund des Königs"', *ZAW* NS 73 (1961), pp. 269-77.

Donner, Herbert, Robert Hanhart and Rudolf Smend (eds.), *Beiträge zur alttestamentlichen Theologie* (Festschrift Walther Zimmerli; Göttingen: Vandenhoeck & Ruprecht, 1977).

Donner, H., and W. Röllig, *Kanaanäische und aramäische Inschriften, mit einem Beitrag von O. Rössler*. 1. *Texte* (Wiesbaden: Otto Harrassowitz, 4th edn, 1979).

Douglas, Mary, *Purity and Danger: An Analysis of the Concepts of Pollution and Taboo* (London: Ark Paperbacks, 1984).

Dozeman, Thomas B., *God on the Mountain: A Study of Redaction, Theology and Canon in Exodus 19–24* (SBLMS, 37; Atlanta: Scholars Press, 1989).

—'Spatial Form in Exod 19:1-8a and in the Larger Sinai Narrative', *Semeia* 46 (1989), pp. 87-101.

Draper, 'Jonathan A., The Twelve Apostles as Foundation Stones of the Heavenly Jerusalem and the Foundation of the Qumran Community', *Neotestamentica* 22 (1988), pp. 41-63.

Drazin, Israel, *Targum Onkelos to Exodus: An English Translation of the Text with Analysis and Commentary* (New York: Ktav, 1990).

Driver, G.R., 'Birds in the Old Testament. II. Birds in Life', *PEQ* 20 (1955), pp. 129-40.

Driver, S.R., *The Book of Exodus in the Revised Version with Introduction and Notes* (CBSC; Cambridge: Cambridge University Press, 1911).

—*Introduction to the Literature of the Old Testament* (Edinburgh: T. & T. Clark, 9th edn, 1913).

—*The Minor Prophets Nahum, Habakkuk, Zephaniah, Haggai, Zechariah, Malachi, Introductions: Revised Version with Notes, Index and Map* (Century Bible, 2; Edinburgh: T.C. & E.C. Jack, 1906).

du Mesnil du Buisson, R., 'Une tablette magique de la région du Moyen Euphrate', in *Mélanges syriens offerts à Monsieur René Dussaud* (Bibliotheque archéologique et historique, 30; 2 vols.; Paris: Librairie Orientaliste Paul Geuthner, 1939), I, pp. 421-34.

Duke, R.K., 'The Portion of the Levite: Another Reading of Deuteronomy 18:6-8', *JBL* 106 (1987), pp. 193-201.

Dumbrell, William J., *Covenant and Creation: An Old Testament Covenantal Theology* (Exeter: Paternoster Press, 1984).

—'Malachi and the Ezra–Nehemiah Reforms', *RTR* 35 (1976), pp. 42-52.

—'The Prospect of Unconditionality in the Sinaitic Covenant', in Avraham Gileadi (ed.), *Israel's Apostasy and Restoration*, pp. 141-55.

—*The Search for Order: Biblical Eschatology in Focus* (Grand Rapids: Baker Book House, 1994).

Durham, John I., *Exodus* (WBC, 3; Waco, TX: Word Books, 1987).

Eastwood, Cyril, *The Royal Priesthood of the Faithful: An Investigation of the Doctrine from Biblical Times to the Reformation* (London: Epworth Press, 1963).

Eichrodt, Walther, 'Covenant and Law: Thoughts on Recent Discussion', *Int* 20 (trans. Lloyd Gaston; 1966), pp. 302-21.

—*Theology of the Old Testament* (trans. D.A. Baker; OTL; 2 vols.; London: SCM Press, 1961–67).

Eissfeldt, Otto, *Hexateuch-Synopse: Die Erzählung der fünf Bücher Mose und des Buches Josua mit dem Anfange des Richterbuches* (Darmstadt: Wissenschaftliche Buchgesellschaft, 1962).

—Jahwe als König', in Otto Eissfeldt, *Kleine Schriften* (eds. Rudolf Sellheim and Fritz Maass; 6 vols.; Tübingen: J.C.B. Mohr, 1962–79), I, pp. 172-93.

—*Die Komposition der Sinai-Erzählung: Exodus 19–34* (Sitzungsberichte der sachsichen Akademie der Wissenschaften zu Leipzig, philologisch–historische Klasse, 113.1; Berlin: Akademie Verlag, 1966).

—*The Old Testament—an Introduction: The History of the Formation of the Old Testament* (trans. Peter R. Ackroyd; New York: Harper & Row, 1965).

Elliott, John Hall, *The Elect and the Holy: An Exegetical Examination of 1 Peter 2:4-10 and the Phrase βασίλειον ἱεράτευμα* (NTSup, 12; Leiden: E.J. Brill, 1966).

Emerton, J.A., 'Are there Examples of Enclitic mem in the Hebrew Bible?', in Fox *et al.* (eds.), *Texts, Temples and Traditions*, pp. 321-38.

—'Priests and Levites in Deuteronomy: An Examination of Dr G.E. Wright's Theory, *VT* 12 (1962), pp. 129-38.

—'The Origin of the Son of Man Imagery', *JTS* NS 9 (1958), pp. 225-42.
Engnell, Ivan, *Studies in Divine Kingship in the Ancient Near East* (Oxford: Basil Blackwell, 1967).
Fensham, F. Charles, 'Covenant, Promise and Expectation in the Bible', *TZ* 23 (1967), pp. 305-22.
—'Father and Son as Terminology for Treaty and Covenant', in Hans Goedicke (ed.), *Near Eastern Studies in Honor of W.F. Albright* (Baltimore: The Johns Hopkins University Press, 1971), pp. 121-35.
—'Malediction and Benediction in Ancient Near Eastern Vassal-Treaties and the Old Testament', *ZAW* NS 74 (1962), pp. 1-9.
Field, Fridericus (ed.), *Origenis Hexaplorum quae supersunt sive veterum interpretum Graecorum in totum Vetus Testamentum fragmenta* (Hildesheim: Georg Olms, 1964).
Fishbane, Michael, *Biblical Interpretation in Ancient Israel* (Oxford: Oxford University Press, 1985).
—*Text and Texture: Close Readings of Selected Biblical Texts* (New York: Schocken Books, 1979).
Fisher, Loren R., 'Creation at Ugarit and in the Old Testament', *VT* 15 (1965), pp. 313-24.
Fisher, Loren R. (ed.), *Ras Shamra Parallels: The Texts from Ugarit and the Hebrew Bible* (AnOr, 49-51; 3 vols.; Rome: Pontifical Biblical Institute Press, 1975)
Fleming, Daniel, 'The Biblical Tradition of Anointing Priests', *JBL* 117 (1998), pp. 401-14.
Fohrer, Georg, 'Altes Testament—"Amphiktyonie" und "Bund"?', in Georg Fohrer, *Studien zur alttestamentlichen Theologie und Geschichte (1949–1966)* (BZAW, 115; Berlin: W. de Gruyter, 1969), pp. 84-119.
—*History of Israelite Religion* (trans. David E. Green; London: SPCK, 1973).
—'"Priestliches Königtum" (Ex 19.6)', in Georg Fohrer, *Studien zur alttestamentlichen Theologie und Geschichte (1949–1966)* (BZAW, 115; Berlin: W. de Gruyter, 1969), pp. 149-53.
Fokkelman, J.P., 'Exodus', in Alter and Kermode (eds.), *The Literary Guide to the Bible*, pp. 56-65.
Fox, Michael V. (ed.), *Temple in Society* (Winona Lake, IN: Eisenbrauns, 1988).
Fox, Michael V., *et al.* (eds.), *Texts, Temples and Traditions: A Tribute to Menahem Haran* (Winona Lake, IN: Eisenbrauns, 1996).
Fraine, J. de, SI, *L'aspect religieux de la royauté Israélite: L'institution monarchique dans l'Ancien Testament et dans les textes Mésopotamiens* (AnBib, 3; Rome: Pontifical Biblical Institute Press, 1954).
Frankena, R., 'The Vassal-Treaties of Esarhaddon and the Dating of Deuteronomy', *OTS* 14 (1965), pp. 122-54.
Frankfort, Henri, *Kingship and the Gods: A Study of Ancient Near Eastern Religion as the Integration of Society and Nature* (Chicago: University of Chicago Press, 1948).
Freedman, David Noel, 'Divine Commitment and Human Obligation: The Covenant Theme', *Int* 18 (1964), pp. 419-31.
—*Pottery, Poetry and Prophecy: Studies in Early Hebrew Poetry* (Winona Lake, IN: Eisenbrauns, 1980).
—'The Name of the God of Moses', in John R. Huddleston (ed.), *Divine Commitment and Human Obligation: Selected Writings of David Noel Freedman*. I. *Israelite History and Religion* (Grand Rapids: Eerdmans, 1997), pp. 82-87.
—'The Twenty-Third Psalm', in *idem*, *Pottery, Poetry and Prophecy*, pp. 275-302.
Freedman, David Noel, and M. O'Connor, 'כרוב', in *TDOT*, VII, pp. 307-19.

Freedman, David Noel and G. Ernest Wright (eds.), *The Biblical Archeologist Reader* (Garden City, NY: Doubleday, 1961).

Fretheim, Terence E., *Exodus* (Int; Louisville, KY: John Knox Press, 1991).

—'The Reclamation of Creation: Redemption and Law in Exodus', *Int* 45 (1991), pp. 354-65.

Friedman, Mordechai A., 'Israel's Response in Hosea 2:17b: "You are my husband"', *JBL* 99 (1980), pp. 199-204.

Frye, Northrop, 'Literary Criticism', in James Thorpe (ed.), *The Aims and Methods of Scholarship in Modern Languages and Literatures* (New York: Modern Language Association of America, 1963), pp. 57-69.

Fuhs, Hans F., 'Heiliges Volk Gottes', in J. Schreiner (ed.), *Unterwegs zur Kirche: Alttestamentliche Konzeptionen* (Freiburg: Herder, 1987), pp. 143-67.

Gadd, C.J., *Ideas of Divine Rule in the Ancient East* (London: Oxford University Press, 1948).

Galling, Kurt, *Die Erwählungstraditionen Israels* (BZAW, 48; Giessen: Alfred Töpelmann, 1928).

Gammie, John G., *Holiness in Israel* (Overtures to Biblical Theology; Minneapolis: Fortress Press, 1989).

Gärtner, Bertil, *The Temple and the Community in Qumran and the New Testament: A Comparative Study in the Temple Symbolism of the Qumran Texts and the New Testament* (SNTSMS, 1; Cambridge: Cambridge University Press, 1965).

Gerstenberger, Erhard S., 'Covenant and Commandment', *JBL* 84 (1965), pp. 38-51.

—'Er soll dir heilig sein: Priester und Gemeinde nach Lev 21,1–22,9', in Frank Crüsemann, Christof Hardmeier and Rainer Kessler (eds.), *Was ist der Mensch...? Beiträge zur Anthropologie des Alten Testaments* (Munich: Chr. Kaiser Verlag, 1992), pp. 194-210.

Gibson, J.C.L., *Canaanite Myths and Legends* (Edinburgh: T. & T. Clark, 2nd edn, 1978).

—*Textbook of Syrian Semitic Inscriptions*. I. *Hebrew and Moabite Inscriptions* (Oxford: Clarendon Press, 1971).

Gileadi, Avraham (ed.), *Israel's Apostasy and Restoration: Essays in Honor of Roland K. Harrison* (Grand Rapids: Baker Book House, 1988).

Gispen, W.H., *Exodus* (BSC; Grand Rapids: Zondervan, 1982).

Glazier-McDonald, Beth, *Malachi: The Divine Messenger* (SBLDS, 98; Atlanta: Scholars Press, 1987).

Goldstein, Jonathan A., *2 Maccabees* (AB, 41A; New York: Doubleday, 1984).

Goldsworthy, Graeme, 'The Great Indicative: An Aspect of a Biblical Theology of Mission', *RTR* 55 (1996), pp. 2-13.

Good, Robert McClive, *The Sheep of his Pasture: A Study of the Hebrew Noun* 'am(m) *and its Semitic Cognates* (HSM, 29; Chico, CA: Scholars Press, 1983).

Gordis, Robert, 'Democratic Origins in Ancient Israel: The Biblical *'edah*', in Saul Liebermann (ed.), *Alexander Marx Jubilee Volume on the Occasion of his Seventieth Birthday* (New York: Jewish Theological Seminary of America, 1950), English section, pp. 369-88.

Gordon, Cyrus H., *Ugaritic Textbook* (AnOr, 38; Rome: Pontifical Biblical Institute Press, 1965).

Gorman, Frank H., Jr, *The Ideology of Ritual: Space, Time and Status in the Priestly Theology* (JSOTSup, 91; Sheffield: JSOT Press, 1990).

Gowan, Donald E., *Theology in Exodus: Biblical Theology in the Form of a Commentary* (Louisville, KY: Westminster/John Knox Press, 1994).

Gray, George Buchanan, *A Critical and Exegetical Commentary on Numbers* (ICC; Edinburgh: T. & T. Clark, 1903).

—*Sacrifice in the Old Testament: Its Theory and Practice* (Oxford: Clarendon Press, 1925).
Gray, John, *The Legacy of Canaan: The Ras Shamra Texts and their Relevance to the Old Testament* (VTSup, 5; Leiden: E.J. Brill, 2nd edn, 1965).
Grayson, A. Kirk, 'Akkadian Treaties of the Seventh Century B.C.', *JCS* 39 (1987), pp. 127-60.
—*Assyrian Rulers of the Third and Second Millennia* BC *(to 1115* BC*)* (The Royal Inscriptions of Mesopotamia—Assyrian Periods, 1; Toronto: University of Toronto Press, 1987).
Greenberg, Moshe, 'Exodus, Book of', in *EncJud*, VI, pp. 1050-67.
—'Hebrew *segulla*: Akkadian *sikiltu*', *JAOS* 71 (1951), pp. 172-74.
—'A New Approach to the History of the Israelite Priesthood', *JAOS* 70 (1950), pp. 41-47.
—*Understanding Exodus* (New York: Behrman House, 1969).
Greenfield, Jonas C., and Michael E. Stone, 'Remarks on the Aramaic Testament of Levi from the Geniza', *RB* 86 (1979), pp. 214-30.
Greengus, Samuel, 'The Old Babylonian Marriage Contract', *JAOS* 89 (1969), pp. 505-32.
Grelot, Pierre, 'Notes sur le Testament araméen de Levi', *RB* 63 (1956), pp. 391-406.
Gressmann, Hugo, *Die Anfänge Israels, von 2 Mose bis Richter und Ruth: Übersetzt, erklärt und mit Einleitung versehen* (Die Schriften des Alten Testaments, 1.2; Göttingen: Vandenhoeck & Ruprecht, 1914).
Gunkel, Hermann, *Die Psalmen* (Göttingen: Vandenhoeck & Ruprecht, 6th edn, 1986).
Gunn, David M., 'New Directions in the Study of Biblical Hebrew Narrative', in House (ed.), *Beyond Form Criticism*, pp. 412-22.
Gunneweg, A.H.J., *Leviten und Priester: Hauptlinien der Traditionsbildung und Geschichte des israelitisch–jüdischen Kultpersonals* (FRLANT, 89; Göttingen: Vandenhoeck & Ruprecht, 1965).
—'Sinaibund und Davidsbund', *VT* 10 (1960), pp. 335-41.
Gurney, O.R., *Some Aspects of Hittite Religion* (Schweich Lectures, 1976; Oxford: Oxford University Press, 1977).
Habel, N., 'The Form and Significance of the Call Narratives', *ZAW* NS 77 (1965), pp. 297-323.
Haelvoet, Marcel, 'La théophanie du Sinaï: Analyse littéraire des récits d'Exode 19–24', *ETL* 29 (1953), pp. 374-97.
Hahn, Scott Walker, *Kinship by Covenant: A Biblical Theological Study of Covenant Types and Texts in the Old and New Testaments* (Marquette University PhD Thesis; Ann Arbor, MI: UMI Dissertation Services, 1995).
Halperin, David J., 'Ascension or Invasion: Implications of the Heavenly Journey in Ancient Judaism', *Religion* 18 (1988), pp. 47-67.
Halpern, Baruch, 'The Ritual Background of Zechariah's Temple Song', *CBQ* 40 (1978), pp. 167-90.
Hanson, Paul D., *The People Called: The Growth of Community in the Bible* (San Francisco: Harper & Row, 1986).
Haran, Menahem, 'The Ark and the Cherubim: Their Symbolic Significance in Biblical Ritual', *IEJ* 9 (1959), pp. 30-38, 89-94.
—'Behind the Scenes of History: Determining the Date of the Priestly Source', *JBL* 100 (1981), pp. 321-33.
—'The *berît* "Covenant": Its Nature and Ceremonial Background', in Mordechai Cogan, Barry L. Eichler and Jeffrey H. Tigay (eds.), *Tehillah le-Mosheh: Biblical and Judaic Studies in Honor of Moshe Greenberg* (Winona Lake, IN: Eisenbrauns, 1997), pp. 203-19.
—'The Complex of Ritual Acts Performed Inside the Tabernacle', *SH* 8 (1961), pp. 272-302.
—'The Priestly Image of the Tabernacle', *HUCA* 36 (1965), pp. 191-226.

—'Temple and Community in Ancient Israel', in Michael V. Fox (ed.), *Temple in Society*, pp. 17-25.

—*Temples and Temple Service in Ancient Israel: An Inquiry into Biblical Cult Phenomena and the Historical Setting of the Priestly School* (Winona Lake, IN: Eisenbrauns, 1985).

Harman, Allan, 'The Interpretation of the Third Commandment', *RTR* 47 (1988), pp. 1-7.

Harper, William Rainey, *A Critical and Exegetical Commentary on Amos and Hosea* (ICC; Edinburgh: T. & T. Clark, 1936).

Harrelson, Walter, *Interpreting the Old Testament* (New York: Holt, Rinehart & Winston, 1964).

Harrison, R.K., *Numbers* (Wycliffe Exegetical Commentary; Chicago: Moody Press, 1990).

Hauret, Charles, 'Moïse était-il prêtre?', *Bib* 40 (1959), pp. 509-21.

Held, Moshe, 'A Faithful Lover in an Old Babylonian Dialogue', *JCS* 15 (1961), pp. 1-26.

Henshaw, Richard A., *Female and Male, the Cultic Personnel: The Bible and the Rest of the Ancient Near East* (Princeton Theological Monograph Series, 31; Pittsburgh, PA: Pickwick Press, 1994).

Hertz, J.H., CH, (ed.), *The Pentateuch and Haftorahs: Hebrew Text, English Translation and Commentary* (London: Soncino, 1952).

Hilber, John W., 'Theology of Worship in Exodus 24', *JETS* 39 (1996), pp. 177-89.

Hillers, Delbert R., *A Commentary on the Book of the Prophet Micah* (Hermeneia; Philadelphia: Fortress Press, 1984).

—*Covenant: The History of a Biblical Idea* (Baltimore: The Johns Hopkins University Press, 1969).

—'A Note on Some Treaty Terminology in the Old Testament', *BASOR* 176 (1964), pp. 46-47.

Himmelfarb, Martha, 'Apocalyptic Ascent and the Heavenly Temple', in Kent Harold Richards (ed.), *Society of Biblical Literature 1987 Seminar Papers* (SBLSP, 26; Atlanta, GA: Scholars Press, 1987), pp. 210-17.

Holzinger, H., *Exodus* (KHAT, 2; Tübingen: J.C.B. Mohr, 1900).

Hooke, Samuel H. (ed.), *Myth, Ritual and Kingship: Essays on the Theory and Practice of Kingship in the Ancient Near East and in Israel* (Oxford: Clarendon Press, 1958).

Horovitz, H.S., and I.A. Rabin, *Mechilta d'Rabbi Ismael cum variis lectionibus et adnotationibus* (Jerusalem: Wahrmann, 1970).

Hort, Greta, 'The Death of Qorah', *AusBR* 7 (1959), pp. 2-26.

Horton, Fred L. Jr, *The Melchizedek Tradition: A Critical Examination of the Sources to the Fifth Century A.D. and in the Epistle to the Hebrews* (London: Cambridge University Press, 1976).

Hossfeld, Frank-Lothar, *Der Dekalog: Seine späten Fassungen, die originale Komposition und seine Vorstufen* (OBO, 45; Göttingen: Vandenhoeck & Ruprecht, 1982).

House, Paul R. (ed.), *Beyond Form Criticism: Essays in Old Testament Literary Criticism* (SBTS, 2; Winona Lake, IN: Eisenbrauns, 1992).

Houtman, Cornelis, *Exodus* (trans. Johan Rebel and Sierd Woudstra; HCOT; 3 vols.; vols. 1 and 2: Kampen: Kok, 1993; vol. 3: Leuven: Peeters, 2000).

Huffmon, Herbert B., 'The Exodus, Sinai and the Credo', *CBQ* 27 (1965), pp. 101-13.

Huffmon, Herbert B., and Simon B. Parker, 'A Further Note on the Treaty Background of Hebrew *yada'*', *BASOR* 184 (1966), pp. 36-38.

Hummel, Horace D., 'Enclitic mem in Early Northwest Semitic, Especially Hebrew', *JBL* 76 (1957), pp. 87-107.

Hurowitz, Victor, *I Have Built you an Exalted House: Temple Building in the Bible in the Light of Mesopotamian and Northwest Semitic Writings* (JSOTSup, 115; Sheffield: Sheffield Academic Press, 1992).

Hurvitz, Avi, 'The Evidence of Language in Dating the Priestly Code: A Linguistic Study in Technical Idioms and Terminology', *RB* 81 (1974), pp. 24-56.

Hyatt, J. Philip, *Commentary on Exodus* (NCB; London: Oliphants, 1971).

Ishida (ed.), Tomoo, *Studies in the Period of David and Solomon and Other Essays: Papers Read at the International Symposium for Biblical Studies, Tokyo, 5-7 December, 1979* (Winona Lake, IN: Eisenbrauns, 1982).

Jackson, Kent P., and J. Andrew Dearman, 'The Language of the Mesha Inscription', in J. Andrew Dearman (ed.), *Studies in the Mesha Inscription and Moab* (ASOR/SBL Archaeology and Biblical Studies, 2; Atlanta: Scholars Press, 1989), pp. 96-130.

Jacob, Benno, *The Second Book of the Bible: Exodus, Interpreted by Benno Jacob* (trans. with an introduction by Walter Jacob in association with Yaakov Elman; Hoboken, NJ: Ktav, 1992).

Jacob, Edmond, *Theology of the Old Testament* (trans. Arthur W. Heathcote and Philip J. Allcock; New York: Harper & Row, 1958).

Jacobsen, Thorkild, 'Primitive Democracy in Ancient Mesopotamia', in Moran (ed.), *Toward the Image of Tammuz and Other Essays on Mesopotamian History and Culture* (HSS, 21; Cambridge, MA: Harvard University Press, 1970), pp. 157-70.

James, E.O., *The Nature and Function of Priesthood: A Comparative and Anthropological Study* (London: Thames & Hudson, 1955).

Jenni, Ernst, and Claus Westermann (eds.), *Theological Lexicon of the Old Testament* (trans. Mark E. Biddle; 3 vols.; Peabody, MA: Hendrickson, 1997).

Jenson, Phillip P., *Graded Holiness: A Key to the Priestly Conception of the World* (JSOTSup, 106; Sheffield: JSOT Press, 1992).

—'The Levitical Sacrificial System', in Beckwith and Selman (eds.), *Sacrifice in the Bible*, pp. 25-40.

—'כהן', in *NIDOTE*, II, pp. 600-605.

Jepsen, Alfred,'*Berith*: Ein Beitrag zur Theologie der Exilszeit', in Arnulf Kuschke (ed.), *Verbannung und Heimkehr: Beitrage zur Geschichte und Theologie Israels im 6 und 5. Jahrhundert v. Chr.* (Festschrift Wilhelm Rudolph; Tübingen: J.C.B. Mohr, 1961), pp. 161-79.

Jeremias, Christian, *Die Nachtgesichte des Sacharjah: Untersuchungen zu ihrer Stellung im Zusammenhang der Visionsberichte im Alten Testament und zu ihrem Bildmaterial* (FRLANT, 117; Göttingen: Vandenhoeck & Ruprecht, 1977).

Jeremias, Jörg, *Theophanie: Die Geschichte einer alttestamentlichen Gattung* (WMANT, 10; Neukirchen–Vluyn: Neukirchener Verlag, 2nd edn, 1977).

Johnstone, W., Exodus (OTG; Sheffield: JSOT Press, 1990).

—'Reactivating the Chronicles Analogy in Pentateuchal Studies, with Special Reference to the Sinai Pericope in Exodus', ZAW ns 99 (1987), pp. 16-37.

Josephus, *Works* (LCL; 9 vols.; London: Heinemann, 1956–65).

Josipovici, Gabriel, *The Book of God: A Response to the Bible* (New Haven: Yale University Press, 1988).

Joüon, Paul, SJ, *Grammaire de l'hébreu biblique* (Rome: Pontifical Biblical Institute Press, 1923).

Junker, Hubert, 'Das allgemeine Priestertum. I. Das allgemeine Priestertum des Volkes Israel nach Ex 19,6', *TTZ* 56 (1947), pp. 10-15.

Kaiser, Walter C., Jr, 'Israel's Missionary Call', in Ralph D. Winter and Stephen C. Hawthorne (eds.), *Perspectives on the World Christian Movement: A Reader* (Pasadena, CA: William Carey Library, 1981), pp. A25-33.

—*Toward an Old Theology Theology* (Grand Rapids: Zondervan, 1978).

—*Toward Old Testament Ethics* (Grand Rapids: Academie Books, 1983).

Kalluveettil, Paul, CMI, *Declaration and Covenant: A Comprehensive Review of Covenant Formulae from the Old Testament and the Ancient Near East* (AnBib, 88; Rome: Pontifical Biblical Institute Press, 1982).

Kapelrud, Arvid S., 'The Covenant as Agreement', *SJOT* 1 (1988), pp. 30-38.

—'The Number Seven in Ugaritic Texts', *VT* 18 (1968), pp. 494-99.

—'The Prophets and the Covenant', in Boyd Barrick and Spencer (eds.), *In the Shelter of Elyon*, pp. 175-83.

—'Temple Building: A Task for Gods and Kings', *Or* NS 32 (1963), pp. 56-62.

Kaufmann, Yehezkel, *The Religion of Israel from its Beginnings to the Babylonian Exile* (trans. and abridged M. Greenberg; London: George Allen & Unwin, 1961).

Kearney, Peter J., 'Creation and Liturgy: The P Redaction of Exod 25–40', *ZAW* NS 89 (1977), pp. 375-87.

Keel, Othmar, *Jahwe-Visionen und Siegelkunst: Eine neue Deutung der Majestätsschilderungen in Jes 6, Ez 1 und Sach 4* (SBS, 84-85; Stuttgart: Katholisches Bibelwerk, 1977).

—*The Symbolism of the Biblical World: Ancient Near Eastern Iconography and the Book of Psalms* (trans. Timothy J. Hallett; London: SPCK, 1978).

Keil, C.F., *Manual of Biblical Archaeology* (trans. P. Christie; 2 vols.; Edinburgh: T. & T. Clark, 1887–88).

Keil, C.F., and F. Delitzsch, *Commentary on the Old Testament* (trans. James Martin; 10 vols.; repr. Grand Rapids: Eerdmans, 1983).

Kiene, Paul F., *The Tabernacle of God in the Wilderness of Sinai* (trans. John S. Crandall; Grand Rapids: Zondervan, 1977).

King, L.W. (ed.), *Babylonian Boundary-Stones and Memorial-Tablets in the British Museum* (London: British Museum, 1912).

Kitchen, K.A., *Ancient Orient and Old Testament* (London: Tyndale Press, 1966).

—'Egypt, Ugarit, Qatna and Covenant', *UF* 11 (1979), pp. 453-64.

—'The Fall and Rise of Covenant, Law and Treaty', *TynBul* 40 (1989), pp. 118-35.

Kleinig, John W., 'On Eagles' Wing: An Exegetical Study of Exodus 19:2-8', *Lutheran Theological Journal* 21 (1987), pp. 18-27.

Kline, Meredith G., *Images of the Spirit* (Grand Rapids: Baker Book House, 1980).

—'The Structure of the Book of Zechariah', *JETS* 34 (1991), pp. 179-93.

Klopfer, Richard, 'Zur Quellenscheidung in Exod 19', *ZAW* 18 (1898), pp. 197-235.

Knierim, Rolf P., 'The Composition of the Pentateuch', in Kent Harold Richards (ed.), *Society of Biblical Literature 1985 Seminar Papers* (SBLSP, 24; Atlanta, GA: Scholars Press, 1985), pp. 393-415.

—'The Vocation of Isaiah', *VT* 18 (1968), pp. 47-68.

Knight, George A.F., *A Christian Theology of the Old Testament* (London: SCM Press, 1959).

—*Theology as Narration: A Commentary on the Book of Exodus* (Edinburgh: Handsel, 1976).

Knohl, Israel, *The Sanctuary of Silence: The Priestly Torah and the Holiness School* (Minneapolis: Fortress Press, 1995).

Knudtzon, J.A., *Die El-Amarna-Tafeln mit Einleitung und Erläuterungen* (2 vols.; Leipzig: J.C. Hinrichs, 1915).

Knutson, F. Brent, 'Literary Genres in PRU IV', in Fisher (ed.), *Ras Shamra Parallels*, II, pp. 155-214.
Koch, Klaus, 'P—kein Redaktor!', *VT* 37 (1987), pp. 446-67.
—'Zur Geschichte der Erwählungsvorstellung in Israel', *ZAW* NS 67 (1955), pp. 205-26.
Korošec, V., *Hethitische Staatsverträge* (Leipziger Rechtswissenschaftliche Studien; Leipzig: T. Weicher, 1931).
Kramer, Samuel Noah, 'The Temple in Sumerian Literature', in Fox (ed.), *Temple in Society*, pp. 1-16.
Kraus, Hans-Joachim, 'Das heilige Volk: Zur alttestamentlichen Bezeichnung *'am qādōš*', in Johann J. Stamm and Ernst Wolff (eds.), *Freude am Evangelium* (Festschrift Alfred de Quervain; BEvT, 44; Munich: Chr. Kaiser Verlag, 1966), pp. 50-61.
—*Psalms 60–150: A Commentary* (trans. Hilton C. Oswald; Continental Commentaries; Minneapolis: Augsburg, 1989).
—*Worship in Israel: A Cultic History of the Old Testament* (trans. Geoffrey Buswell; Oxford: Basil Blackwell, 1966).
Kugel, James, 'The Holiness of Israel and the Land in Second Temple Times', in Fox *et al.* (eds.), *Texts, Temples and Traditions*, pp. 21-32.
—*The Idea of Biblical Poetry: Parallelism and its History* (New Haven: Yale University Press, 1981).
—'Levi's Elevation to the Priesthood in Second Temple Writings', *HTR* 86 (1993), pp. 1-64.
Kugler, Robert A., *From Patriarch to Priest: The Levi-Priestly Tradition from* Aramaic Levi *to* Testament of Levi (Early Judaism and its Literature, 9; Atlanta: Scholars Press, 1996).
Kuntz, J. Kenneth, *The Self-Revelation of God* (Philadelphia: Westminster Press, 1967).
Kutsch, Ernst, 'Der Begriff ברית in vordeuteronomischer Zeit', in Fritz Maass (ed.), *Das ferne und nahe Wort* (Festschrift Leonhard Rost; BZAW, 105; Berlin: Alfred Topelmann, 1967), pp. 133-43.
—'Das sog. "Bundesblut" in Ex. xxiv 8 und Sach. ix 11', *VT* 23 (1973), pp. 25-30.
—*Verheissung und Gesetz: Untersuchungen zum sogennanten 'Bund' im Alten Testament* (BZAW, 131; Berlin: W. de Gruyter, 1973).
—'ברית', in *TLOT*, I, pp. 256-66.
Landsberger, Benno, 'Assyrische Königsliste und "Dunkeles Zeitalter"', *JCS* 8 (1954), pp. 47-73.
Le Roux, J.H., 'A Holy Nation Was Elected (the Election Theology of Exodus 19.5-6)', in W.C. van Wyk (ed.), *The Exilic Period: Aspects of Apocalypticism* (Old Testament Essays; Pretoria: Die Ou-Testamentisse Werkgemeenskap in Suid-Afrika, 1984), pp. 59-78.
Lea, Thomas D., 'The Priesthood of All Christians According to the New Testament', *Southwestern Journal of Theology* 30 (1988), pp. 15-21.
Leibowitz, Nehama, *Studies in Shemot (the Book of Exodus)* (2 parts; Jerusalem: World Zionist Organization, 1976).
Levenson, Jon D., *Creation and the Persistence of Evil: The Jewish Drama of Divine Omnipotence* (San Francisco: Harper & Row, 1988).
—'The Davidic Covenant and its Modern Interpreters', *CBQ* 41 (1979), pp. 205-19.
—'On the Promise to the Rechabites', *CBQ* 38 (1976), pp. 508-14.
—*Sinai and Zion: An Entry into the Jewish Bible* (New Voices in Biblical Studies; Minneapolis: Winston Press, 1985).
—'The Theologies of Commandment in Biblical Israel', *HTR* 73 (1980), pp. 17-33.
—*Theology of the Program of Restoration of Ezekiel 40–48* (HSM, 10; Atlanta: Scholars Press, 1986).

Levine, Baruch A., *In the Presence of the Lord: A Study of Cult and Some Cultic Terms in Ancient Israel* (SJLA, 5; Leiden: E.J. Brill, 1974).

—*Numbers 1–20* (AB, 4; New York: Doubleday, 1993).

—'On the Presence of God in Biblical Religion', in Jacob Neusner (ed.), *Religions in Antiquity: Essays in Memory of Erwin Ramsdell Goodenough* (Studies in the History of Religions, Numen Supplements; Leiden: E.J. Brill, 1970), pp. 71-87.

Lewis, Theodore J., 'The Identity and Function of El/Baal Berith', *JBL* 115 (1996), pp. 401-23.

Licht, Jacob, *Storytelling in the Bible* (Jerusalem: Magnes Press, 1978).

—'גילוי שכינה במעמד הר סיני (The Sinai Theophany)', in Yitschak Avishur, and Joshua Blau (eds.), *Studies in the Bible and the Ancient Near East Presented to Samuel E. Loewenstamm* (Jerusalem: Rubinstein, 1978), pp. 251-68.

Lipiński, E., 'Recherches sur le livre de Zacharie', *VT* 20 (1970), pp. 25-55.

—*La royauté de Yahwé dans la poésie et le culte de l'Ancien Israël* (Verhandelingen van de Koninklijke Vlaamse Academie voor Wetenschappen, Letteren en Schone Kunsten van Belgie. Klasse der Letteren, 27.55; Brussels: Paleis der Academiën, 2nd edn, 1968).

Liver, Jacob, 'Korah, Dathan and Abiram', in Chaim Rabin (ed.), *Studies in the Bible* (SH, 8; Jerusalem: Magnes Press, 1961), pp. 189-217.

Loewenstamm, Samuel E., 'The Divine Grants of Land to the Patriarchs', *JAOS* 91 (1971), pp. 509-10.

—'עם סגלה', in M. Bar Asher *et al.* (eds.), *Hebrew Language Studies Presented to Professor Zeev Ben-Hayyim* (Jerusalem: Magnes Press, 1983), pp. 321-28.

Longman, Tremper, III, *Immanuel in our Place: Seeing Christ in Israel's Worship* (The Gospel According to the Old Testament; Phillipsburg, NJ: P. & R. Publishing, 2001).

Loretz, O., 'ברית—"Band—Bund"', *VT* 16 (1966), pp. 239-41.

Ludwig, Theodore M., 'The Traditions of the Establishing of the Earth in Deutero-Isaiah', *JBL* 92 (1973), pp. 345-57.

Lundquist, John M., 'What Is a Temple? A Preliminary Typology', in Herbert B. Huffmon, F.A. Spina and A.R.W. Green (eds.), *The Quest for the Kingdom of God: Studies in Honor of George E. Mendenhall* (Winona Lake, IN: Eisenbrauns, 1983), pp. 205-19.

Maass, E., 'טהר', in *TLOT*, II, pp. 482-86.

Magnanini, Pietro, 'Sull'origine letteraria dell'Ecclesiaste', *Annali* 18 (1968), pp. 363-84.

Magonet, Jonathan, 'The Korah Rebellion', *JSOT* 24 (1982), pp. 3-25.

Maier, Johann, 'Self-Definition, Prestige, and Status of Priests towards the End of the Second Temple Period', *BTB* 23 (1993), pp. 139-50.

—*The Temple Scroll: An Introduction, Translation and Commentary* (trans. Richard T. White; JSOTSup, 34; Sheffield: JSOT Press, 1985).

Maimonides, Moses, *The Guide to the Perplexed* (trans. Shlomo Pines; 2 vols.; Chicago: University of Chicago Press, 1963).

Mann, Thomas W., *Divine Presence and Guidance in Israelite Traditions: The Typology of Exaltation* (Near Eastern Studies [Johns Hopkins University]; Baltimore: The Johns Hopkins University Press, 1977).

Marinkovic, Peter, 'What Does Zechariah 1–8 Tell Us About the Second Temple?', in Tamara C. Eskenazi and Kent R. Richards (eds.), *Second Temple Studies*. II. *Temple and Community in the Persian Period* (JSOTSup, 175; Sheffield: JSOT Press, 1994), pp. 88-103.

Marriage, Alwyn, *The People of God: A Royal Priesthood* (London: Darton, Longman & Todd, 1995).

Martin-Achard, Robert, 'Israël, peuple sacerdotal', *Verbum Caro* 18 (1964), pp. 11-28.

—'La signification théologique de l'élection d'Israël', *TZ* 16 (1960), pp. 333-41.

Martínez, Florentino García, and Elbert J.C. Tigchelaar (eds.), *Dead Sea Scrolls Study Edition* (2 vols.; Leiden: E.J. Brill, 1997, 1998).
Mauch, T.M., 'Zechariah', in *IDB*, IV, pp. 941-43.
Mays, J.L., *Hosea: A Commentary* (OTL; London: SCM Press, 1969).
McCarthy, Dennis J., SJ, '*berît* in Old Testament History and Theology', *Bib* 53 (1972), pp. 111-21.
—'Compact and Kingship: Stimuli for Hebrew Covenant Thinking', in Ishida (ed.), *Studies in the Period of David and Solomon*, pp. 75-92.
—'Covenant in the Old Testament: The Present State of Inquiry', *CBQ* 27 (1965), pp. 217-40.
—'Exodus 3:14: History, Philology and Theology', *CBQ* 40 (1978), pp. 311-22.
—'Notes on the Love of God in Deuteronomy and the Father–Son Relationship between Yahweh and Israel', *CBQ* 27 (1965), pp. 144-47.
—*Old Testament Covenant: A Survey of Current Opinions* (Oxford: Basil Blackwell, 1973).
—'Three Covenants in Genesis', *CBQ* 26 (1964), pp. 179-89.
—*Treaty and Covenant: A Study in Form in the Ancient Oriental Documents and in the Old Testament* (AnBib, 21; Rome: Pontifical Biblical Institute Press, 2nd edn, 1981).
McComiskey, Thomas Edward, *The Covenants of Promise: A Theology of the Old Testament Covenants* (Grand Rapids: Baker Book House, 1985).
—'Hosea', in *idem*, (ed.), *The Minor Prophets*, I, pp. 1-237.
McComiskey, Thomas Edward (ed.), *The Minor Prophets: An Exegetical and Expository Commentary* (3 vols.; Grand Rapids: Baker Book House, 1992).
McCrory, J.H., '"Up, Up, Up and Up": Exodus 24:9-18 as the Narrative Context for the Tabernacle Instructions of Exodus 25–31', in David J. Lull (ed.), *Society for Biblical Literature 1990 Seminar Papers* (SBLSP, 29; Atlanta, GA: Scholars Press, 1990), pp. 570-82.
McKane, William, *The Book of Micah: Introduction and Commentary* (Edinburgh: T. & T. Clark, 1998).
McKenzie, John L., SJ, *Second Isaiah: Introduction, Translation and Notes* (AB, 20; Garden City, NY: Doubleday, 1968).
McKenzie, Steven L., and Howard N. Wallace, 'Covenant Themes in Malachi', *CBQ* 45 (1983), pp. 549-63.
McNamara, Martin, MSC, *The New Testament and the Palestinian Targum to the Pentateuch* (AnBib, 27; Rome: Pontifical Biblical Institute Press, 1966).
—*Targum and Testament: Aramaic Paraphrases of the Hebrew Bible—A Light on the New Testament* (Shannon: Irish University Press, 1972).
McNamara, Martin, MSC, and Michael Maher, MSC, *Targum Neofiti 1. Exodus; Translated with Introduction and Apparatus; and Notes by Robert Hayward. Targum Pseudo-Jonathan: Exodus, Translated with Notes* (Edinburgh: T. & T. Clark, 1994).
McNeile, A.H., *The Book of Exodus with Introduction and Notes* (Westminster Commentaries; London: Methuen, 1908).
McNicol, Allan J., 'The Eschatological Temple in the Qumran Pesher 4QFlorilegium 1:1-7', *Ohio Journal of Religious Studies* 5 (1977), pp. 133-41.
—'The Heavenly Sanctuary in Judaism: A Model for Tracing the Origin of an Apocalypse', *JRS* 13 (1987), pp. 66-94.
Meier, Samuel A., *Speaking of Speaking: Marking Direct Discourse in the Hebrew Bible* (VTSup, 46; Leiden: E.J. Brill, 1992).
—*The Tenth Generation: The Origins of the Biblical Tradition* (Baltimore: The Johns Hopkins University Press, 1973).

Mendenhall, George E., 'Ancient Oriental and Biblical Law', in Campbell and Freedman (eds.), *The Biblical Archaeologist Reader* 3, pp. 3-24.

—'Covenant Forms in Israelite Tradition', in Campbell and Freedman (eds.), *The Biblical Archaeologist Reader* 3, pp. 25-53.

—*Law and Covenant in Israel and the Ancient Near East* (Pittsburgh: The Presbyterian Board of Colportage of Western Pennsylvania, 1955).

Mendenhall, George E., and Gary A. Herion, 'Covenant', in *ABD*, I, pp. 1179-202.

Merrill, Eugene H., *Kingdom of Priests: A History of Old Testament Israel* (Grand Rapids: Baker Book House, 1987).

—'Royal Priesthood: An Old Testament Messianic Motif', *BSac* 150 (1993), pp. 50-61.

—'A Theology of the Pentateuch', in Roy B. Zuck (ed.), *A Biblical Theology of the Old Testament* (Chicago: Moody Press, 1991), pp. 7-87.

Mettinger, Tryggve N.D., *In Search of God: The Meaning and Message of the Everlasting Names* (trans. Frederick H. Cryer; Philadelphia: Fortress Press, 1988).

—'YHWH Sabaoth—the Heavenly King on the Cherubim Throne', in Ishida (ed.), *Studies in the Period of David and Solomon*, pp. 109-38.

Meyers, Carol L., and Eric M. Meyers, *Haggai, Zechariah 1–8: A New Translation with Introduction and Commentary* (AB, 25B; Garden City, NY: Doubleday, 1987).

—'Jerusalem and Zion after the Exile: The Evidence of First Zechariah', in Michael Fishbane and Emanuel Tov (eds.), *'Sha'arei Talmon': Studies in the Bible, Qumran and the Ancient Near East, Presented to Shemaryahu Talmon* (Winona Lake IN: Eisenbrauns, 1992), pp. 121-35.

Meyers, Carol M., and M. O'Connor (eds.), *The Word of the Lord Shall Go Forth: Essays in Honor of David Noel Freedman in Celebration of his Sixtieth Birthday* (Winona Lake, IN: Eisenbrauns, 1983).

Meyers, Eric M., 'Priestly Language in the Book of Malachi', *HAR* 10 (1986), pp. 225-37.

Milgrom, Jacob, 'Korah's Rebellion: A Study in Redaction', in Maurice Carrez, Joseph Doré and Pierre Grelot (eds.), *De la Tôra au Messie: Etudes d'exégèse et d'herméneutique bibliques offertes à Henri Cazelles pour ses 25 années d'enseignement à l'Institut Catholique de Paris (Octobre 1979)* (Paris: Desclée, 1981), pp. 135-46.

—*Leviticus 1–16: A New Translation with Introduction and Commentary* (AB, 3; New York: Doubleday, 1991).

—'The Priestly Consecration (Leviticus 8): A Rite of Passage', in Stanley F. Chyet and David H. Ellenson (eds.), *Bits of Honey: Essays for Samson H. Levey* (South Florida Studies in the History of Judaism, 74; Atlanta: Scholars Press, 1993), pp. 57-61.

—'Priestly Terminology and the Political and Social Structures of Pre-Monarchic Israel', *JQR* 69 (1978), pp. 65-81.

—'Profane Slaughter and a Formulaic Key to the Composition of Deuteronomy', *HUCA* 47 (1976), pp. 1-17.

—'The Rebellion of Korah: Numbers 16–18 a Study in Tradition History', in David J. Lull (ed.), *Society for Biblical Literature 1988 Seminar Papers* (SBLSP, 27; Atlanta, GA: Scholars Press, 1988), pp. 570-73.

Milik, J.T., '*Milkî-ṣedeq* et *Milkî-reṣa'* dans les anciens écrits juifs et chrétiens', *JJS* 23 (1972), pp. 95-144.

—'Le Testament de Lévi en araméen', *RB* 62 (1955), pp. 398-408.

Miller, Cynthia L., 'Introducing Direct Discourse in Biblical Hebrew Narrative', in Robert D. Bergen (ed.), *Biblical Hebrew and Discourse Linguistics* (Winona Lake, IN: Eisenbrauns, 1994), pp. 199-241.

—*The Representation of Speech in Biblical Hebrew Narrative: A Linguistic Analysis* (HSM, 55; Atlanta: Scholars Press, 1996).

Mitchell, Hinckley G., John Merlin Powis Smith and Julius A. Bewer, *A Critical and Exegetical Commentary on Haggai, Zechariah, Malachi and Jonah* (ICC; Edinburgh: T. & T. Clark, 1912).

Moberly, R.W.L., *At the Mountain of God: Story and Theology in Exodus 32–34* (JSOTSup, 22; Sheffield: JSOT Press, 1983).

Montet, Pierre, *Byblos et l'Egypte: Quatre campagnes de fouilles à Gebeil 1921–1922–1923–1924* (Bibliothèque archéologique et historique; 3 vols.; Paris: Libraire Orientaliste Paul Geuthner, 1929).

Montgomery, James A., and Henry Snyder Gehman, *A Critical and Exegetical Commentary on the Books of Kings* (ICC; Edinburgh: T. & T. Clark, 1951).

Moor, Johannes C. de, 'Contributions to the Ugaritic Lexicon', *UF* 11 (1979), pp. 639-53.

—*The Rise of Yahwism: The Roots of Israelite Monotheism* (BETL, 91; Leuven: Leuven University Press, 1990).

Moran, W.L., SJ, 'A Kingdom of Priests', in John L. McKenzie, SJ (ed.), *The Bible in Current Catholic Thought* (New York: Herder & Herder, 1962), pp. 7-20.

—'A Note on the Treaty Terminology of the Sefire Stelas', *JNES* 22 (1963), pp. 173-76.

Morgenstern, Julian, 'The Ark, the Ephod, and the "Tent of Meeting"', *HUCA* 17 (1942–43), pp. 153-266.

Mosis, Rudolf, 'Ex 19,5b.6a: Syntaktischer Aufbau und lexikalische Semantik', *BZ* 22 (1978), pp. 1-25.

Motyer, J.A., *The Revelation of the Divine Name* (London: Tyndale Press, 1959).

Muilenburg, James, 'The Form and Structure of the Covenantal Formulations', *VT* 9 (1959), pp. 347-65.

—'Form Criticism and Beyond', *JBL* 88 (1969), pp. 1-18.

—'The Linguistic and Rhetorical Usages of the Particle כי in the Old Testament', *HUCA* 32 (1961), pp. 135-60.

Mullen, E. Theodore, Jr, *The Divine Council in Canaanite and Early Hebrew Literature* (HSM, 24; Chico, CA: Scholars Press, 1980).

—'The Divine Witness and the Davidic Royal Grant: Ps 89:37-38', *JBL* 102 (1983), pp. 207-18.

—*Ethnic Myths and Pentateuchal Foundations: A New Approach to the Formation of the Pentateuch* (SBLSS; Atlanta: Scholars Press, 1997).

Müller, H.-P., 'קדשׁ', in *TLOT*, III, pp. 103-18.

Munn-Rankin, J.M., 'Diplomacy in Western Asia in the Early Second Millennium BC', *Iraq* 18 (1956), pp. 68-110.

Muraoka, T., *Emphatic Words and Structures in Biblical Hebrew* (Jerusalem: Magnes Press, 1985).

Naudé, Jacobus A., 'קדשׁ', in *NIDOTE*, VI, pp. 877-87.

Nelson, Harold H., 'The Egyptian Temple', in Freedman and Wright (eds.), *The Biblical Archeologist Reader*, pp. 147-57.

Nelson, Richard D., *Raising Up a Faithful Priest: Community and Priesthood in Biblical Theology* (Louisville, KY: Westminster/John Knox Press, 1993).

—'The Role of the Priesthood in the Deuteronomistic History', in J.A. Emerton (ed.), *Congress Volume: Leuven 1989* (VTSup, 43; Leiden: E.J. Brill, 1991), pp. 132-47.

Neusner, Jacob, *The Idea of Purity in Ancient Judaism* (The Haskell Lectures, 1972–73; Leiden: E.J. Brill, 1973).

Newman, Murray Lee, Jr, *The People of the Covenant: A Study of Israel from Moses to the Monarchy* (Nashville: Abingdon Press, 1962).

Newsom, Carol A., 'He Has Established for himself Priests: Human and Angelic Priesthood in the Qumran Sabbath *Shirot*', in Lawrence H. Schiffman (ed.), *Archaeology and History in the Dead Sea Scrolls: The New York University Conference in Memory of Yigael Yadin* (JSPSup, 8; Sheffield: JSOT Press, 1990), pp. 101-20.

Nicholson, Ernest W., 'The Antiquity of the Tradition of Exodus xxiv 9-11', *VT* 25 (1975), pp. 69-79.

—'Covenant in a Century of Study since Wellhausen', *OTS* 24 (1986), pp. 54-69.

—'The Covenant Ritual in Exodus xxiv 3-8', *VT* 32 (1982), pp. 74-86.

—'The Decalogue as the Direct Address of God', *VT* 27 (1977), pp. 422-33.

—*Exodus and Sinai in History and Tradition* (Richmond, VA: John Knox Press, 1973).

—*God and His People: Covenant and Theology in the Old Testament* (Oxford: Clarendon Press, 1986).

—'The Interpretation of Exodus xxiv 9-11', *VT* 24 (1974), pp. 77-97.

—'The Origin of the Tradition in Exodus xxiv 9-11', *VT* 26 (1976), pp. 148-60.

—*The Pentateuch in the Twentieth Century: The Legacy of Julius Wellhausen* (Oxford: Clarendon Press, 1998).

Niditch, Susan, *The Symbolic Vision in Biblical Tradition* (HSM, 30; Chico, CA: Scholars Press, 1980).

Niehaus, Jeffrey J., *God at Sinai: Covenant and Theophany in the Bible and Ancient Near East* (SOTBT; Grand Rapids: Zondervan, 1995).

North, Francis Sparling, 'Aaron's Rise in Prestige', *ZAW* NS 66 (1954), pp. 191-99.

Noth, Martin, *Exodus: A Commentary* (trans. J.S. Bowden; OTL; London: SCM Press, 1962).

—*A History of Pentateuchal Traditions* (trans. Bernhard W. Anderson; Scholars Press Reprints and Translations Series; repr. Atlanta: Scholars Press, 1981).

—*Numbers: A Commentary* (trans. James D. Martin; OTL; London: SCM Press, 1968).

—'Old Testament Covenant-making in the Light of a Text from Mari', in Martin Noth, *The Laws in the Pentateuch and Other Essays* (trans. D.R. Ap-Thomas; London: SCM Press, 1984), pp. 108-17.

Nötscher, Friedrich, 'Bundesformular und "Amtsschimmel": Ein kritischer Überblick', *BZ* 9 (1965), pp. 181-214.

O'Brien, Julia M., *Priest and Levite in Malachi* (SBLDS, 121; Atlanta: Scholars Press, 1990).

O'Connor, M., *Hebrew Verse Structure* (Winona Lake, IN: Eisenbrauns, 1980).

O'Day, Gail R., 'Jeremiah 9:22-23 and 1 Corinthians 1:26-31: A Study in Intertextuality', *JBL* 109 (1990), pp. 259-67.

Oden, Robert A., Jr, 'The Place of Covenant in the Religion of Israel', in Patrick D. Miller, Jr, Paul D. Hanson and S. Dean McBride (eds.), *Ancient Israelite Religion: Essays in Honor of Frank Moore Cross* (Philadelphia: Fortress Press, 1987), pp. 429-47.

Oesterley, W.O.E., and Theodore H. Robinson, *Hebrew Religion: Its Origin and Development* (London: SPCK, 1955).

—*An Introduction to the Books of the Old Testament* (Living Age Books; New York: Meridian Books, 1953).

Olyan, Saul M., 'Ben Sira's Relationship to the Priesthood', *HTR* 80 (1987), pp. 261-86.

—*Rites and Rank: Hierarchy in Biblical Representations of Cult* (Princeton: Princeton University Press, 2000).

Oppenheim, A. Leo, 'The Mesopotamian Temple', in Freedman and Wright (eds.), *The Biblical Archeologist Reader*, pp. 158-69.

Or, Daniel, '"And they Behold God" (Exodus 24:11)', *Beth Mikra* 101 (1985), pp. 257-58 (Hebrew).
Otto, Eckart, 'Kritik der Pentateuchkomposition', *TRu* 60 (1995), pp. 163-91.
—'Die nachpriesterschriftliche Pentateuchredaktion im Buch Exodus', in Vervenne (ed.), *Studies in the Book of Exodus*, pp. 61-111.
Park, J. Edgar, 'Exodus', in George Arthur Buttrick (ed.), *The Interpreter's Bible* (12 vols.; New York: Abingdon Press, 1952–57), I, pp. 831-1099.
Parrot, André, *The Temple of Jerusalem* (trans. B.E. Hooke; Studies in Biblical Archaeology, 5; New York: Philosophical Library, 2nd edn, 1955).
Paschen, Wilfried, *Rein und Unrein* (SANT, 24; Munich: Kösel-Verlag, 1970).
Patai, Raphael, *Man and Temple in Ancient Jewish Myth and Ritual* (London: Thomas Nelson, 1947).
Patrick, Dale, 'The Covenant Code Source', *VT* 27 (1977), pp. 145-57.
Perlitt, Lothar, *Bundestheologie im Alten Testament* (WMANT, 36; Neukirchen-Vluyn: Neukirchener Verlag, 1969).
Perowne, J.J. Stewart, *The Book of Psalms: A New Translation, with Introduction and Notes Explanatory and Critical* (Grand Rapids: Zondervan, 1966).
Petersen, David, *Haggai and Zechariah 1–8: A Commentary* (OTL; Philadelphia: Westminster Press, 1984).
Petitjean, Albert, *Les oracles du Proto-Zacharie: Un programme de restauration pour la communauté juive après l'exil* (EBib; Paris: J. Gabalda, 1969).
Pfeiffer, Robert H., 'Cherubim', *JBL* 41 (1922), pp. 249-50.
Phillips, Anthony, 'A Fresh Look at the Sinai Pericope', *VT* 34 (1984), pp. 39-52, 282-94.
Plastaras, James, *Creation and Covenant* (Milwaukee: Bruce Publishing Co., 1968).
—*The God of Exodus: The Theology of the Exodus Narratives* (Milwaukee: Bruce Publishing Co., 1966).
Plaut, W. Gunther, 'Exodus', in W. Gunther Plaut, Bernard J. Bamberger and William W. Hallo, *The Torah: A Modern Commentary* (New York: Union of American Hebrew Congregations, 1981), pp. 363-730.
Plöger, O., *Theocracy and Eschatology* (trans. S. Rudman; Richmond, VA: John Knox Press, 1968).
Plumer, William S., *Psalms: A Critical and Expository Commentary with Doctrinal and Practical Remarks* (Edinburgh: Banner of Truth Trust, 1975).
Polak, Frank, 'Theophany and Mediator: The Unfolding of a Theme in the Book of Exodus', in Vervenne (ed.), *Studies in the Book of Exodus*, pp. 113-47.
Polzin, Robert, *Biblical Structuralism: Method and Subjectivity in the Study of Ancient Texts* (Semeia Supplement Series, 5; Philadelphia: Fortress Press, 1977).
—*David and the Deuteronomist: A Literary Study of the Deuteronomic History*. III. *2 Samuel* (Indiana Studies in Biblical Literature; Bloomington IN: Indiana University Press, 1993).
—*Late Biblical Hebrew: Toward an Historical Typology of Biblical Hebrew Prose* (HSM, 12; Missoula, MT: Scholars Press, 1976).
Powis Smith, John Merlin, William Hayes Ward and Julius A. Bewer, *A Critical and Exegetical Commentary on Micah, Zephaniah, Nahum, Habakkuk, Obadiah and Joel* (ICC; Edinburgh: T. & T. Clark, 1912).
Preuss, Horst Dietrich, *Old Testament Theology* (trans. Leo G. Perdue; OTL; 2 vols.; Louisville, KY: Westminster/John Knox Press, 1995, 1996).
—'בוא', in *TDOT*, II, pp. 22-25.
Propp, William H., *Exodus 1–18: A New Translation with Introduction and Commentary* (AB, 2A; New York: Doubleday, 1998).

Puech, Émile, 'Notes sur le manuscrit de *XIQMelkîsédeq*', *RevQ* 12 (1987), pp. 483-513.

de Pury, Albert (ed.), *Le Pentateuque en question: Les origines et la composition des cinq premiers livres de la Bible à la lumière des recherches récentes* (Geneva: Labor et Fides, 1989)

Rad, Gerhard von, 'The Form Critical Problem of the Hexateuch', in *The Problem of the Hexateuch and Other Essays* (trans. E.W. Trueman Dicken; London: SCM Press, 1966), pp. 1-78.

—*Old Testament Theology* (trans. D.M.G. Stalker; 2 vols.; New York: Harper & Row, 1962, 1965).

—'The Royal Ritual in Judah', in Gerhard von Rad, *The Problem of the Hexateuch and Other Essays* (London: SCM Press, 1966), pp. 222-31.

—'βασιλευς: B. מלך and מלכות in the OT', *TDNT*, I, pp. 565-71.

Ramban (Nachmanides), *Exodus* (trans. Charles B. Chavel; Commentary on the Torah; New York: Shilo Publishing House, 1973).

Redditt, Paul L., 'Zerubbabel, Joshua and the Night Visions of Zechariah', *CBQ* 54 (1992), pp. 249-59.

Rehm, Merlin D., 'Levites and Priests', in *ABD*, IV, pp. 297-310.

Renaud, Bernard, *La théophanie du Sinai, Ex 19–24: Exégèse et théologie* (Cahiers de la Revue biblique, 30; Paris: J. Gabalda, 1991).

Rendsburg, Gary, 'Late Biblical Hebrew and the Date of "P"', *JAOS* 102 (1982), pp. 65-80

Rendtorff, Rolf, '"Covenant" as a Structuring Concept in Genesis and Exodus', in Rolf Rendtorff, *Canon and Theology: Overtures to an Old Testament Theology* (trans. Margaret Kohl; Overtures to Biblical Theology; Minneapolis: Fortress Press, 1993), pp. 125-34.

—*The Covenant Formula: An Exegetical and Theological Investigation* (trans. Margaret Kohl; Edinburgh: T. & T. Clark, 1998).

—'The Paradigm Is Changing: Hopes—and Fears', *BibInt* 1 (1993), pp. 34-53.

—*The Problem of the Process of Transmission in the Pentateuch* (trans. John J. Scullion; Sheffield: JSOT Press, 1990).

—'Der Text in seiner Endgestalt: Überlegungen zu Exodus 19', in Dwight R. Daniels, Uwe Glessner and Martin Rösel (eds.), *Ernten, was man sät: Festschrift für Klaus Koch zu seinem 65. Geburtstag* (Neukirchen–Vluyn: Neukirchener Verlag, 1991), pp. 459-70.

—'The "Yahwist" as Theologian? The Dilemma of Pentateuchal Criticism', in John W. Rogerson (ed.), *The Pentateuch: A Sheffield Reader* (Sheffield: Sheffield Academic Press, 1996), pp. 15-23.

Renger, J., 'Untersuchungen zum Priestertum in der altbabylonischen Zeit', *Zeitschrift der Assyriologie* 58 (1966), pp. 110-88; 59 (1969), pp. 104-239.

Reviv, Hanoch, *The Elders in Ancient Israel: A Study of a Biblical Institution* (trans. Lucy Pitmann; Jerusalem: Magnes Press, 1989).

Richter, G., 'Die Einheitlichkeit der Geschichte von der Rotte Korah', *ZAW* 39 (1921), pp. 128-37.

Riekert, S.J.P.K., 'The Struct Patterns of the Paronomastic and Co-ordinated Infinitives Absolute in Genesis', *JNSL* 7 (1979), pp. 69-83.

Ringgren, Helmer, *Israelite Religion* (trans. David Green; London: SPCK, 1966).

Ringgren, Helmer, K. Seybold and H.-J. Fabry, 'מלך', in *TDOT*, VIII, pp. 346-75.

Rivard, Richard, 'Pour une relecture d'Ex 19 et 20: Analyse sémiotique d'Ex 19,1-8', *ScEs* 33 (1981), pp. 335-56.

Roberts, Alexander, and James Donaldson (eds.), *The Ante-Nicene Fathers* (10 vols.; Grand Rapids: Eerdmans, 1980–83).

Rogers, Cleon L., Jr, 'The Covenant with Abraham and its Historical Setting', *BSac* 127 (1970), pp. 241-56.

Rowley, H.H., *The Biblical Doctrine of Election* (Louisa Curtis Lectures, 1948; London: Lutterworth, 1950).

—*From Joseph to Joshua: Biblical Traditions in the Light of Archaeology* (Schweich Lectures of the British Academy, 1948; London: Oxford University Press, 1950).

—*Worship in Ancient Israel: Its Forms and Meaning* (London: SPCK, 1967).

Rudolph, Wilhelm, *Haggai, Sacharja 1–8; Sacharja 9–14; Maleachi, mit einer Zeittafel von Alfred Jepsen* (Gütersloh: Gütersloher Verlagshaus, 1976).

Ruprecht, Eberhard, 'Exodus 24,9-11 als Beispiel lebendiger Erzähltradition aus der Zeit des babylonischen Exils', in Rainer Albertz (ed.), *Werden und Wirken des Alten Testaments* (Festschrift Claus Westermann; Neukirchen–Vluyn: Neukirchener Verlag, 1980), pp. 138-73.

Ryken, Leland, and Tremper Longman, III (eds.), *A Complete Literary Guide to the Bible* (Grand Rapids: Zondervan, 1993).

Sabourin, Leopold, SJ, *Priesthood: A Comparative Study* (Studies in the History of Religions; Numen Supplements, 25; Leiden: E.J. Brill, 1973).

Saggs, H.W.F., *The Greatness that Was Babylon: A Sketch of the Ancient Civilization of the Tigris-Euphrates Valley* (London: Sidgwick & Jackson, 1962).

Sailhamer, John H., 'The Mosaic Law and the Theology of the Pentateuch', *WTJ* 53 (1991), pp. 241-61.

—*The Pentateuch as Narrative: A Biblical–Theological Commentary* (Library of Biblical Interpretation; Grand Rapids: Zondervan, 1992).

Sarna, Nahum M., *Exodus: The Traditional Hebrew Text with the New JPS Translation* (The JPS Torah Commentary; Philadelphia: Jewish Publication Society, 1991).

—*Exploring Exodus: The Origins of Biblical Israel* (New York: Schocken Books, 1986).

Schenker, Adrian, OP, 'Besonderes und allgemeines Priestertum im Alten Bund: Ex 19,6 und Jes 61,6 im Vergleich', in Alois Schifferle (ed.), *Pfarrei in der Postmoderne? Gemeindebildung in nachchristlicher Zeit* (Festschrift Leo Karrer; Freiburg: Herder, 1997), pp. 111-16.

—'Drei Mosaiksteinchen: "Königreich von Priestern", "Und ihre Kinder gehen weg", "Wir tun und wir hören" (Exodus 19,6; 21,22; 24,7)', in Vervenne (ed.), *Studies in the Book of Exodus*, pp. 367-80.

—'Les sacrifices d'alliance: Ex XXIV, 3-8 dans leur portée narrative et religieuse: Contribution à l'étude de la *berît* dans l'Ancien Testament', *RB* 101 (1994), pp. 481-94.

Schmid, H.H., 'Ich will euer Gott sein und ihr sollt mein Volk sein: Die sogenannte Bundesformel und die Frage nach der Mitte des Alten Testaments', in Dieter Luhrmann and Georg Strecker (eds.), *Kirche* (Festschrift Günther Bornkamm; Tübingen: J.C.B. Mohr, 1980), pp. 1-25.

—'In Search of New Approaches in Pentateuchal Research', *JSOT* 3 (1977), pp. 33-42.

—*Der sogenannte Jahwist: Beobachtungen und Fragen zur Pentateuchforschung* (Zurich: Theologische Verlag, 1976).

Schmid, Herbert, 'Jahwe und die Kultustraditionen von Jerusalem', *ZAW* NS 68 (1955), pp. 168-97.

Schmidt, Werner H., *Exodus* (BKAT, 2; 2 vols.; Neukirchen–Vluyn: Neukirchener Verlag, 1974–).

—*Exodus, Sinai und Mose: Erwägungen zu Ex 1–19 und 24* (Erträge der Forschung, 191; Darmstadt: Wissenschaftliche Buchgesellschaft, 1983).

—*Königtum Gottes in Ugarit und Israel zur Herkunft der Königsprädikation Jahwes* (BZAW, 80; Berlin: W. de Gruyter, 2nd edn, 1966).

Schmitt, Hans-Christoph, 'Redaktion des Pentateuch im Geiste der Prophetie: Beobachtungen zur Bedeutung der "Glaubens"-Thematik innerhalb der Theologie des Pentateuch', *VT* 32 (1982), pp. 170-89.

Schneider, Wolfgang, *Grammatik des biblischen Hebräisch* (Munich: Claudius-Verlag, 1974).

Schüssler Fiorenza, Elisabeth, *Priester für Gott: Studien zum Herrschafts- und Priestermotiv in der Apokalypse* (NTAbh, 7; Münster: Aschendorff, 1972).

Schwartz, Baruch J., 'The Priestly Account of the Theophany and Lawgiving at Sinai', in Fox *et al.* (eds.), *Texts, Temples and Traditions*, pp. 103-34.

Scott, R.B.Y., 'A Kingdom of Priests (Exodus xix 6)', *OTS* 8 (1950), pp. 213-19.

Seely, Paul H., 'The Firmament and the Water Above. I. The Meaning of *raqia'* in Gen 1:6-8', *WTJ* 53 (1991), pp. 227-40.

Seux, M.-J., *Epithètes royales Akkadiennes et Sumériennes* (Paris: Letouzer & Ané, 1967).

Shaw, Charles S., *The Speeches of Micah: A Rhetorical-Historical Analysis* (JSOTSup, 145; Sheffield: JSOT Press, 1993).

Sheriffs, Deryck, *The Friendship of the Lord* (Carlisle: Paternoster Press, 1996).

—'Moving On with God: Key Motifs in Exodus 13–20', *Themelios* 15 (1990), pp. 49-60.

Shurden, Walter B. (ed.), *Proclaiming the Baptist Vision: The Priesthood of All Believers* (Macon, GA: Smyth & Helwys, 1993).

Silva, Moisés, *Biblical Words and their Meaning: An Introduction to Lexical Semantics* (Grand Rapids: Zondervan, rev. edn, 1994).

Simpson, Cuthbert Aikman, *The Early Traditions of Israel: A Critical Analysis of the Pre-Deuteronomic Narrative of the Hexateuch* (Oxford: Basil Blackwell, 1948).

Ska, Jean Louis, SJ, 'Ex 19,3-8 et les parénèses deutéronomiques', in Georg Braulik, OSB, Walter Gross and Sean McEvenue (eds.), *Biblische Theologie und gesellschaftlicher Wandel* (Festschrift Norbert Lohfink, SJ; Freiburg: Herder, 1993), pp. 307-14.

—'Exode 19,3b-6 et l'identité de l'Israël postexilique', in Vervenne (ed.), *Studies in the Book of Exodus*, pp. 289-317.

—'Le repas de Ex 24,11', *Bib* 74 (1993), pp. 305-27.

Sklba, Richard J., 'The Redeemer of Israel', *CBQ* 34 (1972), pp. 1-18.

Smend, Rudolf, *Die Bundesformel* (Theologische Studien, 68; Zurich: EVZ-Verlag, 1963).

Smend, Rudolf, 'Essen und Trinken: Ein Stück Weltlichkeit des Alten Testaments', in Donner, Hanhart and Smend (eds.), *Beiträge zur alttestamentlichen Theologie*, pp. 446-59.

Smith, Gary V., 'The Concept of God/the Gods as King in the Ancient Near East and the Bible', *Trinity Journal* NS 3 (1982), pp. 18-38.

Smith, Ralph L., *Micah–Malachi* (WBC, 32; Waco, TX: Word Books, 1984).

Smith, Sidney, 'A Preliminary Account of the Tablets from Atchana', *The Antiquaries Journal* 19 (1939), pp. 40-48.

—'The Practice of Kingship in Early Semitic Kingdoms', in Hooke (ed.), *Myth, Ritual and Kingship*, pp. 22-73.

Smith, William Robertson, *Lectures on the Religion of the Semites: The Fundamental Institutions* (London: A. & C. Black, 3rd edn, 1927).

—*Lectures on the Religion of the Semites, Second and Third Series* (JSOTSup, 183; Sheffield: Sheffield Academic Press, 1995).

—'Priest', in T.K. Cheyne and J.S. Black (eds.), *Encyclopaedia Biblica* (New York: MacMillan, 1902), pp. 3837-47.

Snaith, Norman H., *The Distinctive Ideas of the Old Testament* (London: Epworth Press, 1944).

—'The Priesthood and the Temple', in T.W. Manson (ed.), *A Companion to the Bible* (Edinburgh: T. & T. Clark, 1947), pp. 418-43.

Soden, Hermann Freiherr von, *Die Schriften des Neuen Testament in ihrer ältesten erreichbaren Textgestalt* (2 sections in 4 vols.; Berlin: Alexander Duncker, 1902–13).

Soden, Wolfram von, *The Ancient Orient: An Introduction to the Study of the Ancient Near East* (trans. Donald G. Schley; Grand Rapids: Eerdmans, 1994).

—'Zur Stellung des "Geweihten" (*qdš*) in Ugarit', *UF* 2 (1970), pp. 329-30.

Sohn, Seock-Tae, *The Divine Election of Israel* (Grand Rapids: Eerdmans, 1991).

Solá-Solé, J.M., *L'infinitif sémitique: Contribution à l'étude des formes et des fonctions des noms d'action et des infinitifs sémitiques* (Bibliotheque de l'école pratique des hautes études. Section des sciences historiques et philologiques, 315; Paris: H. Champion, 1961).

Sonnet, Jean-Pierre, SJ, 'Le Sinaï dans l'événement de sa lecture: La dimension pragmatique d'Ex 19–24', *Nouvelle revue théologique* 111 (1989), pp. 321-44.

Speiser, E.A., '"People" and "Nation" of Israel', Finkelstein and Greenberg (eds.), *Oriental and Biblical Studies: Collected Writings of E.A. Speiser* (Philadelphia: University of Pennsylvania, 1967), pp. 160-70.

Sperling, S. David, 'An Arslan Tash Incantation: Interpretations and Implications', *HUCA* 53 (1982), pp. 1-10.

—'Rethinking Covenant in Late Biblical Books', *Bib* 70 (1989), pp. 50-73.

Sprinkle, Joe M., *'The Book of the Covenant': A Literary Approach* (JSOTSup, 174; Sheffield: JSOT Press, 1994).

—'Literary Approaches to the Old Testament: A Survey of Recent Scholarship', *JETS* 32 (1989), pp. 299-310.

Sternberg, Meir, *The Poetics of Biblical Narrative: Ideological Literature and the Drama of Reading* (Indiana Literary Biblical Series; Bloomington: Indiana University Press, 1985).

Steuernagel, D. Carl, *Lehrbuch der Einleitung in das Alte Testament: Mit einem Anhang uber die Apokryphen und Psendepigraphen* (Tübingen: J.C.B. Mohr, 1912).

Stinespring, W.F., 'No Daughter of Zion: A Study in the Appositional Genitive in Hebrew Grammar', *Encounter* 26 (1965), pp. 133-41.

Stoebe, Hans-Joachim, Johann Jakob Stamm and Ernst Jenni (eds.), *Wort–Gebot–Glaube: Beiträge zur Theologie des Alten Testaments* (Festschrift Walther Eichrodt; Zurich: Zwingli-Verlag, 1970).

Stone, Michael E., and Jonas C. Greenfield, 'The Prayer of Levi', *JBL* 112 (1993), pp. 247-66.

Strack, Hermann L., and Paul Billerbeck, *Kommentar zum Neuen Testament aus Talmud und Midrasch* (5 vols.; Munich: C.H. Beck, 1922–28).

Strange, J.F., 'The Idea of Afterlife in Ancient Israel: Some Remarks on the Iconography of Solomon's Temple', *PEQ* 117 (1985), pp. 35-40.

Tal, Abraham, *The Samaritan Targum of the Pentateuch: A Critical Edition.* I. *Genesis, Exodus* (Tel-Aviv: Tel-Aviv University Press, 1980 [Hebrew]).

Talmon, S., 'הר', in *TDOT*, III, pp. 441-42.

Tate, Marvin E., 'Questions for Priests and People in Malachi 1:2–2:16', *RevExp* 84 (1987), pp. 391-407.

—'Satan in the Old Testament', *RevExp* 89 (1992), pp. 461-74.

Teixidor, J., 'Les tablettes d'Arslan Tash au Musée d'Alep', *Aula Orientalis* 1 (1983), pp. 105-108.

Thomas, D. Winton, 'A Note on מחלצות in Zech 3.4', *JTS* 34 (1932), pp. 279-80.

Thompson, J.A., *The Ancient Near Eastern Treaties and the Old Testament* (Tyndale Lecture in Biblical Archaeology; 1963; London: Tyndale Press, 1964).

Thureau-Dangin, F., 'Un acte de donation de Marduk-zâkir-šumi', *Revue d'Assyriologie et d'Archéologie Orientale* 16 (1919), pp. 117-56.

Thureau-Dangin, F. (ed.), *Die sumerischen und akkadischen Königsinschriften* (Vorderasiatische Bibliothek, 1.1; Leipzig: J.C. Hinrichs, 1907).

Tollington, Janet E., *Tradition and Innovation in Haggai and Zechariah 1–8* (JSOTSup, 150; Sheffield: JSOT Press, 1993).

Tournay, R., OP, 'Le Psaume 110', *RB* 67 (1960), pp. 5-41.

Trigger, B.G., *et al.*, *Ancient Egypt: A Social History* (Cambridge: Cambridge University Press, 1983).

Tucker, Gene M., 'Covenant Forms and Contract Forms', *VT* 15 (1965), pp. 487-503.

Uffenheimer, Benjamin, 'From Prophetic to Apocalyptic Eschatology', in Henning Graf Reventlow (ed.), *Eschatology in the Bible and in Jewish and Christian Tradition* (JSOTSup, 243; Sheffield: Sheffield Academic Press, 1997), pp. 200-17.

Utzschneider, Helmut, *Das Heiligtum und das Gesetz: Studien zur Bedeutung der sinaitischen Heiligtumstexte (Ex 25–40; Lev 8–9)* (OBO, 77; Göttingen: Vandenhoeck & Ruprecht, 1988).

—'Die Renaissance der alttestamentlichen Literaturwissenschaft und das Buch Exodus: Überlegungen zu Hermeneutik und Geschichte der Forschung', *ZAW* NS 106 (1994), pp. 197-223.

Van de Walle, R., 'An Administrative Body of Priests and a Consecrated People', *Indian Journal of Theology* 14 (1965), pp. 57-72.

van der Woude, A.S., 'Melchisedek als himmlische Erlösergestalt in den neugefunden eschatologischen Midraschim aus Qumran Höhle xi', *OTS* 14 (1965), pp. 354-73.

—'Zion as Primeval Stone in Zechariah 3 and 4', in W. Claassen (ed.), *Text and Context: Old Testament and Semitic Studies for F.C. Fensham* (JSOTSup, 48; Sheffield: JSOT Press, 1988), pp. 237-48.

Van Dijk, Jacobus, 'The Authenticity of the Arslan Tash Amulets', *Iraq* 54 (1992), pp. 65-68.

Van Seters, John, '"Comparing Scripture with Scripture": Some Observations on the Sinai Pericope of Exodus 19–24', in Gene M. Tucker, David L. Petersen and Robert R. Wilson (eds.), *Canon, Theology and Old Testament Interpretation: Essays in Honor of Brevard S. Childs* (Philadelphia: Fortress Press, 1988), pp. 111-30.

—*In Search of History: Historiography in the Ancient World and the Origins of Biblical History* (New Haven: Yale University Press, 1983).

—*The Life of Moses: The Yahwist as Historian in Exodus–Numbers* (Louisville, KY: Westminster/John Knox Press, 1994).

—'Recent Studies on the Pentateuch: A Crisis in Method', *JAOS* 99 (1979), pp. 663-73.

—'The Yahwist as Theologian? A Response', *JSOT* 3 (1977), pp. 15-20.

VanderKam, James C., 'Joshua the High Priest and the Interpretation of Zechariah 3', *CBQ* 53 (1991), pp. 553-70.

Vanhoye, Albert, SJ, *Old Testament Priests and the New Priest According to the New Testament* (trans. J. Bernard Orchard, OSB; Studies in Scripture; Petersham, MA: St Bede's Publications, 1986).

Vaux, Roland de, OP, *Ancient Israel* (2 vols.; New York: McGraw–Hill, 1965).

—*The Early History of Israel to the Exodus and Covenant of Sinai* (trans. David Smith; London: Darton, Longman & Todd, 1978).

—'Le roi d'Israël, vassal de Yahvé', in Roland de Vaux, OP, *Bible et Orient* (Paris: Cerf, 1967), pp. 287-301.

Vervenne, Marc, 'Current Tendencies and Developments in the Study of the Book of Exodus', in Vervenne (ed.), *Studies in the Book of Exodus*, pp. 21-59.

—'The So-Called Deuteronomic/Deuteronomistic Passages in Exodus', in Ferenc Postma, Eep Talstra and Marc Vervenne, *Exodus: Materials in Automatic Text Processing*. I. *Morphological, Syntactical and Literary Case Studies* (Instrumenta Biblica, 1.1; Amsterdam: Turnhout, 1983), pp. 98-108.

Vervenne, Marc (ed.), *Studies in the Book of Exodus: Redaction, Reception, Interpretation* (BETL, 126; Leuven: Leuven University Press, 1996).

Viberg, Åke, *Symbols of Law: A Contextual Analysis of Legal Symbolic Acts in the Old Testament* (ConBOT, 34; Stockholm: Almqvist & Wiksell, 1992).

Virolleaud, Charles (ed.), *Le palais royal d'Ugarit*. II. *Textes en cunéiformes alphabétiques des archives est, ouest et centrales* (Mission de Ras Shamra, 7; Paris: Imprimerie Nationale Librairie C. Klincksieck, 1957).

—*Le palais royal d'Ugarit*. V. *Textes en cunéiformes alphabétiques des archives sud, sud-ouest et du petit palais* (Mission de Ras Shamra, 11; Paris: Imprimerie Nationale Librairie C. Klincksieck, 1965).

Vogels, Walter, *God's Universal Covenant* (Ottawa: Saint Paul University Press, 1979).

Vriezen, Th.C., *An Outline of Old Testament Theology* (trans. S. Neuijen; Oxford: Basil Blackwell, 1958).

—'The Exegesis of Exodus XXIV 9-11', in M.A. Beek, S.P. Brock and F.F. Bruce (eds.), *The Witness of Tradition: Papers Read at the Joint British–Dutch Old Testament Conference Held at Woudschoten 1970* (OTS, 17; Leiden: E.J. Brill, 1972), pp. 100-33.

Waltke, Bruce K., 'Micah', in McComiskey (ed.), *The Minor Prophets*, II, pp. 591-764.

—'The Phenomenon of Conditionality within Unconditional Covenants', in Avraham Gileadi (ed.), *Israel's Apostasy and Restoration*, pp. 123-39.

Waltke, Bruce K., and M. O'Connor, *An Introduction to Biblical Hebrew Syntax* (Winona Lake, IN: Eisenbrauns, 1990).

Watson, Wilfred G.E., *Classical Hebrew Poetry: A Guide to its Techniques* (JSOTSup, 26; Sheffield: JSOT Press, 1984).

Weeks, Noel K., 'Admonition and Curse' (unpublished manuscript, Sydney, 1999).

Weimar, Peter, 'Sinai und Schöpfung: Komposition und Theologie der priesterschriftlichen Sinaigeschichte', *RB* 95 (1988), pp. 337-85

Weinfeld, Moshe, '*Berît:* Covenant vs. Obligation', *Bib* 55 (1975), pp. 120-28.

—'The Common Heritage of Covenantal Traditions in the Ancient World', in Luciano Canfora, Mario Liverani and Carlo Zaccagnini (eds.), *I trattati nel mondo antico: Forma, ideologia, funzione* (Saggi di storia antica, 2; Rome: L'Erma di Bretschneider, 1990), pp. 175-91.

—'The Covenant of Grant in the Old Testament and in the Ancient Near East', *JAOS* 90 (1970), pp. 184-203.

—*Deuteronomy 1–11: A New Translation with Introduction and Commentary* (AB, 5; New York: Doubleday, 1991).

—*Deuteronomy and the Deuteronomic School* (Winona Lake, IN: Eisenbrauns, 1992).

—'The Loyalty Oath in the Ancient Near East', *UF* 8 (1976), pp. 379-414.

—'ברית', in *TDOT*, I, pp. 253-79.

Weiser, Artur, *Introduction to the Old Testament* (trans. D.M. Barton; London: Darton, Longman & Todd, 1961).

—*The Psalms: A Commentary* (trans. Herbert Hartwell; OTL; London: SCM Press, 1962).

Weisman, Ze'ev, 'The Place of the People in the Making of Law and Judgment', in Wright, David and Hurvitz (eds.), *Pomegranates and Golden Bells*, pp. 407-20.

Weiss, Meir, *The Bible from Within: The Method of Total Interpretation* (Perry Foundation for Biblical Research Publications; Jerusalem: Magnes Press, 1984).

—'Concerning Amos' Repudiation of the Cult', in Wright, Freedman and Hurvitz (eds.), *Pomegranates and Golden Bells*, pp. 199-214.

Wellhausen, Julius, *The Book of Psalms: A New English Translation with Explanatory Notes* (trans. Horace Howard Furness; The Polychrome Bible; London: James Clarke, 1898).

—*Die Composition des Hexateuchs und der historischen Bücher des Alten Testaments* (Berlin: W. de Gruyter, 4th edn, 1963).

—*Prolegomena to the History of Israel* (trans. J. Sutherland Black and Allan Menzies; Edinburgh: A. & C. Black, 1885).

Wells, Jo Bailey, *God's Holy People: A Theme in Biblical Theology* (JSOTSup, 305; Sheffield: Sheffield Academic Press, 2000).

Welten, Peter, 'Die Vernichtung des Todes und die Königsherrschaft Gottes: Eine traditionsgeschichtliche Studie zur Jes 25,6-8; 24,21-23 und Ex 24,9-11', *TZ* 38 (1982), pp. 129-46.

Wenham, Gordon J., *The Book of Leviticus* (NICOT; Grand Rapids: Eerdmans, 1979).

—'Sanctuary Symbolism in the Garden of Eden Story', in *Proceedings of the Ninth World Congress of Jewish Studies*. A. *The Period of the Bible* (Jerusalem: World Union of Jewish Studies, 1986), pp. 19-25.

—'The Theology of Old Testament Sacrifice', in Beckwith and Martin (eds.), *Sacrifice in the Bible*, pp. 75-87.

Westermann, Claus, 'Die Herrlichkeit Gottes in der Priesterschrift', in Stoebe, Stamm and Jenni (eds.), *Wort–Gebot–Glaube*, pp. 227-49.

—*Isaiah 40–66: A Commentary* (trans. David M.G. Stalker; OTL; London: SCM Press, 1969).

Wevers, John William, *Notes on the Greek Text of Exodus* (Septuagint and Cognate Studies, 30; Atlanta: Scholars Press, 1990).

Whybray, R.N., 'Response to Professor Rendtorff', *JSOT* 3 (1977), pp. 11-14.

—*The Making of the Pentateuch: A Methodological Study* (JSOTSup, 53; Sheffield: JSOT Press, 1987).

Widengren, Geo, 'Early Hebrew Myths and their Interpretation', in Hooke (ed.), *Myth, Ritual and Kingship*, pp. 149-203.

—'Royal Ideology and the Testaments of the Twelve Patriarchs', in F.F. Bruce (ed.), *Promise and Fulfilment: Essays Presented to Professor S.H. Hooke in Celebration of his Ninetieth Birthday* (Edinburgh: T. & T. Clark, 1963), pp. 202-12.

Wildberger, Hans, 'Das Abbild Gottes: Gen. 1,26-30', *TZ* 21 (1965), pp. 245-59, 481-501.

—*Jahwes Eigentumsvolk: Eine Studie zur Traditionsgeschichte und Theologie des Erwählungsgedankens* (ATANT, 37; Zurich: Zwingli-Verlag, 1960).

—'סגלה', in *TLOT*, II, pp. 791-93.

Willis, Timothy M., 'Yahweh's Elders (Isa 24,23): Senior Officials of the Divine Court', *ZAW* NS 103 (1991), pp. 375-85.

Winnett, Frederick Victor, *The Mosaic Tradition* (Near and Middle East Series, 1; Toronto: University of Toronto Press, 1949).

Wise, Michael O., '*4QFlorilegium* and the Temple of Adam', *RevQ* 15 (1991), pp. 103-32.

Wiseman, D.J., 'Alalakh', in D. Winton Thomas (ed.), *Archaeology and Old Testament Study: Jubilee Volume of the Society for Old Testament Study 1917–1967* (Oxford: Clarendon Press, 1967), pp. 119-35.

—*The Alalakh Tablets* (Occasional Publications of the British Institute of Archaeology at Ankara; London: British Institute of Archaeology at Ankara, 1953).

—'Archaeology and Scripture', *WTJ* 33 (1971), pp. 133-52.

—*The Vassal-Treaties of Esarhaddon* (London: British School of Archaeology in Iraq, 1958).

Wolff, Hans Walter, *Anthropology of the Old Testament* (trans. Margaret Kohl; Philadelphia: Fortress Press, 1974).

—*A Commentary on the Book of the Prophet Hosea* (ed. Paul D. Hanson; trans. Gary Stansell; Hermeneia; Philadelphia: Fortress Press, 1974).

Worton, Michael, and Judith Still (eds.), *Intertextuality: Theories and Practices* (Manchester: Manchester University Press, 1990).

Wright, David P., 'Day of Atonement', in *ABD*, II, pp. 72-76.

—'Holiness: Old Testament', in *ABD*, III, pp. 237-49.

—'The Spectrum of Priestly Impurity', in Gary A. Anderson and Saul M. Olyon (eds.), *Priesthood and Cult in Ancient Israel* (JSOTSup, 125; Sheffield: JSOT Press, 1991), pp. 150-81.

Wright, David P., David Noel Freedman and Avi Hurvitz (eds.), *Pomegranates and Golden Bells: Studies in Biblical, Jewish and Near Eastern Ritual, Law, and Literature in Honor of Jacob Milgrom* (Winona Lake, IN: Eisenbrauns, 1995).

Wright, G. Ernest, 'The Levites in Deuteronomy', *VT* 4 (1954), pp. 325-30.

—'The Temple in Palestine–Syria', in Freedman and Wright (eds.), *The Biblical Archeologist Reader*, pp. 169-84.

Yardeni, Ada, 'Remarks on the Priestly Blessing on Two Ancient Amulets from Jerusalem', *VT* 41 (1991), pp. 176-85.

Youngblood, Ronald, 'The Abrahamic Covenant: Conditional or Unconditional?', in Morris Inch and Ronald Youngblood (eds.), *The Living and Active Word of God: Studies in Honor of Samuel J. Schultz* (Winona Lake, IN: Eisenbrauns, 1983), pp. 31-46.

Zenger, Erich, *Die Sinaitheophanie: Untersuchung zum jahwistischen und elohistischen Geschichtswerk* (FzB, 3; Würzburg: Echter Verlag, 1971).

—*Israel am Sinai: Analysen und Interpretationen zu Exodus 17–34* (Altenberge: CIS-Verlag, 1982).

—'Wie und wozu die Tora zum Sinai kam: Literarisch und theologische Beobachtung zu Exodus 19–34', in Vervenne (ed.), *Studies in the Book of Exodus*, pp. 265-88.

Zevit, Ziony, 'Converging Lines of Evidence Bearing on the Date of P', *ZAW* NS 94 (1982), pp. 481-511.

—'A Phoenician Inscription and Biblical Covenant Terminology', *IEJ* 27 (1977), pp. 110-18.

Zimmerli, Walther, 'Erwägungen zum "Bund": Die Aussagen über die Jahwe-ברית in Ex 19–34', in Stoebe, Stamm and Jenni (eds.), *Wort–Gebot–Glaube*, pp. 171-90.

—*Old Testament Theology in Outline* (trans. David E. Green; Edinburgh: T. & T. Clark, 1978).

—'Sinaibund und Abrahambund: Ein Beitrag zum Verständnis der Priesterschrift', *TZ* 16 (1960), pp. 268-80.

Zorell, Franciscus (ed.), *Lexicon hebraicum et aramaicum Veteris Testamenti* (Rome: Pontifical Biblical Institute Press, 1984).

Indexes

Index of References

Old Testament

Other Ancient References

INDEX OF AUTHORS